# ART
## IN THE EARLY
# CHURCH

harper ✦ torchbooks

*A reference-list of Harper Torchbooks, classified
by subjects, is printed at the end of this volume.*

WALTER LOWRIE

# ART
### IN THE EARLY
# CHURCH

REVISED EDITION

HARPER TORCHBOOKS \ *The Cloister Library*
HARPER & ROW, PUBLISHERS
NEW YORK, EVANSTON AND LONDON

TO THE MEMORY OF MY DEAR FRIEND
ERNESTO BUONAIUTI
ROMONO DI ROMA
PROFESSOR IN THE UNIVERSITY OF ROME
DISTINGUISHED ROMAN PRIEST
PERSECUTED BY HIS CHURCH FOR WRITING
AN ADMIRABLE *Storia del Christianismo*

ART IN THE EARLY CHURCH
Copyright, 1947, by the Estate of Walter Lowrie
Printed in the United States of America.
This book was originally published in 1901 by The Macmillan Company, N.Y., under the title *Monuments of the Early Church* (in England as *Christian Art and Archaeology*). A completely revised edition was issued by Pantheon Books, Inc., in 1947 under the title *Art in the Early Church*. The present publication was revised by the late Dr. Lowrie for the Torchbook edition.
First HARPER TORCHBOOK edition published 1965 by
Harper & Row, Publishers, Incorporated
49 East 33rd Street
New York, N.Y. 10016

# CONTENTS

Preface to the Torchbook edition     ix

I. INTRODUCTION     1

II. CATACOMBS     20
Inscriptions

III. SEPULCHRAL ART     38
Frescoes: The Orant—The Good Shepherd—The Celestial Banquet—The Eucharist—The Fish—Baptism—The Magi—Daniel and Susanna—Jonah—Noah—Job.

IV. SARCOPHAGI     68
Sarcophagus of Junius Bassus—Philip and the Ethiopian Eunuch—Old Testament Scenes—Sirens—The "Pædagogus"—The Arrest of Peter—The Sacraments — The New Testament Story — The Birth of Christ — The Passion—The Resurrection—The Great Commission—Christ in Glory—"Dominus Legem Dat"—Mercy and Judgment—The Throne of Christ.

V. THE HOUSE OF THE CHURCH     87
The Basilica—The Cross and the Monogram—Constantine and the Apostles—Constantinian Churches in Palestine—The Churches of Justinian.

VI. MONUMENTAL ART     126
Apse of S. Pudenziana—Peter and Paul—The Acanthus—Apsidal Cross—Apse of the Lateran Basilica—Arch of S. Maria Maggiore—Churches in Ravenna—Baptisteries—S. Costanza—The Lateran Baptistery—S. Giovanni in Fonte at Naples—St. John Lateran—Mosaics in St. Peter's—Nave of S. Maria Maggiore — The Nave in General — S. Apollinare Nuovo—Cathedra of Maximianus—Gospel Cover from Murano—Ivory Diptych at Florence—Doors of S. Sabina—The Ivory Box at Brescia—The Ivory Box in the British Museum—Columns of the Ciborium in S. Marco—Diptychs—Ivory Tablet at Trier—Rome after the Barbaric Invasions—Altar Frontal in Salerno—Significance of Attitude and Gesture.

VII. BIBLE ILLUSTRATIONS     179

## CONTENTS

The Vienna Genesis – The Cotton Bible – Rabula Gospel – Rossano Gospel–Joshua Roll–The Four Evangelists–Paris Psalter–Octateuch of Smyrna.

VIII. INDUSTRIAL ARTS (Textile Art)     195

IX. CIVIL AND ECCLESIASTICAL DRESS     206

Bibliography     213

Index to Text and Illustrations     224

# ILLUSTRATIONS

|  | Plates No. | Following pages |
|---|---|---|
| Catacombs | 1-18 | 18, 44 |
| Sarcophagi | 19-31 | 68 |
| Monumental Art | 32-46, 56-71, 145-147, 151 | 86, 126, 134, 206 |
| S. Apollinare Nuovo, Ravenna | 72-78 | 138 |
| Cathedra of Maximianus | 79-89 | 156 |
| Statues and Reliefs | 90-96, 101c-107b | 158, 160, 166, 172, |
| Altar Frontal, Salerno | 107d-118 | 172 |
| Manuscript Illustrations | 119-138 | 182 |
| Industrial Arts | 139-144 | 196 |
| Carolingian Ivories | 148-150 | 206 |

# PREFACE
## TO THE TORCHBOOK EDITION

I was a youth when, fifty-seven years ago, after studying for two years in Rome as Fellow of Christian Archaeology (the first to enjoy that title), I published through Macmillan *A Handbook of Christian Art and Archaeology* (in America the title under which it was sold was different, *Monuments of the Early Church*—unfortunately, for many people ordered both titles and found to their chagrin that they had bought only one and the same book). In fact, at that time there was no other work in English on this theme. That book sold well for forty years, but in spite of many reprintings no opportunity was given me to make revisions and bring it up to date. Therefore I was not ill pleased when the U. S. Government suppressed the book by requiring the publishers through the War Production Board to relinquish the lead plates of the text for making bullets. The illustrations were left, for they were made on copper. There were 154 of them, and gradually I increased that number nearly fivefold.

But I was an old man when eleven years ago I entirely rewrote my first work, making it a bigger and a better book, covering a longer period, enriched with more pictures of early Christian art than were ever presented in a single volume, and gave it to Pantheon Books for publication. Of course they published it well, for they got a prize for it—but perhaps too sumptuously, for the price, $6.50, is beyond the means of the clergy, who chiefly might be expected to buy it.

Now, though tottering on the brink of the grave, I have resolved to salvage this good book by bringing it out (with the kind consent of the original publisher) in a paperback edition at the lowest possible price and with the hope of the greatest possible diffusion. Of course I cannot expect the public to buy any of my own works with the avidity with which they snatched up the cheap editions of my translations from Kierkegaard; but here I offer you a great deal for almost nothing. Here you have the text I wrote eleven years ago when I was still able to write and perfectly conversant with the subject. I am glad to omit a whole chapter and several paragraphs which treated polemically a subject which ought to be irenical—and would be, if all who discuss it were Christians. Having once devoted two pages to the acknowledgment of my debt to forty-two authors as sources of my illustrations, I need not do it again. The bibliography of ten pages made eleven years ago is now somewhat antiquated, and without handling tons of books I could not bring it up to date. It registered 144 authors and 627 volumes. The Index, which refers chiefly to the illustrations and is very full yet not exhaustive, is now placed at the end where one would expect to find it. The Chronology is useful but not essential, and by omitting that we save 14 pages. In all I am able to omit 50 pages and by using thin paper the weight of the book may be reduced to a third of the original (which is important), and I hope the price can be reduced to a fifth. For the 500 and more illustrations have already been paid for, so now I give them to you gratis. Also now they are arranged more conveniently, being here distributed through the book and brought into the closest possible conjunction with the text's comments upon them.

Here at last I can fulfill the desire (impotently expressed in the preface to the last edition) to suppress, at least in the Index, the Latin word *Majestas* (dear to archaeologists) in favor of the Greek word *Doxa* (in English "Glory"). In the New Testament "glory" is used to denote the divine exaltation of Jesus Christ the Lord, which the disciples (not only St. John in his Gospel and St. Paul in his Epistles) detected even in "the days of his flesh." Glory means much more than any earthly majesty, more than the majesty of imperial Caesar.

Therefore the early artists were not content to represent Christ as King: they depicted him as "the Lord of glory." It was a misunderstanding on the part of the Wise Men when they came from the East to do obeisance to an earthly king. It was a misunderstanding on the part of Pilate when over the Cross he set the inscription THE KING OF THE JEWS. This was not true, although it was written in three languages. St. Paul adequately describes what was done when he says, "they crucified the Lord of glory." It was a misunderstanding on the part of a recent pope when he decreed the new festival of Christ the King. I lived in Rome when this innovation was made, and I applauded it, because in modern art, especially in Protestantism, we have made Christ much less than that—we have made him all too human. But I have learned to see that "Christ the King" is more than a misunderstanding: it is a mystification, inasmuch as it is meant to substantiate the claim of the Roman Pontiff as the Vicar of Christ to universal jurisdiction of a political sort. God is not exalted when we make him a sort of Caesar.

*Doxa* belongs properly to God; yet Christians were encouraged to cherish the extravagant hope of sharing the divine glory. The sepulchral art of the early days sought by every means to portray this "hope of glory," "the glory which shall be revealed in us," who, beholding the image of Christ as in a mirror, are "transformed into the same image, from glory to glory." By a figure so inadequate as the celestial banquet, early Christian art sought to represent "what eye hath not seen, neither ear heard, neither hath it entered into the heart of man to believe, the things which God hath prepared for them that love him." In the midst of the corrupion of the tombs it ventured to promise that we "shall be raised in glory," and it sought to vindicate, as subsequent art has hardly essayed to do, the truth of St. Paul's declaration that "to depart and be with Christ is far better." One who has just learned to read may be surprised, as I was, to discover in the New Testament how prominent and pervading is "the hope of the glory of God." Athanasius affirmed nothing more when he said that "God became man in order that men might become divine." This is what it means to be "heirs," or "sons," or "children of God." What else can we mean by "the resurrection of the dead," if by this we mean anything more than the precarious Platonic wager on "the immortality of the soul." Plato called it "a fair risk," *kalon kindynon*. The Platonic doctrine of immortality understands eternity as the infinite prolongation of time—a notion which Hegel stigmatized as *die schlechte Ewigkeit*, spurious eternity. According to the Bible, time is swallowed up in eternity, as death, St. Paul trenchantly says, is "swallowed up in victory." The true eternity is glory.

Men who have not learned to read affirm glibly that apocalyptic eschatology was generally discarded before the end of the second century. But if it is easy to overlook the evidences of eschatology in early Christian literature, it is not possible to ignore a factor which was so prominent in early Christian art. It was, in fact, by the fascination of the heavenly hope that Christianity outbid not only paganism but also Judaism. "Spare the one and only hope of the human race," was Tertullian's adjuration addressed to the Roman emperor. *Fascinans* is the word Rudolf Otto employed to indicate one of the principal notes of religion. This note was plainly manifested in early Christian art, and the other note, the *tremendum*, was associated with it in all the representations of Christ in glory. It is as an expression of the *fascinans* that so much emphasis is placed upon the sacraments in early art. For the experience of spiritual gifts (*charismata*) was regarded as "the earnest of our inheritance." Those who have not yet learned to read cannot get it through their heads that sacraments might have anything to do with eschatology.

WALTER LOWRIE

Princeton, August 1, 1958.

# I

# INTRODUCTION

ALTHOUGH as a whole this book is only an introduction, an introduction to this introduction is needed here to define the point of view from which early Christian art is to be regarded.

First of all it must again be said that we are *not* dealing here with archæology. From the title of this book I deliberately eliminated this word, though naturally enough it characterized my first book, which was written at a time when the frescoes of the Roman catacombs had recently been brought to light by the archæological labors of De Rossi. They were an archæological discovery. But since these pictures, which only with great difficulty can be studied underground, and then not perfectly understood, have now been faithfully reproduced by Wilpert and are available to all students everywhere, Christian sepulchral art need not be treated any longer as a thing by itself, altogether separate from the subsequent developments of Christian art. The carved sarcophagi, though once they were buried in tombs, have not only been brought to light by archæologists but have long been used for the decoration of churches, palaces or public squares, and pictures of them are now accessible to all students. We must get rid of the notion that the study of early Christian art is a department of archæology. "I *can* dig, to beg I am *not* ashamed," is Jowett's witty characterization of the archæologist, but it is not applicable to the student of art in general, however much he might profit by some training in archæology.

It must be asserted emphatically that Christian art should be regarded as a whole—though, of course, not without discriminating the successive stages in its development. The art of the Roman catacombs is the first chapter in a long story. Or one might call it a preface, inasmuch as it intimates the direction which was subsequently followed. The monumental art exemplified by the mosaics which still adorn some of the oldest basilicas and which determined the character of all the minor arts after the fourth century, may be called the second chapter. We cannot say definitely when this chapter began or when it ended. It had, of course, a remote preparation in the catacombs; but it is not plausible to suppose that without a more proximate and appropriate preparation a perfect scheme of mosaic decoration for the churches could have sprung

INTRODUCTION

into existence at the behest of Constantine. A scheme so perfect as a form of art, and theologically so consistent that it dominated the subsequent development for many centuries, could not have been a sudden improvisation. We are obliged to assume that during a century or more before the Peace of the Church a tradition had been formed for the adornment of churches, presumably in fresco, although in Rome the first works of the sort we know were executed in marble and mosaic by the munificence of an emperor.

It is still more difficult to say at what date this chapter ended. When I wrote my earlier book I was obsessed by the notion that in art, as in some other respects, the early Christian period ended with the sixth century. Even so the chapter is a long one. But in fact early Christian art cannot be so definitely circumscribed. In the monumental art of mosaic decoration, and in such minor arts as ivory carving and Biblical illuminations, the early Christian spirit and form persisted well into the Middle Ages, in some places longer than in others. In northern Europe, for example, it was sooner transformed by the Germanic peoples into what we know as mediaeval art; in southern Italy it remained for a long time essentially unchanged; whereas in Byzantium it lasted longest, though in a transfigured form.

The persistence of the early Christian style is demonstrated by the ivory reliefs in Salerno (pl. 107d to 118). I suppose that they were made in the eleventh century, but competent scholars have dated them anywhere from the fifth to the twelfth. It is instructive to confront these reliefs with the twelfth-century mosaics in Palermo (pl. 70b) and in Venice, on the one hand, and on the other hand with the sixth-century ivory reliefs on the chair of Bishop Maximianus at Ravenna (pl. 79 to 89). This comparison makes it plain how deeply mediaeval art was indebted to early Christian, not only for the themes which it borrowed, but for the iconographic form, and for the feeling which inspired it.

By De Rossi and Wilpert the beginnings of early Christian art in the catacombs of Rome are traced to the last years of the first century, that is to say, almost to the Apostolic Age. I agree with them, though many disagree. However, this is not an issue of much importance. Everyone is willing to ascribe the earliest frescoes to the middle of the second century at latest, and those which Wilpert would date earlier include only a couple of distinctively Christian themes and represent a type of decoration which was common not only in Rome but throughout the Empire. It shows, of course, the influence of Greece, through the medium of Hellenistic art, a name which denotes the artistic form and spirit which became dominant everywhere after the con-

INTRODUCTION

quests of Alexander. It goes without saying that Christian art in its earliest stadium, and for a long while after, was dependent upon the forms and conventions of late classic art. Indeed, we may observe that instead of a progressive liberation from classic art there was from time to time a reversion to it, especially in the fourth century when the Church, having conquered the world, was in danger of being conquered by it.

Early Christian art was simply a continuation of late classical art, distinguished only by different themes. From this point of view it must be judged by the norm of an absolute aesthetic and cannot but be regarded as an instance of degeneration, decadence, a relapse into barbarism. Wirth lumps Christian art with all the other manifestations of a post-classical spirit. The beginning of this post-classical art he assigns definitely to the year 275 A.D., when the Emperor Aurelian erected an image of the sun god of Emesa as the highest divinity of the Empire, sanctioning with this a new *Weltanschauung*, and a new *Kunstwollen* corresponding to it. But already for more than two hundred years Christianity had been proclaiming and propagating a new world-view (*Weltanschauung*) which implied a new artistic aim (*Kunstwollen*). Indeed this new intention, before it was commonly manifested in visible form, was trenchantly expressed by Christian writers as *non-Kunstwollen*, or at least as a rejection of what was most admired in pagan art; and from the time when it began to reveal itself as art in the frescoes of the catacombs it was not only anti-Dionysic but anti-Apollonic.

A totally different position is expressed by Wolff, who would derive both the substance and the form of early Christian art from a popular Jewish religious art which had its home, as he supposes, in Alexandria. Since confessedly this art is "lost," it is entirely hypothetical, and no one else looks upon the hypothesis with favor. Strzygowski's contention, if its protean forms can be expressed in a single thesis, is to the effect that the cycle of Graeco-Roman art was terminated by a resurgence of Oriental tendencies, characteristic of various regions and of divers ethnic stocks, which had long been suppressed or thrust into the background. In this Riegl sees simply a relapse into the theory of degeneration which he resolutely opposed.

The fact is that Christian art in its first stadium was similar enough to classic art to be confused with it, and in the Middle Ages it was obviously unclassical. How is this to be explained? We can point to no definite period when this radical change was wrought. Must we not assume that it was implicit in the very beginnings of Christian art?

Here I attach myself more especially to Riegl's key word *Kunstwollen*,

## INTRODUCTION

which already I have used more than once in the sense I find expounded and defended by Panofsky, as the objective and final meaning of art which potentially determines its character. The recognition of the primary importance of purpose delivers us from the necessity of applying everywhere the standard of absolute aesthetics which would stigmatize as decadent all forms of art which are the expression of a new artistic intention, however well they may express it. This is the foundation of a psychologic-historical view of the development of art.

Riegl's view was based upon a study of ornamental art only. That is a narrow basis; but if a specific *Kunstwollen* is apparent in this field, it must be far more evident in pictorial art. In either case it determines the form of art as well as its content; and as the content of Christian art was undeniably new, we have reason to expect that it would be clothed in a new form. Because Riegl was dealing with epochs which were characterized by a common *Weltanschauung*, he did not expressly take into account the possibility, actually realized in the emergence of Christianity, that within a given period and in the same cultural area a particular world view might prompt a minority to express in art an intention peculiar to itself. But this is implied by the view he maintained, and everyone who shares it must reject the notion that early Christian art, though it be accounted a degeneration, was not formally differentiated from contemporary classic art.

Of course it was related to the past. So closely related that, as Wilpert thinks, the first artisans who painted in the Roman catacombs were probably pagans. At all events, they certainly had their training in pagan ateliers. But they worked for Christian patrons, who, not without theological assistance, would prescribe the themes and gradually influence the form.

It is a matter of course that the men who painted the frescoes in the catacombs were loath to remain in the mephitic atmosphere of the tombs and would be inclined to sketch hastily pictures which seldom would be seen, and only obscurely seen by the dim light of little lamps. But for the decoration of the sepulchral chambers (*cubicula*) no one asked for more than a hasty sketch. For where figures were involved the *meaning* was all-important. It was not art for art's sake that was wanted there. Yet it is in this earliest art of the Church that the essential tendency is most clearly revealed.

I summarize here what Dvořák, in his *Anfänge der christlichen Kunst*, has said about the paintings in the catacombs. It is commonly affirmed that the decorative designs in the catacombs were not different from those which were usual in Roman dwellings. But even in this respect the catacombs have a different aspect. The decoration consists of flat lines and bands, having no

# INTRODUCTION

architectural feeling, no solidity or depth. It suggests a new sense of space corresponding to a new artistic purpose. The figures are commonly presented in frontal attitudes, at the same distance from the beholder and without a sense of solidity, yet in coordination with one another.

It is no disparagement of early Christian art to say that it did not aim at sensuous beauty, least of all when depicting the human form. It was, as I have said, not Apollonic. This cannot be explained as an impoverishment of artistic talent; for, if this were the explanation, so sudden a relapse into barbarism would be unprecedented in the history of art. In fact, Roman painters and sculptors were at that moment in full possession of their inherited technical skills. No, it does not represent a rustification; for it is manifest that early Christian art purposefully and consistently suppressed the features characteristic of classic art in all times. It eschewed everything which savored of the old cult of the human body or of naturalism, and in place of this it put new values. The classic interest in ground and background disappeared, together with everything tangible, three-dimensional, or plastic—but not space itself, which became free space, space *an sich*, i.e., an infinite or metaphysical space, which is not merely an optical phenomenon. This is an expression of a new meaning and purpose in art.

In classic art interest in the subject matter, the sacred or mythical figures, had waned to such an extent that they could be used as mere decoration, without suggesting more serious meaning than they did, for example, in Flaxman's designs for Wedgewood pottery. Therefore they could be used without scruple in early Christian art, as they were again in the Eastern Empire when iconoclastic zeal destroyed and prohibited the representation of figures which had a Christian significance. In early Christian art, on the contrary, although epic and dramatic action is lacking, the subjects have evidently the very highest significance. In this art the important thing is not what is visible to the eye but what the mind is prompted to recall. Therefore the cooperation of the beholder was expected and was much more necessary than in the case of classic art. Christian art was subservient to its content, an abstract theological content. In this sense it was symbolical. During the earliest stage it was often content with symbols so abbreviated that in their stereotyped form they resembled hieroglyphs. Of course, classic art, too, had its symbols, which for the most part were anthropomorphic personifications, representing, for example, rivers, cities and oceans. But Christian art coordinated its symbols in significant schemes of thought. Turning away from earthly goods, it fixed attention upon the hereafter. This orientation was not confined to sepulchral art, though there it was obviously appropriate. Impressionism in classic art had already begun to

5

## INTRODUCTION

dematerialize the human figure, but it never carried this tendency to the point of representing the body as temporally and corporally unconditioned—in short, as an image of the soul. Such was the figure of the orant in the catacombs. But that was not the only instance of the sort: it might be said of most of the pictures in the catacombs that they were soul-pictures. The implication is, as Dvořák puts it, that "the soul is everything, the body nothing." Perhaps he puts it too strongly. But one can feel in early Christian art the same sense of the transcendental importance of the body which is evident in mediaeval art.

Essentially, early Christian art is incommensurable with classic art and with that of any ancient time; for instead of aiming to produce sensuous pleasure it seeks to prompt a spiritual experience conformable with the worship of God in spirit which superseded the ancient idolatry.

Even had I been able to say all this as well as Dvořák has said it, I might not perhaps have ventured to affirm on my own authority principles which are at once so broad and so profound.

Since all this can be affirmed of the earliest instances of Christian art in Rome, it is absurd to seek the cradle of this art in the Orient, where not a single example has been found which can be ascribed to so early an age. With regard to a subsequent period, beginning with the fourth century it is not unreasonable to inquire what specific influences were exerted by certain regions, such as Egypt and Syria, which were ethnically distinct and might be expected to show traces of an ancient artistic tradition. Although discoveries which substantiate this presumption have not proved very illuminating, this is a perfectly legitimate field for the exercise of intellectual curiosity. Not much more can be expected of it, for the differences hitherto observed are not substantial. It has been said indeed that the custom of presenting the figures in a frontal aspect was a peculiarity of Syrian art; but, as we have seen, this tendency was evident in the frescoes of the Roman catacombs, and even in Byzantine art the same tendency was only accentuated. There was a substantial reason for it in the fact that the figures were expected to speak to the beholder, to confront him as soul to soul.

One of the most striking differences between early Christian and late classical art is the indifference of the former to landscape painting, of which there is only a single example in the Roman catacombs. This fact is the more significant because landscape painting of an illusionistic character was very much in vogue at the very same time in what is called the baroque period of late classic art. The avoidance of this popular *genre* is evidently in keeping with the feeling for absolute space upon which we have already remarked. In the catacombs the presence of flowers and trees—a mere vestige of the

INTRODUCTION

apparatus of landscape art—served to indicate the celestial paradise. In the frescoes even the figure of the Good Shepherd was not accompanied by the picturesque bucolic adjuncts which were abundantly exemplified in classic art and repeated on many of the sarcophagi. Certain motifs of landscape painting, especially architectural features, were employed later in connection with the illustration of Biblical stories to indicate the place where the event occurred. But landscape as such seems to have had no interest for the Church, except perhaps as a background for the hunting scenes and suchlike secular subjects with which, because of a scruple about the use of religious themes, the walls of some churches are supposed to have been decorated.

In the early frescoes, on the sarcophagi, and in the monumental art of the Church the classical and pre-classical tradition of heraldic symmetry exerted a considerable influence. It prescribed, for instance, that Daniel should be depicted between *two* lions, the Infant Jesus between *two* or *four* Magi, that *two* harts should approach the fountain to drink, and *two* peacocks flank the monogram of Christ. But in general the Greek scheme of triangular composition was abandoned entirely, even where it did not conflict with the aim of depicting a story which involved movement from place to place. Thus one of the standards of absolute aesthetics was discarded.

Here we may consider briefly whether and in what sense early Christian art exhibits an historical interest. But first of all we must distinguish here between sepulchral art on the one hand, and what on the other hand is commonly called monumental art, i.e., the art employed for the decoration of the house of worship, which eventually determined the character of all Christian art, even in its minor forms. In the latter case we can speak of an historical interest in a sense which approximates the meaning we commonly attach to that phrase. For in the nave of the church it was usual to depict Biblical stories, "the Bible of the poor" as it was said, for the instruction of the people. But we must note emphatically that this was *sacred* history, the record of what God had done for His people. Sheer history, or the story of what man has done, had no interest at all for the Church, and of course had no place in the house of worship. The character of "historical" interest manifested by the Church is indicated by the fact that the subjects drawn from the Biblical story were often chosen with the aim of illustrating the typical correspondence between the outstanding events related in the Old Testament and in the New. The Church was interested in these events, not only because they were regarded as real or historical, but because they were significant as the acts of God, and therefore pregnant with the promise of what he could do and would do for His people. For Christian interest (not only in sepulchral art) was

7

decidedly oriented towards the future. Hence the pictorial decoration of the apsidal end of the church dealt with apocalyptic themes, which, even if they were not explicitly eschatological, fixed attention upon the things above and reflected precisely the words of the Liturgy, the *Sursum corda* and the "Holy, holy, holy," the cherubic hymn, which expressed the confidence that the worship of God's people here below was offered in conjunction "with angels and archangels and with all the company of heaven." Thus the "history" in which the Church was interested included past, present and future time. This interest is aptly expressed by St. Paul: "Whatsoever things were written beforehand were written for our learning, that through patience and through comfort of the Scriptures we might have hope" (Rom. 15:4).

In the sepulchral art of the Church everything was designed with reference to the Christian hope of the resurrection of the dead and the life of the world to come. In a subsequent chapter we shall see that from among the "historic" events recorded in the Old and New Testaments precisely those were selected which would substantiate this hope.

From what has already been said it will be seen that Christian art was in some sense symbolical. We have to consider now in what sense this can be affirmed. But here we must deal first of all with a very natural prejudice which disposes many to deny that there was any symbolical meaning at all in early Christian art. They are justly offended by the infinite licence subjective interpreters have been accustomed to use. No one would wish to suppress the exercise of personal freedom in this respect, if it were frankly admitted that this is only for the delectation of the individual interpreter. But it is highly reprehensible, as an infringement of the liberty of other men, when the symbolist insists that the meaning (or the many meanings) which he likes to attach to this or that has an objective importance and must be recognized as the intention of the artist. This brings everything to confusion. Nothing will be said here, of course, to encourage a riot of symbolical interpretations. For, as a matter of fact, the symbolism intended by early Christian art was perfectly definite—even though it cannot be said that the recognition of one symbolical reference must necessarily exclude all others. There doubtless were subjective interpreters in the earliest times. All art, of course, is symbolical in a general sense; but Christian art was symbolical in a more particular sense. It could hardly fail to be, seeing that classic art out of which it grew made much use of conventional symbols, and that the Hebrew religious tradition, though without art, was thoroughly symbolical. Early Christian literature was more symbolical and allegorical than we might wish it to be, and the symbolical interpretation of the Old Testament was richly exploited in the New, espe-

## INTRODUCTION

cially by St. Paul. In view of these facts it would be strange indeed if early Christian art had soberly eschewed the use of symbols. The presumption is in favor of a symbolical interpretation, and the fact is historically attested.

The precise character of early Christian symbolism will be made clear in subsequent chapters. Here in the introduction these general considerations are inserted only for the sake of disposing in advance of a prejudice which would discard the use of all symbolical interpretation for fear of its abuse.

Here at the outset we must encounter also the prejudicial question whether there can be such a thing as Christian art, whether art as such is not foreign and inimical to the Christian religion, the worship of God in spirit and in truth.

To one who is well acquainted with early Christian literature this must seem a grave question. One might think that no pictorial art could possibly arise in Christendom, any more than in Islam, in view of the veto imposed by the Second Commandment of the Decalogue: "Thou shalt not make to thyself any graven image, nor the likeness of any thing that is in the heaven above, or in the earth beneath, or in the water under the earth" (Ex. 20:4).

In fact, many Christian writers understood the Second Commandment as an absolute veto upon pictorial art of a religious sort. It is commonly assumed as a matter of course that the Mosaic prohibition of art was rigidly observed by the Jews of the Dispersion, and that their observance of it, whether within the Church or outside it, must have had great influence in retarding, if not in deterring, the development of Christian art, all the more because it was supported by the opinion of enlightened pagans like Celsus, Varro, Seneca, and the Neo-Platonists in general, who decried every attempt to represent the Deity by means of images. How widespread opposition to the use of religious pictures actually was in the Church is shown by the unanimous condemnation of it by nineteen bishops and twenty-four presbyters at the Synod of Elvira (the ancient Iliberris in Spain) about the year 315, the year before Constantine summoned a larger and more representative synod at Arles, attended by thirty-three bishops, among whom were those of London, Lincoln and York. Although the meeting at Elvira might be regarded as a provincial synod, inasmuch as most of the members were from southern Spain, there was as yet no distinction drawn between a synod and a council, but every meeting in which Christ was assumed to be present claimed œcumenical authority and legislated for the whole Church. The Synod of Elvira must have enjoyed considerable prestige owing to the presence there of Hosius, Bishop of Cordova. And it is an ironical reflection that this distinguished prelate, who was

## INTRODUCTION

to become the favorite bishop in the court of Constantine, at the time when the Emperor was zealously employed in adorning the churches not only with mosaic pictures but with silver statues, had at Elvira subscribed to canon 36, which absolutely prohibited the use of pictures in the churches: *Picturas in ecclesia esse non debere, ne quod colitur et adorabitur in parietibus depingantur.* I must quote the Latin text because it has been subjected to various interpretations. I would translate it: "There should be no pictures in the church building, lest what is worshipped and adored might be painted on the walls." That this decree was prompted by the Second Commandment is clearly established by the fact that the very same verbs which appear here were used in the Vulgate to translate Ex. 20:5, *Non adorabis ea neque coles*—"not bow down to them nor worship them," is our translation.

That the Church should observe strictly the Second Commandment might be considered a matter of course. In fact, the early Christian writers quote it and insist upon it very often. The dangers of idolatry were evidently very real so long as pagan cults were practiced everywhere outside the Church, and Christians were naturally inclined to adopt a rigoristic attitude. Celsus, who of all the opponents of the Church knew best what he was opposing, said of the Christians, "Their eyes cannot bear to behold any temple, or altar, or image of the gods" (Origen: *Cont. Celsum*, VII, 62). Origen himself does not deny this. Indeed in this connection he quotes Ex. 20:4, 5, as decisively binding. His own philosophy did not dispose him to recognize any value in religious art. This is even more evidently true of his predecessor, Clement of Alexandria, who in his *Pædagogus* (III, 11) reluctantly admitted that, if men must wear a ring because of the necessity of having a seal at hand to confirm their signature, they might have engraved upon it "either a dove, or a fish, or a ship scudding before the wind [as a symbol of the Church], or a musical lyre, and if it be a fisherman, one will be reminded of the Apostle and of the children drawn from the water [in baptism]." This was written about the year 200, when already such symbols were common in the Church, though Clement seems to ignore the Christian use of them and refers only to pagan precedents. In this connection he reveals the prevalence of what might be called a puritanical spirit, if it were not more characteristic of the Quakers. For he insists upon the propriety of wearing pure white garments in order to avoid the contamination of dyes. It is the same scruple which prompted John Woolman to wear a gray hat, and which subsequently moved all Quakers to dress in gray.

At about this same time Tertullian in North Africa (*De pudicitia*, 10) mentioned, only to condemn it fiercely, the Christian custom of drinking from

INTRODUCTION

glasses adorned in gold leaf with the figure of the Good Shepherd (pl. 142b). It should be understood that these were not Eucharistic chalices but vessels used at convivial banquets of a semi-religious sort which were associated with funerals.[1] By this furious denunciation of a harmless religious picture Tertullian may evidently be classed as a thoroughgoing opponent of religious art. He thundered against idolatry of all sorts.

In general, Christian writers up to the middle of the fourth century either repudiate the use of art in the Church, or they ignore it so completely that one might suppose it did not exist. Eusebius, Bishop of Cæsarea in Palestine, is an exception, but an ambiguous exception. In his *Letter to Constantina Augusta* he severely rebuked the Empress for requesting him to provide her with a picture of Christ. One might infer from this that he was a resolute opponent of Christian art. But in his *Life of Constantine* he records complacently the Emperor's generosity in adorning many churches with pictures, and mentions without reprobation the statues of the Good Shepherd and of Daniel among the lions which he erected in Constantinople to adorn public fountains. In his *History* he describes without a word of criticism the statue of Jesus which he saw at Cæsarea Philippi and which was said to have been erected as a sign of gratitude by the woman who was healed at Capernaum of an issue of blood. In spite of all this, which was natural in the panegyrist of Constantine, Eusebius is reckoned as an opponent of Christian art.

Nearly all parts of the Church except Italy are represented by such protests. We have already heard voices from Egypt, Africa and Palestine. And well before the end of the second century Irenæus, Bishop of Lyons in Gaul, said scornfully of the Gnostics (*Ad. haer.* 1, 25:6) that "they possess images in painting and in various materials, claiming that a likeness of Christ had been made for Pilate at a time when Jesus lived among them; they deck these images with garlands as the pagans do, and set them up among the philosophers, Pythagoras, Plato and the rest." We are reminded by this that the Emperor Alexander Severus honored in his lararium a figure of Jesus (presumably a medallion) along with figures of Abraham and Orpheus. Writing so scornfully as he does, Irenæus evidently implies that no Catholic Christian would have in his possession what purported to be a portrait of Christ. And in fact all that we know of early Christian art confirms this inference. For a long time the Church was deterred by a very natural scruple from making any attempt to depict the Deity in art, except in a symbolical way. For this reason representations of Christ in the frescoes of the catacombs, on the sarcophagi and in the mosaics of the churches were for the most part frankly symbolical and

[1] See p. 195.

INTRODUCTION

in no case were they regarded as portraits. Therefore the types selected for such pictures could be very divergent, even in the same church, without causing surprise. For more than six centuries after His death no one portrait type was accepted in the Church as a genuine likeness of Jesus. Buddhistic art affords a striking parallel. For during as long a period, i.e., until the first century A.D., Gautama, the historical Buddha, was not represented at all in art except by symbols. Hindu scholars claim that a purely Indian type was developed by that time. But the type which has always prevailed in Mahayana Buddhism and is familiar to us was derived from Hellenistic art, which crept tardily through Bactria into Ghandara, a province in the northeast corner of India. The prominent protuberance upon the cranium of all but the earliest statues of Buddha indicates a misunderstanding of the topknot, the artfully negligent curl, which gentlemen of fashion affected in imitation of Alexander the Great and which is conspicuous on Hellenistic statues of Apollo. The story of the portrait of Jesus which King Abgar is said to have treasured at Edessa, and the many *acheiropoeta* (pictures not made by human hand), are plainly legendary. Especially were Christians reluctant to produce statues, "graven and molten images," of the Deity—though this scruple, of course, did not apply to symbolical figures of the Good Shepherd. For one reason or another statues were rare in the early period. The famous bronze statue of St. Peter which is revered in the Vatican Basilica (as well as the marble statue in the crypt which is not an object of cult) has no good claim to antiquity. The marble statue of Hippolytus in the Lateran Museum (pl. 149c) was made after the year 238 and is the only monument of the sort preserved from early times. It appears that even statues of the emperors were not very common after the Peace of the Church. Perhaps emperor worship, which had been so tragic an obstacle to Christianity, as lately it has been in Japan, might have seemed a lurking danger. But the chief reason for the decline of the art of statuary in Christian times was a new spirit which was strongly adverse to the exaltation of the human body, the cult of man.

A marble statuette of Christ (pl. 102a), recently discovered and now in the Museo delle Terme at Rome, has been widely published as a portrait of Christ. But its admirers are put to some embarrassment by the fact that the breasts are evidently those of a woman. The artist must have taken as his model a statue of Serapis, which he transformed into a statue of Christ by putting in one hand a roll to represent the Gospel, and by elevating the other to imitate the gesture of a teacher. It probably was made about the time Irenæus told of Gnostic groups which claimed to possess a portrait of Christ. I believe Wilpert is right in saying that this likely was a Gnostic production,

INTRODUCTION

and in remarking that the dealer was not far wrong when he described it as "a Hellenistic poetess."

Other writers who do not inveigh against Christian art but ignore it leave the impression that no such thing existed in their time. This therefore was the common opinion before the discovery of the Roman catacombs disclosed not only the existence of a very early and distinctive Christian art but its great extent and characteristic development.

After the middle of the fourth century Christian writers, whether they were opposed to religious art or in favor of it, could no longer ignore it but had to take sides for or against an art "in being." For by that time it was notoriously in being. Encouraged by the munificence of an emperor, the greatest churches East and West, in Rome, in Constantinople, in Jerusalem and in Antioch, were adorned not only with silver and gold and costly marbles but with mosaic pictures. It is astonishing how many men, and how many great men, still opposed it. The great Cappadocians, Basil, Gregory of Nyssa and Gregory Nazianzen, have commonly been counted among the opponents of art; but perhaps it would be more correct to say that they accepted it with reserve. Chrysostom, too, was reserved, but what he tells us about the cult of the martyr Meletius at Antioch suggests how much reason there was to fear idolatry, especially in Syria. It was an idolatry of the saints. Even as late as the fifth century Jerome, being an ascetic, was more than dubious about art; and Augustine, too, was not at ease about it—as appears in the two chapters of his *Confessions* (x, 33 and 34), where he reflects upon the sweet seduction of church music and of pictorial art in the churches. There was in fact a strong dose of Puritanism in the early Catholic Church.

Early in the fifth century Asterius, Bishop of Amasea in Pontus, wrote his homily *De divite et Lazaro* to rebuke the vain and ostentatious perversion of Christian art when rich women had Gospel subjects embroidered upon their garments. But he wrote another homily, *In laudem Euphemiæ,* in which he describes appreciatively pictures he had seen of her martyrdom. In another place he describes, without the least reprehension, pictures he had seen in various churches: Christ among His disciples, healing the paralytic, a blind man, the woman with an issue of blood, forgiving the woman who was a sinner, multiplying the loaves, turning the water into wine, besides pictures of various saints. So Asterius cannot be ranked decidedly on either side of the controversy.

Before the end of the fourth century Prudentius in his *Peristephanon* described in verse pictures of the martyrdom of Hippolytus which he saw in Rome, and others depicting the martyrdom of Cassian which he saw at Imola

INTRODUCTION

(Forum Cornelii). More important is his *Dittochaeon,* which comments upon a cycle of twenty-four scenes from the Old Testament and twenty-five from the New, forming a *concordantia* of subjects regarded as typically parallel, this being a notion which frequently dictated the choice of subjects for church decoration. Evidently Prudentius was an enthusiast for Christian art, and he gives the impression that it was everywhere appreciated.

Yet there is reason to doubt whether at that time all the churches even in Italy were decorated with religious pictures. As late as the fifth century there seems to have been a good deal of reluctance to depict sacred subjects or Biblical scenes. We get a glimpse of this in a letter of Nilus, a hermit of Mount Sinai, addressed to the Prefect Olympiodorus, who had made known his magnanimous intention of building a church which he proposed to adorn with thousands of crosses, with hunting and fishing scenes and all sorts of wild beasts—something like a Persian hunting rug, we can imagine. Such an idea would hardly have entered his head if a decoration of this sort had not been fairly common. We can account for it only by assuming a widespread reluctance to employ a specifically Christian art. Nilus replied by denouncing this idea as "childish." He protested that it was enough to have *one* cross, which should be conspicuous in the apse; and as for pictures, he would have only such as might edify the simple people who were unable to read the Scriptures and which might prompt them to imitate the examples of the saints. Nilus, though he was an ardent ascetic, was a sensible one, who in his writings pointed out the danger and seductions of the monastic life; and, though he was critical of art, he recommends in this letter *Ad Olympiodorum eparchum* the scheme of church decoration which was initiated in Rome in the time of Constantine.

The widespread diffidence with regard to religious art which is revealed by the proposal of Olympiodorus seems to have smouldered in the East until the eighth century, when it was kindled into the violence of Iconoclasm. The violence of this outbreak is exemplified by the council of 754, which denounced "the ignorant artist who with a sacrilegious lust for gain depicts that which ought not to be depicted, and with defiled hands would bestow a form upon that which ought only to be believed in the heart." This was a controversy long drawn out and bitterly contested. It is to be noted, however, that the "images" in question were not statues in the round, for in the East these had never been tolerated. But it must be said that in the East there was and is a tendency to "bow down" to pictures (icons) with a devotion close to idolatry. There were ups and downs in this strife: images were again permitted, to placate the monks, by a council held at Nicæa in 787; but in 815 they were

## INTRODUCTION

again prohibited under the rule of Leo the Armenian; and they were not finally restored until with the death of Theophilus (842) his widow the Empress Theodora put a stop to the persecution and ushered in the Second Golden Age of Byzantine art, which lasted till the Latin conquest of Constantinople at the beginning of the thirteenth century, and is represented in Italy by the twelfth-century mosaics of S. Marco in Venice, in the cathedral at Torcello, the Cappella Palatina at Palermo, and the cathedrals of Monreale and Cefalù, as well as in Constantinople and at Daphne.

In view of what we have seen of the opposition to Christian art, or diffidence towards it, on the part of many of the most notable Christian writers, including many of the Church Fathers, it cannot well be said that the policy of the iconoclastic emperors, with whom most of the bishops agreed, was prompted solely by an irreligious prejudice or by political aims. Rigid and narrow as it was, it did not amount to a thoroughgoing enforcement of the Second Commandment, for it actually encouraged a secular art which dealt with human and animal figures if only it had no Christian meaning. Behind it there must have been a religious motive, such as was exemplified at the end of the fourth century by Epiphanius, Bishop of Constantia (the ancient Salamis) on the island of Cyprus, who in his age was the most redoubtable opponent of religious art. His influence was great, even after his death, because of the high esteem in which he was held for his piety as well as for his orthodoxy. He travelled in Palestine, probably also in the western parts of Asia Minor, where he saw and recorded pictures of Christ, of the Mother of God, of archangels and prophets, of Peter, Andrew, James, John, Paul, and the apostles as a group, of Abraham, Jacob and Moses. He makes no mention of narrative scenes, and perhaps he did not so much object to them. It was the portrait type he thought dangerous, and it was in fact pictures of persons that were commonly venerated in the East. Seeing in a small church in Palestine a curtain on which was woven the image of a saint, he angrily tore it down, regardless of the fact that he was intruding upon the diocese of another bishop, John of Jerusalem, to whom he addressed a letter which shows his animus against art. He wrote also a brochure which was a thoroughgoing attack upon pictures, and a solemn *Testament* to the same effect addressed to the people of his own flock.

But to this picture there is another side. Recent excavations at Dura-Europos, a frontier fortress of the Empire on the middle Euphrates which was destroyed in 256, have brought to light a synagogue painted on all sides with Old Testament scenes (pl. 35), which prove that by that time Jewish scruple against art had so far vanished that it could have had no effect in retarding the development of Christian art. Rather it appears plausible now to suppose,

INTRODUCTION

as some have claimed, that, in the matter of Biblical illustration at least, the Jews may have been beforehand and furnished the models upon which the first Christian illuminators relied. It appears that the first synagogue at Dura (c. 200) had only an ornamental decoration in painting, and that the second had paintings involving human figures only on the wall surrounding the Torah alcove; so that here, it appears, the Jews became emancipated during the first half of the third century.

Happily, too, a church was discovered at Dura at the same time and in the same neighborhood. Both church and synagogue, being close to the east wall, were buried by a protective embankment some time before the town was taken by the Persians, and by this they were preserved. The church is the earliest extant example of a church in a house (pl. 42a). The dwelling house is dated 232 A.D. At some later date two rooms were united by removing the partition wall. One of the rooms retains vestiges of a low dado with Bacchic symbols, but there were no Christian paintings. Presumably this was for the reason that the house was buried so soon after the alteration was made that there was no time for decorating it. For the baptistery on the other side of the house (pl. 36) was richly decorated with appropriate themes chosen from the New Testament and with one from the Old. We shall have occasion to refer to this subject later. It is mentioned here only because it is the earliest monumental proof that church buildings even in small communities were commonly decorated with pictures long before the Peace of the Church.

But to counteract the impression made by the literary opponents of art we do not have to rely solely upon the monuments. There were writers who were eloquent in praising it. Prominent among them was Paulinus of Nola (c. 353 to 431), whose life was almost exactly conterminous with that of Augustine. In spite of his immense wealth he devoted himself to an ascetic life, spending his fortune on works of beneficence which included the building and adorning of churches, one at Nola, a town in the Campania (where he later became bishop), in honor of St. Felix, a confessor, and one at Fundi, where he delighted to resort. No one has written with more eloquence, both in prose and in verse, about the mosaic decoration of the churches. In a letter (xxx, 10) to his friend Sulpicius Severus he describes the themes he chose for the apse of his church at Nola. Incidentally we learn from this correspondence that Sulpicius, who was building at Primuliacum in Gaul a church in honor of St. Martin of Tours, placed there alongside of the patron a picture of Paulinus.

The classical expression of the opinion which ultimately prevailed in the Church is found in a letter addressed by Pope Gregory the Great (c. 600) to Serenus the Bishop of Marseilles who, as was not unnatural in a city pre-

## INTRODUCTION

dominantly Greek, had expressed his objection to pictorial decoration in the churches. "Pictures," said Gregory, "are used in the church, in order that those who are ignorant of letters may by merely looking at the walls read there what they are unable to read in books"—*Idcirca enim picturas in ecclesia adhibetur, ut hi qui letterae nesciunt saltem in parietibus videndo legant quae legere in codicibus non valeant.* Strangely enough, there is no evidence that a contrary opinion was ever expressed in Rome. Certainly it did not prevail.

It is a puzzling problem which confronts us when we review, as we have now done briefly, the literary pronouncements hostile to Christian art, and contrast them with the fact that such an art did actually exist and flourish at a time when most writers ignored it if they did not oppose it. This problem has been fully and fairly dealt with lately by Walter Elliger, a Protestant scholar who writes without sectarian bias.[1] In a book published four years later [2] he dealt with the origin of Christian art. What he says there about the character of Syrian art I desire to summarize in this place.

Taking Jamblichus the Neo-Platonist as a clear exponent of the Syrian mind, he discovers a peculiar danger to the spiritual life in this racial type. For though on the one hand it exalted the spiritual part of man, and perhaps detached it too much from the material, on the other hand it was strongly inclined to make the spiritual visible in material forms, which would thus become objects of worship. This Syrian tendency, though it was utterly un-Hellenic, made itself felt in Asia Minor, a stronghold of Hellenism, before it exercised any influence in the West. The art which it produced was characterized by a strongly accentuated inwardness and transcendental otherworldliness. Interest in the plastic form of the human body yielded to a preference for a flat immateriality associated with a frontal presentation of the figures. The Greek rhythmic-dynamic movement was replaced by static repose and serene gravity; the earthly became a transparent cloak for the Eternal; Greek delight in the present moment and in animal vitality was superseded by a realism which had its ground and goal in the Transcendent. The contribution of Syria to Christian art after the middle of the fourth century is to be found chiefly in the creation of pictures of sacred persons conceived as ideal portraits, portraits of souls. In this *genre* the Syrian mind strove to produce an adequate expression of its distinctive psychic-pneumatic character. It must be admitted that at the long last it was eminently successful in this effort, though one may think that its success was fraught with danger. Byzantine art at its best is

---
[1] *Die Stellung der alten Christen zu den Bildern*, 1930.
[2] *Zur Entstehung der altchristlichen Bildkunst*, 1934.

## INTRODUCTION

documentary evidence of the Syrian's sense of the static repose of the Absolute and fundamentally of all earthly-superearthly being; but by this he betrays the magic realism of his religious thinking. Such pictures differ essentially from Greek reproductions of the natural body, also from the idealistic abstraction of a perfect human form, and from all symbolical expressions of the Divine. They are or were intended to be manifestations of the divine in an earthly medium, a finite but transparent cloak for the Infinite, bearing witness to the immanence of the Divine in the phenomena of this world.

This it seems to me is what is meant, or ought to be meant, by "Asiatic" influence. I see no trace of any other important influence which might be called Asiatic, and I feel no need to seek for such a factor in Persia or elsewhere. The Syrian influence had only to be refined in order to attain at last the lofty expression it ultimately reached in the Justinian Renaissance and in the Golden Age of Byzantine art which followed the Iconoclastic Persecution. Its repercussions upon the West were felt principally at three periods: (1) under Justinian, when the Empire was still united and the difference between East and West was negligible; (2) when the Iconoclastic Persecution drove many eastern artists to Rome (S. Maria Antiqua); (3) when the fall of Constantinople brought to Europe not only its artists but many of the principal works of art.

These general observations must be made in the introduction because there is no place for them in subsequent chapters which deal chiefly with concrete and particular subjects—making easier reading, perhaps, and certainly easier writing.

Here, too, I must say of the subsequent chapters that the chapter on the catacombs is very brief—brief even in comparison with the corresponding chapter in my previous book. It may seem that here there is no place at all for such a subject, since I have announced that this is not a book on archæology. But surely something must be said, if it is not already known, about the situation in which the earliest Christian art originated, which by its tardy discovery made possible for the first time a truly genetic view of the development. And since the views which men still commonly entertain about the Roman catacombs are fabulous and reflect the misapprehensions of more than half a century ago, something may well be said here to dispel the misunderstanding. It requires some self-abnegation on my part to make the chapter so brief. For before I knew much about art I knew a lot about the catacombs, having spent a good part of two years in exploring them, and spent I do not know how much upon the *fossores* who guided me through their labyrinths.

# CATACOMBS

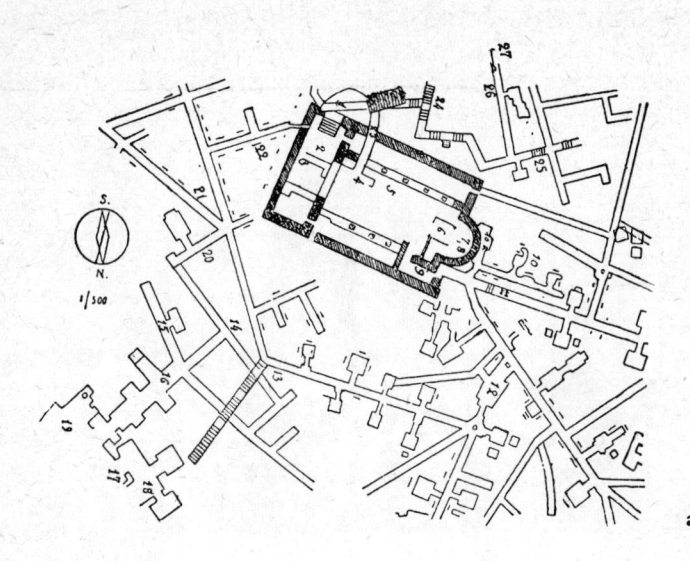

**a.** Plan of part of the cemetery of Domitilla with the basilica built above the tomb of St. Petronilla.—**b.** Section of the cemetery of Callistus showing six levels.

**a.** Entrance to a Gnostic catacomb at Rome. Middle of second century.—**b.** Cubiculum in the Jewish catacomb Rondanini, Rome. Middle of second century.

**a.** Ceiling in the crypt of Lucina in the cemetery of Priscilla. Daniel between the lions; the Good Shepherd alternating with orants and putti. First half of second century.—
**b.** Crypt of Cæcilia with *lucinarium* in the cemetery of Callistus. Third century.

Pl. 4

a. *Cappella greca* in the cemetery of Priscilla. First half of second century.—b. Tombstone in the cemetery of Domitilla. Third century.

Pl. 3

a. Crypt of Januarius in the cemetery of Prætextatus. Decoration representing the four seasons: Flowers, wheat, fruits and olives in the zones; below is the olive harvest. First half of second century.—b. *Arcosolium* in the cemetery of Cyriaca. Moses strikes water from the rock and takes off his shoes at the burning bush; Jonah reposes under the gourd. Third century.

Pl. 5

**a.** A cubiculum in the cemetery of Priscilla. A man points to the Three Children in the fiery furnace; Moses strikes water from the rock. Early second century.—**b.** Fresco in one of the "sacrament chambers" in the cemetery of Callistus. The Samaritan woman draws water from Jacob's well, while Christ reads from a roll of the Scriptures. Third century.

Pl. 6

a. Papal crypt in the cemetery of Callistus. Restored as it was in the fourth century.—
b. Sarcophagus of Livia Primitiva found in the Vatican cemetery, now in the Louvre. Second century.

Pl. 7

**a.** A crypt in Cyrene.—**b.** Fresco in a cemetery in Cyrene.—**c.** Tombstone with graffito representing the raising of Lazarus, now in the Lateran Museum.

Pl. 8

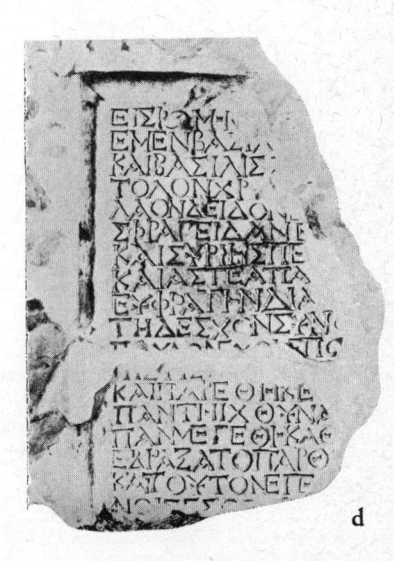

**a.** One of the "sacrament chambers." Cemetery of Callistus. Third century.—**b.** Tombstone in the Museo Kircheriano, Rome.—**c.** *Arcosolium* in the cemetery of Callistus with fresco representing the fossor Diogenes. Third century.—**d.** Fragment of the sepulchral stele of Abercius found in Hieropolis, now in the Vatican. Second century. (See p. 56.)

Pl. 9

**a.** *Above:* An obscure fresco in the catacombs. Third century. *Below:* Wilpert's interpretation: The woman who touched Christ's garment; healing of a blind man; the paralytic carrying his bed; the Samaritan woman at the well.—**b.** Lead coffin from Phoenicia. Fourth century.

## INTRODUCTION

I may say here, too, that the chapter on church architecture is reduced to half the length it occupied before. Yet not much has been sacrificed except a rather technical discussion of architectural problems which have not much bearing upon art. Here I say only so much about church buildings as may serve to reveal the spirit which prompted Christians to build as they did, and to show how appropriate to Catholic worship was the pictorial decoration they devised.

It is unfortunate that a book of this sort must be divided into chapters which deal with such various subjects as catacombs, buildings, frescoes, sarcophagi, mosaics, Bible illustrations, and an omnium-gatherum called industrial arts. This divides things which ought to be united. But this is a *must* which is *unerbittlich*, a stubborn necessity which cannot be altered. I have tried to compensate for it in some measure. But in the main it must be left to the reader to reunite what here is put asunder. For Christian art must be envisaged as a whole. In pursuing iconographical clues I have felt free to ignore to some extent the artificial barriers which the chapters create. But in the space afforded by a handbook I cannot go very far in this direction—not to speak of other limitations which are more personal. But this, after all, is the reader's task. It is not enough for him to read simply what is written. Being furnished here with the most abundant illustrations covering the whole field of early Christian art, he can and must coordinate by the exercise of his spontaneous activity the scattered and disparate data here presented to him. He must always seek to *unite*. There is a perverse activity of mind which distinguishes only to divide and to disintegrate.

*Ceterum censeo*—I say it for the last time—that *Christian art must be envisaged as a whole.*

## II

## CATACOMBS

Although I have expressed my reluctance to deal here with archæology, something must be said, as briefly as I can say it, about the catacombs of Rome, since they were the cradle of Christian art. In view of the diffidence expressed by Christian writers, and the fact that pagan art in its supreme examples was in the service of idolatry, it may be doubted whether a Christian art would ever have been born if it had not been born in the cemeteries, where it was a spontaneous expression of the hope of everlasting life, an expression which in the first instance was not prompted by the theologians, though it was evidently directed by them. When this beginning had been made in response to a popular sentiment and had proved to be innocuous, the Church, at least in the West, no longer felt any serious scruple against the use of art in its houses of worship to express the Christian faith in full.

The catacombs themselves, though they give proof of some skill in mensuration, are very far from being works of art. They have a certain fascination for romantic minds, but it is such a charm as attaches, for example, to the sewers of Etruria, where nothing else is left but cemeteries and sewers to attest a vanished civilization.

Something must be said about the catacombs, if only for the sake of banishing persistent misapprehensions which prevailed in the seventeenth century after the discoveries by Antonio Bosio, and became so firmly fixed that not even De Rossi with his scientific method of exploration was able to dispel them completely. When Bosio rediscovered the catacombs at the end of the sixteenth century men were so amazed at their extent, though they knew then only a small part of them, that they could not well believe the Christians in Rome were numerous enough in the ages of persecution to need so many tombs, or would be allowed to own them, or indeed be capable of carrying out so prodigious a work. On the other hand, they were inclined to exaggerate, to suppose that all the catacombs were connected with one another and with the churches within the walls, so that Christians when they were in danger could escape to a safe hiding place. For it was supposed that the State was ignorant of these underground cemeteries, where Christians could live in times of persecution, and where they commonly resorted for worship. These are misconceptions to which people are inclined to cling only because they are romantic. We know now that the total length of the subterranean galleries is something like <u>five hundred and fifty miles</u>, and that they were made expressly for Christian burial. Not for Christian assemblies certainly, for the galleries were barely a yard wide, and the chambers to which they led were not often large enough to contain fifty people, whereas by the middle of the third century there were forty thousand Christians in Rome. When we read that in times of danger Christians sometimes took refuge in the cemeteries, we are to understand that they dwelt for a time in buildings erected above ground, for no one could live long in the mephitic air of the tombs. Buildings above ground there certainly were, for there was nothing secret about the possession of the cemeteries, and the extent of the area was doubtless defined, as Roman custom prescribed, by an inscription on the portal which indicated so many feet *in fronte* (facing the road) and so many *in agro* (indicating the depth). Consequently the utmost care was exercised not to transgress these limits and encroach upon neighboring properties. To this end the first galleries were commonly traced along the periphery; those which were built later stopped when they met them. Even the catacombs which were separated only by a public road were not united by a tunnel under it.

How the Church when it was a proscribed religion managed to possess property by legal tenure is not clear, but the fact is indubitable. For during periods of persecution both churches and cemeteries were sequestrated and afterwards returned to the Christians as their corporate property, *ad jus corporis eorum*.

The legal status of Church property was simplified in the first instance by the fact that wealthy Christians who gave their houses for public worship and made room in the neighborhood of their private tombs for the burial of their brethren would doubtless retain for a time the legal title to such places. Many of the parish churches, as we would call them, but which the Romans called *tituli*, bore for a long while, and some of them still bear, the names of their donors. So too the cemeteries, if they were not known by a topographic designation, such as *ad duas lauras, ad ursum pileatum, in catacumbas*. Not till the Peace of the Church were such designations superseded by the names of the famous martyrs who were buried in the various cemeteries. But we know that at the beginning of the second century many of the cemeteries, if not all, were recognized as the property of the Church. The biggest of them was then put by Bishop Zephyrinus under the supervision of his deacon Callistus, who was destined to be his successor, and it still bears his name although he was not buried there. At about this time many of the cemeteries were officially administered by the presbyters of the various titles or parochial churches.

## CATACOMBS

We may well wonder how the Church could hold title to its properties within the city, but the cemeteries present a less difficult problem; for Roman Law, which permitted the slaughter of Christian martyrs, protected their tombs. The mere act of burial, without any special act of consecration, made the grave a *locus religiosus* under the protection of the Pontifex Maximus. The legal maxim was: *Religiosum locum unusquisque sua voluntate facit dum mortuum infert in locum suum.* Severe penalties were attached to any violation of a sepulchre, and the protection accorded to the grave was extended to the monument which adorned it, to the surrounding ground allotted to it, the buildings devoted to funeral feasts, and any other property devoted to its maintenance. Such property was not only inviolable but inalienable.

De Rossi proposed a plausible hypothesis to account for the fact that the Church as a society was permitted to possess its cemeteries, at a time when societies in general (not the Christian society alone) were prohibited for fear of political sedition and consequently could hold no meetings. Only one exception was made in favor of the *collegia tenuiorum*, societies formed among the poorer classes to insure a proper burial. Such societies could hardly be disallowed, in view of the fact that the municipalities made no provision for public cemeteries. The members of the burial societies therefore were allowed to possess a common *columbarium* and such buildings as were necessary for the celebration of funeral feasts; and they could meet at stated times to transact business and collect the monthly dues. Plausible as this theory is, we cannot easily imagine that the bishops of Rome, Carthage, or Alexandria would go to the prefecture with tongue in cheek to register as the president of a burial society, or that the State would be deceived by such a statement when it was notorious that the Christian society amounted to many thousands. Duchesne was prompt in criticizing this theory, and it was reduced *ad absurdum* when Hatch and Harnack based upon it the more precarious theory that the organization of the Church was in the first instance not a spiritual but an economic organization. Rudolf Sohm pricked that bubble.

Because of their magnitude and complexity the Roman catacombs suggest that Christians preferred a singular mode of burial. But in fact there was nothing strange about it. The nucleus was the family *hypogeum* or subterranean chamber, which was a common feature of Etruscan and Roman burial. Complexity was due to the necessity of providing for a multitude of burials by exploiting to the utmost the possibilities offered by the character of the ground. In the greater part of the Empire graves were dug beneath the surface, as they are now. Rome by reason of the character of its volcanic soil

22

offered peculiar opportunities for the construction of what we call catacombs. Fortunately, for nowhere else were there so many Christians. At Syracuse, where catacombs were excavated in calcareous rock, the individual chambers and galleries had an amplitude far greater than those in Rome, as had those also at Naples, where they were dug in a harder tufa. The existence of Jewish and Gnostic catacombs at Rome (pl. 2) proves that the Church had not adopted a singular mode of burial. In all cases underground burial was resorted to for reasons of economy.

It was chiefly for economy, economy of space in the burial ground, that incineration (cremation) was practiced commonly, but by no means universally, under the Empire. It was a Greek custom, tardily adopted by the Romans, who originally buried their dead. There seems to have been no religious motive for the change. Many of the older families, the Scipios, for example, continued to bury their dead. The Etruscans, without any change of religion, gave up inhumation in favor of cremation. An immense number of cinerary urns could be accommodated in a single *columbarium*, or dovecote, as the Romans called it. But, in spite of the difficulty of finding a place for burial, the practice of inhumation became common again in Rome in the second century of the Empire. We cannot wonder that the Christians adopted it, since it was the Jewish custom and had a certain relevance to the hope of the resurrection. It was not an essential expression of this hope, for no one imagined that the martyrs who were devoured by fire or by wild beasts were at any disadvantage. With us today the question of inhumation or cremation must again be weighed with a view to economy and convenience—and the advantages are by no means all on one side.

But upon one thing the Christians insisted: they would not be buried with unbelievers, and they preferred to be buried near the martyrs, *ad sanctos*. Hence it was a matter of course that they should have their own cemeteries. "It is permissible to live with the pagans," said Tertullian, "but not to die with them."

It is time now to remark that the name catacomb, though I have used it freely in this chapter, was not used in early times for the subterranean cemeteries of Rome. The word cemetery, which means a sleeping place, is a Greek word, seldom used by the pagans but preferred by the Christians. Not till the Middle Ages was the word catacomb used for Christian cemeteries in general. In the first instance it designated a particular locality near the third milestone of the Via Appia where now we find the Church of St. Sebastian and a "catacomb" bearing the same name. *Kumba* is a Greek word meaning a declivity. How aptly it was applied to this place we did not know till recent excavations under the church, which originally was dedicated by Constantine to the Apostles, revealed a steep ravine lined with tombs. Because of the belief that Peter and Paul had been for a while buried here, this cemetery, which was properly called *ad catacumbas*, was kept open and accessible to pilgrims until the ninth century, when all the other underground cemeteries were forgotten, and for this reason the particular name it bore was attributed to all burial places of the same sort.

About the catacombs, as we shall continue to call them, a general notion of their character is enough for those who are interested chiefly in the art which adorned them. Although not many pictures of the catacombs are furnished here, they are enough to illustrate my brief description.

The plan (pl. 1a) of one level of the cemetery of Domitilla shows how irregular the construction often was. The galleries, barely a yard in width and not much more than a man's height, served principally to reach the burial chambers (*cubiculum* is the word used by archæologists), but eventually they afforded room for undistinguished burials in shelf-like cavities excavated in the walls (pl. 1b, 4b, 7a, 9a), and to afford more room the galleries were often made much higher by sinking the floor lower. Such a grave was originally called *locus*—the archæologists have invented the name *loculus*. The body was simply wrapped in a winding-sheet and not often embalmed. The *loculus* was then closed with a slab of stone (pl. 3a, 7a, 8a), or simply with tiles imbedded in plaster, with or without a painted inscription. A more distinguished grave was the *arcosolium* (as the archæologists call it), which commonly had room for several bodies laid side by side, with the tombstone above it. Sarcophagi of clay, lead or stone, often without ornament, or simply ornamented (pl. 10b), or elaborately carved (pl. 19 ff.), were used for wealthy persons buried in the family chambers or crypts, and at a later time in the churches above ground. The darkly hatched plan of a basilica on plate 1a represents the memorial erected after the Peace of the Church in honor of St. Petronilla. It was common to erect such churches directly above the tomb of a famous martyr, and in order to bring the altar into proximity with the body the floor was sunk, as in this instance, below the level of the ground.

The section of the cemetery of Callistus which is shown on plate 1b illustrates the way the subsoil was exploited to the utmost extent. Here there are six levels. There was a limit, however, imposed by the quality of the soil and the depth at which water would be found. The tufa (a soft stone composed of volcanic ashes and sand) must be neither too hard nor too friable. *Arenaria* (pits from which was taken the *pozzolana* used for Roman mortar), though they were already excavated and ready to hand, were not commonly used for burial because it was difficult to construct *loculi* in such material. Michele Stefano de Rossi, the brother of Giovanni Battista, an engineer who helped him in his excavations, was sometimes able to discover a catacomb by determining where it ought to be, that is, where the soil and the lay of the land was favorable.

The character of the burial chambers (crypts, *cubicula*) is shown well enough in plates 2, 3, 4, 5, 7, 8 and 9. The word crypt is used for the larger chambers or for groups of them, especially for such as were later enlarged and adorned for the commemoration of martyrs (pl. 4b, 7a). *Lucinaria* (pl. 4b, 5a, 7a) were shafts sunk perpendicularly from the surface to provide some light, some ventilation, and to serve for hoisting the soil and stone which had been dug out.

It will be seen that the ceiling (pl. 2, 4, 5) presented the principal field for decoration, the only field not in danger of being destroyed by a new *loculus*—a danger which has overtaken many of the wall pictures.

Evidently such vast works were not constructed haphazard. They required skilled direction, not only for the selection of the sites but for the constant extension of the excavations. In fact, the *fossores* (excavators) constituted a kind of guild. To them was committed the preparation of the dead for burial, as well as their interment. But to their office there attached none of the ignominy which made contemptible the *vespillones* who performed such functions in the pagan community. On the contrary, they were proud of their title and inscribed it upon their tombs as a mark of dignity and merit. In the third century they were counted among the clergy as the lowest grade. In S. Callisto, the official catacomb of the Church, the *fossores* had a *cubiculum* of their own; and from several inscriptions it appears that in the fourth century they had in their hands the management of the cemeteries under the control of the superior clergy. The *Liber Pontificalis* reports that at the beginning of the fourth century Marcellus "instituted twenty-five 'titles' as parishes (the word is *dioceses*) for the baptism and penitence of the multitudes who were converted from paganism and for the burial of the martyrs." This suggests that the cemeteries stood in some relation to the titles or were in some sense parochial cemeteries. There were at that time thirty-two Christian cemeteries on all sides of Rome, and this number corresponds precisely to the twenty-five titles and the seven diaconal churches.

Although the catacombs were not expressly designed for public worship, it is evident that from the earliest times the Eucharist was celebrated there by family groups who came to bury their dead or to remember them a month later and on their anniversaries; for both the "month's mind" and the annual remembrance were observed even by the pagans. The so-called *Cappella greca* (pl. 3a) seems to have been designed for such a use, and the picture above the *arcosolium* represents a family group using the tombstone as an altar for the breaking of bread. There are other crypts even more evidently designed as chapels. The papal crypt (pl. 7a) was furnished in the fourth century with an altar and an episcopal chair. Nine of the popes, from Pontianus to Eutychianus (with the sole exception of Callistus), were buried there. But more numerous gatherings for the celebration of the funeral *agape* or love feast were accommodated in buildings erected above the catacombs. Such celebrations were but half in imitation of an apostolic custom, and half in conformity with pagan usage. They were called *refrigeria*, and because they were likely to be roisterous they were eventually discountenanced. It is evident that in the so-called *Triclia* recently discovered under S. Sebastiano there was a good deal of drinking in honor of Peter and Paul, who for a while were buried near this spot. The twenty-second of February was an annual festival dear to the Romans which was known by the name of *Caristia* or *Cara cognatio*, or simply *Cathedra*, because a vacant seat at the banquet was left for the departed. The numerous stone chairs in the Coemetarium Maius (or Ostrianum) perhaps have some reference to this custom. But the Church knew how to sublimate it by associating the *cathedra* with the episcopate. The festival of the Cathedra Petri was celebrated in Rome precisely on this date. The first reference to it is in the year 354, but Hans Lietzmann supposes that it was introduced early in the fourth century for the sake of counteracting the pagan festival at a time when multitudes were thronging into the Church. The date had nothing to do with any event in Peter's life either at Antioch or at Rome. It had been customary for the bishops of Rome to celebrate the anniversary (*natalis*) of their consecration. As no record had been kept of the dates on which the earlier bishops had been consecrated, they were lumped together on the twenty-second of February. By the fifth century this festival, strangely enough, was forgotten in Rome; but it was observed in Gaul, where for some reason it was transposed to February 18th, and it kept this date when in the ninth century it found its way back to Rome.

After the Peace of the Church the martyrs were zealously commemorated, not only in the memorial basilicas built above the catacombs, but in the crypts themselves, which were enlarged and decorated for this purpose. Consequently the latest pictures in the catacombs are found where the most famous martyrs were venerated, and, ironically enough, the early excavators avoided precisely those regions because of such indications of a late date.

INSCRIPTIONS

The catacombs were not much used for burial after the devastations by Alaric in 410, and subsequent invasions not only rendered the Campagna unsafe but left only too much room within the city for the burial of the dead. Yet pious pilgrims from all lands continued to visit the tombs of the martyrs, and the itineraries prepared for their use proved a precious aid to De Rossi in his search for the catacombs, which were completely neglected when the relics of the saints had been brought during the ninth century within the city and were venerated in the basilicas.

INSCRIPTIONS

To give an adequate account of early Christian epigraphy within the limits of a half dozen pages is, of course, an impossible task; it amounts simply to dismissing the subject in the fewest possible words. It is proposed to give here an account—only in the most general terms, and with but few examples—of the distinctive characteristics of Christian sepulchral inscriptions, of the several classes into which they may be divided, and of the sort of information one may expect to derive from their study. For further and more detailed information one may conveniently consult Marucchi's *Eléments d'archéologie chrétienne*, the first volume of which devotes a disproportionately long section to this subject.

The first distinction which must be marked is that between the original titles and epitaphs, and the later metrical inscriptions with which Damasus and his imitators adorned the tombs of the martyrs and signalized their deeds. Of the first class it is convenient to distinguish between such as present only the simplest data, a name, a date, or some merely conventional formula; and such as, with richer content and more characteristic form, throw light upon dogma, or upon the conditions of the civil and religious life. The earliest Christian epitaphs are very brief, and one can seldom derive from them important inferences about ecclesiastical dogma or custom. This characteristic brevity detracts considerably from their importance as sources of information; and the student needs to be warned that early Christian epitaphs are commonly appealed to far too loosely in proof of the prevalence of this or that doctrine or custom, as though it made no substantial difference whether they were proved for the second, the third, or the fourth century. We have to rely upon the inscriptions of the early period for the proof of the existence of certain customs; but when it is a question of dogma or ritual the very point at issue is usually the ascertainment of the *earliest* date to which they may be ascribed within this period,

27

CATACOMBS

and epitaphs which cannot be securely assigned even to an approximate date ought not to be used except in mere illustration of doctrines and practices which are otherwise attested for the age in question.

Most of the more elaborate inscriptions are late, but it does not follow that all simple inscriptions are early, for brevity was the rule throughout the history of the catacombs. It has already been mentioned that many tombs were without name, and were distinguished only by the familiar possessions of the deceased which were pressed into the fresh plaster. It was also in the fresh plaster that the friends sometimes scratched the date of the "deposition" of the body.

This custom of indicating the day of the month upon which burial took place, and this name for the act of burial—*depositio*, *depositus* (κατάθεσις), contracted, D., D.P., etc.—are peculiar to Christian inscriptions, and characterize all but the very earliest. The word "deposition" expresses the hope which illuminated the Christian burial; it indicates the committal to the earth of a treasure which shall be restored. The term of life of the defunct was indicated according to pagan custom: *Vixit annis* ..., *mensibus* ..., *diebus* ... (V.A...M...D...). From the third century this datum was often given with less precision: *Vixit annis plus minus* ... (Q.VIX.AN.P.M.XXX). The name was commonly accompanied by these formulas only; or also by the name of the person dedicating the monument, by some affectionate epithet (*filio dulcissimo*), or by some exclamation denoting the Christian hope for the departed—*in pace* (ἐν εἰρήνῃ), *in Deo*, *in Cristo*. Such exclamations were the earliest adjunct to the mere name which alone marks the tombs of the most primitive period. They were expressed also by the symbols of the dove, the anchor, the fish, and later by the so-called Constantinian monogram.

The three names which were characteristic of Roman citizenship (*prænomen*, *gentilitium*, and *cognomen*) had begun to fall into disuse with the end of the first century, and their presence upon Christian monuments denotes a very high antiquity. The *prænomen* was generally dropped, and still more commonly a single name appears, sometimes of a strictly Roman character, sometimes of Eastern, or barbarian derivation, denoting a Jewish or perhaps a servile origin. Some of them are evidently names taken in baptism, with a Christian signification or association. *Petrus* occurs several times in Rome in the second century, *Petronilla* is associated by tradition with the first, *Paulus* also occurs, and later *Maria*. Such names as *Martyrius*, *Adeodatus*, *Evangelius*, are evidently of Christian formation; so also are a considerable number of names expressing humility—as *Projecticius*, *Fimus*, *Stercorius*—which one encounters already by the end of the third century. The names *Fides*, *Spes*, *Agape*, *Eirene*, etc., are very ancient; and the name *Lucina*—which probably

28

denotes the illumination received in baptism—is associated with the burial place of St. Paul and with the earliest nucleus of the cemetery of Callistus.

How much historical significance may lie in the simplest inscriptions—even in a mere name—one can judge fairly only by consulting De Rossi's own minute studies, which, for all their subtlety, approve themselves anything but rash. It is especially for the early period, in the case of purely Roman names, and by reason of the rigorous system of personal and family nomenclature which the Romans used, that such arguments can be securely drawn. The very title of the cemetery of Domitilla is sufficient to connect it with the imperial Flavian family. Domitilla (feminine diminutive) was a common cognomen in this family; it corresponded to the masculine Domitianus. It is known that in the first century a vast estate (*predia amarantiana*—now corrupted to *Tor Marancia*), in which this cemetery is situated, belonged to a branch of this family. The cemetery itself brings the proof that it was, as a matter of fact, to the Christian branch of the family it belonged. A pagan *stele* was found there which records that the family tomb which it marked was obtained EX INDULGENTIA FLAVIÆ DOMITILLÆ. Another reads: FLAVIÆ DOMITILLæ divi VESPASIANI NEPTIS EIVS BENEFICIO HOC SEPVLCHRVm MEIS LIBERTIS LIBERTABVS POsui. Among the Christian epitaphs of the cemetery there are a number of names of the Flavian *gens*; for example:—

ΦΛ. CABEINOC KAI TITIANH AΔΕΛΦΟΙ.

That is, "Flavius Sabinus and Titiana, brother and sister." All of this renders plausible the form in which De Rossi completes a mere fragment which appears to have belonged to the inscription placed over the entrance of the cemetery:—

Sepulc R V M
Flavi O R V M

At all events, there is no doubt that as early as the first century this was the burial place of the Christian members of the imperial Flavian house. These mere names suffice to connect this cemetery with the illustrious converts of the *gens Flavia* whom the Church could already count within the Apostolic age. It has been suspected, from the language in which Tacitus describes him (*mitem virum abhorrentem a sanguine et cædibus*), that Titus Flavius Sabinus, elder brother of the Emperor T. Flavius Vespasianus, was the first of the family to be converted to Christianity. He was for the first time Prætor in 64 under Nero, and it is certain that as a duty of his office he must have examined into the causes of the Christians who were executed for their religion. During the thirty years of absolute peace and tranquillity which the Church enjoyed after the death of Nero there is no mention of Christians of this name. The relation of the family to Christianity becomes first publicly known by reason of the persecution of Domitian, and it is attested by pagan as well as by Christian historians. The first to fall a victim was the Consul Titus Flavius Clemens, son of the above-mentioned T. Flavius Sabinus and first cousin of the Emperor. While Clemens was beheaded, his wife, Flavia Domitilla, niece of Domitian, and another Flavia Domitilla, who was a niece of Clemens, were exiled to the islands of Pandataria and Ponza. In explanation of these harsh measures, it must be supposed that Domitian considered the profession of this strange religion by members of his own family a proof of political disaffection. It suggests food for the imagination to reflect that but for this outbreak of suspicion a Christian emperor might have occupied the throne of the Cæsars before the end of the first century; for it was the two sons of Clemens and Domitilla whom Domitian had adopted as his succesors, changing their names to Vespasianus and Domitianus.

The memory of the Flavian converts and martyrs has been preserved in the Church and hardly needed the confirmation of the monuments. But another illustrious convert and martyr of the first century is known as such only through inscriptions discovered in the cemetery of Priscilla. Manius Acilius Glabrio, Consul in 91 with Trajan and head of one of the noblest Roman families, was also put to death by Domitian. He was made to fight with a bear or a lion, and, proving victorious in this contest, was beheaded. Though no memory was preserved in the Church that he died a Christian, yet the terms in which Suetonius records the charge which was brought against him and other members of consular and senatorial rank who suffered with him (*molitores rerum novarum*) has led several historians to suspect that they were martyrs for the Faith. That the Acilii Glabriones were Christians was put beyond a doubt in 1889 when, in the central and primitive region of the cemetery of Priscilla, there was discovered an extensive and richly ornamented *hypogeum* which contained fifteen inscriptions in Latin and Greek of members of this family. Originally there must have been more, for the epitaph of the Consul himself is missing; the very richness of the marble decoration specially marked this crypt for destruction, and only fragments of the sarcophagi and their inscriptions remain. One of them reads:—

αΚΙΛΙΟC ΡΟΥΦΙΝΟC
ΖΗCΗC ΕΝ ΘΕΩ

Acilius Rufinus live in God—a sure sign of the Christian character of the sepulchre. Another reads:—

M ACILIUS V · ·
C · V ·
et PRISCILLA C · ·

*Manius Acilius vir clarissimus (et) Priscilla clarissima (femina)*. The title *clarissimus vir* leaves no doubt that this personage of senatorial rank belonged to the family of the consul who was put to death under Domitian. The name Priscilla suggests a relationship with the family of the senator Pudens from whose wife Priscilla the cemetery took its name. In this cemetery were likewise buried that Aquila and Priscilla (Prisca) who were companions of St. Paul, and the site of whose house upon the Aventine is marked by the church of S. Prisca (*contraction* for Priscilla). Their common use of the name Priscilla, together with the fact that both families were buried in the same cemetery, suggests some close tie between the family of the tentmaker upon the Aventine and the senatorial family of the Esquiline.

There is something to be learned from the very brevity of the early inscriptions; there is argument to be drawn from their silence. During the first four centuries of the Church no single mention is made of a slave, and but rarely of a freedman, among the thousands of inscriptions of the catacombs—justifying the Christian boast that master and slave recognized their equality in the Church. In a later time the inscriptions occasionally record the manumission of slaves in suffrage of the departed.

In contrast to the pagan custom, even the noblest of the Christians recounted none of the honors of their offices and rank, except that the initials V. C. (*vir clarissimus*), C. F. (*clarissima femina*), were not uncommonly inscribed to indicate membership in the senatorial order. The Christian attitude was that of looking forward beyond the tomb, rather than back over the course of earthly honor and success: *recessit a sæculo* became a familiar formula in the fourth century. In the third and fourth centuries the profession of the defunct was often mentioned in the inscription or indicated by picturing the tools of his trade. We have in general in the catacombs a thorough vindication of Tertullian's boast (*Apol*. 37) that the Christians were to be found in every rank and in every profession.

Nothing could be more simple than the epitaphs of the Roman bishops in the papal crypt at St. Callistus. The earliest which have been preserved in this crypt are those of Anteros (236) and Fabianus (250):—

ANTEPΩC · EIII (Anteros, bishop).

ΦABIANOC · EIII · M̄P̄ (Fabianus, bishop, martyr).

The inscriptions of this crypt prove that Greek was still the official language of the Roman Church.

The next pope, Cornelius, was buried in a distant region of the same cemetery, the very region, in fact, which seems in origin to have been the property of the Cornelii and the Cæcilii. This probably explains the fact that the epitaph of this pope is not in the official language of the Church, but in Latin:—

CORNELIVS · MARTYR
EP

The word "martyr" here is original; on the epitaph of Fabianus, however, it was a subsequent addition.

Most of the very early inscriptions in the Roman catacombs were in Greek, and the same language persisted here and there to a comparatively late period. Greek inscriptions were sometimes written in Latin characters, and Latin sometimes in Greek. The very general traits of Christian epigraphy which can here be noticed serve as well for the Greek as for the Latin, for the East as for the West. It seems not unlikely, however, that early inscriptions in the Orient may have been more elaborate than those of the same period which we know in Rome.

The use of the *stele* or *cippus* was not altogether rare in the Church, although the vast majority of inscriptions are upon plaques of stone. Despite their pagan significance, the initials D · M · (*Dis manibus*) are sometimes found upon Christian tombs; partly because the plaques were thus inscribed as they were bought at the shops, and partly, perhaps, because they were so much the ordinary sign of a tomb that their more specific significance was forgotten. B. M. (*bonæ memoriæ*) was sometimes substituted in a later age.

In point of orthography De Rossi distinguishes two classes of the primitive Roman inscriptions: those painted in red (in Pompeian fashion), which are characteristic of S. Priscilla; and those cut in the stone, which are elsewhere almost universal. The orthography is for the most part careless, and after the second century there begin to appear frequent mistakes which reflect the popular pronunciation and the popular idiom.

Even in the concise terms of the early epitaphs there sometimes lies a clear testimony to early dogma. In the third century a greater fullness and variety appears. There are a number of prayers, particularly in Greek, which suggest a liturgical origin. Metrical inscriptions are rare until the fourth century; the earliest examples of them are commonly brief, and show a dependence upon, if not an actual quotation from, the Classical poets. But there are also inscriptions in *quasi versus*, a variety of verse invented by Commodian, a Christian poet of the third century. It is not of much interest to record that the inscriptions, early and late, testify to belief in God, in Christ as God, in the Holy Spirit, and in the Resurrection; it would be a matter of startling consequence if they did not. Of more importance are the references to baptism, particularly the baptism of infants; and to the widows and virgins of the Church.

Of all the dogmatic notices which the inscriptions furnish, none have so sympathetic an interest, and none may be accounted of such importance, as those which illustrate the custom of prayer to and for the departed. We may distinguish three classes: those containing a prayer for the peace of the departed; those petitioning the prayers of the departed in behalf of those who remain below—these two often being combined; and those calling upon all who read the inscription to pray for the person it commemorates. Such forms are fairly frequent after the middle of the second century.

To another class belong the appeals for the intercession of the martyrs. It was hardly before the fourth century that the martyrs were regarded as advocates before God for the souls of the departed. For this period, however, the popularity of the view is proved, not only by inscriptions, but by some of the paintings of the catacombs which represent the soul introduced into heaven by the saints, and the same theme appears later in the mosaics of the basilicas. It is in this cult of the martyrs that we find the roots of the later doctrine of the saints; in the official recognition of martyrdom, and in the special efficacy which was attributed to the martyr's intercession, we have the essential factors of the mediæval doctrine. It was this conception of the martyrs as advocates in the Judgment which made burial near them seem so desirable. The following inscriptions are of the fourth century:—

    CVIQVE PRO VITAE SVAE TESTIMONIO
  SANCTI MARTYRES APVD DEVM ET CRISTVM
          ERVNT ADVOCATI
        (Cemetery of Cyriaca.)

     DOMINA BASILLA COM
    MANDAMVS TIBI CRES
    CENTINVS ET MICINA
  FILIA NOSTRA CRESCEN . . .
 QVE VIXIT MENS X . ET DES . .
      (Cemetery of Basilla.)

*Domina* (*dominus*) was the title given to martyrs. The latter inscription reads: "O lady Basilla, we commit to thee Crescentinus, and our tiny daughter Crescen(tia) who lived 10 months and . . . days."

Another, from Aquileia,

> MARTYRES · SANCTI
> IN · MENTE · HAVITE
> MARIA

reads, "Holy martyrs, remember Mary."

But to return to the earlier forms which regard all the faithful departed without distinction: I have spoken of them as a sympathetic subject of study, because they are so human, so naive, and spring so promptly from the heart. The prayer for a place of refreshment, of light and peace, of rest in God, in behalf of the departed soul, was impossible from the standpoint of the pagan, simply because the other world was not conceived in such terms. To the Christian, on the other hand, these were the ideas which were naturally associated with the death of the believer; and if there was nothing in the Christian teaching which positively required such prayers, there could at least be no more solid objection brought against them than the claim that they were superfluous. What more natural, however, than that the Christian hope for the dead should at the very tomb itself be expressed as a prayer? What more natural than that such prayers should appear upon the tombstones before they were formulated in the liturgies, and before the doctrine of a purgatory of pain had turned their glad confidence into a tearful and doubtful supplication? The simple exclamations we here record bear evidence of being the fruit, not of any clear doctrinal conception, but of a popular and natural fantasy.

> · · vIBAS
> IN PACE ET PETE
> PRO NOBIS

"Live in peace! and pray for us," reads an ancient inscription in S. Domitilla. The following, of the fourth century, gives the theological ground which justifies such a prayer to the dead, "Pray for us because we know that thou art in Christ":—

> GENTIANVS FIDELIS IN PACE QVI VIX
> IT ANNIS XXI MENSS VIII DIES
> XVI ET IN ORATIONES TVIS
> ROGES PRO NOBIS QVIA SCIMUS TE IN CHRISTUM [1]

---

[1] The name of Christ is represented by the monogram.

That prayer for the dead was not associated with harrowing doubt about their fate we see, for example, in an early Greek inscription in S. Domitilla, which at the same time demands the prayer of the departed in behalf of the surviving friends:—

ΖΗCΑΙC · ΕΝ · ΚΩ · ΚΑΙ · ΕΡΩΤΑ · ΥΠΕΡ · ΗΜΩΝ

"Mayest thou live in the Lord! and pray for us." This is simply the realization of the communion of saints.

Of the third or fourth century is the following:—

ANATOLIVS FILIO BENEMERENTI FECIT
QVI VIXIT ANNIS VII MENSIS VII DIE
BVS XX ISPIRITVS TVVS BENE REQVIES
CAT IN DEO PETAS PRO SORORE TVA

"Thy spirit rest in God: pray for thy sister."

The demand for prayer in behalf of one's own soul seems to manifest a too anxious solicitude about one's fate; but it is found as early as the end of the second century in the epitaph of the Phrygian bishop, Abercius, written by himself (page 75). The following metrical inscription from S. Priscilla belongs probably to the fourth century:—

EVCHARIS · EST · MATER · PIVS · ET · PATER · EST · · ·
VOS · PRECOR · O FRATRES · ORARE · HVC · QVANDO ·
VENItis
ET · PRECIBVS · TOTIS · PATREM · NATVMQVE · ROGATIS
SIT · VESTRAE · MENTIS · AGAPES · CARAE · MEMINISSE
VT · DEVS · OMNIPOTENS · AGAPEN · IN · SAECVLA ·
SERVET

There is unfortunately but little space left to treat of the inscriptions with which Damasus adorned the tombs of the martyrs. They deserve more attention than can here be given them. They are interesting, not only as a type of Christian poetry which was admired by contemporaries and frequently copied in succeeding centuries, and because of the beautiful and characteristic letters in which they were cut; but for the fact that they reveal several pages of the history of the martyrs which but for them would be absolutely unknown, that they testify clearly to the character of the cult which was rendered to the martyrs in the fourth century, and that they make it possible to identify in each cemetery the position of the most venerated tombs. There was no cemetery at Rome which had not at least one such inscription, and still others were placed in the cemeterial basilicas and chapels. Most of the original inscriptions have totally perished, many of them at the hands of the Goths; but the text of about forty of them has been preserved through the copies made by the pilgrims. In consequence of this lucky preservation a mere fragment of the original marble suffices for the restoration of the whole inscription and serves often to fix its original location.

One of them, to cite an instance of the puzzles archæologists must solve, though the marble slab was broken into one hundred and twenty-five pieces, has been almost completely restored and put in its original place at the end of the crypt of the popes in the cemetery of Callistus (pl. 147). I give here the translation, which must suffice for an example of Damasus's poems: "Here, if you inquire, lies crowded together a throng of the righteous, the venerable tombs hold the bodies of the saints, their lofty spirits the palace of heaven took to itself. Here the companions of Sixtus who bore trophies from the enemy; here a number of the leaders who ministered at the altars of Christ; here is placed the priest who lived in long peace; here the holy confessors whom Greece sent; here young men and boys, old men and their pure descendants, who chose to keep their virgin modesty. Here, I confess, I Damasus wished to deposit my body, but I feared to disturb the holy ashes of the righteous." It is not unreasonable to suppose that a "throng" of martyrs were often buried in a single tomb, particularly such as suffered together in the same persecution. In the case of such as were burned or thrown to the beasts, often only very small portions of their bodies could be recovered. Sixtus II and his companions in martyrdom are here mentioned, although Damasus set up in this same crypt a special inscription in his honor. Those "who ministered at the altars of Christ" are probably unnamed deacons and presbyters; and the "*sacerdos*" of the next verse may refer to the Roman bishops who were buried here (using the singular for the class), though De Rossi understands Miltiades, who was the first pope to enjoy the peace given by Constantine. The "confessors" from Greece are unknown, but they may have been Hippolytus and his companions. The last lines seem intended as a rebuke to those who disturbed the bodies of the martyrs in their zeal to be buried near them.

Damasus was in fact buried in a little basilica connected with the cemetery of Domitilla, in which he prepared also the tombs of his mother and sister. For himself and for them he composed inscriptions. This chapel has not yet been discovered, but a small fragment of an inscription found near the church of SS. Cosma e Damiano was recognized by De Rossi as belonging to Damasus's inscription to his sister, the text of which was known. This piece was again lost, and has been rediscovered in the course of the excavation of the Forum. It awakens surprise that it is not inscribed in the customary Damasian letters; but this is explained by the fact that the sister died before Damasus became pope and before he had adopted the type of letter which is associated with his name.

De Rossi has traced the author of these beautiful letters, which though frequently imitated in a later age were never precisely copied. On the marble which contains the inscription to St. Eusebius, discovered in St. Callistus, there is at each end a line of smaller letters which read from top to bottom: *Damasis Pappæ cultor atque amator Furius Dionysius Filocalus scribsit*—"Furius Dionysius Filocalus the reverer and lover of Pope Damasus wrote it." This famous personage was the secretary of Damasus. In this inscription one is struck not only by the false spelling, but by the character of the letters, which in fact are only a distant imitation of the Damasian. This is explained by the fact that the original inscription had been broken, and was restored again about the end of the sixth century, perhaps by Pope Vigilius; it was then cut on the back of an inscription of Caracalla.

The interesting inscription which has been translated above is enough to show that Damasus was not a great poet; his verses are not always regular, and he shows a lack of invention in his frequent repetition of favorite words and phrases, many of them taken from Virgil. But his style was accounted elegant by Jerome (*elegans in versibus scribendis*), and he seems to have been a conscientious historian. The historical researches which he must have made about the martyrs were doubtless facilitated by the fact that he was archivist of the Roman church before he was made pope.

In the composition of metrical inscriptions Damasus had imitators among the popes. Many such inscriptions were in dedication of basilicas; some of them we shall have occasion to notice in connection with the mosaics. Suffice it to say here that with the end of the sixth century poverty and ignorance had become so general that hardly any inscriptions were produced, except the rude epitaphs of popes or of other rulers.

# III

## SEPULCHRAL ART

The earliest Christian art of which we have any knowledge is what I call here sepulchral art. It is not a very nice name, but it indicates clearly enough that this was an art appropriate especially to the tomb, because it expresses the hope of a survival of bodily death.

We have seen that early Christian writers, prompted by the fear of idolatry, expressed great diffidence about pictorial art, so that the discovery of the catacombs presented us with a surprise. It seemed almost incredible that while these good men were writing there actually was being developed in the cemeteries just such a religious art as they dreaded and reprobated. There it sprang up and developed as a spontaneous expression of the Christian faith and hope. If it had not gained so early a foothold in the cemeteries, the Church, we may imagine, might have eschewed pictorial art as absolutely as did Judaism and Islam. What a dreadful possibility to contemplate! Christendom then would have been cut off from one of the loftiest expressions of human culture. As a matter of fact, the decoration of the basilicas, or what I call more generally monumental art, was encouraged by this precedent and developed so early that in turn it could exert a marked influence upon sepulchral art in its final phase.

The Church entertained a lively hope of everlasting life, expressed concretely by belief in the resurrection of the dead. The art employed in the cemeteries was oriented, more thoroughly than may at first appear, towards that hope. Some pagans cherished a hope of immortality, but vaguely, not as "the sure and certain hope" we are bold enough to express in the Burial Office, where we affirm concretely our belief in "the resurrection unto eternal life, through our Lord Jesus Christ, at whose coming in glorious majesty to judge the world, the earth and the sea shall give up their dead, and the corruptible bodies of those who sleep in Him shall be changed and made like unto His glorious body, according to the mighty working whereby He is able to subdue all things unto Himself." We shall see that the sepulchral art of the Church, in its whole tenor and in every individual instance, affirmed this concrete faith. Life after death, life in spite of death, in spite of every presumption to the contrary which the dissolution of the body compels us to face, though it is evidently not a human possibility, and therefore is paradoxically called by Karl Barth "man's impossibility," is nevertheless the possibility of God, for "with

God all things are possible" (Mk. 10:27). This is the foundation of the Christian hope.

The Platonic hope of immortality, because it took no account of the possibility of God, but was recommended only by a non-religious myth which suggested that the human soul is by its nature indestructible, was held with so much diffidence that St. Paul could say of the Gentiles generally that they are "without hope and without God in the world" (Ephes. 2:12). Indeed it was proposed by Plato only as a *kalon kindynon*, "a fair chance." About the beginning of the Christian era several pagan cults known as "mysteries" made a strong bid for popularity by seeking to substantiate by religious myths the hope of immortality. But because these were known to be myths this hope was hardly raised above the plane of wishful thinking. Christianity successfully outbid all these cults because it appealed not to myths and legends but to what were believed to be historical facts. Myths which vaguely supported the hope of immortality were depicted upon a small minority of pagan sarcophagi. The Christian sarcophagi recounted the mighty acts of God. In the garden of the church where I ministered in Rome stood a pagan sarcophagus which bore witness to the hope of immortality: the door was unlocked and half open, and the genii, guardians of the tomb, held their torches aloft, not dejectedly extinguished as custom prescribed. I often reflected how pallid was that hope compared with the pictures inside our church. By far the greater number of the pagan sarcophagi had no reference to life beyond death but dwelt upon the fullness of life here below, expressed by Bacchic symbols, by scenes of the chase, by battles with the Amazons, etc. But sepulchral art of the Greeks attained its highest expression and its profoundest pathos when it depicted the fond farewell of dear ones who were never to meet again.

## FRESCOES

Christian art had something totally new to say, and it said it first in the frescoes of the Roman catacombs. It is obvious that during the centuries of persecution it could say it only in the underground chambers where it was customary to bury the dead. There were many other catacombs besides those of Rome, not only in Italy and North Africa, but as far north as Cologne. The Roman catacombs, however, were incomparably the most extensive, and since they are also the earliest we know of, there is a strong presumption that there Christian art began. The commoner custom of digging graves in the soil (*sub divo*), as we do, gave no scope for the development of sepulchral art.

## SEPULCHRAL ART

Whatever date is ascribed to the burial chambers in the Roman catacombs, it is certain that the first intent of the frescoes was simply decorative, an effort to make the tomb more cheerful. In the cemetery of Priscilla, which is supposed to be the burying-place of the Acilii before the end of the first century, the subjects are purely ornamental; and in the vestibule of the cemetery of Domitilla, the Flavian hypogeum of the same date, the only Biblical pictures are those of Noah and Daniel. There is no evidence that before the middle of the second century the Christian burial chambers were obviously different from others, except for the fact that themes connected with pagan religions were avoided, and that decorative subjects were preferred which, like the cycle of the four seasons (pl. 5a), had a significant application to human life. The mosaics in S. Costanza (pl. 62) show that even after the Peace of the Church this same theme was popular. Such subjects as the Good Shepherd and the orant could be used decoratively, especially on the ceilings (pl. 4a, 9a), without suggesting to the pagans a specifically Christian meaning.

It is a striking fact that many of the earliest pictures in the catacombs were from the Old Testament. I have mentioned Noah in his ark and Daniel between two lions as the earliest we happen to know of. It seems likely that the story of Jonah, which became the most popular subject of all, may have appeared as early, though we have no record of it. In the second century we have Moses striking the rock, and the companion picture of Moses taking off his shoes at the burning bush likely emerged at the same time, though we have no instance of it before the third century. The deliverance of Susanna was one of the earliest themes, but it happens that the scene in which Daniel confounds the elders is not found before the third century. The story of the deliverance of the Three Children from the fiery furnace was one of the earliest and most popular. It was associated by the artists with the Magi; for both groups wore the Persian dress, and it may have been thought naively that when the Three Children refused to worship the golden image which Nebuchadnezzar had set up, they forthwith followed the star which led them to Bethlehem, where they worshipped the Infant Christ. In the third century we have Tobias with his fish and Job in his affliction. In the fourth century, Moses and Aaron threatened by the Hebrews, the rain of manna, the fall of Adam and Eve, David with his sling, and (on the sarcophagi) Isaac saved from sacrifice and Elijah carried up to heaven. As early as the second century we have the following New Testament subjects, to mention only those which denote deliverance: the raising of Lazarus, the healing of the woman with an issue of blood, the paralytic carrying his bed, and the Samaritan woman. After the beginning of the third century, the raising of Jairus' daughter, the healing of a blind man

40

and of a leper and a demoniac. It will be noticed that Old Testament subjects predominated. This will not seem strange when we reflect that until the New Testament Canon was definitely formed about the middle of the second century the Church had no Bible but the Old Testament. The New Testament writings were read in the Church and esteemed as apostolic, but until they were canonized they did not enjoy the same reverent estimation as Holy Scripture. It was a matter of course that themes from the New Testament were multiplied after it had been raised to the same level as the Old.

The subjects enumerated above may seem at first to have little or no connection with one another. The secret was in part divulged when I spoke of several of these subjects as signal instances of deliverance. The connection was more concretely explained by Edmund Le Blant in the Introduction to his *Sarcophages de la ville d'Arles*, where he drew attention to a prayer which is still used in the Roman Church: *Ordo commendationis animæ quando infirmus est in extremis*. After a long litany we find the following supplications:

> *Receive, O Lord, thy servant into the place of salvation which he may hope of thy mercy.*
> *Deliver, O Lord, the soul of thy servant from the pains of hell, etc.*
> *Deliver, O Lord, his soul as thou didst deliver Enoch and Elijah from the common death of the world.*
> *Deliver, O Lord, his soul as thou didst deliver Noah from the deluge.*
> *Deliver, O Lord, his soul as thou didst deliver Isaac from sacrifice and from the hand of his father Abraham.*

And so the prayer continues with the same formula, mentioning the deliverance of Daniel from the den of lions, of the Three Children from the burning fiery furnace and from the hand of the wicked king, Abraham from Ur of the Chaldees, Job from his sufferings, Lot from Sodom and from the flame of fire, Moses from the hand of Pharaoh, king of the Egyptians, Susanna from false accusation, David from the hand of King Saul and from the hand of Goliath, Peter and Paul from prison, and Thecla from horrible torture.

It is remarkable that among these examples of signal divine deliverance there are very few subjects which are not represented in early Christian art, and they are such as did not lend themselves to pictorial treatment—as the deliverance of Enoch and the departure of Abraham from Ur. On the other hand, this list includes almost all of the Old Testament subjects which were employed in sepulchral art. Many of these subjects are repeated in other prayers which are connected with the Roman funeral liturgies, and it is to be remarked that Lazarus and Jonah, omitted here, are elsewhere added to the list.

This explanation was promptly welcomed, and it is accepted gratefully by all who seek any significance in the sepulchral art of the early Church. It needed only the support of a broader basis, and this was provided by Victor Schultze who pointed to analogies in early Christian literature, noting that the Bible itself encourages us to regard some of these instances as typical of the deliverance of the soul from death, and that the miracles of Christ, which soon were added to the Old Testament cycle, are properly regarded as manifestations of the divine power which is able to save to the uttermost. Although the Roman prayer is not nearly as old as the pictures in the catacombs, the same argument is exemplified by Jewish prayers which are contemporary with them, and which appear as early as the fourth century in the *Apostolic Constitutions* (v, 7); that is, in a Christian context, with the addition of Christ's miracles: "He who raised Lazarus on the fourth day and the daughter of Jairus and the son of the widow, and rose also Himself; who after three days brought forth Jonah living and unharmed from the belly of the whale, and the Three Children from the furnace of Babylon, and Daniel from the mouths of lions, shall not lack power to raise us also. He who raised the paralytic, and healed him who had the withered hand, and restored the lacking faculty to him who was born blind, the same shall raise us also. He who with five loaves and two fishes fed five thousand and had twelve baskets over, and who changed the water into wine, and who sent the stater which he took out of the mouth of the fish to those who demanded tribute by the hand of me Peter, the same shall also raise the dead."

Clearly we here have the thread which connects such various subjects as I have enumerated and explains how appropriate they were in the Christian cemeteries. They were a demonstration of God's omnipotence, a confirmation of the faith that "with God all things are possible" (Mk. 10:27). The miracles of the Old and of the New Testament combined to prove this principal article of the Christian faith. Jesus Himself ascribed all His miracles of healing to the power of God when He said, "If I by the finger of God cast out devils, then is the kingdom of God come unto you" (Lk. 11:20).

The most notable instance of God's deliverance of His people was the passage of the Red Sea. This theme presented insuperable obstacles to the artists who painted in the catacombs, but it was carved upon several of the sarcophagi.

Many of the favorite subjects in the catacombs I have hitherto omitted to mention because they do not belong strictly to the line of thought we have been following. As early as the second century we find the allegorical figure of the Good Shepherd, which subsequently was embellished with various bucolic additions. In the third century Orpheus was sometimes depicted as the mythological expression of the same idea. For, like Orpheus, the Good Shepherd was one who delivers souls from death. This thought was suggested by the twenty-third Psalm.

Themes so important as the symbols of Baptism and of the Eucharist will be dealt with later, and here it is enough to say that they emerged in the second century. Pictures of the celestial banquet, of the souls of the deceased entering paradise and being presented to Christ are not found earlier than the third century. In the fourth century the shepherds appear along with the Magi at the manger. Incidentally we have in the second century the Annunciation, Balaam pointing to a star above the Mother and Child (pl. 18c), the baptism of Christ, a single picture of His crowning with thorns (pl. 15a), His appearance as Judge, and the parable of the wise and foolish virgins. Not till the fourth century, and presumably as a reflection of the art of the basilicas, did Christ appear as the Teacher of the world, seated in the midst of His apostles, and as the Lamb of God upon a mountain from which flow four rivers. Personifications of Love and Peace, of sun and moon, of rivers and seas, were early adopted from classical art, as were dolphins, doves and peacocks, the latter, a bird which among pagans has a reference to life beyond death. This is a bare enumeration, and though it does not pretend to be complete, I mention finally the fact that the proprietors of some of the tombs had their professions depicted—as *fossores,* as provision merchants, etc.

The predominance of Old Testament subjects in the earliest art of the Church gives some countenance to the precarious contention that Christian art in its first stage was in a measure dependent upon the illustrated Bibles of the Jews. There is no evidence of such Bibles. But it is barely possible that the Jews, under the influence of such an environment as Alexandria, were so far able to forget their scruples against pictorial art. There is no evidence of it. But recently the presumption to the contrary was somewhat weakened by the discovery at Dura, a remote outpost of the Empire on the Persian border, of a synagogue (pl. 35) which was completely decorated with Biblical scenes before or shortly after the middle of the third century. The subjects, so far as they can be identified, were as follows: Moses was conspicuous on the west wall, immediately above the niche which enshrined the Torah (the books of the Law), under which was a majestic seat for the rabbi who presided. Moses was there depicted before the burning bush and in the act of receiving the Law. The pictures on either side of this central theme and on the other walls are arranged in three zones. In the uppermost zone on one side is the crossing of the Red Sea in three scenes. In the lowest zone we have the infancy of

Moses. Flanking one side of the niche are Esther and Mordecai, and opposite them Samuel in the act of anointing David. Other subjects which can be identified are the Temple, the Ark of the Covenant, and Miriam's well. On the side walls, which have been half destroyed, we can identify Jacob's dream, the capture of the Ark by the Philistines and its return to Zion (?). A long section is devoted to Elijah: the widow's cruse, the sacrifice on Carmel (1 Kings 18), and the slaughter of the priests of Baal. But the raising of the widow's son is on the west wall, and on the east Elijah is fed by ravens. One can discover no principle upon which these many subjects were selected and arranged. This is the more surprising because Christian art, whether in the catacombs or in the churches, was obviously purposeful in the choice of subjects and in their arrangements, and it may be observed that the pictures in the baptistery at Dura were appropriately chosen. The decoration of such a synagogue could not have served as a model for the Christian house of worship, even if it had been early enough to affect the development of Christian art; and the discoverers of Dura present evidence to show that in this instance the scruple which restrained the Jews from the production of pictorial art had been overcome gradually, and not completely overcome in that community until the middle of the third century. For it seems that shortly before that time they had ventured to depict only the figure of Moses, and that until then it had no pictorial decoration. This meant the tardy triumph of a liberal faction, and it cannot be assumed that many Jewish communities were equally emancipated. But even if frescoes like these were abundant, they were far too late to influence the beginnings of Christian art in the catacombs. It may be surmised that the Biblical stories could not have been depicted so well without a long period of preparatory exercise employed in illustrating the texts of Biblical manuscripts; but as yet there is no proof that the Jews ever engaged in such an activity. If anywhere, it must have been in Alexandria, a liberal center of learning where such a radical innovation might have been possible. But the frescoes at Dura exhibit none of the peculiarities of Alexandrian art. They are, of course, decidedly "Eastern"; but nothing more definite can be said about their style.

After the Peace of the Church, when New Testament themes became predominant, a few subjects were added to the Old Testament cycle, like Daniel killing the dragon, but they were not popular enough to be often repeated. That the miracles of the Old and the New Testaments were regarded as an assurance of the hope of personal deliverance from death is shown by the fact that sometimes in the place of Noah in the Ark or of Daniel amongst the lions

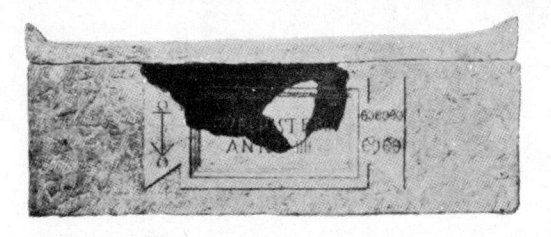

**a.** Fresco from a syncretic tomb. A "good angel" conducts Vibia to paradise, where she is seated at the celestial banquet. Fourth century.—**b.** Fresco from the cemetery of Petrus and Marcellinus. A more typical picture of the celestial banquet. Fourth century. (See p. 52.)—**c.** Sarcophagus in the cemetery of Priscilla. Early fourth century.

Pl. 11

**a.** Fresco in the cemetery of Domitilla. Veneranda introduced into paradise by St. Petronilla. Fourth century.—**b.** Orant with dalmatic and veil in the cemetery of Callistus. Third century.—**c.** Symbol of the Eucharist. A characteristic example. (See p. 54.)

Pl. 12

a. *Fractio panis* in the *Cappella greca*. Before the middle of the second century. (See p. 53.)—b, c. Eucharistic symbol in the crypt of Lucina. A glass of red wine shows through the mesh of the basket. Middle of second century. (See p. 54.)

Pl. 13

**a.** Fresco in one of the "sacrament chambers." Cemetery of Callistus. Symbols of baptism and the Eucharist: Moses strikes water from the rock; a fisherman; Christ eating with the six disciples by the Sea of Tiberias. Third century.—**b.** Fresco in the cemetery of Callistus. Daniel's judgment of the elders who accuse Susanna. Second century.—**c.** Fresco in the cemetery of Petrus and Marcellinus. Visit of the Magi. Third century.

Pl. 14

**a.** Fresco in the cemetery of Praetextatus. Christ crowned with thorns and smitten with a reed. First half of second century.—**b.** Fresco in the cemetery of Callistus. Symbol of the Eucharist. A man (in *pallium* and *tunica exomis*) blesses the loaf and fish on the tripod; the orant symbolizes the Church in prayer. Third century.—**c.** Lid of sarcophagus: The Three Children; Visit of the Magi. Third century.—**d.** Tiles with painted inscription closing the loculus of Julia, a martyr. Third century.

Pl. 15

Fresco in the cemetery of Priscilla over the tomb of a consecrated virgin. The bishop bestows the veil; the deceased as orant; the Mother and Child as an example of virginity. Third century.

Pl. 16

a. Fresco in the cemetery of Priscilla. Noah as orant in the ark, and the dove with the olive branch. Early second century.—b. Bust of Christ, central figure in a fresco in the cemetery of Petrus and Marcellinus. Fifth or sixth century.

Pl. 17

**a.** Ceiling fresco in the cemetery of Petrus and Marcellinus. The Good Shepherd. Third century.—**b.** A portrait orant. Cemetery of Thrason. Fourth century.—**c.** Fresco in the cemetery of Priscilla. Balaam, pointing to a star, foretells the birth of the divine Child. Middle of second century.—**d.** Fresco in the cemetery of Priscilla. An orant. Second century.

Pl. 18

appeared a picture of the deceased, who in this case was clothed in his ordinary dress and in the attitude of prayer, i.e., as an orant.

## THE ORANT

Orant (or orans) is a word invented by archæologists to describe one of the earliest symbols used in the catacombs. In general it is to be understood as a symbol of the soul, the disembodied soul. In its most abstract use it was a female figure, even on the tomb of a man. For this reason the word orant is preferable, and in English it is more convenient than orans because the "s" can be added to indicate the plural. Thus we can speak of two orants which alternate with the Good Shepherd in the decoration of a ceiling (pl. 4a). It is commonly said that the outstretched hands reflect the common attitude of prayer. It would be more correct to say that this is the characteristic attitude of the Christian in prayer. "Lifting up holy hands" is a Biblical expression, but it does not indicate how high the hands were lifted. Presumably the Jews raised them as high as the ears, and there spread them out, as they do now to express deprecation. The pagans raised them higher, stretching them towards heaven, in the attitude exemplified by the beautiful statue of the praying boy in the Lateran Museum, who, moved by the *élan* of a naive religion of immanence, is happily unconscious of the paradox of prayer, unaware that it might be presumptuous for man to speak to God. The Christians adopted a very significant attitude in prayer, which early writers (among them Tertullian, *De orat.* 14) described as the attitude of Christ on the cross. Modern pictures of the Crucifixion suggest to us that this must mean that the arms were stretched out horizontally—an attitude which the American Indians learned from the Spaniards. But no, what was meant is clearly indicated by one of the earliest representations of the Crucifixion, which is illustrated on plate 93b. This was the attitude of the orant (pl. 18b, d), and it is still the attitude of the priest at the altar.

Not all the Old Testament characters who were depicted as examples of divine deliverance were represented in the attitude of prayer, i.e., as an orant. We may reflect that Moses had something else to do with his hands, whether he was taking off his shoes, or receiving the Law, or striking the rock. Jonah, who had prayed in the belly of the whale, could not be depicted as an orant at the moment when he was spewed out; Abraham held in his hand the knife, and Isaac's hands were bound. Noah, Daniel, Susanna, and the Three Children were the only Biblical figures depicted in the attitude of an orant. The New

Testament figures who were healed by Christ were naturally employed in supplicating Him for help.

The orant in its most frequent use, whether in frescoes or on the sarcophagi, represented the soul of the deceased, either abstractly or conceived as a spirit portrait (pl. 12a, 16, 18b, 23c, 24b, 25b).

This attitude expresses the belief that the soul in question had entered into blessedness. The inscriptions, *in pace*, in peace, in Christ, with the martyrs, were declarative, not precative, although prayers for the dead, ejaculatory prayers, were as common as they were natural, and they were inscribed on many tombs.

But what was the fundamental significance of the orant? About this there is no unanimity. Many opinions have been advanced. Wilpert in his last book said rather presumptuously, "It is incredible these various suggestions should be made, seeing that the right interpretation was given by me thirty-eight years ago." Wilpert understands the orant to mean that the deceased are praying for the loved ones who survive them on earth. This is a consolatory reflection, and in fact many of the inscriptions addressed to the departed (and not only to eminent saints) ask for their prayers: *Pete pro nobis*. But this is not the only meaning of prayer. I have the impression that Wilpert insists upon this one meaning because he is intent to make out that the Virgin Mary, when she is depicted in this attitude (as she never is in sepulchral art, and not in any art before the Peace of the Church), is to be regarded as the Intercessor for mankind. *Deesis* is the word he uses for this notion. But certainly this notion cannot be attached to the figures of the Old Testament heroes, Noah, Daniel, etc., nor does it apply to the generic figure of the orant which was conspicuous in the earliest art of the Church. If the abstract figure of the orant may be associated with anything concrete, it must be with the Church. The orant in the catacombs is evidently praying for *himself*, supplicating God for deliverance or giving thanks to him for it. In any case the attitude of the orant expresses faith, for prayer is an expression of faith. To the eye of the beholder it is an assurance that the individual depicted in that attitude is saved, that his prayer has been heard, and that he has entered into paradise, for the essence of prayer is faith. I say like Wilpert, "it is incredible" that modern archæologists propose so many explanations of the orant, and fail to recognize that to the early Christians it was first of all a symbol of faith. Hope had its symbol in the anchor, love (*agape*) in the Lord's Supper, and if we do not find the symbol of faith in the orant, there is no other place we can look for it. Yet the Church must have had a symbol for faith, which was the distinctive quality of the Christian.

## FRESCOES

So distinctive of the New Covenant, it may be objected, that the Old Testament has almost nothing to say about it. St. Paul (Rom. 4:9, 17, 22; Gal. 3:6, 11) exploits the only two passages which exalt faith: "Abraham believed God" (Gen. 15:6); and "The just shall live by faith" (Hab. 2:4). Yet no one will venture to say that the author of the Epistle to the Hebrews was guilty of an anachronism when in the eleventh chapter he regarded all the heroes of the Old Testament as examples of faith: "By faith Abel," etc. This notion was not strange to the Jews; for in the Septuagint it is said of Daniel (6:23) that he was delivered from the lions because he "believed in his God"; and the faith of Jonah is assumed when it is said (3:5) that as a consequence of his preaching the people of Nineveh believed God. The divine acts of deliverance as they are depicted in the sepulchral art of the Church are so closely parallel to that list of the heroes of faith which we find in the Epistle to the Hebrews that they too must have been thought of as examples of faith. The fact that the objects of Christ's mercy are not represented in the attitude of the orant does not separate them from the other group, for Jesus Himself said to them, "Thy faith hath saved thee."

Understanding faith as "the substance of things hoped for, the evidence of things not seen," the Epistle to the Hebrews rightly attributes such a faith to the heroes of the Old Covenant: "By faith Abel ..., by faith Enoch ..., by faith Noah ..., by faith Abraham ..., by faith Isaac ..., by faith Moses ..." In this list David is expressly included, and though Daniel is not mentioned by name, nor the Three Children, Shadrach, Meshach and Abednego, they are embraced by the phrase, "who stopped the mouths of lions, quenched the powers of fire." So all the Old Testament examples of deliverance which were depicted in the early art of the Church are included here among the heroes of faith, excepting only Job, Jonah and Susanna. For this reason they were depicted as orants. I do not know how it could be made plainer than fundamentally the orant was understood to be the symbol of faith. When this symbol was used generically and with no relation to a particular individual it must have been understood to mean the faith of the Church, or the Church itself, the Church which manifested its faith by prayer.

It may be remarked here incidentally, for it must be said somewhere, that the appeal to history which is made by depicting these many instances of God's gracious intervention to deliver His people is characteristic of the Jewish-Christian tradition as a whole. The Greeks had no such interest in history as such; they were interested in stories, and this interest could be satisfied by myths. The Christians appealed to historical facts and founded upon them an irrefragable argument: Such things God has done in the past; we can therefore trust Him to save to the uttermost. This was the fulcrum which enabled the Church to overturn the pagan world. Early Christian writers were keenly aware of their advantage, and they pressed it triumphantly. To them history was significant because it registered the acts of God, who because He was one God might be assumed to have one constant purpose. Many gods means no history of any real importance. On the assumption that there is no god at all history becomes the grim proof of determinism which not only Karl Marx has made of it. The ancient pagan world was won over to the Christian view of history—but not easily; for Gnosticism stoutly withstood it, rejecting not only the history of the Old Testament but repudiating its God. The Christian view of history can be impugned only if it can be shown to be fallacious as a whole. It is not overthrown by the consideration that particular stories, like that of Daniel, are not historical, and that the stories of Job and Jonah did not pretend to be. Such stories have argumentative value insofar as they are believed to be historical, and they may be true, significantly true, even though they are not factual.

On the other hand, the art of the catacombs exhibits no interest in narrative for its own sake. The stories which it brings to mind are not told in detail, for they were familiar to all and needed only to be indicated by conventional formulas which resembled hieroglyphs. If they were told at all, it was without any of the scenic embellishments characteristic of Hellenistic art in its romantic phase which testifies to the Greek interest in story telling. Only one picture which has the character of a landscape has been discovered in the catacombs. In picturing the miracles of Jesus, even He, the agent, might be left out, if the story could easily be identified without introducing Him as the healer. A man carrying a bed on his back sufficed to recall the whole story of the paralytic, or rather the two stories, both of them rich in picturesque details, with which this unusual act was associated.

From this it is evident that Christian sepulchral art was not meant to be didactic, as the art employed for the decoration of the churches very properly was. In didactic art the picturesque details in the two stories of the paralytic were supplied as far as could be (pl. 74b, 75a). In the tombs men had only to be reminded of what they well knew. Fundamentally the sepulchral art of the Church was argumentative, presenting "the evidence of things not seen," and only in a limited way was it meant to be pedagogically edifying. "Dare to be a Daniel!" might in times of persecution serve as exhortation and encouragement.

To return to the orant—it cannot be said that this is the only symbol of the Church, for the ship, a ship in peril miraculously preserved, was commonly used to symbolize "the ark of Christ's Church" in its external, one might say its negative, aspect. It was used to illustrate the dictum universally accepted in early times, and not even by John Calvin rejected, that outside the Church there is no safety or salvation, *extra ecclesiam nulla salus*. But the orant exhibited it in its essential character, as "in God," "in Christ," the believing and praying Church. For this reason among others the generic figure of the orant had to be a woman, for the word *ecclesia* (church) is a feminine noun. A mosaic of the fifth century in S. Sabina (pl. 68a) uses *two* female figures to distinguish "the Church from among the Gentiles" and "the Church from the Circumcision." The former holds a Bible written in Greek characters, the other has one with Hebrew letters. Because the inscriptions indicate here how these figures are to be understood, we must interpret in the same sense an earlier mosaic in S. Pudenziana, where two women place garlands (*coronæ*) upon the heads of the two Apostles Peter and Paul, who represent respectively the mission to the Jews and to the Gentiles. These personifications of the Church are not depicted in the posture of the orant, for in both cases they have something else to do with their hands. But there is a panel on the wooden doors of S. Sabina (pl. 94a) dating from the same period, in which a woman in the attitude of the orant stands between Peter and Paul, looking up with them where the cross points, beyond the firmament of heaven to Christ in glory. Although Wilpert and many others interpret this figure as the Mother of the Lord, the early artists were never guilty of the anachronism of placing her alongside of St. Paul, and therefore this figure must be understood as the personification of the Church. Faith as "the substance of things hoped for, the evidence of things not seen" was never more perfectly represented in art.[1]

This interpretation of the orant as a symbol of the Church triumphant through faith is in a measure confirmed by the frequent juxtaposition of this figure with that of the Good Shepherd, especially where both occur in the symmetrical patterns used for the decoration of ceilings (pl. 4a). This combination is meaningful when we understand that the Good Shepherd is paired with the Church which he saves.

---

[1] See p. 161.

### THE GOOD SHEPHERD

Everyone knows that the Good Shepherd was a favorite symbol in the catacombs and on the sarcophagi (see index *s.v.*). The appropriateness of this symbol in sepulchral art is plain enough. The shepherd of the twenty-third Psalm leads his sheep "through the valley of the shadow of death"; in the Synoptic Gospels the shepherd of the parable (Lk. 15:4-6) finds the lost sheep and "layeth it upon his shoulders rejoicing"; and when the parable is interpreted allegorically in Jn. 10:1-18, Christ Himself is "the Good Shepherd who giveth his life for the sheep," the point is clearly eschatological. From the parable of the lost sheep the artists derived the familiar figure of the youthful shepherd carrying the sheep upon his shoulders, either holding the four feet in one hand in front of his breast, or two feet in each hand—the modes in which shepherds were commonly seen carrying their wounded sheep. The artists found a model ready to hand in the pagan statues of Hermes Criophoros. For this reason the Good Shepherd sometimes carries a kid or a goat. Hence in these pictures there was in fact no such pathos as Matthew Arnold discovered in his famous line,

*And on his shoulders not a lamb—a kid.*

Later the Good Shepherd was depicted in the performance of the multifarious activities of his idyllic profession. After the middle of the fourth century this figure sometimes was given the features conventionally attributed to St. Peter (pl. 25c, d). We must remember that every bishop was regarded as a "pastor," and Peter in particular had received from the Lord the charge, "Feed my sheep" (Jn. 21:16, 17). But it is to be understood that Peter did not carry the sheep to paradise, like the Good Shepherd, but back to the Church.

The figure of the Good Shepherd, though in the first place it was used in sepulchral art, had obviously a broader interest, and Eusebius in his *Life of Constantine* records that the Emperor used this and the figure of Daniel between the lions to adorn fountains in Constantinople. They were likely bronze statues. It is significant that this is the only theme in Christian art which was often presented as a statue. The Church frowned upon carving in the round, because it might easily lead to idolatry. The Good Shepherd was so plainly a symbol that it was not liable to be abused. But portrait statues were rare, even those of emperors, and the only statue of a martyr we know is that of St. Hippolytus (pl. 101c). The use of statues in the churches can claim no sanction in early tradition. In the Eastern Church they were never used, and there the violence of the iconoclasts was aimed only at the reverence paid to pictures.

## THE CELESTIAL BANQUET

No subject in early Christian art had a more obvious reference to life beyond the grave than the celestial banquet, a picture of the *refrigerium* in paradise. It is commonly remarked that this subject was suggested by one particular saying of Jesus: "They shall come from the east and from the west and from the north and the south and recline at table in the kingdom of God" (Lk. 13:29). But in fact this same notion emerges more often in the Gospels than we commonly observe. Matthew's version of this saying (8:11), "recline with Abraham, Isaac and Jacob," taken together with the saying about Lazarus lying "in Abraham's bosom" (Lk. 16:22, 23; cf. Jn. 13:23), suggests that this was a notion familiar to the Jews. Jesus led His disciples to expect such heavenly refreshment when at the Last Supper He said (Mk. 14:25), "Verily I say unto you, I will no more drink of the fruit of the vine until that day when I drink it new in the kingdom of God." The implication is that He will then drink again with them, and the word "new," which signifies the heavenly change which everything must undergo in the kingdom of God, relieves this conception of all grossness. In my understanding of the improvised banquet near Bethesda (the feeding of the multitude, Mk. 6:32-45 and the duplicates) it was primarily a pledge that the disciples who ate with Him there would be His guests at the celestial banquet.[1]

But these intimations in the Gospels are so slight that we commonly ignore them—even mistranslate them. It can hardly be thought that they alone furnished the suggestion which prompted the artists in the catacombs to depict the celestial banquet. One might say rather that they furnished a Christian sanction for adopting a pagan symbol for the peace, abundance and refreshment to be expected in the life beyond death. Refreshment, *refrigerium*, meant not only drink but substantial food. Many pagan sarcophagi depict the traveller who has said farewell to his dear ones and, accompanied by his faithful dog, reaches the place of rest and plenty where the dog too has his bone. For the pagans this was wishful thinking. Many savage tribes have dreamed of happy hunting grounds. The Christian pictures are quite like the pagan, except that the dog is austerely excluded, and that the fish (which often appears in pagan pictures) is the only viand presented on the table. In

---

[1] See my *Short Story of Jesus*, pp. 107ff.

both cases bread was served as a matter of course, and the *petits pains* bear the mark of the cross, inasmuch as they were customarily folded in that fashion. The Christians, no doubt, saw a special significance in this. In one instance such breads are carved on a sarcophagus (pl. 11c) with the monogram of Christ, and are thus distinguished as Eucharistic bread. The number of guests at the celestial banquet is invariably seven, and by this it is distinguished from pictures of the funeral feast, which also was celebrated by Christians and pagans alike. But seven was also the number depicted in the symbols of the Eucharist. It seems to have been prescribed by the consideration that six disciples ate with the risen Lord on the shore of the Sea of Tiberias (Jn. 21:1-14). The celestial banquet is distinguished by the fact that servants are on hand to serve the wine (pl. 11). Wine was commonly drunk warm, and it always was mixed with water because it must have a high alcoholic content in order to keep for any time in "bottles" of skin or clay. Plate 11 furnishes fair examples of the celestial banquet, where, as in the Eucharistic symbol, the guests recline upon a semicircular sofa (*cline*) about a table called a *sigma* because of its resemblance to the Greek letter "s." In this instance the servants are named Peace and Love. One of the guests cries, "Peace, mix me wine"; another, "Love, give me warm wine." The picture on plate 12a represents a lady named Veneranda who is introduced into paradise by her "good angel"; and there she is seen seated at table. The place of honor was at the "right corner" (which is the left as viewed by the beholder), and accordingly it is there Christ is placed in pictures of the Last Supper. The place next in importance was at the other corner.

Except for its association with the Eucharist and with an appearance with the risen Lord, the picture of the celestial banquet is not sublime. Yet it represents the desire for rest, peace and refreshment which is encouraged by the Bible. Our activistic age, not satisfied with this ideal, demands an opportunity for "service" in heaven, and to satisfy this we have revised the Book of Common Prayer. The revisers, I take it, must have been young men, exuberant exponents of muscular Christianity and the strenuous life, to whom it might seem better to serve in hell than reign in heaven. At my age, after a laborious life, I long for rest, and in these times especially it is consoling to think that in heaven there will be someone to serve me.

The word "celestial" is not exactly appropriate in this connection; for these early Christians were in one respect not so naive as we; they did not ignore the consideration that the perfect consummation of bliss is not to be attained until the Last Day, with the resurrection of the dead. But encouraged by Christ's word to the dying thief (Lk. 23:43), they dared to believe that after death their souls would be in paradise. It has been said that scenic art was rare in the catacombs; but it was used, very sparingly, it is true, to depict the delights of paradise. For heaven itself a very different glory was imagined, yet not arbitrarily imagined, for it reflected in every detail the Revelation of St. John.

The celestial banquet is a theme which did not emerge in the catacombs till the third century, at a time when the Church had grown less fearful of following pagan precedents. It therefore did not influence the form in which a distinctively Christian theme, the Eucharistic feast, was presented a century earlier. Although the Eucharist cannot be reckoned among the proofs of immortality which were furnished by the mighty acts of God recounted in the Old and New Testaments, it is nonetheless evidently appropriate in sepulchral art; for both Baptism and the Eucharist were more than proofs, they were the pledge of eternal life.

## THE EUCHARIST

Although baptism was represented realistically as well as symbolically in the frescoes of the catacombs, the Eucharist could be represented only by symbols, for the reason that the ceremony was surrounded by so much mystery that outsiders were not permitted to behold it, and the early Christian writers were chary about describing it. Not till the Middle Ages did any artist venture to depict the Eucharist as it was actually celebrated in the Church (pl. 151, 148, 150). It seems to us that by maintaining such secrecy the Church exposed itself needlessly to the horrible suspicions which were current among pagans, that in this sacrament the Christians murdered infants in order to drink their blood. The only picture which is in a certain degree realistic is a fresco in the *Cappella greca* (pl. 13a), where we see a little group gathered in this very crypt to celebrate the sacrament in memory of their dead, using the tombstone for an altar. The number of persons present is seven, as at the celestial banquet; but the veiled woman in the midst suggests a different interpretation, and this is borne out by the striking gesture of the man who is breaking the loaf, for "the breaking of bread," *fractio panis*, was so characteristic of the Eucharist that it was often denoted by this name, and so far as we know the phrase was never used in any other connection. The meaning is made perfectly clear (in spite of some archæologists who are inclined to be contentious) by the seven baskets which are ranged on either side.

This picture, without the realistic traits to which I have called attention, was often repeated in the catacombs. It seems to have been the earliest symbol of the Eucharist; and it is supposed that the more concise symbols, the baskets, the loaf, and the fish, were abbreviations of it. In its fullest form it depicted seven men seated in a half circle (*sigma*) about a round table or a tripod on which is displayed the principal viand, a fish, the symbol of Christ (pl. 12c), and on either side are ranged the seven baskets. I have already intimated that the number of persons was determined by the story (Jn. 21:1-14) of the appearance of the risen Lord to six disciples on the shore of the Sea of Tiberias, where He gave them bread and fish to eat. In one picture (pl. 14a) the disciples, being fishermen just landed from their boats, are properly represented with very scanty clothing, which is what the Gospel means by "naked" (Jn. 21:7). The seven baskets refer more obviously to the feeding of the four thousand (Mk. 8:8), and the two fishes which are commonly seen on the table are mentioned in the other story of this miracle (Mk. 6:41). On plate 13 we see the "two fishes," and alongside of them two baskets containing the fragments of bread which were left over. In this case, to make the reference to the Eucharist more abundantly clear, a glass of red wine can be discerned through the mesh of the baskets. Originally these figures flanked a picture of the Eucharistic feast, which was destroyed to make place for a new grave.

We were ill-prepared to understand that there could be a relation between the feeding of the multitude and the sacrament of the Eucharist such as is expressed by the earliest art of the catacombs, and even now many are disposed to regard it as a vain conceit. For, in fact, the Synoptic Gospels give no hint that this miracle had any connection whatever with the Last Supper or with the Eucharistic sacrament; and, strangely enough, no one was ready to take at its face value the sixth chapter of St. John which assumes the closest connection. St. John, who for reasons of his own, did not mention the Last Supper, brings the feeding of the multitude into an immediate relation with Christ's Eucharistic discourse about the true bread from heaven which giveth life. In St. John's Gospel the eschatological implications of the sacrament are expressed as strongly as they were by the artists of the catacombs and by writers of the same period: "He that eateth My flesh and drinketh My blood hath eternal life, and I will raise him up at the last day." The short liturgy in the *Didache* regards the Eucharist as the nourishment of eternal life; St. Ignatius called it "the medicament of immortality, the antidote of death"; and St. Clement of Alexandria, "the provender of eternal life." In Protestantism this range of thought has vanished completely, and in Catholicism it is only vaguely apprehended. The Roman and the Protestant liturgies are alike in seeing not much more in the Eucharist than the memorial of Christ's atoning death. <u>Hardly a trace is left of the forward-looking, eschatological emphasis which was predominant in early Catholic thought.</u> In spite of St. John, no one before Albert Schweitzer perceived the eschatological implication of the Synoptic account of the miracle. In my *Short Life of Jesus* (pp. 110 ff.) I sought to justify St. John as well as the early Christian artists, and more recently I have said more to the same effect in my book on *Essential Action in the Liturgy*. The fact that this thought emerged in the earliest art of the catacombs, and appears to have been well established by the middle of the second century, raises the presumption that it was entertained earlier, and perhaps bears witness to a tradition which antedates the Fourth Gospel.

## THE FISH

I have already remarked that the choice of the fish as a symbol of Christ seems in the first instance to have been due to the mere fact that two fishes were included in the repast near Bethsaida. The most summary abbreviation of that story is the picture of two fishes. Commonly they flank the anchor, symbol of hope (pl. 55d). Perhaps the earliest use of the single fish is on the sarcophagus of Livia Primitiva (pl. 7b), where it is paired with the anchor, the Good Shepherd being in the middle. This is a hieroglyph for the common epitaph *spes in Christo*.

But it is certain that this symbol owed its great popularity to the invention of the famous acrostic which discerns in ΙΧΘΥΣ, the word for fish, the initial letters of the Lord's full title: Ἰησοῦς Χριστός Θεοῦ Ὑιός Σωτήρ, i.e., Jesus Christ Son of God, Saviour. This in a way deepened the meaning of the fish symbol in its relation to the Eucharist, emphasizing the fact that the food there offered is Christ Himself, and at the same time it freed it from this exclusive association, so that it might be used with reference to baptism, and still more broadly as the symbol of Christ in whatever connection He was thought of. Prosper of Aquitaine speaks of Christ as "giving Himself as food to the disciples by the seashore, and offering Himself to the whole world as *Ichthys*." Irenæus affirms (*Adv. hær.* IV, 18:5) that "bodies when they receive the Eucharist no longer belong to corruption but have hope of immortality."

The fish appears from the second to the fourth century and well beyond that in a great variety of connections and upon all sorts of monuments, upon amulets, carved stones and rings. Clement of Alexandria counselled Christians, if they were to wear rings at all, to wear them on the little finger of the left hand where they would be no impediment to labor, and to engrave upon them Christian symbols, the fish and the dove, the anchor, the lyre and the ship. That his advice was followed we see from several seals which are illustrated here (pl. 55d, e, 54a). I leave it to the reader to decipher them. The game is worth the candle. The dolphin was, of course, thought of as a fish, and because it was reputed to be friendly to man it was the more commonly used in decorative art. It gained a sepulchral significance from the fable that it carried the souls of the departed to the islands of the blest. Fishing scenes were common in classical art where the interest was purely decorative; but in Christian art (see index *s.v.* fisherman) a profound significance was attached to them. The fisherman represented the apostolic "fishers of men," for not only was Christ a fish, but His disciples as well. Tertullian says: "We little fish, after the image of our Ichthys Jesus Christ, are born in the water, nor otherwise than swimming in the water are we safe." This, of course, refers to baptism.

This symbolism is summed up in the epitaph of the third or fourth century written for a certain Pectorius of Autun. It is an acrostic, the first letter of each line forming the word ichthys: "Divine progeny of the heavenly Ichthys, receive with pious heart among mortals the immortal spring of divinely cleansing waters; refresh thy soul, my friend, with the perennial waters of the wisdom which maketh rich; receive the delicious food of the Saviour of saints; eat, hungry one, holding Ichthys in thy two hands."

Of far higher importance for the whole character of early Christian symbolism is the famous metrical epitaph of Abercius, discovered by Dr. Ramsay and now in the Vatican (pl. 9d). Abercius has been plausibly identified as the bishop of Hieropolis, a small town in Phrygia. He lived in the latter part of the second century, and presumably made his visit to Rome in the time of the Antonines. The inscription was known only from manuscripts until Dr. Ramsay discovered large fragments of the sepulchral *stele*. It reads as follows:

"I, a citizen of an elect city, have in my lifetime erected this monument, to have a place to put my body when time shall require it.

"My name is Abercius, a disciple of the holy Shepherd who feeds His sheep upon the hills and plains, who has great eyes which see through all, who taught me the sure learning of life, and sent me to Rome to see the royal city and the queen clad in a golden robe and with golden shoes. There I saw a people who had the gleaming seal. I saw also the plains of Syria and all cities,

## FRESCOES

Nisibis, beyond the Euphrates. Everywhere I found fellow believers, Paul . . . ; everywhere Faith was my guide, and gave me everywhere for food the Ichthys from the spring, the great, the pure, which the spotless Virgin caught and ever puts before the Friends to eat. She has also delicious wine, and she proffers wine mixed with water along with bread. I, Abercius, dictated this to be written in my presence when I was seventy-two years old. Let everyone who shares my confession and understands this inscription pray for Abercius.

"No man may lay another body in my grave. But if it be done, he must pay to the Roman treasury two thousand gold pieces, and to my dear native city Hieropolis one thousand gold pieces."

It is implied here that the mystic symbolism of this inscription would be understood only by fellow believers. The enigmatical language is due partly to the consideration that baptism and the Eucharist were secrets jealously guarded by the Church. Yet the Eucharist, as we have seen, is appropriately mentioned in a sepulchral inscription, and in the account of such a journey it belongs essentially as the customary expression of communion with a visiting bishop. Abercius speaks mysteriously of Christ as "the Fish," and having begun in this vein, he proceeds rather fantastically to speak of the Virgin Mother as the one who "caught" the fish. He says also, strangely enough, that it is she who offers this food to the Friends. The queen clad in gold must mean the Church in Rome, and the "gleaming seal" is, of course, the sacrament of baptism. So it was commonly called. This was suggested by Rev. 7:4 ff., and in the baptismal ceremony the last act was marking the sign of the cross with oil upon the forehead of the neophyte—a rite which in the West was subsequently deferred and regarded as a separate sacrament of confirmation. Faith was his guide, for everywhere he found fellow believers, and everywhere substantial uniformity in ritual.

## BAPTISM

Not only the Eucharist but also the seal of baptism was a pledge of immortality. For this reason baptism figures frequently in the art of the catacombs. Cyril of Jerusalem (*Catechesis*, 111:11) says that "by baptism the sting of death is destroyed," and (in his *Introductory Catechism*, 16) that "baptism is a holy and unbreakable seal, the chariot to heaven, the rapture of paradise, the title to heavenly citizenship," and Irenæus (*Adv. hær.* iv, 18:5) calls it "the bath which insures incorruptibility" (cf. Hermas: *Simil.*, ix, 16).

Although various sacred acts were commonly called *mysteria*, or in Latin sacraments, baptism and the Eucharist, because they were instituted by Christ, were in a class by themselves, and the effort to discover pictures of other sacraments in the so-called sacrament chapels of the cemetery of Callistus is an anachronism. One might think that the picture of the paralytic carrying his bed was meant as a symbol of the sacrament of penance, seeing that Jesus in healing the paralytic at Capernaum had said with challenging emphasis, "Thy sins be forgiven thee" (Mk. 2:1-12). But in fact the solemn reconciliation to the Church of members who had lapsed during the Decian persecution, though it was an important precedent, had not yet become a customary sacrament for the discipline and edification of believers. And although this figure often appears in early Christian art (see index *s.v.* paralytic), it appears probable that the artists of the catacombs had in mind rather the other case of a man who was told to take up his bed and walk (Jn. 5:8), the impotent man by the pool of Bethesda (Bethsaida in the Vulgate), and that it was associated with baptism because of the angel which descended and "troubled the waters" (Jn. 5:4).

Many of the allusions to baptism were as farfetched as this. Tertullian (*De bapt.*) enumerated as symbols of baptism: the creation of the world when "the Spirit of God moved upon the face of the waters," the healing of the impotent man by the side of the pool, the deliverance of Noah from the Flood, the passage of the Red Sea, the waters of Marah (Ex. 15:23-25), and the water struck by Moses from the rock. Cyprian (*Epist.* 63:8) adds to these the Samaritan woman at the well, which was in fact a favorite theme in the catacombs and in later art, partly because it is an instance of Jesus' interest in persons who were not Jews, and perhaps chiefly because of the saying, "Whosoever drinketh of the water that I shall give him shall never thirst, but the water that I shall give him shall become in him a well of water springing up unto eternal life" (Jn. 4:14; cf. 7:38). But it would seem that water which enters into a man, or "proceeds out of his belly," has not much to do with baptism. Cyprian reduces to an absurdity the symbolical method of interpretation when he affirms that "as often as water is mentioned in the Holy Scriptures baptism is meant." Because of such licentious use of symbolism sober-minded men are disposed to make no use of it at all, and will not even recognize a symbol when they see it. But from what has already been said it is evident that the art of the catacombs was in fact symbolical in several senses of the word. The extravagant use of symbolism by Christian writers leads us to expect it. Visitors to the cemeteries might be inclined to attach a variety of meanings to the pictures they saw there; but we, if we are sober, will be content with the primary symbolism.

## FRESCOES

It is certain that the figure of a fisherman was regarded as a symbol of baptism. It occurs frequently on the sarcophagi but only four times in fresco. In one of the sacrament chambers the fisherman has thrown his line into the waters which Moses strikes from the rock, and close to him is a picture of the meal of the disciples by the Sea of Tiberias. In another case the fisherman is close to the impotent man who was healed as he lay beside the pool of Bethesda. But this perhaps is not very significant, inasmuch as the artists practiced economy by making use of any water that happened to be available. On the sarcophagi the fishermen take advantage of the water supplied by the Flood on which the ark of Noah floats, or of the sea where Jonah is swallowed by the monster (pl. 22a, b, 25b).

Pictures of the baptism of Jesus are fairly frequent in the catacombs, and may be distinguished from ordinary baptisms by the descent of the dove. It seems to us a matter of course that this subject should occur; but pictures of Christ's infancy, of His "life," and of His suffering are rare in the catacombs, and it is likely that the pictures of His baptism were prized as a support for the sacrament which was practiced by the Church. The lack of such themes is the more striking because they were prominent in the decoration of the churches and even on the sarcophagi. We must remember that before the Peace of the Church pictures illustrating distinctively Christian themes could not be carved in the shops or publicly displayed. The elaborate sarcophagi were made after the Peace, but the greater part of the frescoes in the catacombs antedated it, and was therefore in a sense pre-theological. It reflected the popular understanding of Christianity at a time when the Trinitarian and Christological questions which agitated the fourth and fifth centuries had hardly been broached. A growing apprehension of the importance of these questions is manifested by the pictures which were chosen to decorate the churches. This art was reflected in the later pictures of the catacombs, and still more clearly by the sarcophagi. It is significant that pictures of Adam and Eve, illustrating the fall of our first parents, came into vogue after the Peace—as a sign that the problem of sin and redemption had begun to replace the problem of natural death with which the earlier art had been exclusively concerned. Hence the Incarnation and the Passion acquired immense significance, not only with a view to the forgiveness of sin, but for life itself, if it is profoundly conceived. Athanasius concluded his book *De incarnatione* with the affirmation that the Logos "became human that we might become divine; and He manifested Himself through the body that we might receive an idea of the invisible Father; and He suffered the insolence of men that we might inherit immortality." From this point of view, which was that of the Church Fathers, the Incarnation, the Passion and the Resurrection of Christ were absolutely the most appropriate themes for sepulchral art, being the most evidential support of the hope of eternal life.

In his *Dogmengeschichte* (ii, p. 155) Adolf Harnack says: "Natural theology as developed by the Greeks covered the ground so thoroughly that it could be challenged only by an historical fact of eminent uniqueness. Such a fact—'the newest of the new, yea, the only new thing under the sun'—was known to the Greek Fathers: *the Incarnation of the Son of God*. This of itself counterbalanced the whole system (so far as it was counterbalanced) and exercised upon it a decisive influence. But it applied with perfect clarity to one particular point, *the fact of death*, which appeared all the more irrational in proportion as a higher worth was attached to it. Death, the dreadful paradox, is resolved by the most paradoxical fact conceivable: *that God became man*." I rub my eyes; for this is the voice of Kierkegaard, though the hand is the hand of Harnack!

Doubtless the more refined points of the theological controversy were not perfectly understood by the people in the fourth century; but all were interested, and all were aware that *vere Deus et vere homo* expressed the gist of it. Accordingly, the pictures in the churches, though they did *not* imply any biographical interest in what we call "the life of Jesus," emphasized the Incarnation, the Passion and the Resurrection. This corresponded with the liturgical emphasis upon Christmas, Holy Week and Easter. Though this emphasis is reflected in the sarcophagi, the frescoes of the catacombs were for the most part too early to be affected by this new and profounder train of thought. The Peace of the Church, though with worldly triumph it brought worldly corruption, coincided nevertheless with a profounder conception of Christianity, which gradually had resulted from the study of the Old and New Testament Scriptures. Without this background of Hebraic tradition the teaching of St. Paul could not be rightly understood, nor could the potent influence of Greek philosophy be offset.

In spite of the fact that since the middle of the second century the Roman baptismal creed (the Apostles' Creed, as we call it) emphasized the faith that Jesus was born of the Holy Ghost of the Virgin Mary, that He was crucified under Pontius Pilate, and was buried, and rose again the third day, these themes, which were duly stressed in the baptisteries and the basilicas, were, as we have seen, hardly depicted at all in the catacombs. In sepulchral art there is no picture of the Annunciation, and of the Visitation there is only one instance (on a sarcophagus in Ravenna). The adoration of the shepherds was not depicted before the Peace, though the angels telling them the good news emerged earlier. Pictures of the Mother and Child are the more interesting because they are rare. The oldest and most significant picture represents Balaam pointing to a star above the head of the Infant (pl. 18c), an allusion to his prophecy (Num. 24:17): "I see Him, but not now; I behold Him, but not nigh: there shall come forth a star out of Jacob, and a scepter shall rise out of Israel." In another instance (pl. 16) the Mother and Child are introduced as an example of virginal continence, in a scene in which a bishop gives the veil to a consecrated virgin who was buried in the tomb below and appears in the center of the picture in the posture of an orant.

The catacombs give evidence of a strong reluctance on the part of Christians to portray the Saviour realistically, and as great a reluctance to depict His passion. It is well known that the Crucifixion was not represented realistically before the fifth century (pl. 93b, 95c). There is only one picture in the catacombs which depicts the crowning with thorns (pl. 15a), and when it appears on the sarcophagi it is a wreath (*corona*) a soldier places daintily upon His head (pl. 27b). For all that, it is astonishing to observe that the catacombs contain no scenes of the Resurrection of Christ, though this theme is evidently more pertinent to the hope of life beyond death than is the raising of Lazarus and the widow's son at Nain. In the catacombs it is sometimes disconcerting to find that pictures which strike us as peculiarly congenial belong to the latest period, such, for example, as the very modern figure of Christ illustrated on plate 17b. All of the pictures which represent Christ seated in the midst of the apostles are at least as late as the fourth century. This theme appears more commonly on the sarcophagi (pl. 20b, 26b, 30, 31), but there too it was a reflection from the apsidal mosaics (pl. 57, 69b). In this scene Christ is not only Teacher but Judge, the judge of all mankind. But sepulchral art had in mind, not the universal judgment, but the individual scrutiny every soul must be prepared to undergo upon departing from the body. The deceased is brought personally into the presence of Christ. For example, a handsome sarcophagus illustrated on plate 26b, although it was bought to bury the body of a bishop, was intended for a married couple, and the man and wife at either end are introduced humbly into the presence of Christ and His apostles.

## THE MAGI

In view of what has been said above about the dearth of pictures in the catacombs which have to do with the infancy of Jesus, it is surprising that the adoration of the Magi was a favorite theme (see index *s.v.* Magi). There may have been more than one reason for this preference, and perhaps it was not at first prompted by a dogmatic interest. The Church from among the Gentiles showed a predilection for stories which illustrated the attraction which Christ exercised upon individuals outside the pale of Judaism. The Magi presented a case of peculiar interest; for they were not simply "wise men from the East" but as priests of Zoroastrianism they represented the ancient religion of Persia which in old times had made a profound impression upon the Jews during their exile, and in its latest phase as Mithraism, a cult disseminated throughout the Empire, especially among the soldiers, became in the third century the chief rival of Christianity. We must also take into account the fact that the festival of the Epiphany, the manifestation of Christ to the Gentiles, celebrated on the sixth of January, enjoyed unrivalled popularity until, near the middle of the fourth century, Christmas was celebrated on the twenty-fifth of December, the winter solstice as it was then, and the pagan festival *solis invicti,* of the unconquered sun. This is one of the indications that Constantine confused Christianity with sun worship, especially with that form of it which was exemplified by Mithraism. Some of his coins bear the Mithraic motto *Soli invicto comiti* (pl. 55b), the gist of which Kipling in his hymn to Mithras expressed very well in the refrain, "For he was a soldier too." Although we find no mention of the festival of Christmas before the time of Constans, it is plausible to suppose that Constantine established it.[1] The earlier festival, because it celebrated the manifestation of Christ to the Gentiles, involved, of course, the Magi—and for the same reason it did not involve the shepherds, who were Jews, nor the ox, nor the ass. In Italy this festival, Befania, is still the more popular of the two.

But there is reason to believe that what attracted the Magi into the cycle of sepulchral art was a more trivial circumstance, namely, a formal likeness to the Three Children in the fiery furnace, which was one of the earliest subjects in the catacombs. The Magi, of course, were Persians; and in representing the Three Children (see index) the artists faithfully followed the Biblical description (Dan. 3:21): "in their mantels, their hosen, and their hats, and their other garments." That is to say, they wore the dress which in

---

[1] For Constantine's interest in the sun see pp. 97, 111.

Roman art was conventionally attributed to Persians: the Phrygian cap, a short fluttering cape fastened above the right shoulder, a short girded tunic, and tight-fitting pants. With better reason the Magi were dressed in the same way (pl. 14c), and ultimately their number (which is not indicated in the Bible) was fixed at three, to correspond with Shadrach, Meshach and Abednego. The fact that the gifts they brought were of three sorts was not understood to imply that there were just so many givers; and in the third century a liking for symmetry led the artists to depict two Magi or four. Not till the Middle Ages did they acquire the names of Balthazar, Melchior and Casper, three kings of Orient, representing the three principal races of mankind.

We are not told in the third chapter of Daniel whether the golden image Nebuchadnezzar set up was the image of himself or of his god. But the Christians preferred the former and less plausible alternative because the refusal of the Three Children to worship the image of a king had profound pathos for them, who might at any time be thrown to the lions or burnt at the stake for refusal to worship the image of an emperor. The scene of their brave refusal resembled closely the picture of the Magi before Herod. The earliest form in which the Three Children were presented in the catacombs was standing in the furnace where a stoker is engaged in heating it seven times more than usual. The fact that they were saved nevertheless is indicated by their attitude as orants, and also by the presence among them of a fourth figure "like a son of the gods." When the story was told more elaborately, the likeness with the Magi was so close that the two subjects were often depicted side by side, and sometimes they were merged by placing the star above the Three Children. It looks as if the artists may have been naive enough to think of this as a real sequence—as though the Three Children, refusing to worship the image, were guided by a star to Bethlehem where they worshipped the divine Infant.

This combination, especially when the Magi were paired with the shepherds, made a long frieze which hardly could be contained on the side of a sarcophagus and was therefore commonly carved on the lid, where the surface available was long but narrow, requiring small figures.

The fact that both these "historical" stories were fictitious, even if this had been recognized, would not have rendered entirely vain the purpose for which they were depicted in sepulchral art. In a little book called *The Birth of the Divine Child* I made an effort twenty years ago to justify the use of religious myth. That book has been generally ignored—perhaps because it was little. At all events, there is no room for such an argument here.

## DANIEL AND SUSANNA

It is rather astonishing (perhaps disquieting) that many of the "historical" themes which were popular in the earliest art of the catacombs were drawn from the Book of Daniel, several of them from parts of that book which are not contained in the Protestant Bible and are stigmatized as apocryphal. One of them was the story of Susanna (Dan. 13:1-6 in the Vulgate), who by the wise judgment of Daniel was exonerated from the false charge brought against her by the two elders. The judgment scene (pl. 14b) depicts the climax of this story; but it sufficed if with the brevity of early Christian art Susanna was represented as an orant between two wolves (or as a lamb between wolves), like Daniel between two lions.

Protestants are not all of them aware that Daniel was *twice* thrown to the lions. In the first instance (Dan. 14 in the Vulgate) he was the victim of popular indignation because he had pulled down the statue of Bel and slain the dragon which they of Babylon worshipped. It was on this occasion the angel carried the prophet Habakkuk by the hair of his head from Judæa to Babylon in order to give to Daniel in the lions' den the bowl of pottage and bread he was on the point of taking to the reapers in his field. This story must be known because it is frequently depicted in early Christian art (pl. 19a, c, 20a, 93a). But commonly the artists perferred a perfectly symmetrical composition: Daniel standing alone between two lions. Daniel was naked, like our first parents and Jonah. These were the only naked figures in Christian art. If an orant fully clothed appears between two lions, we are to understand that this represents the soul of the deceased delivered from death and the powers of evil. In one case illustrated here we see a boy (pl. 25b), in another an apostle (pl. 28).

## JONAH

Another "historical" subject many times repeated is the story of Jonah (see index). Garrucci published thirty-five instances, and Wilpert as many more. It may be that even the early Christians, in spite of the novelistic features of this story, did not recognize it as a sublime invention to stir up interest in foreign missions. But at least they were not troubled by the inept objection of modern scoffers who insist that the "great fish" of the Biblical story must have been a whale, and more particularly a right whale, which is said to have a gullet so small that it cannot swallow a herring. The sperm whale, on the other hand, can easily swallow a man. But the early Christian artists made use of the sea monster or dragon which was common in classic art, especially in the story of Perseus and Andromache. This beast could easily swallow Jonah, but it remained a puzzle how he could have turned in so narrow a belly so as to come out head first after he had entered head first. I know of only one case where the artist has deliberately avoided this perplexity by putting him in feet first (pl. 22b). Wilpert mentions another where he comes out feet first. But not many would be troubled by such trifling incongruities in a fabulous story. It was enough that Jesus had associated Jonah with His own resurrection (Mt. 12:39 f.).

In the catacombs and on the sarcophagi this story was commonly depicted in three scenes, the last of which represents the prophet lying naked and in idyllic ease under an arbor covered with ivy or with a gourd. "Ivy" was Jerome's translation, which may have been suggested by the artistic tradition. Augustine corrected it by "gourd." No worm gnawed this gourd, nor did it ever fade; for the Christian artists meant to depict everlasting bliss. The figure of Jonah is so beautiful because they took as their model classical pictures of Endymion, the symbol of enchanted sleep and eternal youth. This story, like that of the Three Children and the Magi required so much room that it was often carved on the lid of a sarcophagus. But artists who had a *horror vacui* contrived to find place on the side of a sarcophagus for an abbreviated presentation of the subject, the last scene being always preferred, because it contained the gist of the story.

## NOAH

Noah, a prehistoric theme, was one of the earliest and most popular subjects both in the frescoes and on the sarcophagi (see index). This story was prized as a symbol of deliverance, and it was so succinctly told that room could be found for it anywhere, if only there was water, such as the sea into which Jonah was thrown. For in early Christian art the Ark was far from being a seaworthy ship—it was merely a cubical box, having a lid and a lock. Christian artists did not invent this form: the word "box" was used in the Septuagint, and precisely such a box as we see in the catacombs was used in classic art to tell the story of Danaë and Perseus set adrift in the sea, or of Deucalion and Pyrrha in the Greek myth of the Flood. The same box appears on a coin (pl. 54b) minted in the reign of Septimius Severus for the small state of Apamea in Phrygia which was proud of the distinction of containing within its boundaries the great Mount Ararat on which the Ark grounded. The Biblical story is faithfully followed so far as space would permit. Noah and his wife stand in the Ark, and a second time they are represented standing on dry ground, holding up one hand in a prayer of thanksgiving for deliverance. The raven as well as the dove with the olive branch perches on the rim. The Christian picture was still more concise: Noah in the posture of the orant stands alone in the box—we are left to imagine the wife, the sons, the daughters-in-law and the animals. Today a child's comment would be, "But what became of the dear little animals?"

### JOB

The patriarch Job, as the hero of a profound poem of suffering, constancy and deliverance, is a subject eminently suitable for sepulchral art, but it did not appear in the catacombs till the third century, and only on the sarcophagi was it depicted with any art. On the sarcophagus of Junius Bassus (pl. 28) Job's wife brings him food as he sits on the heap of potsherds; but fearful of approaching too near she presents it on the end of a forked stick and covers her nose with her garment (Job 19:17).

All of the subjects which might be mentioned here were enumerated briefly at the beginning of this chapter, and as I am not writing a complete treatise, I do not propose to describe all of them in detail. The index will enable the student to follow each particular subject, and about some of the subjects which subsequently were depicted with more art I shall have to speak in another chapter. Moses' reception of the Law was not painted in the catacombs but was common on the sarcophagi. It is the counterpart of the reception of the Law by Peter from the hand of Christ, which was common in sculpture and church mosaics. The raising of Lazarus, one of the earliest themes, occurs fifty times in the frescoes of the catacombs, and as often on the sarcophagi. The convention which the artists followed is strange enough to require some notice. Lazarus is almost always depicted as a mummy standing upright in an edicule (*tugurium*) such as can be seen now, though on a larger scale, among the tombs which flank the Roman roads. But this was a mode of burial nowhere practiced, the corpse was never left standing on its feet. We have reason to be surprised that the artists ignored the clear indication of the Gospel (Jn. 11:38) that the grave was in a cave and a stone lay upon it, and we are surprised again that they preferred to depict a mode of burial which was never in use. Perhaps Lazarus was standing in order that he might promptly respond to the command, "Come forth"; but how could he come when, as the Gospel says, he was "bound hand and foot with grave clothes"?

About the frescoes of the catacombs, though much more remains to be said, I shall say no more, except to remark briefly that not all of them represented religious subjects. Artisans and merchants were sometimes human enough to wish to depict in their tombs the trades by which they made a living.

## IV

## SARCOPHAGI

So evident is my failure to separate completely the frescoes and the sarcophagi that I may as well confess it frankly. The division indicated by the title of this chapter could not be drawn rigidly without involving tiresome repetition. It amounts in effect to a division between earlier and later, between the cryptic or esoteric style of the earliest art, and the pictures more clearly self-revealing which were developed when the times of persecution were past, and especially on the sarcophagi. However, the earliest themes persisted for a long time, and in describing them one cannot stop short with the frescoes. Now we shall deal exclusively with themes which appear only on the sarcophagi or are most adequately represented there.

The elaborate sarcophagi we have to study were expensive luxuries, made in big ateliers, perhaps by pagan artists, or at all events in conformity with old conventions which in different parts of the Empire prescribed various styles. Rome, as the most cosmopolitan city, exhibits the greatest variety of styles. It is lightly assumed by some that the sarcophagi found in Rome were many of them made elsewhere, chiefly in the East where marble was abundant. But this is a very precarious assumption. For, though it can be argued that the finished product would weigh less than the rough block, it obviously could not be so safely transported from a great distance. It seems certain that in some cases, like the sarcophagus of the two brothers (pl. 19a) and the "theological sarcophagus" (pl. 19c), the design complied with the instructions of the future occupant or his survivors. But not many would be more provident than men are today. Roman law allowed scant time for burial, and the survivors would have to seek hurriedly for a proper sarcophagus among the many which were displayed in the shops, to suit the various tastes of purchasers. We see in many instances that the portrait of husband and wife (*imago clypeata*) was roughly carved with the expectation of moulding in wax the exact lineaments of the pair who might purchase the sarcophagus. Plate 26b illustrates a beautiful sarcophagus which was evidently designed for a married couple (who are introduced at each end), but was bought for a clergyman, "Concordius the son of Blanda," who as bishop signed the decrees of the Council of Valence (374). The most elegant of all the Christian sarcophagi (pl. 28) was probably not made for Junius Bassus, Prefect of Rome, who, like Constantine, was baptized upon his deathbed. No lid had been made to match

## SARCOPHAGI

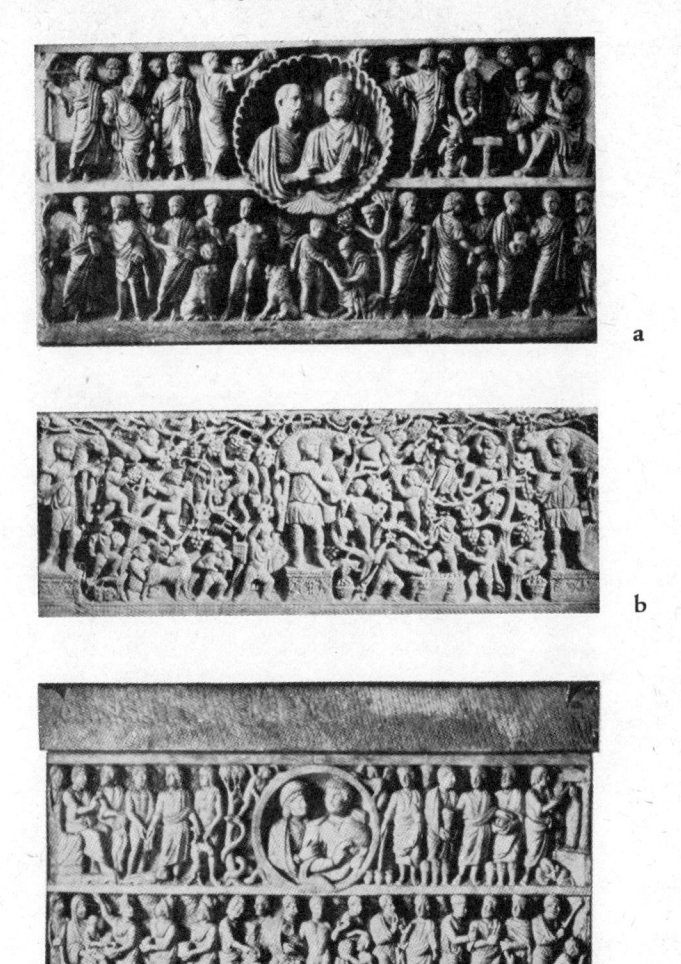

**a.** Sarcophagus of the Two Brothers. Lateran Museum. Raising of Lazarus; Peter's denial; Moses receiving the Law; sacrifice of Isaac; Christ before Pilate; Peter strikes water from the rock; Daniel; Peter's arrest; healing of a paralytic and a blind man; the miracle of the loaves and fishes. Fourth century. (See pp. 64, 73, 76-78.)—**b.** The Good Shepherd. Sarcophagus of the third century. Lateran Museum.—**c.** "Theological sarcophagus," Lateran Museum. The Trinity creating man; the Fall; miracle at Cana; the loaves and fishes; raising of Lazarus; the Magi; healing of a blind man; Daniel and Habakkuk; Peter's arrest; Peter striking water from the rock. Fourth or fifth century. (See p. 72.)

Pl. 19

**a.** Sarcophagus. Lateran Museum. Compared with pl. 19a, b, the only new subject is Jonah. Fourth century. (See p. 64.)—**b.** Sarcophagus. Lateran Museum. An example of Majestas. Fourth century. (See p. 82.)—**c.** Fragment of a sarcophagus. Lateran Museum. Elijah carried up to Heaven in a chariot. Fourth century.

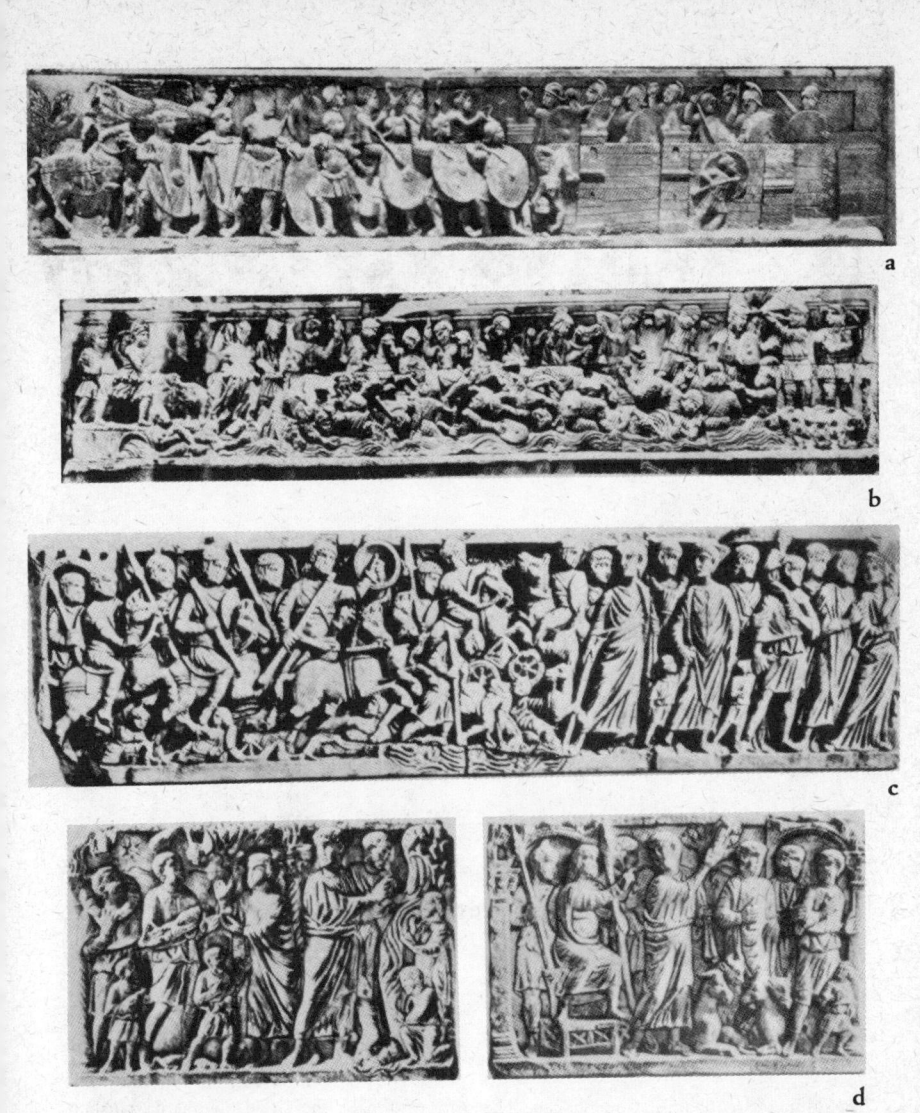

a. A relief on the Arch of Constantine. The taking of Susa.—b. A relief on the Arch of Constantine. Defeat of Maxentius at the Milvian Bridge.—c. Sarcophagus. Aix. Pharaoh and his hosts drowned in the Red Sea. Fourth century.—d. Ends of the same sarcophagus. Quails in the desert and water from the rock; story of St. Menas.

Pl. 21

**a.** Roman sarcophagus. Copenhagen. The story of Jonah; the Good Shepherd; a fisherman. Fourth century.—**b.** Crude carving from Tarsus. Metropolitan Museum, New York. Jonah enters the monster feet foremost. Fourth century. (See p. 65.)

Pl. 22

**a.** Fragment of a sarcophagus. Museum of St. Callistus. Ulysses bound to the mast escapes the sirens. Fourth century.—**b.** Fragment of a sarcophagus, same date and source as the one above, except that two of the sirens are dressed as philosophers; they are the heretical teachers.—**c.** Sarcophagus. S. Maria Antiqua. Story of Jonah (only the *horror vacui* accounts for the three rams above his gourd); the Good Shepherd; the baptism of Jesus; (in the center) Christian catechesis. Fourth century. (See p. **76**.)

Pl. 23

**a.** Roman sarcophagus. Louvre, Paris. The Good Shepherd delivers a soul from the roaring lions. Fourth century.—**b.** Another sarcophagus in the form of a bath, the earliest representation of catechetical instruction. Second century. (See p. 76.)—**c.** Lid of a sarcophagus. Lateran Museum. Christ dividing the sheep from the goats. (See p. 83.)

Pl. 24

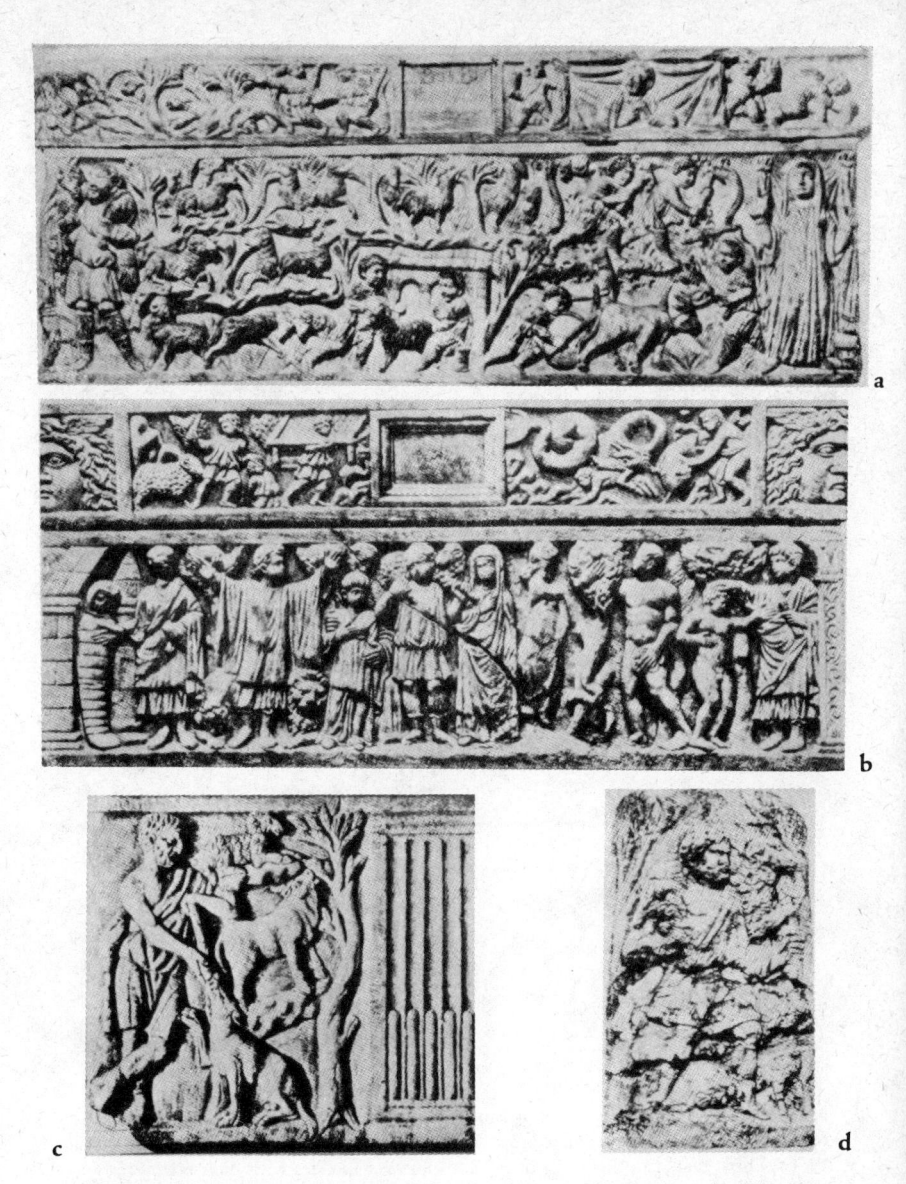

**a.** Polychrome sarcophagus. Lateran Museum. Good Shepherd; an orant; bucolic scenes. Third century.—**b.** Sarcophagus of the Lungara. *On the lid:* The Good Shepherd absolves the paralytic who goes off carrying his bed; story of Jonah; a fisherman. *Below:* The raising of Lazarus; the deceased boy as Daniel saved from the lions; the same boy and his mother under the protection of the Good Shepherd; the fall of man; the baptism of Jesus. Fourth century.—**c.** Part of a sarcophagus. Lateran Museum. Peter as shepherd. Third century.—**d.** Relief on a marble block. Vatican. Peter as shepherd.

Pl. 25

**a.** Strigilated sarcophagus. Lateran Museum. A fisherman and the Good Shepherd; the orant is the Church surrounded by doves. Third century.—**b.** Sarcophagus. Museum, Arles. Christ seated in the midst of his apostles; the apostles with their Scriptures (on the lid); the wife is introduced at one end, the husband at the other. Fourth century.—**c.** Lid of a sarcophagus. Lateran Museum. The Magi and a shepherd. Fourth century.

Pl. 26

**a.** A relief. Museo delle Terme, Rome. Philip the deacon expounds Isaiah to the Ethiopian eunuch. Third century. (See p. 73.)—**b.** *Via crucis;* Christ crowned (not with thorns); Christ led before Pilate. *Center:* The guards asleep at the tomb (the cross surmounted by the triumphal monogram). Lateran Museum. Fourth century.—**c.** Ends of a sarcophagus. Lateran Museum. Moses (Peter) receives the Law and strikes water from the rock; Peter's denial (in the background the Constantinian buildings in Palestine). Fourth century.

Pl. 27

Pl. 28

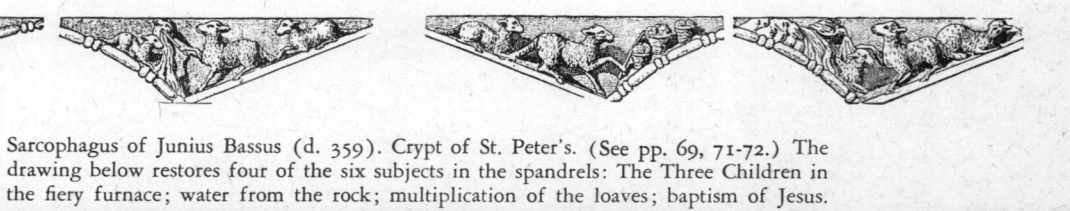

Sarcophagus of Junius Bassus (d. 359). Crypt of St. Peter's. (See pp. 69, 71-72.) The drawing below restores four of the six subjects in the spandrels: The Three Children in the fiery furnace; water from the rock; multiplication of the loaves; baptism of Jesus.

a. Sarcophagus used for the burial of Brother Ægidius, a companion of St. Francis, but made for a husband and wife who are introduced to Christ (a boyish figure of *Majestas*). *On the lid:* The story of Jonah. Museum, Perugia, ca. 350.—b. Sarcophagus of Theodore, Bishop of Ravenna. Ravenna. Fifth century.—c. Sarcophagus. Ravenna. Paul and two apostles offer their crowns to Christ; Peter with his cross. Fifth century.

Pl. 29

A sarcophagus decorated on all sides (it includes the side shown on the next page (Fig. a). S. Ambrogio, Milan. A representation of the Missio. (See pp. 61, 81, 85.) On one side, Christ is seated, on the other he is standing, the *Agnus Dei* and two women suppliants below him. *Lid:* The Three Children refuse to worship the image; the three Magi. *Ends:* Sacrifice of Isaac; the four Evangelists; ascent of Elijah; Noah in the ark; water from the rock. Fourth century.

Pl. 30

**a.** Side of sarcophagus. S. Ambrogio, Milan. Fourth century.—**b.** and **c.** Sarcophagus of Sextus Petronius Probus (d. before 395) and his wife, Anicia Faltonia Proba (d. after 410). Museo Petriano, Vatican. An example of the Missio (see p. 61, 81), which here is addressed to 22 disciples, including 12 on the ends. Peter stands at the right.

Pl. 31

it, and because the lid which was used displayed Bacchic scenes, they had to be covered with cement.

In Christian as well as in pagan times a great number of artists were employed in this business, and consequently there was a great diversity in their products, with respect to style as well as to quality. The uniformity of the sarcophagi made in Ravenna may be attributable to the fact that Theodoric granted a monopoly to one firm.

As for the various styles in vogue, it must suffice to indicate the principal categories which are here illustrated. The so-called frieze sarcophagus is the style most characteristic of Rome, and the one in which the *horror vacui* is most in evidence (pl. 19). To afford room for still more pictures the field was often divided into two zones. Another sort was the colonnaded sarcophagus, which also might be divided into two zones, diversified by arcades, or replaced by them (pl. 20b, 27b, 28, 29a, 31). The so-called city gate sarcophagus (pl. 30) is another named variety. The contention that arcades indicate an Eastern origin cannot be made to seem plausible in view of the fact that almost all the examples we know were actually found in the West.

The front edge of the lid was usually decorated. It was a comparatively narrow strip even when the lid had the form of a gabled roof. This was the place for an inscription, and sometimes also for portraits of the deceased, generally man and wife, with their right hands clasped, that being a significant part of the marriage ceremony. It may be noted that the woman is always on the right of the man, in Christian as well as in pagan pictures. I do not know why, nor precisely when, this custom was inverted in the Christian marriage ceremony. There is reason to think that the new custom was not generally followed before the sixteenth century. For until the Reformation the old custom was observed at Hereford, whereas the use of Sarum and York was followed by the Reformed Church of England, if the phrase in the rubric, "the man on the right hand," means, as it is commonly taken to mean, on the right hand of the priest. On pagan sarcophagi Juno Pronuba often appears behind the couple to confirm their union. This convention was so firmly fixed that we see it repeated sometimes on Christian sarcophagi, where the female figure may have been interpreted as the Church. In a few instances Christ occupies this place and blesses the couple.

For the most part sarcophagi were decorated only on the front, with the expectation that they would be placed against a wall. But even if they were so placed the ends would be visible, and therefore they were sometimes decorated (pl. 21d, 27c, 31c). In exceptional cases all four sides were decorated with equal care (pl. 30, 31). Purely ornamental features, such as the *strigil* (pl. 24a, 26a) and perpendicular channels (pl. 25c), were equally common on Christian and pagan sarcophagi. Although the sarcophagi were rectangular, an elegant variation was suggested by the bath (pl. 24), which in Rome was commonly of marble.

The subjects which predominated in the earliest stage of sepulchral art were not suppressed in the later stage which is represented by most of the sarcophagi, but they were supplemented, especially by themes from the New Testament. Not all the new subjects were as obviously pertinent to sepulchral art, for they were taken in part from the mosaics which adorned the basilicas. But no topics of Christian theology are entirely impertinent to the hope of eternal salvation. They are appropriate to the tomb if they are appropriate to the Church.

Beneath the illustrations there is not space enough to describe fully the many themes which are crowded upon a single sarcophagus, and the publisher, for aesthetic reasons, counsels me to make the captions briefer even than the limitations of space require them to be. Therefore here in the text I have to describe in more minute detail than is compatible with literary elegance the many subjects which are crowded on the sarcophagi, and on some of the smaller monuments, such as ivory boxes, where they are even more numerous. For example, the ivory box at Brescia [1] displays on one field a pretty complete inventory of early Christian art. To this grim necessity of being or seeming to be pedantic I yield the more readily because I remember that from the first this book was designed to be instructive rather than beautiful.

## SARCOPHAGUS OF JUNIUS BASSUS

I say nothing here about the costly sarcophagi of porphyry which were made for the mother and sister and daughter of Constantine and now adorn the Vatican Gallery, for the subjects depicted on them were not Christian, not even religious. But of the sarcophagi properly called Christian the most beautiful is that of Junius Bassus, preserved in the crypt of the Vatican (pl. 28). It is a perfect example of what the Roman archæologists now describe as *lo stile bello*. The implication of this phrase is that the pursuit of the beautiful was not a predominant trend in Christian art, that the artists were commonly not intent upon making holy men look beautiful. They recognized clearly enough that beauty is an aesthetic category which does not adequately render

[1] Pl. 94, 96. See p. 164.

the idea of the Holy. The most specious characterization of the Apostles Peter and Paul (pl. 65b) ascribes to them no personal beauty. In Buddhistic art we have a perfect parallel: the arhats or original disciples of Gautama are strongly characterized but have no beauty we could desire of them. Under the Church of S. Sebastiano, where Peter and Paul were for a time buried, many fragments have been found of their effigies which exemplify both *lo stile bello* and the opposite tendency—the two tendencies which at various times have prevailed in the Church. In Italy the early Renaissance strove with might and main to make Christ and His apostles beautiful, but a different tendency prevailed in the baroque. It has been said that the early literary sources emphasized the words of Isaiah (53:2), "no form nor comeliness, no beauty that we should desire Him," but that Christian art emphasized the beauty of Christ. This judgment is not quite true.

But it is not surprising that on the sarcophagus of Junius Bassus the figure of Christ enthroned above the heavens is Apollonic, for this was not conceived of as a portrait of Jesus: it represented what archæologists call *majestas*. But the same idyllic and youthful figure appears below in the triumphal entry into Jerusalem, and also in the scene where Christ stands before Pilate. It is natural enough that the first parents are beautiful in their nakedness, for so they were always represented. Abraham and Daniel (who here is elegantly clothed) are noble Roman types, and even Job is a handsome man. Pilate is good-looking, although his assessor has a sinister Roman face. The artist seems to have felt that Pilate had exonerated himself by washing his hands, and by making the *corno*, the protection against the evil eye, as a sign of his distrust of the Jews. But we are embarrassed by the effort to make Peter and Paul so beautiful that they can hardly be distinguished. Where they stand on either side of Christ we know that Peter must be on the left; but in the upper zone where one of the apostles is arrested we might think because of the noble head that it was St. Paul—were it not that it is certainly St. Paul who, in the lower zone, is led to his execution in the swampy region of the Tre Fontane which here is indicated by tall reeds.

Incontestably this is a beautiful sarcophagus; but the most attractive feature to me is the series of pictures in the spandrels which under the form of lambs represent the Three Children in the fiery furnace, Moses (or rather Christ) striking water from the rock, the multiplication of the loaves, and the baptism of Jesus.

The inscription on the lid records that Junius Bassus was a neophyte when at the age of forty-two years he died as Prefect of Rome. Maybe like Constantine he felt that the political duties he had to perform were not always compatible with the obligations imposed by baptism. Tertullian took it as a matter of course that for a Christian it was impossible to be an emperor. But we know that also many private persons were prone to defer baptism till death was near. Rather than accept the obligations of the Christian way of life, they preferred to remain catechumens. For they rightly felt, more keenly than men do today, "that baptism representeth unto us our profession; which is to follow the example of our Saviour Christ and be made like unto Him." It is ominous that from the American Book of Common Prayer these solemn words were recently deleted—and yet we cannot well defend ourselves against Kierkegaard's searching question: "How is it possible to be a Christian without being a disciple, or a disciple without being a follower?" If in this age we were not accustomed to baptize infants, I wonder how many baptisms there would be. In our land a great majority of the people are baptized, but not quite a half profess to be Christians, and less than a quarter make any effort to practice Christianity.

A man so young as Junius Bassus would hardly be provident enough to order his sarcophagus beforehand and prescribe the themes which should adorn it. Evidently this beautiful sarcophagus was not made expressly for the Prefect but was bought in the shop after his death. It was not even then complete, for an appropriate lid was lacking, as we have seen, and its place was hastily supplied by one decorated with Bacchic scenes which had to be obliterated with cement—a very hard cement which Msgr. de Waal removed by patient and fruitless labor.

One illustration depicts a sarcophagus which was intended for a husband and wife but was bought for the burial of an unmarried priest. Some of the sarcophagi illustrated here (pl. 24b, 25b) were evidently made expressly for the persons who actually were buried in them, but doubtless not before their death. The so-called "dogmatic sarcophagus" (pl. 19c) must have been made to order; for though most of the subjects which adorn it are conventional, the scene at the left of the upper zone is unique. The three figures engaged in the creation of man must have been meant to represent the Trinity, and it is Christ as the Logos who allots to Adam and Eve their respective labors: tilling the ground and spinning the wool of the sheep. The fourth and fifth centuries were nothing if not theological. This interest predominated over *lo stile bello*.

Busts of the deceased, commonly a man and wife, were often carved on the sarcophagi upon a shield (*clypeus*) or a shell. Sometimes the portraits are strikingly well done, as on the "sarcophagus of the two brothers" (pl. 19a) and one represented on plate 20a. This does not necessarily imply that the portraits were made from life. The Chinese found a way of making portraits of ancestors after their death. Commonly the faces are so roughly sketched that they barely indicate the difference in sex. They were made ready for any purchaser, with the understanding that the portrait would be finished in wax.

### PHILIP AND THE ETHIOPIAN EUNUCH

The popularity of this subject (pl. 27a) was due not only to the fact that it is an instance of a Gentile, and an African at that, who was converted to Christianity in the first days of the Church, but also to the consideration that it contained a striking argument against the far too common practice of deferring baptism. For the eunuch as soon as he had heard the doctrine and reached a place where there was water exclaimed impetuously, "What doth hinder me to be baptized?" (Acts 8:36). In the third century, however, the Church was not so expeditious as was Philip in baptizing converts. Converts were first subjected to a long course of instruction and probation, which perhaps was suggested by the initiation to pagan mysteries. The Apostolic Age regarded baptism as the first step in the long way of becoming a Christian. Baptism is hardly a necessary sacrament if one can become a Christian, and even an eminent one, without being baptized. Constantine's position was comical; for he boasted of being "a peer of the apostles" when he was not even baptized.

The story of the eunuch's conversion as it is depicted here is very interesting. It shows that Christian art when it emerged from the catacombs became as much interested in picturesque detail as was Hellenistic art. The eunuch is depicted as a *delicatus*, an effeminate man, sharply contrasted with the rude vigor of Philip. Philip puts his fingers together in the way Italians now do when they argue earnestly and make a cogent point. Before the chariot runs a *cursor*. Here he has a sack slung over his shoulder, and in other instances he carries a staff to clear the way. In this case he is giving a piece of money to a poor woman, while a child holds out his hand for a gift. It was customary to give alms after baptism. On other reliefs the *pedisequus* carries a basket of provisions. The account of the journey is, of course, exceedingly abbreviated. After passing a sundial the chariot reaches the tenth milestone, and from there on, as in the vicinity of Rome, the road is flanked by great tombs. But the poor woman is supposed to be within the city—and there, on the balcony of her palace, wearing a crown, Queen Candace awaits the return of her favorite minister.

## SEPULCHRAL ART

### OLD TESTAMENT SCENES

The Old Testament subjects which were dear to the artists of the catacombs were repeated on the sarcophagi, although the New Testament themes had begun to predominate. Noah appears thirty-six times in the frescoes and forty times on the sarcophagi. This is Styger's estimate. The Good Shepherd [1] was still a favorite theme, and in sculptural reliefs it was embellished with more picturesque details. Daniel remained a favorite subject for the sarcophagi, but as it belonged essentially to the cycle of sepulchral art it had no place in the basilicas. Moses receiving the Law had a more enduring interest as the counterpart of the reception of the New Law by Peter. As has been remarked already, Adam and Eve, representing the creation of man and his fall, emerged in the fourth century, as an indication of a profounder theological comprehension, and therefore appeared for the first time on the sarcophagi. The ascent of Elijah to heaven was also a new theme, although it was evidently appropriate to sepulchral art. In sculpture the story was very well told, for pagan art provided a model in the pictures of the sun god and his chariot (pl. 20c, 30, 93a). Jonah remained as popular as ever (see pp. 64f.). Because this theme was appropriated by sepulchral art the missionary point of the story was ignored and the scene under the gourd was interpreted as the blissful repose of eternity, *requies aeterna*. Jonah's sleep under the vine, which in the Biblical story was an episode, became in the artistic tradition the culminating point (pl. 23c). Usually the artists make it clear that the vine was a gourd, but in a few instances we see ivy leaves (pl. 29a). It is strange that Jerome ignored this tradition, translating the word by *hedera*, ivy. Augustine rightly corrected this by *curcubita*, for only a gourd could grow so rapidly and be destroyed so promptly by the worm as the story represents (Jonah 4:5-7). The scene was admirably represented in Christian art, for the artists used as a model pagan pictures of Endymion's sleep. Here, as in the case of Adam and Eve and of Daniel, the Christian artist, without giving offense, could exhibit his virtuosity in depicting the nude. In some instances Jonah is represented as casting himself into the sea. This correctly interprets his sacrifice as a willing one, for he had in fact asked to be thrown overboard (1:12).

---

[1] See p. 49.

SARCOPHAGI

## THE SIRENS

In the story of Ulysses and the sirens classical mythology provided a moral lesson which the Church was glad to appropriate. Ulysses bound to the mast but with ears open to the seductive music of the senses is several times represented on Christian sarcophagi. In one picture we have an interesting variation of this theme: only one of the figures is just a plain siren, whereas the others, wearing the philosopher's mantle and holding a scroll, allude to the seduction of heretical doctrines and the "false teachers" of which the Scripture bids us beware (2 Pet. 2:1).

## THE "PÆDAGOGUS"

Another subject which was drawn neither from the Old Testament nor from the New is the *pædagogus* or *grammaticus*. I use here the Latin words because they mean more than we commonly mean by pedagogue or grammarian. Clement, who was the head of the Catechetical School in Alexandria, revealed the importance of doctor or teacher in the early Church when he entitled one of his books *Pædagogus*. These men, although they taught the teachers and informed the minds of bishops, were not themselves reckoned among the clergy. It is true that Origen was ordained presbyter by the Bishop of Jerusalem, but in Alexandria the bishop was loath to recognize the validity of his orders. About the middle of the second century Justin Martyr was conspicuous as a lay teacher, and earlier than that Hermas, who seems to have been a brother of Pius the Bishop of Rome, complained that no seat was allotted to him among the presbyters, though he was regarded as a prophet. Other teachers of the sort we would describe as philosophers or theologians. At least as late as the fourth century there were many laymen who were recognized as more competent to teach than were the bishops or presbyters. Although the Bishop alone was called pastor, these men exercised a pastoral ministry in the deepest sense.

I dwell at some length upon this subject because the suggestions we derive from literary sources are corroborated and made more concrete by scenes which appear on the sarcophagi and are often erroneously interpreted. Plate 23c illustrates a sarcophagus in the middle of which is seated a man holding a scroll. Archæologists commonly speak of this figure as "the reading man." This noncommittal description is true enough but not illuminating, and it is too broadly used when it is applied to the picture of Peter's arrest. It should be understood that the man is not merely reading the Scriptures but expounding them, as a catechist, *pædagogus* or *grammaticus* would be expected to do. Although here no living auditor is visible, the place of the pupil is occupied by the orant, representing the soul of the deceased woman who owed her saving knowledge of Christianity to the good teacher whom she gratefully commemorates on her sarcophagus, reproducing in wax his face as well as her own. This evidently is a sarcophagus which was made to order.

This introduces us to the more difficult problem presented by plate 24b—which like the sarcophagus depicted above it has the form of a Roman bathtub. In some respects the meaning is plainer here—indeed it is plain enough, if we understand that the ideal theme of the Good Shepherd and the orant which intervene between the teacher and his pupil is not to be thought of as separating them. The teacher who, like the two adult men beside him, is dressed as a philosopher, is expounding the Scriptures, to the great delight of his interested hearers. The water clock (*clepsidra*) visible at the extreme left was a common appurtenance of the schoolroom. Opposite the teacher sits a dignified matron, holding in her left hand a roll of the Scriptures and demonstrating with her right, hearty assent to the teaching she hears. Behind her chair stands a young girl, presumably her daughter, who listens as eagerly. Alas, this beautiful girl died when she was still a young woman, and for her the mother had this sarcophagus made, representing her as an orant standing beside the Good Shepherd, gratefully recalling the Christian instruction she had received.

### THE ARREST OF PETER

Where Peter's arrest is represented on the sarcophagi along with that of Paul (as on pl. 28), it may be that his arrest in Rome was intended, but in other cases it is certainly his arrest by Herod (Acts 12:3-19). This is represented many times in substantially the same way (pl. 19a, c): two soldiers distinguished by a flat hat without a brim lay hold upon Peter as he sits reading the Scriptures. This peculiar hat was, without any reason, supposed to distinguish the Jews, and the scene was therefore interpreted as the revolt of the Israelites against Moses—with some plausibility because it often occurs in conjunction with the picture of Moses striking water from the rock. Wilpert identified this hat as the *pileus pannonicus* which was distinctive of certain branches of the Roman military service, which was priced at about two dollars in the maximal tariff of Diocletian, that mischievous experiment with ceiling prices which served no good purpose but to inform us of monetary values of all sorts of articles used in the fourth century. It is not creditable to archæologists that this discovery was made so late, for everyone had seen such hats on the porphyry figures at the southwest corner of S. Marco, figures of Roman officers dating from the early days of the fourth century.

Once it is understood that we have to do with Roman soldiers, the application to Peter is plain. It is all the plainer because just such soldiers (not Israelites) are represented in many reliefs as drinking from the water which issues miraculously from the rock—a scene which is commonly found alongside the arrest of Peter (pl. 19a, c). Clearly it is Peter who strikes this baptismal water from the rock, and Wilpert is justified in associating this scene with Peter's baptism of the centurion Cornelius, the first Gentile convert (Acts 10). Wilpert argues plausibly that it was the conversion of Cornelius which prompted Herod to arrest Peter (Acts 12:3-19). This connection, at all events, is assumed by the reliefs on the sarcophagi. On the "sarcophagus of the two brothers" (pl. 19a) Peter is arrested at the moment he strikes water from the rock, and near him stands the angel (an angel without wings) who later was to deliver him from prison—just as beside Daniel on this same sarcophagus stands Habakkuk.

The Canaanitish woman (Mk. 7:24-30), because she was the first Gentile who came into saving contact with Christ and hailed Him as "Lord," was often paired with Cornelius, and sometimes it is Peter who brings her to Christ—though in fact the disciples wanted to have her request granted only that she might be "sent away" so that they would be rid of her importunity. Archæologists often confound this woman with the woman healed of an issue of blood, and also with Mary, the sister of Lazarus. But by their gestures the three are clearly distinguished: only the woman with an issue touches Christ's garment, the Canaanitish woman kneels in an attitude of supplication, while Mary, as an expression of her gratitude, stoops to kiss Christ's hands or His feet.

I was taken aback by Wilpert's contention that through his experience of imprisonment Peter was prompted on leaving Palestine to go to Rome. But I see that Harnack in his *Chronologie*, i, p. 244, makes the same suggestion, supposing that Peter went to Rome in the year 42. Acts 12:17 says only that "he departed and went to another place," and it is said in verse 19 that at first "he went down from Judæa to Cæsarea and tarried there."

On the sarcophagi we see sometimes the arrest of Peter, and sometimes his release. In view of what has been said above it is easy to understand that it is the arrest of Peter which is represented in the central scene on the "sarcophagus of the two brothers" (pl. 19a), where a man is seated upon a stool reading the Scriptures, while one soldier threatens to take the book from him, and another spies upon him through the branches of a tree. This has been a hard nut for interpreters to crack: there have been no less than twelve explanations, including "the seated man," which explains nothing at all. No doubt it is Peter whom the military spies have succeeded in finding and apprehending. But when Wilpert called this scene "*cathedra Petri*" he used a very inappropriate name for a picture in which the seat is so inconspicuous.

## THE SACRAMENTS

The sacraments of Baptism and the Eucharist were as prominent on the sarcophagi as in the frescoes of the catacombs. Indeed they were represented more frequently at a time when New Testament themes had begun to predominate. More than a hundred instances are known, but almost all of them are dated after the Peace of the Church. The Miracle of Cana was added to the symbols of the Eucharist and is usually found alongside of the miracle of the loaves and fishes, for wine was an essential element in this sacrament, and that was not prefigured in the feeding of the multitude. The scheme followed by the artists was simple and economical of space: Christ touches with a magic rod the jars of water, and holding out both hands He blesses the loaves and the fish which the disciples present to Him (pl. 19a, 20a). The significance of the scene is indicated further by baskets full of bread. I need not labor again to show how pertinent the sacraments were to sepulchral art. Both of them were pledges of immortality. The story of the Samaritan woman at the well, which was associated with both sacraments, was represented on the sarcophagi more frequently than in the early frescoes.

## THE NEW TESTAMENT STORY

It has been remarked already that on the sarcophagi New Testament subjects predominated, and incidentally I have mentioned some of the miracles of Jesus. The healing of the blind and of the lame and of the paralytic were frequently depicted, in one instance the healing of a leper, more often the cure of demoniacs. The raising of Lazarus, which occurs fifty times in the frescoes, was repeated as often on the sarcophagi. There are seventeen instances of the raising of the widow's son at Nain, but only two of the raising of Jairus' daughter (cf. 94c). We are not to suppose, however, that these subjects when they appear on the sarcophagi were suggested by a historical or a didactic interest, that is, for the instruction of the people, as they were in the decoration of the basilicas, or that they express the biographical interest which we see in them as episodes in the public ministry of Jesus. They were adduced here, just as they were in the early frescoes of the catacombs, as instances of the mighty power of God. We have to take into account the fact that the sepulchral art of the fourth century and later was influenced to some extent by the didactic pictures seen in the churches; but even the early mosaics, though they were clearly meant to be instructive, did not aim, any more than did the Gospels themselves, to illustrate the "Life of Jesus" in the biographical sense which we attach to that phrase. Even such long cycles as we have in the nave of S. Apollinare Nuovo, the ivory chair of Maximianus, the alabaster columns in S. Marco, and the ivory altar frontal at Salerno, do not betray the biographical interest which is prominent in our modern "Lives of Jesus." Like Matthew and Luke they lay emphasis upon the miraculous birth, and they accord with all the Gospels in concentrating attention upon the few days which spanned the whole story of the Passion and the Resurrection. So it was too with the sarcophagi, though for lack of space they could not depict any of these subjects so freely and fully as they were depicted at the same period in mosaics and in reliefs which were not so much hampered by lack of space.

### THE BIRTH OF CHRIST

On the sarcophagi as in the frescoes the wonderful birth of Christ was attested by the visit of the Magi; but now for the first time the shepherds appear along with them, and we have the apocryphal addition of the ox and the ass beside the manger (pl. 26c).

The subjects next enumerated (the Passion, the Resurrection, the commission to the disciples, and Christ in glory), though they were very prominent on the sarcophagi, had hardly any precedents in the early frescoes of the catacombs. They were doubtless a reflection of the monumental art of the basilicas.

### THE PASSION

The Lord's Passion begins with the entry into Jerusalem (pl. 28), which is followed by the kiss of Judas, the arrest of Jesus, Peter's denial (though the scene before Caiaphas is only once depicted), the judgment of Pilate (which is very frequent), the crowning of Christ by the soldiers (not with thorns!), the *via crucis* and the cross in various forms, but not the Crucifixion.

### THE RESURRECTION

We have reason to wonder that the Resurrection of Christ, which is very prominent on the sarcophagi, does not appear at all in the earliest cycle of sepulchral art, for St. Paul regarded it as the basic argument for the hope of life after death. The Resurrection was commonly indicated by the empty tomb, to which the women came on the "third day," bearing ointments to anoint the body, and found the guards asleep. The form of the tomb is not derived from the account in the Gospels but from the monuments commonly seen along the Roman roads. Perhaps the artists had a vague intention of representing the Holy Sepulchre at Jerusalem as it was transformed by Constantine. It is not so obvious to us that the cross itself, especially in the form of the Constantinian monogram, was a symbol of triumph, the triumph of the Resurrection (pl. 27b). The fragment of the so-called Gospel of St. Peter, verse 39, expresses this view.

The cross as it appears on the sarcophagi has often a close likeness to the standards which were carried before the Roman armies, on which the transverse bar supported the banner bearing the images of the reigning emperors, the *sacri vultus*. Thus the standards had the form of the letter *tau* (T), which was in fact the most realistic form of the cross, as Tertullian (*Apol.* 16) and Justin Martyr remark. When this is understood we can see the relevance of St. Ignatius' words in his Epistle to the Smyrneans 1:2: "The Lord Jesus Christ was for our salvation under Pontius Pilate and Herod the Tetrarch truly fastened to the cross with nails, in order by His Resurrection to raise up unto all generations the *standard* for His saints and faithful followers from among the Hebrews and the Gentiles united in the one body of the Church." With this we may compare the well-known line of the hymn by Fortunatus: "Vexilla regis prodeunt," the banners of the king advance.

It would be appropriate to consider here, in connection with the Resurrection, the representations of the risen and glorified Christ, which were frequent on the sarcophagi; but about these themes so much has to be said that they must be treated separately under the titles *Missio* and *Majestas*.

## THE GREAT COMMISSION

*Missio* is the name archæologists have chosen for this theme. It is a good name, for it reminds us that the commission given by the risen Christ to His disciples was emphatically and explicitly a *mission*, a sending (Mt. 28:16-20): "All authority hath been given unto Me in heaven and on earth. Go ye therefore, and make disciples of all nations, baptizing them into the name of the Father and of the Son and of the Holy Ghost, teaching them to observe whatsoever I commanded you. And lo, I am with you always, even unto the consummation of the age." These last words of the Gospel of St. Matthew are, not without some justification, described by critics as "secondary." This is meant to be a disparaging term; but we must not forget that Christians of an early day had good reason to regard them as *primary*, as the exact expression of what the Church is for.

That the primary importance of Christ's commission was well understood in the fourth century is shown by the impressive pictures of it upon the sarcophagi. They are the more significant because it is certain that they reflect precisely pictures which appeared in the apsidal mosaics, the field reserved for the most central and important themes. Although only two of the apsidal mosaics which represent Christ seated in the midst of His apostles have been well perserved (pl. 57 and 69b), we can be sure that once they were very numerous, perhaps the predominant theme for apsidal decoration. This is proved by the sarcophagi and by late frescoes in the catacombs.

The Great Commission which I have quoted from St. Matthew is distinctly articulated, and so it was also on the sarcophagi. Although the discreet items contained in this theme cannot be divided, they must be dealt with separately.

## CHRIST IN GLORY

Christian art at a later period singled out for particular treatment the Ascension (pl. 93a, 118) and the more difficult subject of Christ in Glory (pl. 101b, 94a, 125b); but on the sarcophagi the *whole* theme was presented in one picture, often reproduced without substantial variation (pl. 20b, 28, 29a, 30, 31a). In this picture Christ is majestically seated above the firmament of heaven, or standing upon the "mountain" in Galilee, addressing His disciples and delivering unto them His law. This picture archæologists have aptly enough described as *Majestas*. It represents more than kingly majesty, more even than is commonly understood by *Christus Rex*, the title of the festival inaugurated by Pope Pius XI, which is disquieting because it hints at a claim to temporal power on the part of Christ's Vicar. It expresses perfectly the meaning of the words which introduce the Great Commission: "All power is given unto Me in heaven and on earth." This is a stupendous declaration! The artists were ideally justified in representing Christ as speaking from heaven, for though it was on earth He gave this commission to His disciples, it was the risen, the heavenly Christ who spoke. He had called His disciples "apostles" when He sent them out upon their mission in Galilee: they were apostles (missionaries) in a larger and greater sense when they went out, clothed with His authority, to make disciples of all nations. That the Great Commission conferred power as well as imposed a duty was well understood in the early Church. Jesus with amazing modesty had foretold that His disciples would do greater works than His (Jn. 14:12). Alas, this is a prediction which has not yet been fulfilled. The Church invites contempt because faint-heartedly it claims so little. In the endeavor to appease secular society it is unfaithful to God's law. If it should be said that this spirit of appeasement does not predominate in the Church of Rome, it ought to be remarked at the same time that it was not characteristic of the English Puritans or the Scotch Covenanters, nor can we reprove in this respect the Mennonites and similar sects, who at least as objectors are consistent and "conscientious."

## "DOMINUS LEGEM DAT"

"The Lord gives the Law" is the motto often inscribed upon the scroll which Christ hands to Peter. It is the exalted Christ who gives the Law, even though the "commandments" to which the Great Commission refers were pronounced in the days of His humiliation, "the days of His flesh."

The prominent place accorded to this theme in the apsidal mosaics is not to be understood as a repudiation by the Catholic Church of St. Paul's antithesis between law and grace, a relapse, as some have thought, into Jewish legalism; for St. Paul himself, even in the epistle where the exigencies of controversy led him to sharpen this contrast most exceedingly, did not hesitate to speak of the necessity of fulfilling "the law of Christ." He never thought of faith as a substitute for "walking" in Christ's ways, or of grace as a dispensation from duty. The *doing* of Christ's commandments was as important to him as to St. John. He affirmed even of the old law that "it is holy, righteous and good." Psalm 119 shows that pious Jews regarded the Law not as a hard exaction and a heavy burden but as a gift, the most precious gift of God. So we must regard the "new commandment." The newness of Christ's law is sometimes indicated by the early Christian artists who inscribed on the scroll handed to Peter the monogram of Christ. But if the new law was written upon the heart, not on tables of stone, it was none the less a "must," something to be *done,* and the Catholic emphasis upon the commandment is thoroughly evangelical. This picture, however, does indicate that the early Catholic Church was not seriously concerned about the controversial antithesis St. Paul had drawn between law and grace. It did not understand it as a repudiation of all law. The reaction of the early Church is expressed by the so-called Second Epistle of St. Peter, where it is said of the epistles "of our beloved brother Paul" that therein "are some things hard to be understood, which the ignorant and unsteadfast wrest (as they do also the other Scriptures) to their own destruction." In the long run, the doctrine of justification "by faith alone" (*sola fide*), which is a travesty of Paul's doctrine, has inevitably obscured the primary conception, so clear in the Gospels, that Christianity is the law of life, is "the way."

## MERCY AND JUDGMENT

The majestic figure of Christ we are here considering represents Him not only as Ruler but as Judge, "the most worthy Judge eternal." This is a clear implication, and sometimes it is expressed by the picture of Christ in His exaltation separating the sheep from the goats (pl. 24c). It was appropriate that in the frescoes of the catacombs the individual judgment of departed souls was more often depicted, but on the sarcophagi, which reflected the art of the basilicas, it is natural enough that we find an allusion to the picture of the universal judgment which confronted men in the mosaics of the apse. It is not true that the early Catholic Church, though it had ceased to expect Christ's coming soon, had lost the direction prescribed by eschatology, a decisive orientation towards the future, towards the "last things," the End. The pictures at the apsidal end of the church, and also upon the façade, were predominantly apocalyptic, and were derived from the Revelation of St. John the Theologian. We can understand this in view of the fact that St. John's picture of the worship in heaven was a reflection of the worship of the Church on earth, so that it is our most complete and authentic witness to the essential character of Christian worship in the Apostolic Age; and in the fourth century the Church was glad to think that the worship it performed was a reflection of the cult in heaven as St. John described it. Nevertheless this predilection for the Apocalypse is surprising because at that time Christians were inclined to be content with the world as it was, with the peace which Constantine had bestowed upon it. There is good reason to think that Constantine and the bishops of his court resented the otherworldliness and the relative disparagement of this world which eschatology implied. Zahn affirms that Eusebius, Bishop of Cæsarea, to whom was committed the task of preparing the sumptuous copies of Scripture which Constantine presented to the greater Churches, intentionally omitted the Apocalypse from these important manuscripts, and thereby nearly succeeded in excluding it permanently from the Canon. It is all the more surprising that a different tendency prevailed in Christian art. It prevailed also more widely. For just at this time earnest men who found this good world too good a place for Christians to live in were prompted to desert it and betook themselves by thousands to Egypt and Syria, there to live as hermits in the desert. And after the death of Constantine his triumphant cross, the monogram, was commonly accompanied by the most striking eschatological symbol (pl. 103b), Alpha and Omega, the Beginning and the End (Rev. 21:6).

It is incredible that men who have read the four Gospels can say of Christ as the poet does, "His voice sweet-toned and blessing all the time." Yet one might conceive that Christ as He is depicted on the sarcophagi and in the apsidal mosaics as high and lifted up is engaged only in blessing. For the gesture of His right hand is one which we associate with benediction, whether in the so-called Greek manner or the Roman. But this is a misapprehension, which I have sought to correct in a section devoted to gesture. Suffice it to say here that Christ's gesture has no such significance. It was the gesture commonly used by orators. It means therefore neither blessing nor condemnation —or rather it may mean either, it is ambiguous (pl. 20b, 26b, 28, 29a, 30, 31a, 69, 64a). We must stick to the point that this is a common gesture of address, alloquy. Christ delivers His Law, the Great Commission, not only with His left hand to Peter, but with His right hand He addresses it to all His disciples.

Certainly the thought of mercy and truth predominates in this picture. But the *Agnus Dei* which commonly accompanies it, "a lamb standing as though it had been slain" (Rev. 5:6), makes it clear that the benediction of Christ is not an easygoing indulgence. On the sarcophagi, as Wilpert justly observes, the whole picture—Resurrection, Ascension and *Majestas*—spells, for those who know how to read, the comfortable words which St. Paul pronounced in 1 Cor. 15:54-57: "Death is swallowed up in victory. O death, where is thy sting? O grave, where is thy victory? The sting of death is sin, and the power of sin is the law: but thanks be to God who giveth us the victory through our Lord Jesus Christ." But it was salutary for men to be confronted in the church by Christ as the Judge "who condemned sin in the flesh, that the ordinance of the law might be fulfilled in us who walk not after the flesh but after the spirit" (Rom. 8:3).

It is possible to trace plainly enough the development of a sterner conception of Christ as Judge. It becomes fully evident in the prodigious Pantocrator of Byzantine art, which in its mildest form emerged in Roman art as early as the fifth century and is to be seen on the triumphal arch of S. Lorenzo (pl. 67a). Under this picture of Christ seated upon the globe of the world might have been inscribed the motto: *Securus judicat orbis terrarum*. This development can be traced through the centuries, and even in Michelangelo's tremendous picture of the Last Judgment we can discover some kinship with the *Majestas* of the sarcophagi and the apsidal mosaics. The gesture of Christ's hand is still equivocal: He seems to be raising the blessed to eternal felicity—and at the same time pressing down the damned.

In the Middle Ages the sterner conception of Christ had become so predominant that men felt the need of a gentler mediator, the Madonna.

### THE THRONE OF CHRIST

It goes without saying that in early Christian art there was nothing vindictive about the figure of Christ as Judge. But it may need to be said again that the note which predominated was neither mercy nor judgment but majesty. This is clearly expressed by the throne, which was a favorite theme at least as early as the fifth century (pl. 32, 33, 104b, and on the arch of S. Maria Maggiore, though it is not shown on pl. 65). This was a throne upon which no one sat, but it was clearly designated as the throne of Christ by the dove which hovered above it, by the cushion (a wool-sack, as the English call the seat of the Lord Chancellor), by the cross, or by the book with the seven seals.

In Byzantine art this was understood to refer exclusively to the Last Judgment, and the name *etimasia* (or *hetimasia*), which means preparation, was given it in allusion to Psalm 9:7: "The Lord sitteth as King forever: He hath prepared His throne for judgment"; and Psalm 89:14, which in the Septuagint reads: "Judgment and justice are the preparation of Thy throne." Wilpert affirms that this name is a misnomer, and that in early Christian art the throne carried no suggestion of the Last Judgment, however well it was "prepared." He points to the bronze relief above the principal door of St. Sophia in Constantinople, which was spared by the Moslems because it included no human figure (pl. 107b). Here under an arch is depicted a throne covered with a rich (purple?) cloth and with a cushion supporting an open Gospel on which we can read in Greek: *The Lord said: I am the door of the sheep; by Me if any man enter in, he shall find pasture.* "This," said Wilpert, "spells HAGIA SOPHIA—ma bisogna saper leggere."

Because the principal theme of apsidal decoration (the exalted Christ giving the Law to His disciples) is most frequently found on the sarcophagi, it has been necessary to deal with it here, anticipating the subject of another chapter; and because the empty throne cannot well be separated from the theme of *Majestas*, I have gone on to speak of it in this connection, although it does not appear on the sarcophagi. But about Peter and Paul, who figure in almost all of these pictures, so much needs to be said that a special place must be allotted to this subject in the sixth chapter.

## MONUMENTAL ART

**a.** The throne of Christ, with cushion and royal mantle, the book with seven seals, and the dove. S. Matrona in S. Prisco near Naples. Early fifth century.—**b, c.** Baptistery of the Orthodox, Ravenna. In the mosaics of the dome the throne alternates with the Holy Table bearing the four Gospels. *ca.* 450.

Pl. 32

**a.** The Christ invisible upon the throne, is hailed by Peter and Paul. Chapel of S. Zeno in S. Prassede, Rome, 817–824.—**b.** Baptistery of the Arians, Ravenna. *ca.* 520.

Pl. 33

a. Figure of an apostle. Baptistery of Naples. After 350.—b. St. Agnes heading the procession of virgin martyrs. S. Apollinare Nuovo, Ravenna. Cf. pl. 72.—c. Portrait of St. Ambrose. Chapel of St. Victor in S. Ambrogio, Milan. Early fifth century.

Pl. 34

Synagogue at Dura-Europos. *ca.* 250. (See pp. 16, 43-44.)—**a.** The walls of the synagogue were decorated with Biblical pictures in three zones. The shrine of the Scriptures, with the seat of the rabbi, is at the left.—**b.** One episode in the story of Moses: The child is found in an ark among the bullrushes, and when he becomes a boy he is presented to Pharaoh.

Pl. 35

Baptistery at Dura-Europos. Before 256. The font with a picture of the Good Shepherd; on the lower wall is what appears to be the visit of the three women to the Holy Sepulchre; above, Peter essays to walk on the water, and Christ heals the paralytic, who then walks off with his bed, as may be seen in the picture presented on a larger scale above.

Pl. 36

# CHURCH BUILDINGS

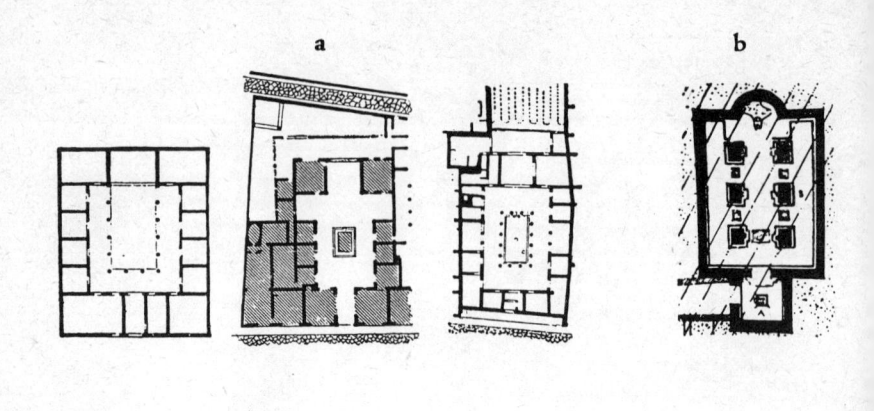

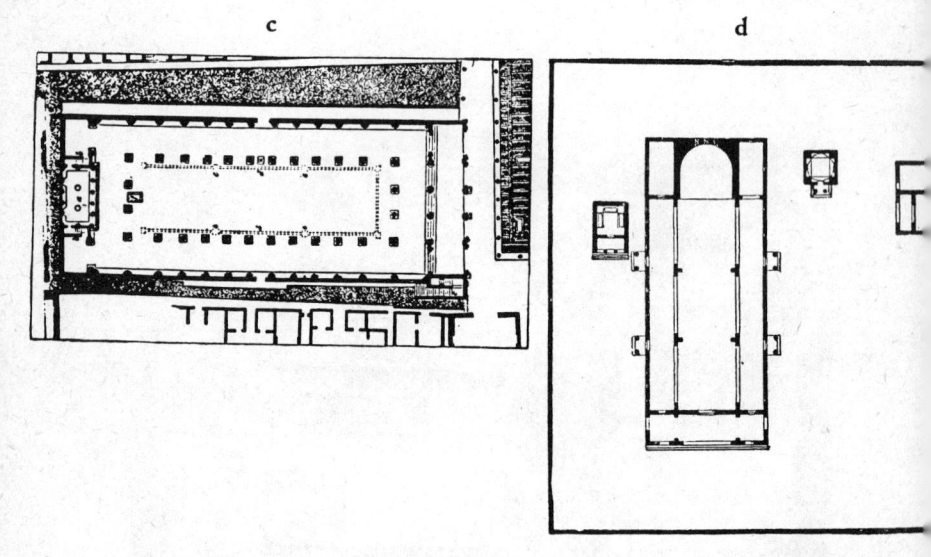

**a.** Plans of Greek and Roman houses which may have determined the form of the Christian basilica.—**b.** Plan of underground chapel of a mystic cult found outside of Porta Maggiore.—**c.** Plan of a civil basilica at Pompeii.—**d.** Peribolos about the church in Ruweha, North Syria.

Pl. 37

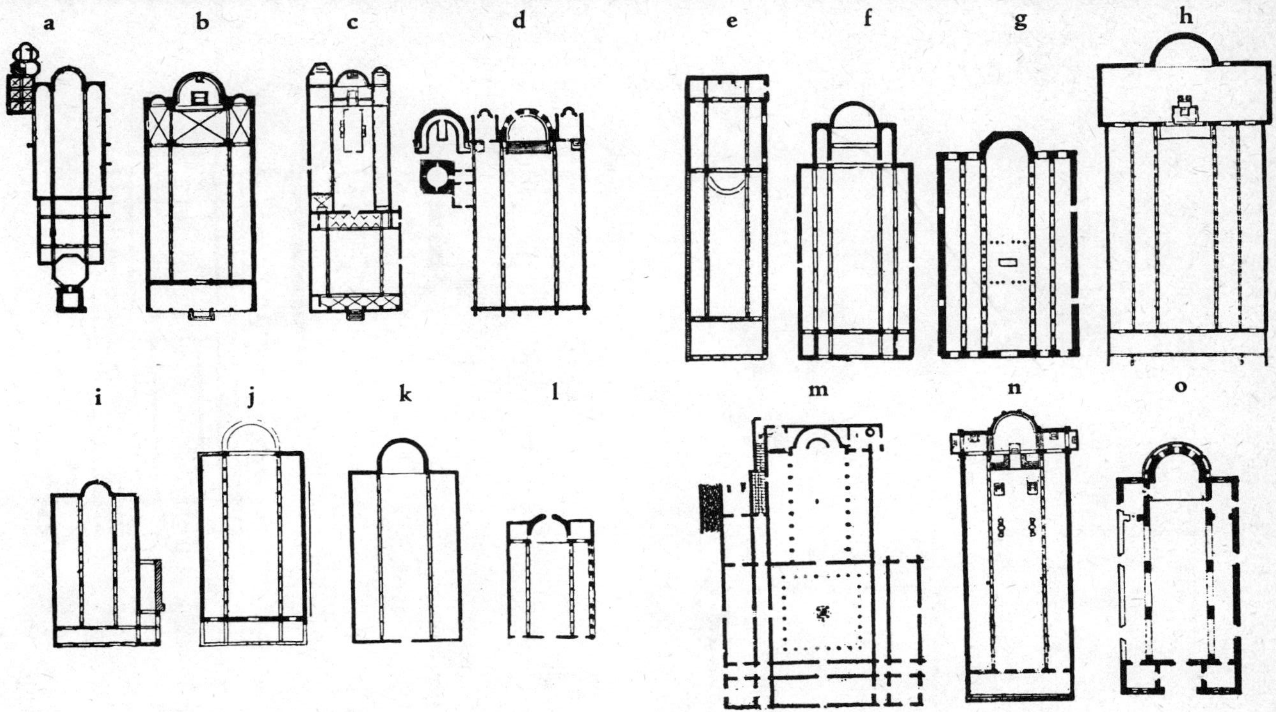

Plans of basilicas. **a.** Cathedral of Parenzo.—**b.** S. Pietro in Vincoli, Rome.—**c.** S. Clemente, Rome.—**d.** S. Apollinare in Classe.—**e.** S. Lorenzo, Rome.—**f.** Church in Ruweha, North Syria.—**g.** Basilica Ursiana, Ravenna.—**h.** St. Paul's, Rome.—**i.** S. Maria in Cosmedin, Rome.—**j.** S. Apollinare Nuovo, Ravenna.—**k.** S. Agata, Ravenna.—**l.** S. Spirito, Ravenna.—**m.** Xenodochium, Porto.—**n.** S. Maria Maggiore, Rome.—**o.** Basilica in Kalb-Luseh, North Syria.

Pl. 38

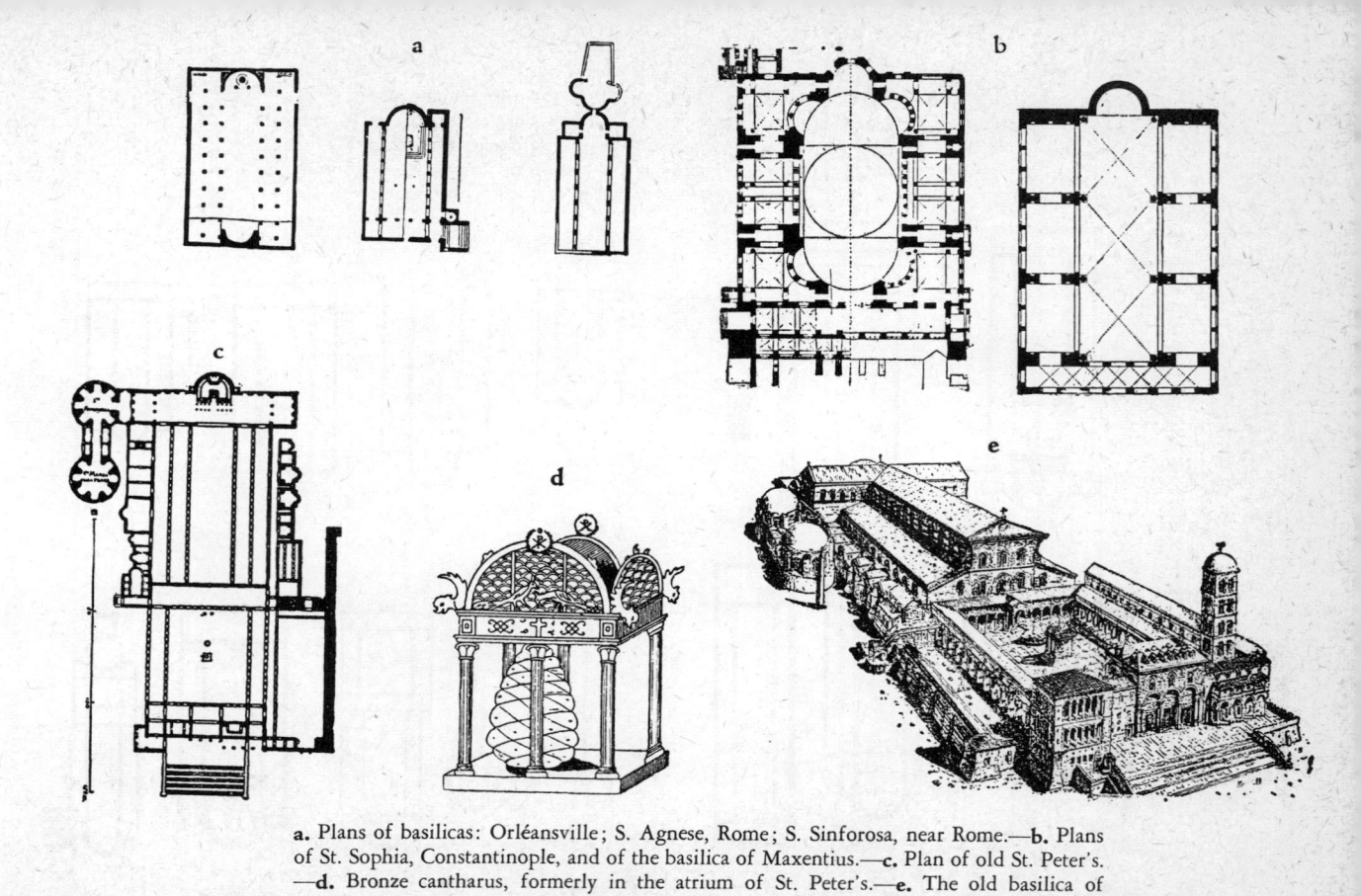

a. Plans of basilicas: Orléansville; S. Agnese, Rome; S. Sinforosa, near Rome.—b. Plans of St. Sophia, Constantinople, and of the basilica of Maxentius.—c. Plan of old St. Peter's.—d. Bronze cantharus, formerly in the atrium of St. Peter's.—e. The old basilica of St. Peter.

Pl. 39

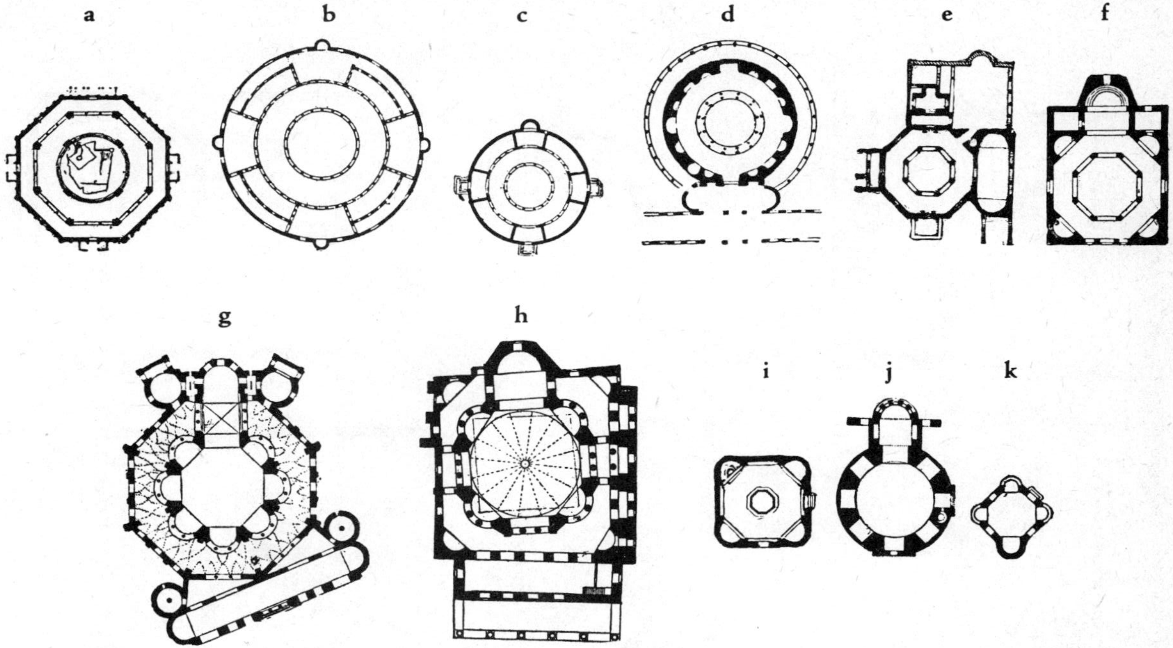

Plans of centralized buildings. **a.** Mosque of Omar, Jerusalem.—**b.** S. Stefano Rotondo, Rome.—**c.** Church of the Ascension, Jerusalem.—**d.** S. Costanza, Rome.—**e.** Lateran Baptistery.—**f.** St. George, Ezra.—**g.** S. Vitale, Ravenna.—**h.** SS. Sergius and Bacchus, Constantinople.—**i.** Orthodox Baptistery, Ravenna.—**j.** St. George, Thessalonica.—**k.** Arian Baptistery, Ravenna.

Pl. 40

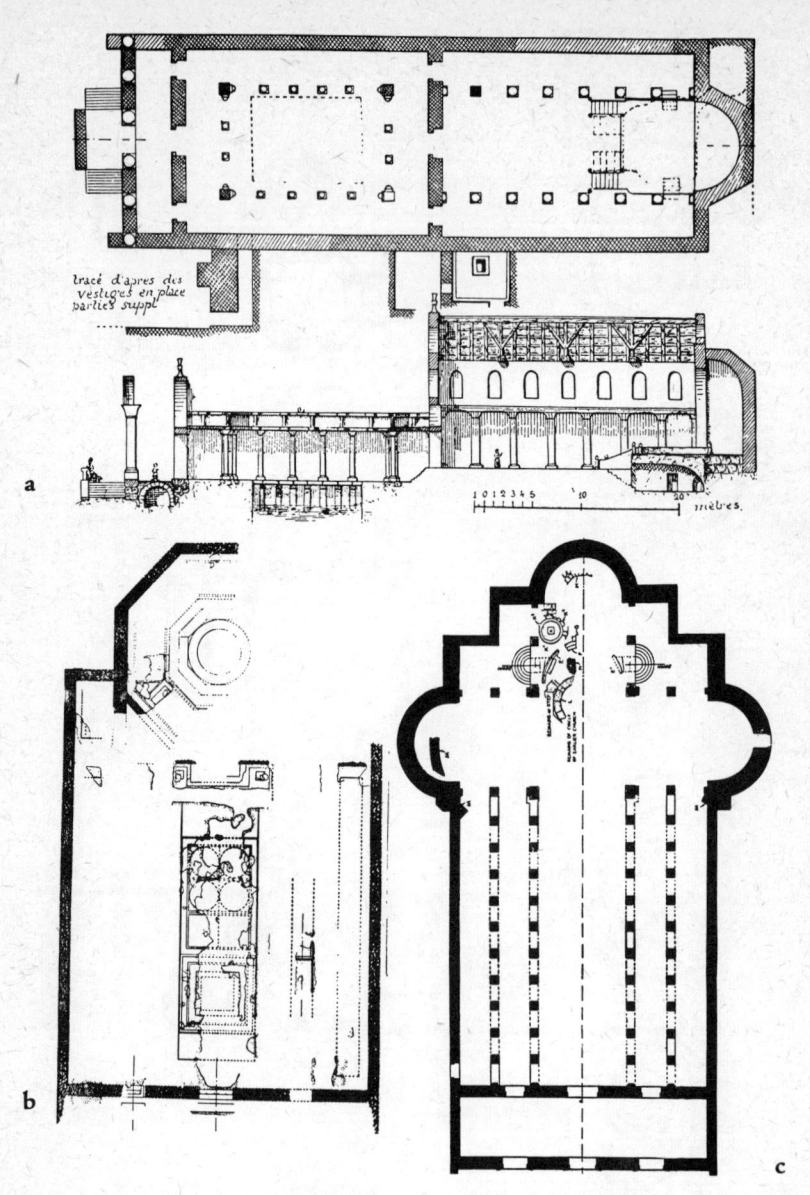

**a.** Plan of Constantinian church of Eleona, Mount of Olives.—**b.** Plan of Constantine's church at Bethlehem.—**c.** Plan of Justinian's reconstruction of same.

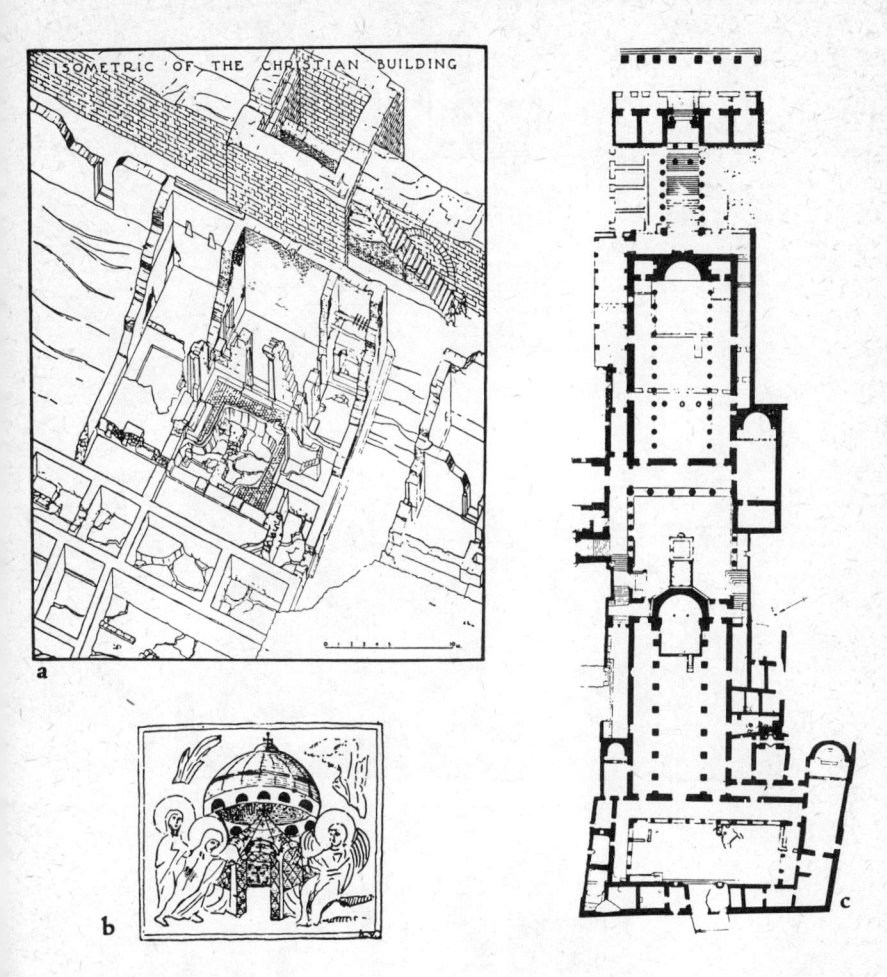

**a.** Plan of the church at Dura (before 256).—**b.** The Holy Sepulchre, a miniature.—**c.** Plan of Fountain Court Church at Gerasa.

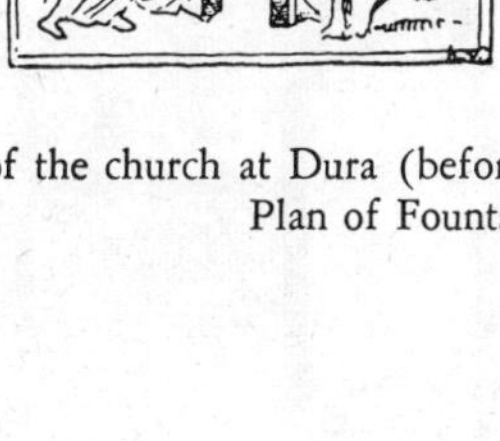

Pl. 42

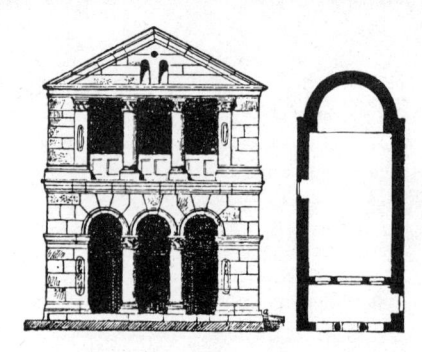

**a.** Basilica at Turmanin, North Syria. Sixth century. A restoration.—**b.** Basilica at Turmanin, as De Vogüé saw it.—**c.** Church at Babuda, North Syria. Sixth century. (Restored.)

Pl. 43

**a.** Mausoleum of Galla Placidia, Ravenna.—**b.** Interior of the Mausoleum.—**c.** Section of church in Ruweha, North Syria.—**d.** Bronze lamp in the form of a basilica. Fifth century.

Pl. 44

a. Interior of St. Paul's Church, Rome.—b. Interior of S. Maria Maggiore, Rome.

Pl. 45

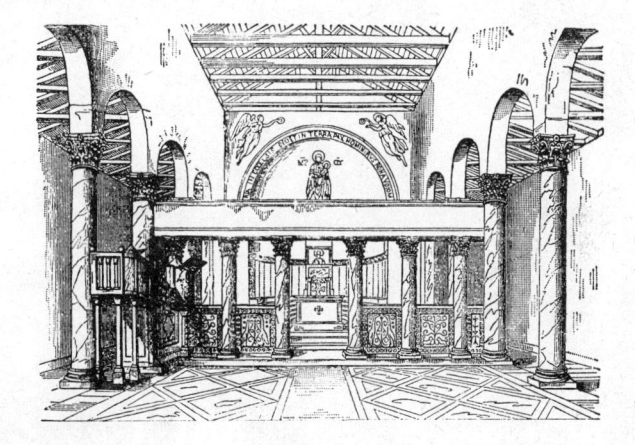

a. Interior of S. Vitale, Ravenna. Sixth century.—b. Cathedral of Torcello. Seventh century.

Pl. 46

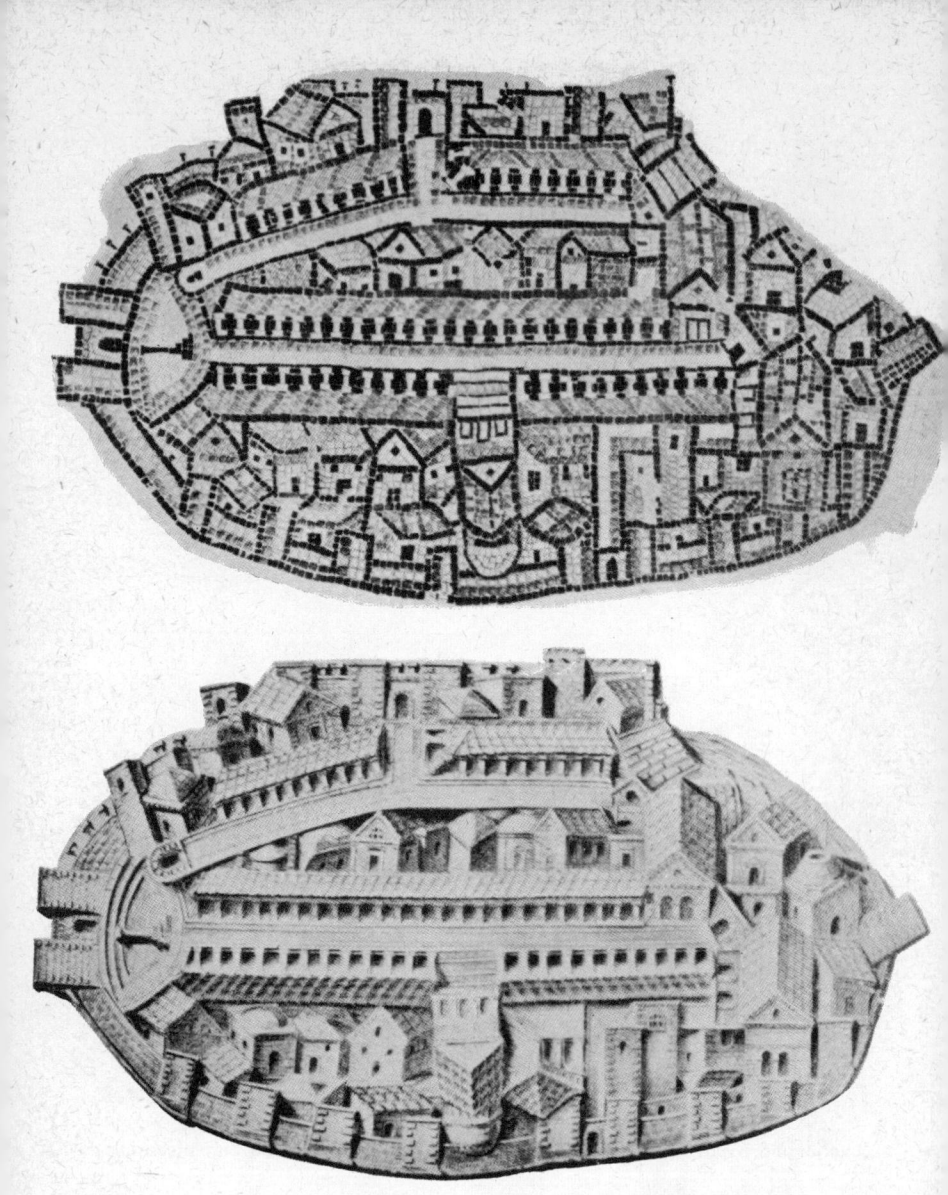

Plan of Jerusalem. Part of mosaic map of Palestine on the floor of a church at Madaba. Opening on the colonnade is the Constantinian Church of the Holy Sepulchre (Anastasis). It is interpreted in the picture beneath by Heisenberg.

Pl. 47

a. Church of St. Sophia, Constantinople, with Turkish minarets.—b. Basilica at Kalb-Luseh, North Syria. Seventh century.

Pl. 48

a. St. Sophia, looking across the nave.—b. St. Sophia, looking west.

Pl. 49

a. S. Maria in Cosmedin, Rome; restored as it was in the twelfth century.—b. Cathedral of Parenzo. Sixth century.

Pl. 50

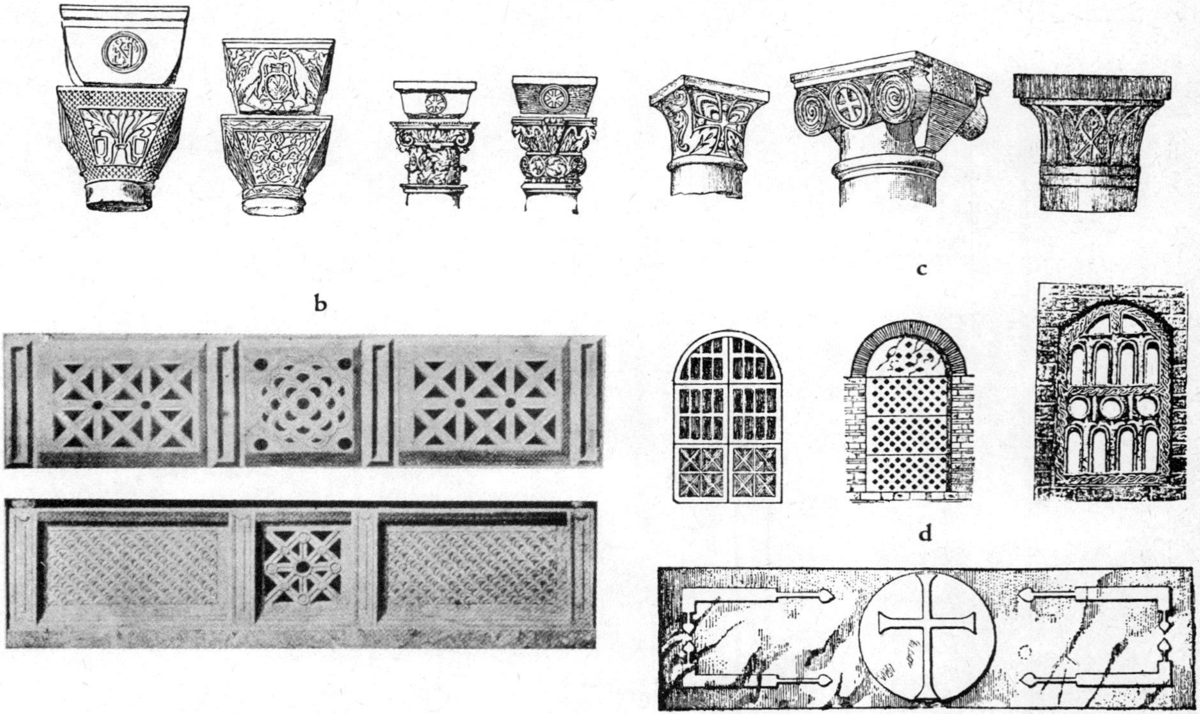

a. Early Christian capitals designed to support arches.—b. Chancels of fourth and fifth centuries.—c. Stone windows.—d. A chancel in S. Clemente, Rome. Sixth century.

Pl. 51

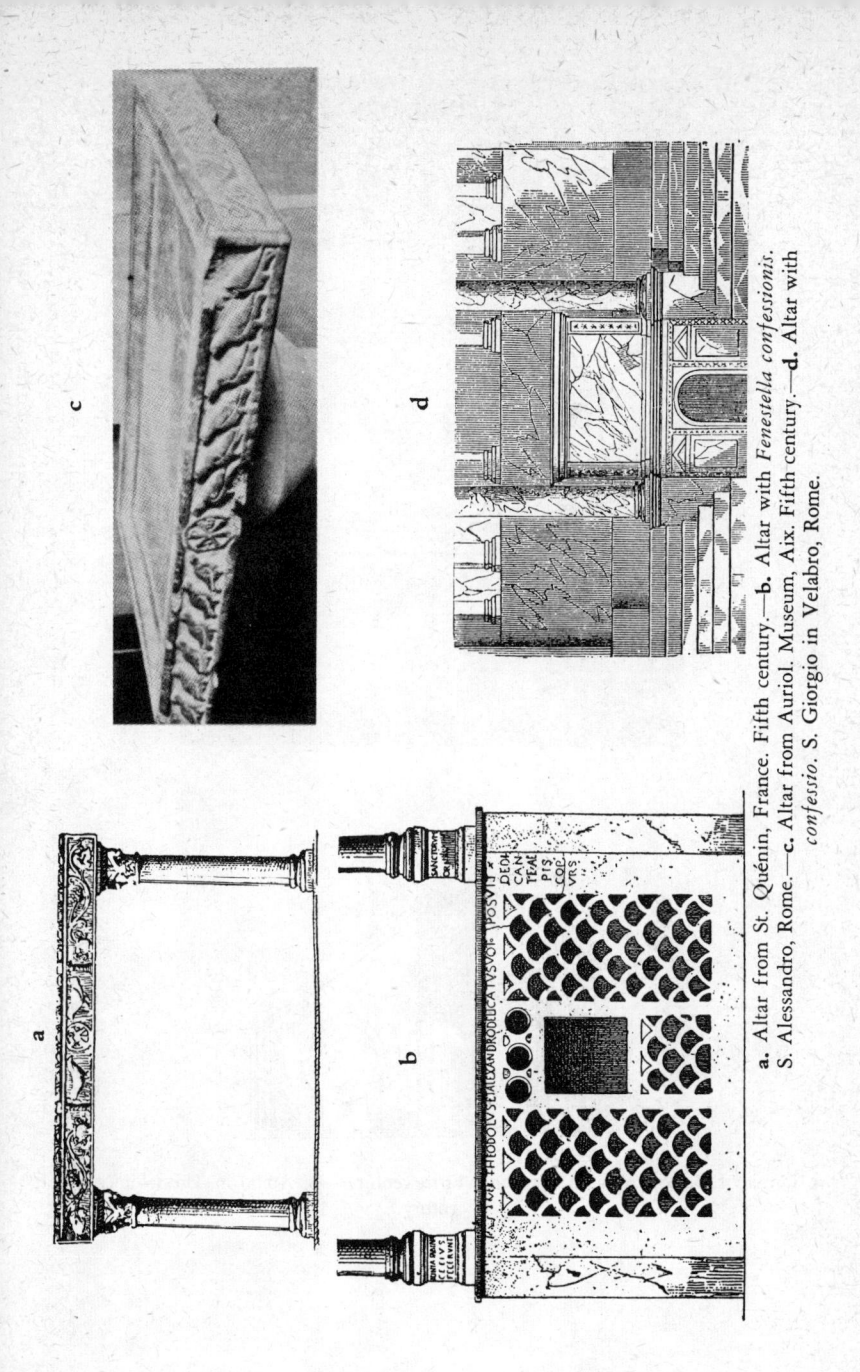

**a.** Altar from St. Quénin, France. Fifth century.—**b.** Altar with *Fenestella confessionis*. S. Alessandro, Rome.—**c.** Altar from Auriol. Museum, Aix. Fifth century.—**d.** Altar with *confessio*. S. Giorgio in Velabro, Rome.

Pl. 52

**a.** Pulpit of Bishop Agnello. Ravenna. Fifth century.—**b.** Ambo in Thessalonica. Fifth century.

Pl. 53

# V

# THE HOUSE OF THE CHURCH

THE TITLE of this chapter means that I do not propose to write a treatise on church architecture, as I did in my earlier book.

Here, without dwelling upon the strictly architectural character of church architecture, I seek to show that the forms actually adopted in early times were strikingly appropriate to the purpose of housing the Church of God, the assembly of God's people, meeting in His presence; that it was precisely adapted to the Christian cult; and (as will appear in the sequel) that the pictorial decoration, as it was finally employed, was absolutely apt.

In a sense, therefore, this chapter is an interruption of the orderly study of pictorial art to which the remainder of this book is devoted. But it is not a needless interruption. From sepulchral art to the monumental art which adorned the basilicas there is no direct sequence, and the chapter which here is interposed between these two themes is a most necessary introduction to the latter. The monumental art of the early Church cannot be well understood without some understanding of the buildings it was meant to adorn.

But I am interested in the church building for its own sake. How the Church resolved the problem of making for itself an appropriate house, a terrestrial home, is one of the most interesting themes in early Christian history. The most adequate and appropriate appellation for the building which we commonly call a church is "the house of the Church" (*domus ecclesiæ*, τῆς ἐκκλησίης οἶκος). *Domus* means also a home, and a home reflects the character of its occupants. The Church was intimately at home in the type of building it devised.

Here at the outset we may consider other names which were commonly used. The Greek word ecclesia in its Christian use properly denoted the assembly of God's people; but as early as the fourth century it was used also for the meeting house, and in southern Europe the words derived from it (*chiesa*, *église*, etc.) are still used with the same ambiguity. Unfortunately, in English and in all the tongues of northern Europe we are troubled by the same ambiguity, although the word church (kirk, *Kirche*, etc.) meant primarily the edifice, described as God's property (*kyriakē*). The Latin equivalent was *dominicum*. But in early times the pagans as well as the Christians sought to distinguish the society from the edifice in which it worshipped. Even in a pagan source we find the church called *domus columbæ,* house of the dove. To emphasize the sacred character of the edifice it was called *domus Dei,* the house of God, or as the place of prayer (*proseuxerios*). Only the pagans spoke of Christian houses of worship as temples or *sacraria*. Christians described the church as *basileios 'oikos,* royal house, meaning the house of the divine king; and the corresponding word basilica (royal), which was commonly used to denote halls built by imperial order for public use, seemed to the Christians an appropriate name for the house of God.

In its secular use the word basilica did not precisely define the character of the building, or the public use to which it was put (Vitruvius, vi, 8). It was used as broadly almost as the word hall, and it was applied even to private halls in the palaces of wealthy patricians. The Christians used this appellation more definitely for an oblong rectangular hall with interior colonnades and an apsidal prolongation (pl. 38). Hence this name was not used for baptisteries, which were built on a round or a polygonal plan, nor for cemeterial chapels of similar shape, and it was not commonly applied to the churches of a central type which Justinian made popular.

So far as we know, the name basilica was used for the first time by the Bordeaux Pilgrim (333), but not much later Eusebius used it four times (*V. C.* iii, 31, 32, 53), and in one place (*H. E.* x, 4) he spoke of the church as "the royal house."

## THE BASILICA

The type of building which we call a basilica proved to be so suitable for Christian worship that it was adopted everywhere throughout the Empire, and in the West it held its ground, almost undisputed, for a thousand years. Indeed it was never completely superseded in the West; for at least the oblong plan and the arcades were conserved in Gothic churches, and even when the dome became a favorite feature. The tenacity of the traditional type is shown by the fact that the great church of St. Peter in Rome remained essentially a basilica when it was rebuilt in the sixteenth century. It did not take the shape of an equal-armed cross (which was suggested), although that plan would have enhanced immensely the effect of Michelangelo's dome, which can be seen to advantage only from behind the apse.

No one now will maintain that the Christian basilica was an invention of Constantine, or that the earliest extant examples of it were actually the first. We assume that prior to the fourth century this type was well established as the result of a gradual development—even though we have to admit that there is more truth than evidence in favor of this assumption.

The recent discovery at Dura on the Euphrates of a church which can be dated definitely before the year 256 is exceedingly important because it is absolutely unique. We have no other ocular demonstration for the belief that churches were built or adapted expressly for Christian worship before the Peace. And yet the fact is not doubtful. It results indirectly from the unimpeachable record that many were destroyed, either during the periods of persecution, or during the intervals of comparative peace when the progress of the Gospel compelled the Christians themselves to pull down their old churches and build greater ones (Eusebius, *H. E.* viii, 1). "How can we describe," says Eusebius, "the multitudes which gathered in these churches, or the distinguished people who flocked to the places of prayer?" It is likely that most of the churches built before the days of Diocletian were destroyed in the terrible persecution which he inaugurated. And there is good reason to believe that a dozen at least of the parochial churches in Rome (the *tituli*, as they were called) existed in some form before they were rebuilt in the time of Constantine. But probably not much is left of the earlier buildings, for Eusebius affirms (*H.E.* x, 2) that the churches rebuilt after the Peace were much greater than the original houses of worship. At Rome there were also buildings belonging to the Church outside the City, in connection with the catacombs; for the *Liber Pontificalis* says of Fabian (236–250) that he built there many edifices—*multas fabricas per cymeteria fecit*. Minucius Felix in his *Dialogue*, which was certainly written before the time of Diocletian, represents the opponent of Christianity as saying, "The odious sanctuaries (*sacraria*) of this impious sect are springing up throughout the whole world." Lampridius, an enemy of Christianity, relates in the *Life of Alexander Severus* (c. 49) that when to this emperor (222–235) there was submitted the question of a property which had been bought by the Christians but was claimed by a guild of cooks, he decided the case justly by saying, "It is better for God to be worshipped there in one way or another than the place be given to the cooks for a tavern." We are carried much further back by the chronicle of the city of Edessa, where it is recorded that in 201 "the temple of the Church of the Christians was destroyed by a flood." Eusebius narrates (*H. E.* vii, 30:9) that when Paul of Samosata had been excommunicated but tried to retain possession of "the house of the Church" at Antioch, the Emperor Aurelian (270–275) rendered a just decision when he decreed that the house should be delivered "to those persons to whom they of Italy and the bishop of the doctrine in the city of Rome should write letters."

We cannot doubt that churches were built before the days of Constantine since we have the proof that many were sequestrated or destroyed. The persecution by Diocletian began on February 23, 303, by the burning of the Scriptures and the destruction of the church which was near the imperial palace at Nicomedia. At the end of this persecution, according to Lactantius (*De mort. pers.* c. 48), the Nicomedian ordinance of Licinius, which was published in the year 313, restored all the ecclesiastical properties to the Churches, which it recognized as legal corporations—*ad jus corporis eorum, id est ecclesiarum, non hominum singulorum pertinentia.* At about the same time, that is, just before Constantine obtained the imperial power, an edict of Galerius, though it rebuked the Christians for their contumacy, permitted them "to rebuild the houses in which they were accustomed to worship," and expected them "in return for this clemency to supplicate their god for the safety of the emperor" (Eusebius, *H. E.* viii, 19:9). The edict of Maximinus (Eusebius, *H. E.* ix, 10) permitted the Christians to adhere to their sect without fear of molestation, to perform their cult, and to rebuild "the Lord's houses." "And to make our generosity appear the greater," it went on to say, "we decree that if any houses and lands formerly pertaining to Christians have by the order of our parents been allotted to the public treasury, or occupied by any city government, or have passed by sale or by gift into the hands of any private persons, they shall all revert as of old to the Christians as their rightful property." An earlier persecution was brought to an end when the Emperor Valerian was taken prisoner by the Persians (about 260), and his son Gallienus restored to the Christians the Church properties which he and his father had confiscated. This we learn from a rescript addressed to Dionysius, Bishop of Alexandria, and his Egyptian colleagues (Eusebius, *H. E.* viii, 13). The edict to which this refers described the clergy as "ministers of the Word" and expressly permitted them to exercise their ministry.

Instances enough have been cited here to prove that long before the Peace of the Church Christians possessed appropriate houses for worship; and since the form which we call the basilica was appropriate in the highest degree and is exemplified in all the earliest churches extant, we have reason to believe that this type of building was not simply adopted from the style which was prevalent in public buildings, nor invented by the architects of Constantine, but was gradually developed during the ages of persecution to fit the purpose for which it was employed. It is a garment which fitted the Church so well that it must have been made to order. This assumption is so plausible that no one now will be inclined to reject it. But when we ask more particularly what factors determined this development, there is plenty of room for controversy.

## THE BASILICA

Before considering this debatable question we must have a general notion of the features which fundamentally distinguish the early Christian basilica (pl. 38). It was an oblong rectangular hall, nearly twice as long as it was wide, and was divided longitudinally into three (or sometimes five) aisles. The central aisle (the nave) was nearly twice as wide as the side aisles and more than twice their height. The nave was covered with a gable roof of timber, the beams of which were commonly hidden by a flat wooden ceiling. Although the height of the ceiling was not much greater than the width of the nave, the penthouse roof of the side aisles was so much lower that the windows of the clerestory provided plenty of light and ventilation. Usually there were no windows in the lower walls, and the doors (except in northern Syria) were at one end, corresponding in number to the number of the aisles. At the other end the nave terminated in the apse, a semicircular room surmounted by a half-dome. On the chord of the apse, or in front of it, was the altar, and behind that the seats of the clergy. I mention here only the fundamental and invariable features. Usually the apse projected beyond the rectangular walls, but sometimes it was inscribed (pl. 37d)—a difference which was not observable within the church. Sometimes each of the three aisles ended with an apse; but this innovation, apart from considerations of symmetry, was prompted by the necessity of providing a place for the altar of prothesis, which was a peculiarity of the Syrian Liturgy, and therefore we find it only in the East.

We can distinguish four stages in the gradual development of the Christian house of worship. The first was a brief stage, during which the disciples in Jerusalem worshipped with their Jewish brethren daily in the Temple, but performed their distinctive cult, the breaking of bread, "from house to house" (Acts 2:46). In the second stage the synagogues were used with some success for the initial effort to win the Jews to the Gospel (Acts 9:20; 13:13-14:3; 17:1-4; 18:4; 24-26); but Christian worship, centering in the Eucharist, was still performed in private houses (Acts 20:7-11). We are told in one place (Acts 19:9) that at Ephesus Paul rented a lecture hall (*schola*). But this was for preaching, that is, for missionary propaganda among the Gentiles, and we may be sure that Christian worship was still conducted in private houses. The third period extended well into the third century, and during this period it is likely that private houses used for Christian worship, even if they were nominally held by the original owners, were put permanently and completely at the disposition of the Church, serving incidentally perhaps as the residence of the bishop. At Dura, for example, the Church managed to adapt to its use an ordinary dwelling house by removing the partition wall which had separated two large rooms, by furnishing another room as a baptistery, and utilizing, as it seems, an intermediate room for the *agape*. But in the larger cities the fourth stage must have begun well before the middle of the third century. When Gentiles were thronging into the Church in great numbers it must have been necessary to construct appropriate houses of worship on a large scale and in a form which determined the character of the greater buildings constructed after the Peace.

So far there is not much room for controversy. But when we ask more precisely what were the principal factors which determined the ultimate form of the basilica, the answers are various. Ten solutions of this problem have been proposed, if we may include the antiquated notion that the Christian basilica was the invention of Constantine. The name rather than the form suggests the easy answer that the Christian basilica was simply a copy of the public basilicas. That it was determined by the form of the synagogue or of the lecture hall (*schola*) are theories for which there is no evidence, though they have been dear to Protestants because they are inclined to project back into early Christian times the sort of worship to which they are accustomed, which consists exclusively of instruction and prayer. The reading of the Scriptures, the sermon, and the prayers did in fact constitute a great part of Christian worship in the second century, as we learn from Justin Martyr; but we learn from him also that this all culminated in the Eucharist. The house of the Church must therefore have been, as indeed it was, appropriate for all these parts of worship. If the breaking of bread had been performed without the accompaniment of instruction and prayer and song, the church would have had the form of a dining room (*triclinium*). Some derive the form of the Christian basilica from the private basilicas (the Egyptian hall, as Vitruvius calls it) which were sometimes found in the mansions of the rich, and may have been in some cases put at the disposition of the Church. Others trace it to chapels in the catacombs, or to the memorial *cellæ* built above the tombs of the martyrs. Some are content with the notion, true enough in itself, that the Christian house of worship grew organically to fit the growing needs of the Liturgy. True as this is, it does not go far enough to explain certain peculiarities of the Christian basilica. In time past I argued hotly for the belief that the most striking peculiarities of the Christian basilica are explained by the custom of worshipping in the atrium, especially the peristyle atrium, of the private house. But this does not explain the apse, nor does it explain why the nave was always covered with a roof, or why it was flanked by the colonnades, instead of being surrounded by them, as was the atrium and the middle space of the public basilica. I observe that in the Christian house at Dura it was not the atrium which was used for worship. I feel obliged to attach a good deal of weight to the view that the form of the Christian church was influenced by the type of chapel adopted by the mystery cults for a purpose not very dissimilar since it involved a sacred meal. Such a building is exemplified by the underground chapel discovered at Rome outside Porta Maggiore (pl. 37b).

Faced by so many divergent theories, I asked one of my archæological colleagues what I had better say about this perplexing subject. He astutely advised me to leave the choice to the reader, admitting that something might be said in favor of all of these views. As for the reader, I cannot hinder him from making his own choice. But for myself I cannot combine views which seem to me mutually exclusive. Being a champion of either/or, I am not disposed to accept an and-and-and—especially when it runs to ten ands. But I have sufficiently intimated my preferences, and more will be said about them in the sequel. I will say here only that the effort to trace the Christian basilica to chapels in the catacombs inverts the historical sequence. For such chapels as there were underground were evidently modelled after the rooms in which Christians were accustomed to worship above ground. And the memorial *cellæ*, though they have an apse, have no colonnades, and the apse is commonly a triple one, a trefoil. The synagogue, the lecture hall, and the public basilica I would leave entirely out of the account. It is certain that in the time of Constantine at least one private basilica contained in a sumptuous palace was turned into a church. There may have been other instances in Rome; but they were certainly not numerous enough to constitute a precedent. Although I cannot share the fond belief of Richter and Taylor that the immense hall which is now S. Maria Maggiore was originally the private basilica of a wealthy Roman patrician and was given to the Church as early as the third century, I take pleasure in the thought that such conspicuous opulence was once possible, as indeed it was in Rome when Rome was the capital of the world. Today who can repress a nostalgic feeling at the reflection that then it was no uncommon thing for one man to have a thousand servants? In the fifth century there were distinguished Christians leading an ascetic life whose lands, it is said, were measured not by acres but by kingdoms. Such a one was St. Paulinus of Nola.

The reader is of course perfectly free to make his choice, but perhaps what I have said here may serve to guide it. I subscribe heartily to the notion that the church was made to fit the Liturgy; but it is my belief that both the Liturgy and the Christian basilica are exponents of the same will-to-form, the same *Kunstwollen*; and perhaps we do not see so deep into the millstone

—that is, into the genesis of early Christian form-construction—as we pretend to see.

The motive which explains the early Christian forms of art is obscure to us because, whether we be Catholics or Protestants, we do not fully share it. Hence today there are not many who would be satisfied with the basilica as a house of worship. It is an acquired taste, and it can be acquired only by a prodigious effort to put ourselves back into the skin of early Catholic Christianity. This effort is never wholly successful. Therefore when we build a basilica it is denatured to suit our taste, unless a purely antiquarian interest predominates.

I shall speak in another connection of the early churches which were built on a central plan with domes and vaults, which clearly indicate another will-to-form. In the West the *plan* of the basilica predominated, almost to the exclusion of any other; but with respect to the vertical axis there was a steady movement away from the early ideal. Already in Lombard architecture the nave was much higher, and to add to the impression of height the flat ceiling was discarded, so that the eye might wander and be lost among the rafters and trusses. In the Gothic church not much remains to remind us of the basilica except the oblong plan and the position of the altar—if it is not thrust against the east wall. The side aisles, which are a structural necessity in very large buildings, have no longer the significance which was attached to the colonnades, and in the most beautiful of the smaller churches they were advantageously eliminated.

It is notorious that today, except in the Eastern Church, there is no concordant will-to-form—not even in the particular denominations. The nearest approach to it is found in the extremer Protestant sects, which want first and foremost a convenient auditorium—and no more than that. In the Roman Church the will-to-form is distracted by various precedents which compete with one another. Where men are no longer content with the baroque and the rococo, they are likely to revert to earlier styles of Renaissance architecture, or they go still farther back to the Romanesque, or to the Lombard pattern, which economically has so much to recommend it that lately it has been adopted in Rome for a great number of parochial churches. But they rarely go back to the basilica. And if Roman Catholics and Anglicans revert to the Gothic, it is chiefly in an antiquarian spirit. On the other hand, only Roman Catholics and Lutherans are bold enough to cast aside all tradition and build thoroughly modernistic churches.

I enumerate here the principal characteristics of the basilica which in old times endeared it to many generations of Christians. The points upon which

I dwell, though they are not all of them invariable, are I believe typical. It is the more necessary to mention them because they are not always observed, nor are they in every case plainly observable. In this way, I think, we can approach an apprehension of the will-to-form which was characteristic of early Catholic times, if not of an earlier age. Here it is not merely a question of *form*, if I am right in thinking that the urge which resulted in the Christian basilica is the very same urge which was expressed in the Liturgy.

It has been said that the Christian basilica is the pagan temple turned inside out, or rather outside in. This is a witty remark, but it is far more than that, for it indicates a radical change in the spirit of worship. The pagans worshipped outside their temples—and so did the Jews, for they stood in the courts. Even the pagan altar was outside the temple. But the Church as the Body of Christ needed a house in which to assemble. They needed a meeting house—not in the banal sense in which this word is used by Quakers and Congregationalists, as a place where men meet one another, but in the deeply religious sense that there they meet together with God, in the sense in which the Tabernacle in the wilderness was the tent of meeting, the place where God's people met God. The congregation, the Ecclesia, was profoundly united by the sense that it met in the presence of God, although superficially this human-divine encounter has the effect of isolating the particular individual. Because of this mystical sense of personal and collective encounter with God the *inside* of the church had to be decorated and not the outside. The colonnades of the Greek temple were transferred to the interior. It is astonishing how indifferent the early Christians were to the external appearance of their churches. They treated their churches as they did their houses, which needed to be glorious only within. It is hard for us to credit the evidence that even in the twelfth century the glorious church of S. Marco at Venice showed on the outside plain brick walls which were not yet covered with the marble veneer which makes them now so beautiful. In Constantinople the church of St. Sophia, viewed from without (pl. 48a), is still plain brick, disfigured by enormous buttresses which were added in the thirteenth century, and embellished only by the minarets supplied by the Turks. To this the richly decorated interior presents the greatest possible contrast.

Only the façade of the basilicas was sometimes decorated with mosaics. This means simply the gable and so much of the wall of the nave as was not hidden by the colonnade of the atrium. The churches of the fifth and sixth centuries in northern Syria are an honorable exception; for being built of stone in a good tradition of masonry, they are embellished on all sides with appropriate architectural designs, and in some cases (pl. 43a), the façade is adorned with two towers. It appears that towers were characteristic of palace architecture (pl. 94b) in Syria, recalling a time when even palaces had to be fortified. Nowhere else were they used in connection with churches, for there they had no relevancy. So long as church bells were not in use, there was no reason for a campanile, steeple, or spire. The round brick towers erected close to some of the churches at Ravenna were built in the eighth century to afford a refuge in case of a sudden incursion of Saracen pirates.

Although the walls of the basilica actually served to support the roof, the structural purpose of them was ignored and they were regarded simply as a screen against the outside world, a hostile or uncomprehending world—in short, "the world," as the New Testament calls it. Viewed from within, the walls produced a satisfying sense of *enclosed space*, a protected space within which was salvation. I venture to speak of it as a *magic* space. Historians who pay serious attention to the peculiarity of the early Catholic mind do not hesitate to use the word "magical" to describe the notions it attached to the sacraments. Those who repudiate Catholicism rather relish the use of this word, understanding it as a condemnation. I do not, for it is not easy to dispose of the suspicion that St. Paul's notion of the sacrament of the body and blood of Christ might be described by this word (1 Cor. 11:30), or the sacrament of baptism when it is regarded as "the laver of regeneration" (Tit. 3:5). The sacramental system of the Pentateuch is described by Goldberg (*Die Wirklichkeit der Hebräer*) as "magic realism." If we are inclined to repudiate this phrase, it is chiefly because Protestantism has in the long run succeeded in rationalizing the religious conceptions of the Old Testament and of the New.

I admit that I use the word "magic" provocatively, challengingly; and it goes without saying that I attach to it the best meaning it will bear, not the base conceptions of savages and medicine men. Because this word denotes the extremist antithesis to our rationalistic conceptions, it may serve to startle men into an apprehension of the essentially *religious* character of Christian worship. If we discard the word magic because of its baser connotations, we must find another to use in place of it. We might say *mystical*—but then we must use this word in a more realistic sense than we commonly do. I should be content to say *numinous*, if I could be sure that a word so recently coined would be generally understood to denote the feeling of dread *and* fascination which is prompted by a sense of the presence and operation of God. It was only in a dream that Jacob saw the ladder on which angels ascended and descended, yet he exclaimed, "Surely the Lord is in this place! How dreadful this place is, this is none other but the house of God, this is the gate of heaven"

(Gen. 28:17). How much more *tremendum* and *fascinans* the house in which men meet with God, in which they are endued with "ghostly strength," in which they are fed with bread from heaven, and encouraged to believe that with God all things are possible! The sacraments of the Church are not in the baser sense magical, but clearly they are attestations of a profound religious realism, and not conventional symbols of trivial beliefs. If it is thought perverse of me to use the word magic at all, it will be seen at least that I use it as a protest against a far worse perversion which is prevalent in Protestantism, where the "idea of the holy" is rarely attached to the house of God, and no clear line is drawn between the sacred and the secular. As religion, Christianity is denatured by Protestantism, even if it is stressed as dogma. And because Christianity is life, religion is the more important factor.

The search for a magic space self-enclosed against the world led the mystery cults to build their sanctuaries underground. The Christians may have been moved by the same feeling when they constructed chambers in the catacombs and adorned them as chapels. Although the basilicas were built aboveground, they had no windows which afforded a view of the world or obtruded a sense of its existence. The windows of the clerestory admitted light and air, but the stone or wooden grille with which they were filled did not permit even a view of the sky. Windows were not often pierced in the side walls, unless there were five aisles, the outermost of which would be left in darkness, and then they were too high to afford a view. The exception proves the rule. For when the church was oriented with the altar towards the east the occasional use of windows in the apse had the purpose of permitting the rising sun to shine upon the altar. It seems that Constantine, who had his own reasons for venerating the sun, preferred to have it shine through the portal (as is said particularly of the church at Tyre), and therefore put the apse at the west end. But the danger of confounding Christianity with sun worship ended with his death. Christianity, though it did not discourage men from finding God in nature, was very far from being an example of Natural Theology. Its dogmas were not only concerned with the supernatural, but they were supernaturally revealed. Within the numinous space enclosed by the church walls, these doctrines were proclaimed and believed, the gifts of the Spirit, charismatic gifts, were received, and the hope of the kingdom of God, a totally otherworldly hope, was heartily cherished. For this reason windows were not wanted to communicate with the outside world, "this miserable and naughty world." For this reason Stoicism, the chief exponent of Natural Theology, was abhorred, in spite of its austere morality. And we should remember that we are speaking of an age which was anterior by a millennium and a half to the Romanticism which in our day has been brought to a pitiable end by the Darwinian picture of "nature red in tooth and claw" which with raving shrieks against our creed. Outside the house of the Church is Nature: inside is grace abounding, from the baptistery to the altar.

It may seem natural enough that in the ages of persecution the house of the Church was closed against a hostile world. But so it remained after the Peace when the political world was friendly. It was characteristic of the Greek and Roman dwelling house, the home of the family, that it had no windows opening upon the outside world and had hardly any external adornment. In Gothic architecture at the height of the Middle Ages we note a striking difference. The walls which had no architectural function were discarded, and the church was all windows. It is true that the sense of enclosed space remained, the eye was unable to discern through the colored glass the commonplace aspects of the world, yet sublimer subjects were presented to it in a thousand forms. Angels flock in through the windows, attesting along with holy men and monarchs that the Church is surrounded with a cloud of witnesses. This new feeling was shown also by the fact that the beauty of the outside of the building was as important as the inside. The Gothic church was the pride of the Christian city in a land where all were Christians.

In the basilica the sense of enclosed space was all the more mysterious and "magical" because it was differentiated space. It was space separated by the colonnades into large and smaller parts, into still smaller parts by the parapets of the choir, by a row of columns in front of the presbytery, by the apse which determined the position of the altar, by curtains, and in some instances by galleries. All of these spaces were significant, and the smaller spaces served to enhance the effect of the great. From the early Christian point of view the Church of St. Peter in Rome is condemned when it is said of it that all is on so vast a scale that there is nothing to indicate how big it is. It was once said boastfully of the Cathedral of St. John the Divine in New York that St. Sophia has no columns so great as the monoliths which adorn its apse, and even St. Peter's has nothing bigger. The truth is that the columns in St. Sophia are on a small scale in order to enhance the grandeur of the whole.

It is commonly said in favor of the basilica that the long colonnades lead the eye irresistibly towards the altar as the center of devotion, while the flat ceiling hinders the glance from straying far above it. This is very plausible. In some cases (pl. 72) a procession of saints depicted above the colonnade moves towards the altar. We are told of other cases where a river carries the eye in the same direction. Yet this ignores the fact—a fact which is very strange to us—that the worshippers did not stand in the nave but in the side

## THE BASILICA

aisles, behind the colonnades, where the altar was hardly visible, even if it were not obscured by curtains. What the people saw were the pictures on the high walls of the nave. That was an attractive sight. In order that it might be seen the better, the horizontal architrave characteristic of Greek architecture was soon superseded by the archivolt, turning the colonnade into an arcade such as appears for the first time at the beginning of the fourth century in the palace of Diocletian at Spalato. The ceiling, it is true, was generally flat. This was desirable because the church was also an auditorium where the Scriptures were read and expounded. But this ceiling, gilded, or painted blue to represent the heavens, attracted the eye to itself. Still more powerfully the eye was attracted to the half-dome of the apse which represented the dome of heaven and in which only heavenly scenes were depicted. We cannot exaggerate the symbolical importance of the dome. It was the favorite form for tombs, whether they were pagan or Christian, and it surmounted the baptisteries. In the church the ciborium (the canopy above the altar) was in its earlier form a dome. In every case the dome meant heaven, and under it men's feelings were encouraged to expand. Thus even in the basilica there were intimations of the great dome which in the East ultimately dominated the church, in spite of the fact that the Liturgy required the altar to be far from the center and therefore stressed the horizontal axis which conflicted with the perpendicular axis of the so-called central churches.

This long disquisition about the basilica serves incidentally to show how perfectly adapted such a building was for Christian worship in early Catholic times. But here, in a chapter introductory to pictorial art, my chief purpose is to show that the walls of the basilica in their whole extent were available for pictures, if the Christians chose to use them. It may be that for a century or more they made no use of them. It seems that in certain parts (Strzygowski says Armenia) they were for a very long time content with bare walls and the sense of enclosed space, *Raumgefühl*. But it is clear how and where pictures must be used if they were to be used at all. They must be used to enhance the sense of religious mystery in the enclosed space, complementing and accompanying the Liturgy by presenting to the eye the world of spiritual realities which it implies and evokes. Whereas in the glass windows of the Gothic churches the spiritual realities in which the Church lived and moved and had its being were obscurely intimated, the earlier age sought to produce clear pictures of historical scenes and even of the ineffable mysteries. The mysteries of the faith would naturally be represented, not as in Gothic cathedrals over the portal where every passer-by could see them, but on the apsidal wall behind the altar. There the triumphant cross was depicted, or

Christ was depicted in glory, giving to His apostles the new commandment. It was natural too that from the walls of the nave the stories of the Old and of the New Testament spoke to the people with a sober didactic purpose and recalled the mighty acts of God in history.

Before describing particularly the great basilicas erected immediately after the Peace of the Church, whether at Rome or in Palestine, buildings which presumably reflected an early Catholic tradition, and which certainly served to fix permanently a uniform style, something more must be said about the distribution of the significant parts of space within the basilica. To complete the picture of a typical basilica I will therefore describe certain features which might almost be regarded as furniture, if they were not invariable and essential aspects of the architectural scheme.

No one would speak slightingly of the Holy Table as a piece of furniture, since more than anything else it determined the form of the house of the Church. Yet in size it was insignificant. It never was enlarged in proportion with the size of the building, but in the immense churches erected after the Peace it retained the size, a size determined only by its use, which had sufficed for the earliest houses of worship. It was almost square, and tradition limited it to something like a yard and a quarter in its greater dimension. Not till late in the Middle Ages did the custom of burying beneath the altar the body of a saint require that the length should be approximately that of a man. The altar needed to be large enough only to support the eucharistic elements and the book of the Gospel, or later the Missal. It might be of wood or stone or even of precious metals. In any case it was clearly in the form of a table, supported by four legs or more rarely by a pedestal. For illustrations of the altar consult this subject in the index.

Whatever the size of the altar, its importance was sufficiently indicated by the ciborium (*q.v.* in the index), a dome above the altar which was supported by four columns, and which might vary in size to comport with the magnitude of the building. The bronze baldachino in St. Peter's does not look big in that place, although it is 95 feet high. In early times, however, the ciborium was never of great size. It was distinguished in the greater churches by the costly material used for its construction. The silver ciborium erected in the old church of St. Peter by Leo III weighed 2704 pounds, and that in the Lateran, 1227 pounds. The Greek word *Kiborion* means a cup. It was an inverted cup, forming a dome, which, as we have seen, was felt to be the appropriate covering for sacred things and sacred persons—an empress, by way of example (pl. 107b).

How the altar was covered is shown by several illustrations (pl. 64c, 63b,

150b). They represent a cloth of white linen superimposed upon one of heavier material which also was of linen but woven with wool to present geometrical designs in color. Later a solid frontal was used. It might be of marble, silver, gold, or ivory. When the body of a martyr was found at some depth beneath the altar this was enclosed on all sides, leaving only a small aperture (the *confessio*) through which might be thrust a handkerchief, which impregnated with the sanctity of the place would be treasured as a relic. This was a magical but rather innocent way of obtaining relics before men began in the eighth century to rifle the tombs of the saints to obtain their bones. By this macabre industry the Church became a *bottega*, a shop for petty gains. Another innocent way of accumulating relics was to take oil from the lamps which burned continually before the great shrines in Rome and Palestine. This precious oil was taken home in small leaden flasks (*ampullæ*) impressed with pictures of the place (pl. 103a). A number of these have been preserved in the Lombard cathedral at Monza. It must be remembered that candles were not much used except in processions, and that they were not placed upon the altar. It hardly needs to be said that the pretty pagan practice of strewing the altar with flowers was not adopted by the Church. So long as the celebrant stood behind the altar facing the people, a cross or crucifix upon the altar would have been an intolerable obstruction.

Although the plan of the basilica was determined by the altar, this could not be placed in the center, even if the church were built on what we call the central plan. Yet in a sense it stood in the middle, for it was placed between the clergy and the people, so that the congregation as a whole might be said to surround it. Even in the earliest times when all sat at table to partake of the Lord's Supper, the position assigned there to apostles, prophets, bishops, presbyters and deacons was the most ostensible indication of their rank. At a later time, when Christians were too numerous to sit together at a common board, the clergy alone sat behind it and the people stood in front. The seat of the bishop in the middle, against the apsidal wall, (his *cathedra* or *sede*—whence the name episcopal see) clearly defined his place and function in the Church; for in presiding at the Lord's Supper he occupied the place of Christ. At the time we have now in mind the clergy and the laity, if not more substantially distinguished, were more sharply separated when the raised platform, the presbytery, was divided from the rest of the church by stone parapets (chancels), and often by a row of columns erected in front of the altar (pl. 46b, 50a), adumbrating the rood screen. Because the bishop presided at the Holy Table, his cathedra was directly behind it, and the presbyters had their seats on either side of him.

The deacons, as the character of their service required, were expected to stand, as did the acolytes, and, of course, the rest of the congregation. The inventory of church furniture did not include pews, nor even movable seats. The area defined by the apse, although generally it had the same width as the nave, was often not large enough to accommodate all of the clergy, but it could easily be enlarged by placing the altar farther to the fore. This did not involve any substantial change in the architecture. But in some of the greater churches, like the Lateran basilica and the basilicas dedicated to St. Peter and St. Paul, the presbytery was immensely enlarged by building a transept, which in some cases, like the three I have mentioned, protruded beyond the rectangular plan of the basilica and gave it the form of the so-called Latin cross. Although the transept was not common even in Rome, pilgrims coming from the north would naturally regard it as normative, since they found it in the great shrines which were the principal object of their visit. The transept was marked off from the body of the church not only by chancels, but by a great arch which corresponded in size with the half-dome of the apse. This so-called triumphal arch afforded a favorite field for mosaic decoration (pl. 57, 69a).

It was customary for the bishop to sit in his chair when he preached (*ex cathedra*), as Jesus did, like the Jewish rabbis, as Greek philosophers did, and as professors do today. But it seems impossible that in the greater basilicas he could be heard from this remote position, unless he were making merely allocution to the clergy. At all events, there were pulpits in the churches, called *ambo* or *bema*, both words being derived from *anabaino*, to ascend. There were commonly two of them because they were used principally for reading the Epistle and the Gospel. The hymn called the gradual (from *gradus*, a step) was sung while the deacon mounted the higher pulpit to read the Gospel. In Rome it was customary as early as the sixth century to thrust the choir with its chancels out into the nave (pl. 50a), and very advantageously the pulpits were erected there where the Scripture and the sermon could be better heard. Professor Baldwin Smith tells me that in northern Syria some of the churches have in the middle of the nave traces which suggest that a pulpit might have been erected there. That is quite likely. For, strange as it seems to us, the nave was not much in use. Hence a pulpit as well as the choir might be intruded into it. As we have seen, it was occupied, not by the faithful, but by the "hearers" (we would call them inquirers), by catachumens and by certain classes of penitents, who were formally dismissed in turn after they had heard the Scriptures and the sermon, since they might not participate in the sacramental Liturgy. Various forms of dismissal are still recited in the Greek rite, but in the Roman Mass nothing of the sort remains but the dismissal of the whole congregation with the dry words, *Ite, missa est,* from which comes the name mass.

This brings us to the curtains, which is the last item of furniture I shall mention. We may reflect that in antiquity curtains were used more generally than they are with us, who think of them chiefly as an adornment for windows. Perhaps in ancient times they were not much used for windows, but they were used for doors (pl. 147) and were hung between the columns of an arcade (pl. 74a). It is likely that curtains were used in the basilica to separate the side aisles from the nave, and thus to hide the men from the women. It is certain that they were hung from the architrave which connected the columns in front of the altar, in order that at certain moments they might be drawn across the nave to hide the liturgical acts of the celebrant. This we know because the metal attachments for such curtains are still to be seen in some places. By the same token we know that curtains were hung about the ciborium. According to the *Liber Pontificalis,* Gregory IV (ninth century) made for St. Paul's a great curtain (*velum*), which presumably was in two parts, and twenty-four smaller ones (*cortinæ*), which likely were in pairs between the twelve columns in front of the presbytery. This custom seems strange to us. And indeed it was neither a natural nor an innocent thing. In the Eastern Church it resulted in the iconostasis, a thin but permanent partition covered with sacred pictures which at all times hides the altar from the people. We can understand that the curtains, many of them covered with sacred figures, added to the sense of mystery. It was a mystery far too magical, it seems to me, for it evidently was prompted by the Greek mystery cults which only because they had a mock resemblance to Christianity had for a while some influence upon it. This unholy game with curtains lasted for a long time even in the West, but fortunately it has left no trace upon the Roman ritual—unless the rule that certain parts of the Mass are to be said *secrete* (i.e., in a voice audible only to those who are standing near) may be a sort of substitute for curtains. Many Roman priests observe this rule reluctantly. "Spikes" in the Anglican Communion who do this sort of thing are without excuse, for they cannot claim that their Church imposes such a rule. This is a Catholic custom which cannot pretend to be apostolic, for we cannot forget that the disciples were accustomed for a long time to sit at a common table and to hear every word the "president" pronounced.

In the Eastern Church the tradition has been maintained that there may be but one altar in a church. In the Roman Church the custom of building many altars close to the walls and hardly at all separated from the people has encouraged an almost irreverent familiarity, at the greatest possible remove from the mysterious veneration encouraged by the use of curtains.

<u>But in a memorial basilica the altar was not always in the apse, and even in early times there might be more than one altar.</u> Such was the case in the Constantinian church now called S. Sebastiano but originally dedicated to the Apostles. There excavators in recent times sought in vain for traces of an altar in the apse, but found the original site of it in an eccentric position in the nave, where it *had* to be because immediately below it was the tomb in which the bodies of Peter and Paul once lay. And in this church there was another altar sacred to St. Sebastian, because his body lay beneath it.

Until the Middle Ages, except in the Baptistery of the Lateran, for which Constantine provided bronze doors taken from a secular building, and in the rare case that a pagan temple was used for a church, wooden doors sufficed for the basilicas, but sometimes they were richly sculptured (pl. 93). Commonly the doors in front of the church corresponded in number to the aisles. Not even the central portal was especially striking or inviting, as it became in the development of the Gothic church. It was hid by the colonnade of the atrium, or by the vestige of it which remained in front of the church when there was no room for a square court. The atrium (pl. 39e) was characteristic of Rome and of the churches in Palestine which were built by Constantine in the Roman style. It was not often used in the Eastern Church, and consequently we do not find it at Ravenna. For lack of an atrium, the fountain which usually stood in the middle of it (pl. 39d, e), to serve for ceremonial ablutions before entering the church, was transferred to the door (pl. 147). In any case it was running water—more hygienic than the holy water which lies stagnant in little basins. According to the mind of the early Church, water did not need to be blessed by man in order to perform the cleansing function for which God had created it. The only conspicuous portal was the propylæum which sometimes ornamented the entrance to the atrium. In the East, where the atrium was rarely used, it was not uncommon to surround the whole church with a wall like the peribolos of a Greek temple (pl. 37a).

I must not omit a piece of furniture which was peculiar to the Eastern Church where it was required by a distinctive feature of the Syrian liturgy. It was the "table of prothesis," located in a room near the sanctuary, where the bread which was to be used in the Eucharist was first wounded and slain and buried before it was carried to the altar. This certainly was a significant ceremony! But is it not too histrionic?

The character of the Christian basilica is best exemplified by the great churches erected in Rome immediately after the Peace, most of them by the munificence of the Emperor. Some of them were built at great cost, on an immense scale and with a magnificence which has not often been surpassed. Doubtless some of the parochial churches (*tituli*) were still standing and others were restored at that time, but because they were rebuilt on a greater scale during the fifth century, there is none to which we can refer as an example of the earliest Christian basilicas, though a dozen of them at least occupy the sites of churches which existed in the third century.

It is likely that in Rome, as in smaller cities, the first pictorial decoration was in fresco; but nothing of the sort has been preserved, and the earliest pictures we know were produced in the more costly medium of glass mosaic, an art which the Church ardently appropriated as peculiarly suitable to its purposes, and carried on to a degree of development which was not approached in pagan art. But in this chapter I am speaking of the buildings, not of their decoration. The names which many of the older churches still bear support the tradition that they were built where once stood the houses which wealthy patrons put at the disposition of their Christian brethren. One church bearing the name of Pudenziana is connected with Pudens, a Roman senator, who was a disciple of Peter and Paul (2 Tim. 4:21), the name being used here as an adjective (Pudentian church), which later was misunderstood as the name of a daughter of the senator. In ancient Catholic practice the names of founders or benefactors were attached to a church with no more scruple than Protestants feel when they speak, e.g., of the Jones Memorial Church. Only memorial basilicas built above the cemeteries (therefore outside the City) were known by the name of a particular saint, i.e., of the martyr buried beneath.

Plausible as is the tradition which connects many of the churches in Rome with men or women who were mentioned in the New Testament or were prominent in subsequent times, the connection is not in any instance conclusively proved. It is true that when excavations are made beneath any of these churches the remains of a private house are sure to be found. But one cannot dig anywhere in Rome without finding ancient dwellings; and under these churches it is disconcerting to find more than one dwelling house, and sometimes (as under S. Clemente) a pagan shrine. In the fifth century there were twenty-five titles in Rome, but it is not likely that more than half of them can trace their origin as far back as the third century.

The church which Constantine built above the tomb of St. Peter was the largest in Christendom, a basilica of five aisles preceded by an atrium (pl. 39c, e). The emperor built a smaller basilica over the tomb of St. Paul, another (now called S. Sebastiano) over the place where the bodies of both Apostles were for a while buried together, another over the tomb of St. Lawrence, and another in honor of St. Agnes, and near that the round mausoleum (now known as S. Costanza) which was meant for his own family. All of these were cemeterial churches, therefore outside the walls. Only the Church of St. Peter was near enough to be included within an extension of the old wall which was built by Leo the Great (440–461) and called after him the Leonine Wall.

The emperor gave to Sylvester, Bishop of Rome, the great palace of the Lateran, which had been an imperial property since it was confiscated by Nero from the senator Plautius Lateranus. A part of it was given by Maximian to his daughter Fausta who in 307 became the wife of Constantine and died in 326. This great palace served not only as the episcopal residence, and for all the business of the diocese, but the imposing basilica connected with it became the principal cathedral of the bishop, although his throne was erected in every church. The Church of St. John Lateran was originally dedicated to the Saviour—tradition says in 324, but it is also said that in 313 a council was held there under Melchiades. It was an immense basilica of five aisles, which has been altered only by incorporating the columns two by two in heavy pillars of masonry, which impaired the appearance of the ancient building but insured its stability. Alongside of it Constantine built an imposing baptistery, the first building of the sort in Christendom, which was called by the name of St. John the Baptist, a name which subsequently was applied to the basilica. This great baptistery remains intact, except for the loss of its decorations in mosaic, in marbles and in precious metals with which Constantine adorned it.

The baptistery was appropriately built beside the bishop's church. There was but one baptistery for the whole diocese, and no baptismal fonts in the parish churches. For though the bishop had been obliged to yield to the presbyters the right to celebrate the Eucharist in their several churches, it was he who baptized. At a solemn ceremony on Easter Even, the catachumens, who had been prepared by a long course of instruction, were admitted to the Church and introduced into the basilica for their first communion, after they had received the washing of regeneration and the anointing (*consignatio*, confirmation) which naturally followed the bath.

The fact that the cathedra of the bishop was conspicuous in every basilica indicated that his authority extended to every Christian assembly, and that the presbyter who celebrated the Eucharist in his absence, seated in his place, was acting as his agent. It meant indeed far more than that, for it is an expression of a fact not obvious to the eye that when Christians in a great city were too numerous to meet commonly in one place, they were still one Church, one fold with one shepherd, and shared the same Eucharist. By this symbolism, expressed in every parish, the unique authority of the bishop was sufficiently defined. Yet in Rome there was the additional provision that the presbyter of a parochial church might not consecrate the Eucharist until from the altar at which the bishop presided there was brought a particle of the host, called "the leaven," which had been consecrated there. The bishop himself was present from time to time, following an orderly rotation, in every one of the churches, and the word "station" is still used in Rome to indicate the place where the bishop will be (or the Cardinal Vicar, as it is now), and thither the people flock in great numbers.

Since baptism was a bath and was always performed by immersion, baptisteries were built as bath houses commonly were, on a round or polygonal plan and with a domed roof, and this tradition was followed for more than a thousand years. The octagonal baptistery erected by Constantine and his round mausoleum, both of them surmounted by domes, afford proof enough that it was not a lack of technical skill which obliged the Church in the West to adhere for centuries to the traditional type of the basilica, even when the dome had become the favorite fashion in the East.

Upon his mother Constantine bestowed the great Sessorian palace, and there Helena, who shared with her son a special veneration for the cross, and had a part in discovering it at Jerusalem, transformed the great hall of the palace into a church, where a piece of the True Cross was displayed. This transformation was easily accomplished by adding an apse, although the hall had no colonnades. Not till the twelfth century was it provided by Pope Lucian with this traditional feature, and even then no ceiling was added to hide the rafters of the roof. This Church of S. Croce was first called *Basilica Sanctæ Crucis in Hierusalem*, or was known simply as Jerusalem. This exemplifies the tendency to repeat in Rome the great churches in Palestine, where, as Eusebius ventures to say of Constantine, "he created the New Jerusalem which was spoken of by the prophets."

Roman tradition ascribes to Liberius (352–366) the church now known as S. Maria Maggiore (St. Mary Major, as the English quaintly call it). It is a church with three aisles, originally without a transept (pl. 45b). At first it was known simply as the Liberian Church, and presumably it was Liberius who decorated the nave with mosaics. It was first associated with Mary when the Council of Ephesus affirmed to her the title of Theotokos, Mother of God, and Sixtus III, to celebrate this event, adorned the east wall above the apse with pictures of the infancy of Jesus (pl. 65). But even before that it was associated with Bethlehem for the fact that a replica in wood of the Saviour's crib was treasured there and came in time to be regarded as the original. For this reason S. Maria Maggiore has long been the station for the midnight Mass at Christmas. Until very lately it was the only place where a midnight Mass was celebrated in Rome. In the pontificate of Theodore (642–649) this church was known as Beata Maria ad Præsepe, because this pope, who was a native of Jerusalem, had deposited in it a stone hewn from the cave in which Christ was born. We learn through Jerome that in Bethlehem it was believed that the original crib was made of clay.

It is not easy to account for the fact that Constantine, when over the tomb of St. Peter he built a great basilica, and one of considerable size over the place where the bodies of both Apostles had lain for some time, contented himself with erecting a small basilica over the tomb of St. Paul. For at that time St. Paul was not held in less honor. Constantine himself showed the same reverence for both Apostles by enclosing the bodies of each of them in a bronze box adorned with a heavy golden cross. Eventually the inequality was redressed when the small building Constantine had erected over the tomb of the Apostle to the Gentiles was replaced by a great basilica of five aisles known as the Church of the Three Emperors, meaning Valentinian II, Theodosius the Great and Arcadius (pl. 45a). The inscription above the triumphal arch (pl. 69a), *Theodosius cepit perfecit Honorius aulam doctoris mundi sacratam corpore Pauli,* ascribes to Theodosius and Honorius "this hall dedicated to the body of Paul the teacher of the world," and the inscription below indicated that the decoration was completed by the filial piety of Placidia, daughter of Theodosius the Great, and by the zeal of Pope Leo the Great (440–461). Although in 1823 this basilica was destroyed by fire, a danger which constantly threatened wooden roofs, it was rebuilt so precisely in the same form that today it is the only monument which gives an adequate impression of the grandeur of a great basilica of five aisles, like the original Church of St. Peter. It is adorned now with an immense variety of Italian marbles, chiefly from the quarries of Carrara, so that it served me as a sampler when I went there with my *marmista* to choose stones for the decoration of the American Church of St. Paul-within-the-walls. It seems to me, however, that the numinous character of this church has been irreparably destroyed by fire.

The small church which Constantine built over the tomb of St. Paul was, like most of his churches, oriented in such a way that the portal was at the east in order to admit the rays of the rising sun. The present Church of St. Peter retains the original orientation which Constantine had given this church. It is said plausibly enough that the position of Peter's tomb on the slope of the Vatican Hill made any other orientation very difficult. But on the alluvial plain of the Tiber, where Paul was buried, there was no such difficulty. To orient the apse towards the east involved only the suppression of a secondary road, and that could have been accomplished by Constantine as easily as it was by the decree of the three emperors. The Constantinian Church of S. Lorenzo also had its portal at the east end, and this orientation was inverted by Pelagius II in the sixth century. In view of the fact that most of the churches built by Constantine had the same orientation, exactly the opposite of that which afterwards prevailed, it is vain to attempt to explain in each individual case why it must have been so; for it evidently represents a strong predilection of this emperor, and there is no evidence that before his time Christians had any interest in giving their churches a particular orientation. They had no disposition, like the Jews, to worship with their faces turned towards Jerusalem. But we know that Constantine had a peculiar interest in the sun. And well he might, for the prodigy he beheld in the sky and interpreted as a cross was a solar phenomenon. It seems likely that the one god his father worshipped was the sun, and having this inheritance, Constantine was only too liable to confound Christianity with sun worship. On some of his coins (pl. 55b) the sun god appears, with the Mithraic motto, *Soli invicto comiti*, comrades at arms of the invincible sun. It happened that the first day of the week, the day of Christ's Resurrection, was known as Sunday; and in the Edict of Milan which made this a day of rest Constantine described it, in a phrase more pagan than Christian, as "the great and venerable day of the sun." Although until the reign of his son Constans no mention is made of the celebration of Christmas on the twenty-fifth of December, it is likely that Constantine was responsible for this innovation, for on this date (which in the Julian calendar was the winter solstice, the moment when the sun began to regain its power) was celebrated the festival of the unconquered sun, *festis invicti*. The orientation of the portal towards the sun was due perhaps to the consideration that traditionally the apse had no windows through which the sun might be seen, whereas through the portal its rays could enter the church—as Bishop Paulinus remarked with satisfaction in the panegyric he pronounced at the dedication of his church at Tyre (Eusebius, *H. E.* x, 4:17). Perhaps when the Christians tardily bethought themselves of making windows in the wall of the apse it seemed to them more appropriate to turn that end of the church towards the rising sun.

## THE CROSS
## AND THE MONOGRAM

The cross was never held in greater honor than in the early centuries with which we are now dealing. Several Christian writers dwelt fondly upon its symbolical significance. They saw it dissimulated in many of the commonest objects, in the letter T, in the yards of a ship, in the crosspiece of an anchor, in the trophy, in the standards of the army, in the traditional attitude of prayer, and in the constitution of nature with its four points of the compass and its four winds (swastica). We know that it was frequently used as a gesture in private prayer. Tertullian says, "Before beginning any action, when we enter the house or leave it, when we put on our clothes or our shoes, when we seat ourselves at table, at lamp-lighting, or on going to bed, we trace on our foreheads the sign of the cross."

It may seem strange therefore that in the earliest Christian art the cross was not depicted realistically. But we can understand that Christians were loath to depict the common patibulum or gallows upon which the worst criminals suffered. This would subject them to the cruellest misunderstanding. A graffito scratched upon the wall of the pages' room on the Palatine shows a figure with the head of an ass attached to a cross, and the inscription under it reads: "Alexaminos adores his god." Thus was a young Christian derided by his companions. The picture belongs to the end of the second century, and it is the earliest representation of the Crucifixion we know of. The cross which first appeared upon the monuments was the triumphal cross of Constantine, often in the form of the monogram he beheld in his vision.

In the pagan symbols which resembled the cross Christians were inclined to see a presage of the Gospel. But the only symbol of this sort which they used before the fourth century was the swastica, an ancient pagan representation of the four winds, which had come to be little more than a decorative motif (fig. A on pl. 55a). We see it on the garment of a fossor (pl. 9c). The so-called Nile key was sometimes employed on Egyptian tapestries after the fifth century (pl. 143e, 144a). To the Egyptians it symbolized life (fig. K on pl. 55a), and Christians regarded the cross as the tree of life. The triumphal

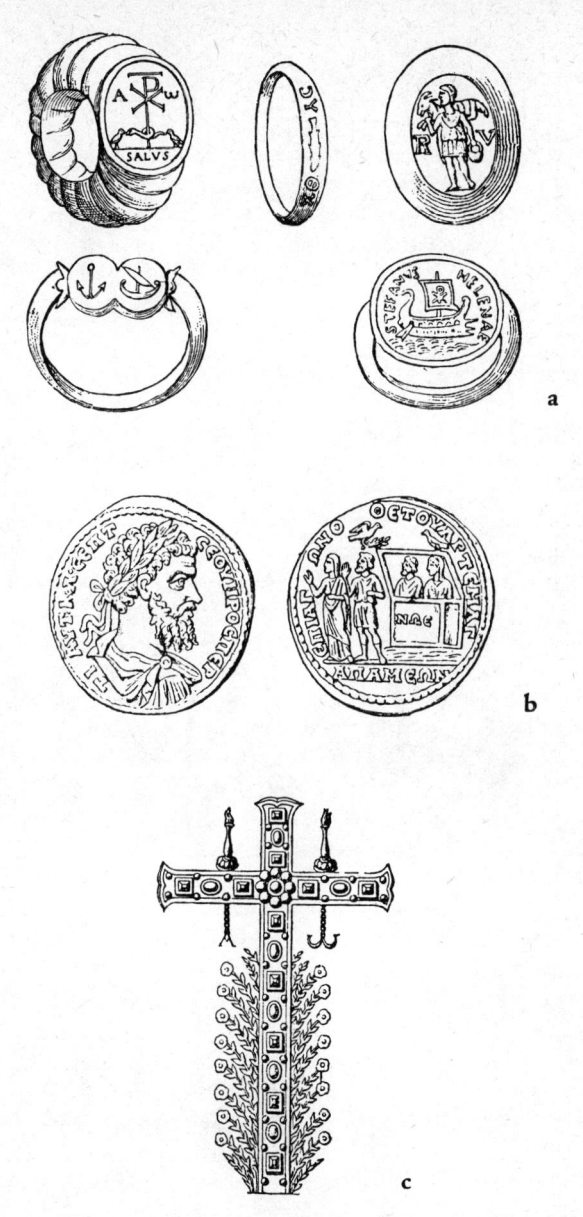

**a.** Early Christian rings.—**b.** A coin of Apamea, Phrygia, representing Noah and the ark. Reign of Septimius Severus. (See p. 65.)—**c.** *Crux gemmata.* Fresco in the cemetery of Pontianus. Eighth century.

Pl. 54

SYMBOLS

Pl. 55

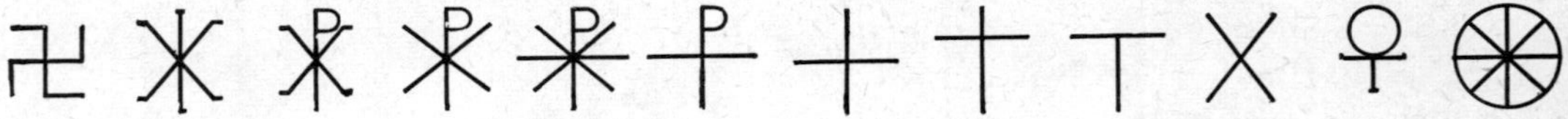

**a.** Various forms of the monogram and cross.—**b.** Four coins of Constantine.—**c.** Coins of Nepotianus, Eudoxia, and Galla Placidia.—**d.** Carved gems of second and third centuries.—**e.** The fish on early Christian seals.

cross as it was depicted in the basilicas was not only studded with jewels but burgeoning with flowers. A cross of this sort painted in the vestibule of the cemetery of Pontianus (pl. 54c) is a reflection of the art of the basilicas. The cross was often surrounded by a wreath, as was the Constantinian monogram, which, as we must remember, was always understood to be the cross.

The equal-armed cross appears on coins before the Christian period simply as a monetary sign, but it is possible that Constantine meant it as a cross when he used it on one of his coins (fig. A on pl. 55c), where on the other side of the sun-god a star is to be seen, and around it the Mithraic inscription: *Soli invicto comiti*.

Knowing that Constantine was prone to confound Christianity with sun worship, there is reason to believe that the cross which he saw in the sky was the sun wheel (fig. L on pl. 55a). On this same plate the figures B to E show five forms of the so-called monogram as it appeared on early Christian monuments. D is symmetrical, and it was the earliest form. But there was a tendency to depict an upright X, to make it clear that it is the first letter of the Greek word Christ. The P is evidently the second letter, for in Greek it is the letter R, and perhaps it was to make this letter resemble an R that in the fifth century the loop of the P (rho) was not brought around to meet the staff but terminated in an outward curve (pl. 29b).

No one knows the derivation of the word *labarum*, which denoted the military standards adorned by the Constantinian cross. In no other way was the official adoption of the Christian religion so plainly marked. Different legions were distinguished by the shape of their standards, several of which are depicted on plate 55b. Fig. B has the cross above the banner on which three dots indicate the portraits of the emperor and his sons. The staff transfixes the serpent, symbol of evil, and the inscription, *Spes publica*, hails the cross and the Christian religion as the hope of the people. This motto expresses the significance of the cross (doubtless the monogram) which Constantine erected in the Roman Forum. It was the triumphant cross bearing the motto, "In this sign you conquer," and in this light nothing could be more perverse than Carducci's vibrant lines: "Rome no more conquers since a Galilean ascended the Capitol, threw down a cross of his and said, 'Follow and serve.'" We find a similar device on a ring illustrated on plate 54a. The same idea is expressed in a silk brocade found at Achmim in Egypt and ascribed to the fifth century (pl. 144c). Above, the imperial eagle attacks an evil beast: below, Christ slays the dragon (crocodile) with a spear which ends in a cross. The Empire and the Church are united in the task of suppressing evil. This expresses Constantine's thought. Essentially it was the idea of the Holy Roman Empire.

Very early, but not in the time of Constantine, the monogram was accompanied by the Greek letters Alpha and Omega, to affirm the divinity of Christ who was both the Beginning and the End (Rev. i:8). On a well-known sarcophagus in Ravenna (pl. 29b) these letters appear in connection with the monogram in its original form and in the simpler form of a cross (fig. H on pl. 55a) which became common in the fifth century. A contemporary sarcophagus presents the monogram without the letters and without a wreath (pl. 55c). The best representations of it are in a bronze plate found at Aquileia and in a mosaic at Albegna, both belonging to the latter part of the fourth century (pl. 103b, 58b). On a lead coffin of the fourth century found in Phœnicia the monogram is surrounded by the letters of the Greek word for fish (IXΘYS) which spell Jesus Christ Son of God Saviour (pl. 10b).

The monogram, being the sign of triumph, was not commonly used in the West after the fatal date when Rome was conquered by the Goths. The undisguised cross of suffering displaced it. The patibulum (fig. I on pl. 55a), an upright stake with a transverse bar above it, is the most realistic form of the cross on which criminals were hung; but for the Christians it was too realistic. They had some reason for using the so-called Latin cross (fig. H), for the superscription which Pilate affixed to the cross of Jesus must have been supported by an upright staff. But the equal-armed cross (fig. G) was more commonly used both in the East and the West. When we call this the Greek cross we think of a distinction which was not made before the Middle Ages. The term Latin cross has perhaps more justification, for it appears that it was used in the earliest apsidal pictures (pl. 58a). But the common use of the Latin cross dates from the sixth century, the time of the Arian rule in Ravenna. It seems to have grown out of the use of processional crosses, which required a long staff (95a). It was carried by Christ (pl. 61a, 88, 89b, 95b), by saints (64a), and by Peter as his especial emblem (pl. 29c). Probably it was from such pictures of the cross that later artists got the notion that when he was crucified Christ was raised high above the ground. The earliest pictures of the Crucifixion (pl. 95c) do not support this notion.

## CONSTANTINE
## AND THE APOSTLES

There can be no doubt that the New Rome which Constantine built on the Bosphorus as the capital of his empire was adorned by him with many magnificent churches, but strangely enough Eusebius tells us almost nothing about them, though he tells of churches built at Tyre, at Antioch, at Nicomedia, at Heliopolis, and describes at great length the notable churches in Palestine, which was the land of his birth. But we know that there was an early church of Hagia Sophia which was replaced by the far greater church built by Justinian. There was also a church of Irene (peace), built to celebrate the peace he brought to the Empire, which doubtless was suggested by the Ara Pacis of Augustus. The only church which Eusebius mentions (*V. C.*, 58–60) was the Church of the Apostles. In this Constantine took a particular interest, for it was built as his mausoleum. It was said to be a very lofty building surmounted by a vast dome. The dome, as we have seen, was appropriate to a mausoleum, and we may suppose that when Justinian rebuilt this church in the domed style he made current, he did not change it essentially. It may indeed have been the model for the centralized churches we associate with his name. At all events, Justinian's church did serve as a model for S. Marco in Venice. Constantine adorned his church with the utmost magnificence, and under the dome he erected twelve columns representing the apostles, and the place designated for his tomb was the center of this circle. For he thought of himself as the "peer of the apostles"—not without some reason, for no apostle could claim to have done so much to expand the Church. Perhaps he thought he was more than a peer, for by locating his tomb amidst these "pillars" of the Church he assumed for it the place he allotted to Christ when around the Holy Sepulchre he erected twelve columns. He certainly did not mean to put himself on a par with the bishops when he said that he was "bishop of external affairs." He was the only bishop of that sort, and it was not merely over external affairs he claimed authority when he presided at the Council of Nicæa.

Constantine introduced no new note into Catholic theology when he emphasized the importance of the apostles, for they had always been regarded as the cornerstone of ecclesiastical authority and the criterion of pure doctrine. But his interest in this theme, as in the cross and in the sun, probably had a considerable influence upon monumental art. The *Liber Pontificalis* records that Constantine presented to the church which he built over the tomb of St. Peter, not only four porphyry columns (which doubtless supported the ciborium), but twelve spiral columns of marble brought from Greece, which stood in a line before the presbytery of this church until it was demolished. Eight of them are still preserved as adornments of the balconies under the dome of St. Peter, and one may be seen in the chapel next to the north door, where it is described naively as a remnant of the Temple of Solomon. These columns, which were characteristic of fourth-century baroque, served as a model for the immense bronze columns which Bernini made in the sixteenth century to support his baldachino.

But the influence of Constantine's devotion to the apostles is shown chiefly by the fact that in his time the picture of Christ seated among His apostles and giving them the Great Commission suddenly attained enormous popularity. This scene is frequently depicted on the sarcophagi (see index *s.v.* Christ, Twelve, and *Missio*), and at the same time it found its way into the catacombs. From this we may infer securely that it had already become a favorite theme for apsidal decoration, whether in fresco or mosaic, although the mosaic in the Church of S. Pudenziana (pl. 57) is the only important example preserved to this day. Only in the apse could the full significance of this picture be felt. Directly beneath it the bishop was seated in the midst of his presbyters, reflecting the heavenly analogy which prompted Ignatius to liken the bishop to Christ and the presbyters to the apostles.

## CONSTANTINIAN CHURCHES IN PALESTINE

Eusebius was himself a native of Palestine, and it is perhaps for that reason he devoted so much space in his *Life of Constantine* to the churches which the emperor built in the Holy Land. Yet he did not devote too much attention to them, seeing that pilgrims had already begun to flock from all parts of the Empire to visit these shrines. The Bordeaux Pilgrim came in 333, and not many years later Etheria, the superior of a group of Spanish nuns, who until lately was supposed to be Silvia of Aquitaine, gave a more vivid description of the cult which was performed at Jerusalem and Bethlehem. This was about the time when Rufinus with his disciple and patron Melitia, and when Jerome with his disciples and benefactors Paula and Eustachium, lived for a long time in Jerusalem or Bethlehem. We get the impression that, except for the pilgrims, and the anchorites of both sexes who had taken up their abode in Palestine, there were not very many Christians at hand to worship in the churches of Jerusalem and Bethlehem. In the fourth century there were few regions where Christ had so few disciples as in Judæa and Galilee.

The churches which Constantine built in the Holy Land are interesting for themselves, for they are unlike any others we know; and of course they are peculiarly interesting for the sacred sites they commemorate. Because the Churches of the Nativity and of the Holy Sepulchre are each of them unique, the description Eusebius gives of them is not clear enough to obviate very discordant views about the shape of them. And because the perennial interest of Christians in these sites has prompted men to transform the original buildings in many ways, not enough is now left of them to elucidate the literary descriptions. Only recently has archæological research discovered a basis for a concordant view of the Constantinian churches.

There is no doubt that the churches of Jerusalem and Bethlehem were lavishly decorated by the munificence of Constantine. In his letter to Macarius, Bishop of Jerusalem, and to his colleagues in Palestine he promised to provide all the marbles and precious metals they might see fit to use, requiring only that these churches must be the most beautiful in Christendom. By the richness of the decoration he would compensate for their exiguous size; for the basilica erected near the Holy Sepulchre was barely 120 feet long, and that at Bethlehem was not much greater. Eusebius remarks upon the gilded ceilings, the noble columns, the incrustations of precious marbles, the polished pavements, and the careful masonry which was smooth even on the outside. The pilgrims were impressed by the glitter of marble and gold, and especially by the splendor of the lamps which burned perpetually in the Holy Sepulchre and in the Grotto at Bethlehem.

With all this nothing is said about mosaic pictures, and from this negative testimony some are inclined to infer that pictures had no part in the decoration. There is something to be said for this view, since there is reason to think that at least in North Syria there was a deep-seated aversion to religious pictures. De Vogüé's opinion that in this part of Syria no pictorial decoration was used has been confirmed by later explorers. Mosaic tesseræ have been found there, but it is supposed that they were used for arabesque ornament. The argument from silence, however, is weakened when we reflect that gleaming marbles and gold, which were a more costly decoration than mosaic pictures, would be more likely remarked upon. We know that there were admirable mosaics in the baptistery of the Lateran, but only the marble and the silver and gold were described by contemporaries. And whatever may have been the prejudice of Syria, we cannot think that Constantine, who adorned the churches of Rome with mosaics, would have been content to see the churches of Palestine without this significant adornment, especially when he expected them to be the most beautiful in the world. It is certain that by the sixth century some of the churches of Palestine were richly decorated with religious pictures. The description which Choricius gives of St. Sergius at Gaza shows that it was decorated as completely as any church in Rome. We happen to know that in 614 the church at Bethlehem was spared by the Persians because they saw the Magi depicted on the façade in their national dress.

From this we can infer that the inside of the church was decorated with pictures of the Nativity. My dear "colleague" Professor Albert Friend, who knows so much and publishes so little, has reasons of his own for believing that the churches of Jerusalem and Bethlehem, especially the church on Mount Sion, which commemorated the place where Jesus celebrated the Last Supper, were decorated elaborately by Eudoxia with appropriate mosaics. I see reasons enough for believing that the Constantinian churches in Palestine were adorned with pictorial mosaics which were appropriate to the sacred sites they celebrated. And I am inclined to think that the pictures of the Nativity, of the Passion and of the Resurrection, which at this same time became popular throughout the world, owed their vogue to Constantinian mosaics in the churches of Jerusalem and Bethlehem.

Constantine's first care was to honor the tomb in which the Lord had been buried and from which He rose triumphantly on the third day. We speak commonly of this church as the Holy Sepulchre, but the name first given to it was Anastasis (resurrection). This more aptly expressed the Christian faith, for in fact it was an empty tomb.

Remembering that the place where Christ suffered and was buried and rose again was outside the walls of Jerusalem, it may at first seem strange to us that the Anastasis was precisely in the center of the city. But we must remember that the old city had been destroyed, and that eventually a new city was built by Hadrian outside the walls and given his name of Aelia. This was a pagan city, in which the Church had no deep roots and not many adherents; for the Jews had been driven from Jerusalem, and the Jewish-Christian community, warned by Christ's prophecy, had left the doomed city before the siege and removed to Pella. They never returned to the neighborhood of Jerusalem, but it is plausible to suppose that the sites made sacred by the Lord's Passion and Resurrection had not been forgotten, even though they were defiled by pagan cults. It was not by any miracle that the Lord's tomb was identified. Eusebius assumes that it was well known, in spite of the pagan efforts to hide it by building there a temple of Venus upon a high superstructure. Constantine removed this great mass of material polluted by demons and replaced it with fresh earth brought from afar. The wonder is that beneath this mass the tomb was actually discovered—and unexpectedly the hill called Golgotha, and not far from that the true cross, which was thenceforth preserved at the place where it was found, under the basilica which was subsequently erected.

The buildings constructed in the sixth century, the destruction wrought later by the Mohammedans, the rebuilding done by the Crusaders, and the subsequent division of the property between various national Churches, have so obscured the original plan that archæologists have felt free to interpret as they liked the long but vague description given by Eusebius. Most of them made only one church out of it, a basilica ending in an apse which was supposed to cover the tomb. Even Père Abel understood Eusebius' "hemisphere" as an apse, although that is only a quarter of a sphere. If archæologists had taken literally two expressions which Eusebius uses emphatically to describe the building erected over the tomb (namely, "hemisphere" and "head of all"), we need not have waited so long for the true interpretation of his words, which eventually was forced upon us by the floor mosaic (a map of Palestine) in the church at Madaba (pl. 47), and by the apsidal mosaic in S. Pudenziana (pl. 57),[1] both of which represent the building above the tomb as a domed structure, a true hemisphere, as distinct from the basilica as the head is from the body. Starting with this perception the whole complex can be described with tolerable accuracy. We begin with an imposing propylæum which opened to the west upon the principal street, a street which, as the map at Madaba shows, was adorned on both sides by a colonnade. This led to the square atrium in front of the basilica. The atrium had on all sides a colonnade of two stories, and doubtless had a fountain (cantharus) in the middle of it. From the atrium three doors gave entrance to the basilica of five aisles. In the East the three doors, representing the Trinity, were traditional. In this case the five aisles were required, not because of the size of the church, but because of its importance. The first aisle on either side was separated from the nave by a row of columns, likely surmounted by arches, while the side aisles had ornate pillars. There were galleries (exedra) above the aisles for the use of women, who in the East were more strictly separated from the men. For this reason galleries were rarely used in the West. S. Agnese was the only instance in Rome, and the churches built by Justinian in Ravenna reflected the practice of the East. The gilded ceiling has already been mentioned. Etheria gives to the basilica the name of Martyrium, a name commonly used in Rome for a cemeterial basilica. Such a basilica sometimes abutted upon the tomb it was built to honor, as in the case of S. Sinforosa near Rome (pl. 39a). So it was at Jerusalem: the Martyrium abutted upon the Anastasis, which Eusebius described as the "hemisphere" and "head of all."

The Anastasis or Church of the Resurrection had therefore the form appropriate for a tomb: it was a round building surmounted by a dome, which, as Eusebius tells us, was covered with lead and had the same height as the basilica. A Roman architect would have built the dome in masonry or cement;

[1] See p. 126.

but this was likely of wood, built according to a technique which is said to have originated with the Persians and was used by the Mohammedans. The great mosque of Omar on the side of Solomon's Temple has such a dome, and the bulging domes of the Russian churches could be built only in this way. It is certain that in Syria timber domes were common after the fifth century. Therefore Justinian's use of this feature was not violent innovation, and the domed churches of the Renaissance had a precedent in early Christian tradition. An early miniature representing the Holy Sepulchre (pl. 42b) strongly suggests a wooden dome; and yet we cannot be sure of it, for it appears that pillars were used for its support, and this suggests a heavier structure. But there was a gallery, and the pillars may have been used to support that. In another place I have remarked upon the twelve detached columns disposed in a circle around the tomb. They supported nothing, but stood free in front of the pillars to represent the twelve apostles. The tomb itself was by the architect hewed profanely to the dimensions which suited his plan, though this involved the sacrifice of its vestibule. The whole rock, when it was reduced to a symmetrical form, was surrounded by a gilded grille and crowned (as the miniature shows) with a conical roof. Within this sanctuary, resplendent with the light of many lamps, the bishop entered alone, to lead the people in prayer and to bless them. Here, because it was a tomb, he burned incense, many centuries before this was done in ordinary churches at the celebration of the Eucharist. We can see that in the pictures which represent the women at the empty tomb there was some effort (not very successful) to depict this sacred monument.

An open court "paved with gleaming stones" surrounded the Martyrium and the Anastasis. But these buildings did not stand there alone. In Syria a single church was sometimes surrounded like a Greek temple with a peribolos (pl. 37d); but there are many more examples of a court which contained a complex of sacred buildings, one of them the Fountain Court at Gerasa (pl. 42c), and we may suppose that they reflect the custom established by the first and most eminent church in Jerusalem. The Martyrium and the Anastasis were contiguous, but to go from one to the other the worshippers, it seems, had to pass through the court. It was from the court one approached the stairway which led down to the chamber under the basilica where the True Cross was conserved but not exhibited. One building opening upon the court is plausibly identified as the baptistery, and that too was probably built by Constantine. But the most interesting feature in the court was Calvary. This rock having been discovered unexpectedly, had to be left of course in the eccentric position where it was found, but it was cut down sharply on all sides to make it fit the restricted space, surrounded by a metal grille and surmounted by a high cross richly adorned, which likely was the prototype of the jewelled crosses which were often depicted in apsidal mosaics. The mosaic in S. Pudenziana was meant to be a true picture of Calvary and its cross (pl. 57). Strangely enough, Eusebius makes no mention of this important monument, though certainly he must have seen it. Perhaps his silence implies an historian's scepticism. Etheria describes the daily services performed beneath Calvary as well as the special ceremonies on Good Friday. Some were held "before" and some "behind" the cross. The bishop's throne was set up before the cross for the more numerous services. In the mosaic of S. Pudenziana, where Christ is enthroned in front of Calvary, we may see a reflection of this custom. But on Good Friday it was behind Calvary an altar was set up for the display of the remnants of the True Cross—which the devout were permitted to touch with the forehead and the eyes, but not with the hands or with the lips . . . lest they might slyly filch a fragment of it, as some pious persons had done with their teeth. The Three Hours' Devotion as it was performed there might well be a model to us, for it consisted of nothing else but the reading of appropriate passages from the Scriptures. At another service held beside the cross on Good Friday the bishop preached, and every presbyter in turn was expected to do the same.

At the instigation of his pious mother Constantine erected the church called Eleona, the local name for the Mount of Olives on which it stood. It was a small basilica with an atrium (pl. 41a), built over the cave which legend associated with Christ's last discourse to His disciples (Mk. 13:3-37). At a later time a church was built on the site of the Ascension.

On his own initiative Constantine built a church near the oak of Mamre where Abraham talked with God (Gen. 18), his indignation being aroused when he heard that this sacred spot was profaned by idolatrous sacrifices, since in a way it was sacred also to people of various religions.

It seems to have been again at Helena's solicitation that Constantine furnished the means for building a sumptuous church at Bethlehem, over the cave in which Christ was born. To us the word cave does not suggest a stable; but in Palestine it was common enough, as it still is in Italy, to use a natural or an artificial cave for the shelter of cattle. The Protevangelion of James calls the stable in which Christ was born a cave; Justin Martyr, who was a Syrian, understood it to be a cave; and Origen, who early in the third century was a long time in Palestine, told Celsus that there still exists at Bethlehem the cave in which Christ was born and the manger in which He was swaddled. Epiphanius takes it for granted that the Gospel indicates a cave, and Jerome states that until Constantine's time Thamus-Adonis was worshipped in this cave. This interpretation, which determined the character of the earliest pictures of the Nativity, cannot easily be rejected. At all events, this tradition was sanctioned when Constantine built a basilica over the cave at Bethlehem.

Eusebius, though he exalts the importance of the Church of the Nativity, does not describe it, and in their attempt to reconstruct the Constantinian basilica archæologists have until lately been left in the lurch. The problem is complicated by the fact that this church was rebuilt by Justinian—as was asserted in the tenth century by Eutychius, the Patriarch of Alexandria. Because the archæologists would not believe his report, all their efforts were foredoomed to failure. Not being an archæologist, I can tell without blushing the story of their failure. Heisenberg enumerates complacently a dozen futile attempts to reconstruct the original church before he solved the problem ... in a way equally false. The most eminent archæologists, Strzygowski in the van, but also Diehl and Wiegand, persisted in believing that the present building (pl. 41c) dates from Constantine. Père Vincent judged rightly that the end of the basilica above the cave is more recent, but he concluded wrongly that the building was completed with an ordinary apse. In 1908 William Harvey, a young English engineer, was asked by the British government to examine the whole structure, and he reported that it was Constantinian throughout. This is rather ironical because it was the same Harvey who in 1934, when Britain as the mandatory power in Palestine had authority to make excavations, discovered under the floor of Justinian's church mosaic pavements of the time of Constantine and the complete outline of the original church (pl. 41b), and thus brought a long controversy to a close.

It is now known that the Constantinian basilica at Bethlehem was completed, not by an ordinary apse, and not by the trefoil apse of Justinian, but by an octagon having the whole width of the nave and the first two aisles. As no supports were provided for a masonry dome, it was certainly roofed with timber like the rest of the basilica.

I quote Crowfoot's description. At the east end "in the middle of the nave a flight of steps led up to an octagonal chapel or *memoria* which is the most striking of all the recent discoveries. On a smaller scale—it is only about half as wide—the octagon at Bethlehem corresponds with the Anastasis at Jerusalem. In both places the architect had to design a building which would enable pilgrims to see all that was to be seen of a holy relic. At Jerusalem the shrine was a tomb which the architect surrounded with an open grille. At Bethlehem the shrine was a subterranean cave, and the architect made a large breach in the roof so that pilgrims could look down a shaft or well into the grotto below. The mouth of the shaft was circular, about 12 feet across, and it was surrounded by a stone kerb.... Round the stone circle there were two steps on an octagonal plan, and the floor between the lower step and the outer sides of the octagon was paved with another splendid series of mosaics." I remark, as Crowfoot does, that there seems to be no place for an altar.

We can be sure that Helena and her son provided lavishly for the adornment of the shrine at Bethlehem. It was likely she who replaced the clay manger with one of silver, which provoked Jerome to say in a sermon preached at Bethlehem on Christmas Day, "Oh, if I might see the crib in which the Lord lay! Now, as though to do honor to Christ, we have done away with the clay and replaced it with silver."

## THE CHURCHES OF JUSTINIAN

Not wishing to dwell upon questions of architectural technique and having no ambition to make this work complete by describing local peculiarities, whether of Africa, Egypt or the East, I conclude with a brief account of the development of the central style of architecture by the architects of Justinian.

But I make one exception in order to call the attention of the reader to the interesting development of the basilica in northern Syria, where an abundance of good building stone and an admirable tradition of the art of masonry accounts for the fact that there the churches were carefully finished on the outside and even adorned with architectural ornament. The lack of marble columns or of the material for making them encouraged the use of pillars which supported broad archivolts, and the paucity of wood discouraged the use of ceilings (pl. 43a, b, c, 44c, 48b). The roofs of course were built of timber, and so too were the domes, which formerly were thought to be of masonry. It was a timber roof which covered the column of St. Simeon Stylites towards which four buildings of the basilical type converged, forming a great cross. This in a sense was a central type, but the arrangement was evidently prompted by the desire to honor this sacred column, and it has nothing to do with the central churches we are about to consider. The cruciform mausoleum of Galla Placidia at Ravenna is a centralized building in the strictest sense, but it was not a church. We have seen that a centralized plan, whether round or cruciform or square, was traditional for tombs. For this use it was appropriate, as it was also for baptisteries. But it is not obvious how a centralized building could be used for Christian worship, since liturgical considerations prescribed that the altar might not be placed in the center of such a building towards which the architectural lines pointed as the place of chief importance. For this reason the oblong plan of the basilica held its own in the West for more than a thousand years, indeed was never wholly abandoned, even when columns gave place to pillars and timber roofs to vaults, when the Romanesque gave place to the Gothic, or even when the domes of Brunelleschi and Michelangelo were erected over the Cathedral at Florence and the Church of St. Peter at Rome.

On plate 40 it will be seen that among the eleven plans of centralized buildings only four were built to serve as churches. The first is a Moslem mosque; the second, S. Stefano Rotundo, was originally a meat market and never was successfully adapted for Christian worship; the fourth is a mausoleum; three of them are baptisteries; the third was appropriately built to mark the site of the Ascension. It will be remarked how eccentric was the emphasis upon the apse and presbytery in the four churches which were designed expressly for Christian worship. Yet the churches built by Justinian in the East and at Ravenna established a precedent which has been followed generally in Greece and in Slavic lands, so that now the timber dome is the most striking feature of Orthodox churches. In spite of my predilection for the antique basilica, I cannot deny that these buildings, from an architectural point of view, are far superior, and that the emphasis placed upon an elongated apse made them suitable for worship. They not only raised new problems but solved them triumphantly in a variety of ways. Until the Gothic style reached its full development there were no other churches so interesting to the architect. As an example of perfect equilibrium which is visible from within as well as from without they are superior to Gothic churches.

But what was it that prompted so radical a change in church architecture? I am inclined to think that the basilica, with its long colonnades and comparatively low ceiling which emphasized exclusively the longitudinal axis, failed to satisfy a longing for "heaven-uphoistedness"—to use the word by which an old guide in the Adirondacks expressed the feeling he experienced on the summit of Mt. Marcy. Eventually this want was met completely by the lofty Gothic vaults, at an immense expense for a structure incomparably more costly than the early basilica, at the expense, moreover, of the acoustic value of a flat roof, and at the expense of a feeling precious to the early Christians, the feeling that by the walls and roof they were not only protected from the outside world but were pressed close together in a charismatic fellowship. But this was a want no longer felt. The other want, that for a greater stress upon the perpendicular axis, had already been supplied in part by the high walls of the Lombard churches. It was supplied more fully by the ogival dome over the Cathedral in Florence, and by many other domed churches which did not sacrifice the basilical plan. The dome, a symbol of the dome of heaven, is in itself as appropriately used over an assembly of living Christians as it is over their tombs, it is as appropriate to mature Christians as to the neophytes who enter the baptistery. If any mystical significance was attached to the half-dome of the apse which surmounted the presbytery, or to the small dome of the ciborium which covered the altar, the same sense must have attached to the great dome which covered the people of God assembled for worship. The round and octagonal shrines at Jerusalem and Bethlehem, being known throughout Christendom, had sooner or later an influence throughout the world. The chapel Charlemagne built at Aix was surely a reminiscence of the Anastasis, then known as the Church of the Holy Sepulchre, which the Templars frankly copied in their Temple at London. The use of galleries in the East made this sort of church more adequate for Christian worship, and the deep sanctuary contrived by the architects of Justinian made it perfectly suitable for the celebration of the Eucharist. The basilica (Martyrium) at Jerusalem did not in length much exceed its width, and in conjunction with the "hemisphere," the "head of all," it was a close approach to the centralized plan. The church at Bethlehem, being almost square (apart from the octagon), approached it more closely. It was still more closely assimilated to the central type when it was rebuilt by Justinian (pl. 41a). The form, or rather the many forms which the architects of Justinian developed afford an almost perfect solution of the problems which they faced. Auguste Choisy characterizes very well the advantages of the so-called Byzantine architecture. "It is not merely," he says, "the feeling of unity one experiences in viewing a Byzantine interior, but also a sort of tranquillity and calm which is simply the satisfaction of the spirit before a work where all the combinations which account for the equilibrium are clearly apparent. Our Gothic buildings arouse a sort of inquietude and uneasiness, owing to the fact that the buttressing elements are relegated to the exterior. At first sight one does not take account of the equilibrium. Quite different is the effect of the Byzantine structures. Here the buttresses are within the building, the eye embraces in one glance the dome which covers the edifice and the elements which support it. One sees nothing which does not explain itself. This is the clarity of Greek art." This applies to all the types produced by the architects of Justinian, to the thoroughly centralized plan of the Church of Saints Sergius and Bacchus at Constantinople and S. Vitale at Ravenna, but equally to the churches which in one way or another preserved the oblong form of the basilica, as did St. Sophia. It applies of course to the scheme which ultimately became universal in the Eastern Church: a square plan with a large central dome and four smaller domes which support it. The Justinianian Church of the Apostles at Constantinople, which served as a model for S. Marco in Venice and for one of the great churches in Provence, emphasized the longitudinal axis by using three domes to cover the nave, which were supported on either side by heavy vaults and smaller domes, and at the ends by the narthex and the half-dome of the apse. St. Sophia, though it was never imitated, is the supreme example of this art. The whole nave is covered by the one great dome supported by two half-domes of the same diameter. This, because of the variety it introduces, is far more elegant than the elliptical roof of the Mormon Tabernacle at Salt Lake City; but it has not the same acoustic quality, nor is it so stable. For though today, owing to the immense buttresses added on the exterior, it is still standing, in ancient times it twice collapsed. Choisy says of St. Sophia: "Throughout the whole length of this nave the details are framed in three large divisions; the main lines produce a simple impression; the details, multiplied within measure, make the size evident. Suppress the lateral colonnades and there is nothing to emphasize the extraordinary breadth of the cupola. They are needed to furnish a scale and to spare St. Sophia the strange praise bestowed upon St. Peter's, that there is nothing to indicate how big it is."

In comparison with the basilica this type of church offered a far greater field for pictorial decoration. In this respect we may compare two churches which are completely decorated with mosaics: the Cathedral of Monreale and S. Marco in Venice. Since the side walls of the basilica were low and insufficiently illuminated, the space available for pictorial decoration was limited to the apsidal wall (sometimes augmented by a triumphal arch) and the clerestory. The west wall was not often decorated because the people did not face it. On the other hand, buildings of the central type made available to the artists, not only the interior walls as a whole, but the vaults and domes which roofed the church and the massive pillars which supported them. Moreover, the narthex or vestibule which was common in the East furnished an opportunity for depicting upon its walls and vaults and cupolas the introduction to the Gospel, the story of Creation.

Columns were still used as well as pillars, but they were subsidiary, they no longer supported the walls and the roof. They were highly important, however, as a decoration. Polished shafts of marble comported perfectly with lustrous mosaics and with the marble incrustations which covered the lower walls. The classical capitals, on the other hand, were felt to be inappropriate because they could not be polished. Hence even in the basilicas they were gradually transformed by using an ornament in low relief which could be polished or gilded. The use of the drill was found effective for the production of light and shadow without making the raw stone visible. Such capitals were evidently not appropriate in Gothic architecture, and therefore they were no longer used when the stone texture of the walls was nakedly apparent. The form of the "Byzantine" capitals had to be changed essentially to meet the requirement of supporting, not an architrave, but an arch. It had to be strengthened at the corners, and eventually a stone cushion was introduced with the intent of concentrating the weight which it supported (pl. 46, 47).

The illumination of the domed churches was even more adequate than that of the basilica. In both cases it was from above, and in order that it might not be too glaring it was customary to fill the windows with grilles of wood or stone or with slabs of alabaster (pl. 51c). It was essential that the light should come from above, for only when it was reflected to the eye of the beholder at an angle of 45 degrees did one see the glint of the glass tesseræ, especially the gold glass. Pictured glass was not used in the windows. This may seem to us an impoverishment of the early churches. It is true that the scarcity of the material made it impossible to develop the art of stained glass. But so long as the churches were decorated with mosaics this art was not wanted. The introduction of colored lights would mar the effect of the mosaics. You cannot have your cake and eat it too: if you want mosaics, or even frescoes, you must forego the glamor of stained glass windows. In the Gothic church, where the walls have no longer any structural importance, they are appropriately replaced by stained glass windows. Where there are no walls mosaics are out of the question. In Italy, where men clung to the custom of decorating the churches with frescoes, even the Gothic churches, especially those built by the Franciscans, did not sacrifice for windows all the walls but reserved them for frescoes, and because of this attachment to fresco painting the art of stained glass was not highly developed. In the twelfth century the Cosmatesque artists lavished upon the floor rather than upon the windows a brilliant polychrome decoration (50a).

# VI

# MONUMENTAL ART

IN CHAPTER IV, dealing with sarcophagi art, much was said about the picture of Christ seated in the midst of His apostles and giving them the Great Commission. This theme belongs properly here, for it is certain that it first emerged in the monumental art of the basilicas as a subject, perhaps the favorite subject, for apsidal decoration. I had to anticipate the consideration of this important subject because the sarcophagi furnish the most numerous examples of it. Its great popularity was due, I suppose, to Constantine, to whose peculiar interest in the twelve apostles I have called attention. It is likely that he used this theme in the apse of the church which he dedicated to the apostles (now S. Sebastiano). We may be sure that the Apostles Peter and Paul appeared in the apse, for it was over their temporary tomb that the church was erected. It probably was used in the Church of St. Peter, for we have seen that twelve columns were erected in front of the presbytery in memory of these "pillars." But the earliest apsidal mosaic of this sort which remains to our day is that in S. Aquilino at Milan, which was built about the year 350—not long after Constantine's death, but late enough for the introduction of the Alpha and Omega as accompaniments of the monogram which is inscribed in the halo behind the head of Christ (pl. 69b).

I remark here, by the way, since I have not had occasion to say it before, that in earlier times the halo was used only to distinguish Christ. In the sixth century, when it came to be used for angels and saints, the halo of Christ was differentiated by an inscribed cross (pl. 56a, 64a, 73b).

## APSE OF S. PUDENZIANA

The theme with which we are now dealing is most perfectly presented by the mosaic in the apse of S. Pudenziana (pl. 57), a church built about the year 384, in the pontificate of Siricius, upon a site, it is believed, where Christians had worshipped since the days when Pudens, a Roman senator, associated by tradition with both Peter and Paul, had opened his house to accommodate the Church. This was certainly one of the most ancient "titles" in Rome. The name *pudentiana* was originally understood as an adjective, indicating that

# MONUMENTAL ART

a. Bust of Christ. Archiepiscopal Palace, Ravenna. *ca.* 500.—b. Bust of Christ in the mosaic of S. Pudenziana, Rome. P. 182.

Pl. 56

Apsidal mosaic. S. Pudenziana, Rome. 412–417.

Pl. 57

Pudens was the founder, but it has led naturally enough to the popular notion that Pudentiana, a daughter of the senator, was the patron of the church. In the mosaic Christ holds an open book on the pages of which we read: *Dominus conservator ecclesiæ pudentianæ* (pl. 57).

I have remarked already that when this subject was depicted in the apse one could not but reflect that directly below were seated the bishop and his presbyters exactly in the position in which Christ and His apostles were represented. This was the heavenly analogy which led St. Ignatius to liken the bishop to Christ and the presbyters to the apostles. It is not likely that any of the mosaics which have disappeared presented this theme so adequately. Yet as we see it now it has suffered not only from the ravages of time but from a barbarous restoration perpetrated in the sixteenth century by a cardinal who took his title from this church and wanted to bring it up to date, the date of the baroque. He wanted a shallow apse, and to this end he sacrificed a part of the mosaic, cutting off an apostle at each end and parts of the living creatures which symbolize the Gospels. At a later date a new baldachino obscured the *Agnus Dei* beneath the throne. The modern character of some of the faces is due to a restoration made in 1831. For all that, it is a noble picture. The figure of Christ (pl. 56b) is unspoiled, except for half of the face.

Here we have one of the earliest pictures of the four living creatures (Ez. 10:14; Rev. 4:7) which were often represented in or above the apse or upon the façade. They mean to us the four Gospels, or the Evangelists Matthew, Mark, Luke and John, though in the first instance it was not definitely decided to which of the Evangelists they referred. They mean indeed much more, for the common use of these figures implies that even in the fourth century apocalyptic eschatology was not totally discarded. And this was not the only apocalyptic subject used in the mosaics. It was commonly accompanied by the four-and-twenty elders casting their crowns at the feet of the Lamb which had been slain before the foundation of the world.

In this picture the four angelic figures, floating in the sky, surround the triumphal cross erected upon Mount Calvary in the midst of the New Jerusalem in which Christ is enthroned (cf. pl. 69a, 60b, 94a). Christ is clad in a pallium which shimmers with gold. His gesture is that of the teacher, but of a teacher to whom all power is given in heaven and on earth. No earthly teacher is seated upon a throne and clad in cloth of gold. This is not Jesus in His humiliation as He taught beside the Lake of Galilee: it is the risen and glorified Christ who gives to His apostles the Great Commission. There is in His gesture an ambiguity which is at once terrifying and comforting; for evidently this Teacher is also the Judge. The apostles acclaim Him as Lord.

In the background stand two women ready to crown with a garland the heads of Peter and Paul, who are seated respectively on the left and on the right of Christ. It has been supposed that these figures represent the daughters of Pudens—an absurd notion, for however saintly Santa Pudenziana and Santa Prassede may have been, it was not for such as they to crown the Apostles. If they had been represented at all in this picture (where Pudens does not appear), it must have been as suppliants. The only possible explanation of these figures is that which is forced upon us by the dedicatory mosaic on the west wall of the Church of S. Sabina (pl. 68), where two female figures are distinguished by the inscription as *Ecclesia ex circumcisione* and *Ecclesia ex gentibus* (the Church from the Circumcision and the Church from among the Gentiles). Only lately has it been observed that these two figures are distinguished plainly enough by their dress: the woman who represents the Church of the Gentiles is dressed as a Roman matron, having under her veil the white ruche which was commonly worn in the fifth century. The books they hold are distinguished by the lettering as Hebrew and Greek, the Old Testament and the New. It had not been forgotten that *Una Sancta* was composed of two Churches which once had been in strife with one another, and that Peter and Paul represented divergent tendencies. Pictures of the sacred cities Jerusalem and Bethlehem were often introduced in the apsidal mosaics (pl. 65a, 64a, 63a) to indicate this division. Bethlehem, because of the visit of the Magi, the Epiphany to the Gentiles, was always on the side of St. Paul, and that was at the right hand of Christ, the place of honor. For the Romans, much as they were inclined to exalt St. Peter, could not ignore the fact that predominantly they were the Church from among the Gentiles.

From an archæological point of view this picture is especially interesting because the artist has represented more or less realistically the churches which Constantine built to adorn the city of Aelia Capitolina. "This," said Eusebius in his *Life of Constantine*, "is perhaps the New Jerusalem which was foretold by the prophet." This is an impious "perhaps." It expresses his distaste for apocalyptic eschatology. Zahn affirms that because of it he omitted the Revelation of St. John from the costly codices Constantine charged him to prepare for many of the greater churches, and thereby nearly succeeded in excluding it permanently from the Canon. But it was natural that the artists who essayed to depict Christ enthroned in the New Jerusalem should take as a model the Holy City as it then was, and amalgamate with it the church at Bethlehem. We see on the ends of a sarcophagus shown on plate 27c that these churches were used as a background for historical scenes connected with the story of

Jesus. This anachronism was innocent enough, for it depicted Palestine as the pilgrims saw it.

We have seen that the principal street of Jerusalem was flanked by colonnades (pl. 47). The steps and the propylæum leading to the Anastasis interrupted this colonnade in the middle, and there Christ's throne is placed, directly in front of Golgotha and the jewelled cross which surmounted it. In the background are the churches of Jerusalem and Bethlehem. In this case, for no reason we can descry, Jerusalem corresponds to the position of St. Paul. For the round building just above his head can only be the Anastasis (Church of the Resurrection), and the rectangular building contiguous to it, but almost hidden by Calvary, must be the Martyrium. Above St. Peter is the octagonal end of the Church of the Nativity at Bethlehem with its square basilica.

## PETER AND PAUL

There are many mosaics in which Peter and Paul, "the princes of the apostles," appear alone on either side of Christ. Only five of them are illustrated here (pl. 33, 69a, 64a, 63a). On the sarcophagi such cases are innumerable (pl. 20b, 28, 29c). The chief Apostles sufficed to represent the whole order, and in Rome especially they would be exalted because it was the boast of that Church that they could point to their "trophies" or tombs as those of their founders and martyrs. The limited space on a sarcophagus often exacted the economy of representing all the apostles by these two. Although in the apse there was room for a larger composition, the room was often wanted for other purposes, especially for the patrons of the church or its donor (pl. 64a, 63a). To introduce these persons to Christ the two Apostles sufficed.

Something must be said here in general about Peter and Paul in Christian art—even if this interrupts the consecutive study of apsidal mosaics. In my little book on *SS. Peter and Paul in Rome* I said pretty much all I then knew about this subject. But lately I received from Professor Rosenstock-Hussey further enlightenment about the shrewd exploitation of the Apostle Paul during the Middle Ages, first by an emperor, then by a pope—information which I cull from his book *Out of Revolution*, pp. 503-561, 765-768. In view of this new light I must rehearse briefly what I said six years ago.

We are accustomed to put Peter first, saying "Peter and Paul," because actually Peter had the priority in point of time, and because the Church of Rome now insists upon this order. But this order was not always observed in

Rome. In the so-called *triclia*, a hall used for semireligious festivities near the tomb where the bodies of both Apostles once lay, the numerous graffiti scratched upon the wall in the first years of the fourth century acclaim indifferently Peter and Paul or Paul and Peter. This clearly reflects the fact that till then these two Apostles enjoyed equal honor in Rome. Rome took equal pride in the two apostolic martyrs whose tombs they venerated. They were compared to the Dioscuri (Castor and Pollux, "the heavenly twins") whom the pagans had regarded as the special guardians of Rome. Even in the sixteenth century Peter and Paul have this role in Raphael's picture of the battle at the Milvian Bridge, and when the bronze statue of Peter was placed upon the column of Trajan, Paul was given as honorable a place upon the column of Marcus Aurelius. But in the eighth century, when the Church of Rome founded its claim to preëminence upon the authority bestowed upon Peter, Paul suffered an eclipse in the West, and was all the more exalted in the East as the Universal Apostle, the Apostle to the Gentiles, "the teacher of the world," as the inscription by Honorius upon the triumphal arch in his church proclaims: *doctoris mundi sacratam corpore Pauli*. We have seen that in early times there was a disposition to accord the first place to St. Paul. On the sarcophagi and in the apsidal mosaics (with the single exception of the arch in S. Lorenzo, pl. 64a) Paul has the place of honor, on the right of Christ. Some pious archæologists allege that in ancient times the left was the place of honor; but that is a vain attempt to escape the implications of early Christian art, for this allegation is simply not true. In recognition of the fact that the right is really the place of honor, the ecclesiastical authority in Rome has in recent times reversed the traditional position of the two Apostles. Under the triumphal arch of St. Paul's Church, where the Apostle to the Gentiles is on the right and the Apostle to the Circumcision on the left, the statues of Peter and Paul which lately were erected below reverse their positions, and to humiliate St. Paul more clearly the episcopal throne in his own basilica was by Leo XIII adorned with the scene in which Christ says to St. Peter, "Feed my sheep." More recently Pius XI, because of his enthusiasm for missions, did what he could to reinstate St. Paul, the great missionary. But since the Reformation the Roman Church has felt obliged to play down St. Paul because Luther, with some exaggeration, played him up.

A similar situation occurred in the Middle Ages when St. Paul was chosen with great political sagacity as the principal support of the imperial theocracy in its crusade against the "pornocracy" of the papacy. Perhaps it was Otto III (983–1002) who first bestowed upon St. Paul the sword as his distinguishing symbol. Judging from similar instances in art we are inclined to associate the sword with his martyrdom, or perhaps to think of it as "the sword of the Spirit" (Ephes. 6:17); yet nothing would serve the purpose of the emperor but to equip St. Paul with the sword of civil authority, in reference to his dictum that the ruler "does not bear the sword in vain" (Rom. 13:4). It was then, and in reply to this challenge, that St. Peter, for the first time in art, was equipped with the keys. It may be seen (pl. 69a) that in the fourth-century mosaic, in St. Paul's Church, St. Peter carries the keys, but this is a little improvement made by the restorer in the nineteenth century. It is true that in several early pictures Peter receives the keys, receives them in behalf of the Church, but does not carry them as the symbol of his unique authority. The authority expressly bestowed upon him was held, as St. Cyprian claimed, by all the apostles *in solidum*.

The popes at first submitted supinely to the highhanded appropriation by the emperors of the Apostle to the Gentiles, the Teacher of the world. But Hildebrand, the monk of Cluny who became Pope Gregory VII (1073-1085), had the sagacity to reclaim St. Paul as the support of the papal theocracy over *urbs et orbis*, the city of Rome and the whole world. The religious policy of the papacy had associated St. Peter so exclusively with the *urbs* that he could not be used as an œcumenical authority. But St. Paul could, and to this end he was equipped with *two* swords, to make it abundantly plain that he possessed the civil as well as the spiritual sword, though the former might be wielded, for the advantage of the Church, by the "secular arm." Hildebrand had listened to his friend Peter Damianus, who (in *De picturis principium apostolorum*, c. 2) said of St. Paul, who belonged to no particular city and had no special cathedra, that "he plainly exercises the power of the right hand of God," that "he is God's right arm extended over the whole earth." Thus in the interest of his high political policy Hildebrand restored Paul to a perfect parity with Peter. Dr. Rosenstock publishes three bronze tesseræ which at that time were stamped for the pilgrims who visited Rome. They represent Peter and Paul seated side by side. On two of them each Apostle holds a key—a recognition that the key to the kingdom of heaven, the authority to bind and to loose, to retain and to remit sins (Mt. 16:19; 18:17, 18; Jn. 20:23) was held by the Apostles as a corporate authority—and on the third, where Peter alone has the key, Paul has the sword.

The Vatican has a bronze medallion of the third century (pl. 65) which depicts the characteristic traits of the two Apostles more plausibly than any other ancient monument—even Dürer did not characterize them more plausibly—and yet we cannot reasonably indulge in the assumption that after two centuries their portraits had been preserved or their traits accurately remembered.

## THE ACANTHUS

Here where we are engaged in the study of pictorial art in the churches we cannot ignore the fact that some of the mosaics preserved to us from the earliest period are simply decorative. Paulinus of Nola, who himself was so zealous in adorning with mosaics the churches which he built, affirms that in the fifth century, even in Italy, pictures involving human figures were "rare." Doubtless he was thinking of churches in provincial towns. But even in Rome there was a predilection for purely ornamental designs in mosaic. The acanthus, though it has no symbolical significance, was preferred to the vine, and, contrary to its nature, but with striking decorative effect, it was indefinitely elongated in vinelike convolutions, which because of their thickness filled the space more adequately than the thin stems of the grape and were more pleasing to the eye.

The mosaic in the eastern apse of the vestibule of the Lateran Baptistery is filled with the convolutions of a bright green acanthus which against a dark blue background produces a very rich effect. In spite of the small field it occupies, the impression is prodigious. In the way of pure decoration it could hardly be surpassed. Of the mosaic which adorned the west apse of the vestibule not a trace is left, yet Wilpert, guided by a sketch made in the sixteenth century, and by later mosaics which were likely inspired by it, is bold enough to describe it. He thinks that convolutions of the acanthus like those at the other end enclosed in a mandorla (as in S. Clemente, pl. 58a) a cross "occupied" by doves, as is the monogram in the fifth-century mosaic in the baptistery at Albegna near Naples (pl. 58b). The apsidal mosaic in S. Clemente, though in its present form it is very late, may reasonably be cited here, for substantially this may be regarded as a work of the fourth century which was altered only by the introduction of Mary and John on either side of the cross. This theme of Mary and the beloved disciple at the foot of the cross, though it was suggested by the Fourth Gospel, was not used by early artists. Perhaps the first instance of its use is in an eighth-century fresco in S. Maria Antiqua (pl. 75b). Wilpert might well have referred to the apsidal mosaic in S. Maria Maggiore, where, except for the coronation of the Virgin Mary in the center, there is nothing to indicate that the rich convolutions of the acanthus are not ancient. Wilpert supposes, moreover, that in the mosaic he essays to reconstruct the hand of God (*dextera Domini*) appeared at the top of the dome, as in S. Clemente; that the four rivers of life gushed from beneath the cross; and that four pastoral scenes at the bottom were framed by the stems of acanthus. It is essentially in these terms Paulinus describes the apsidal mosaic of the church which he built at Nola in honor of St. Felix. But he mentions besides this a medallion of Christ, who holds a book in His hand and is acclaimed by Peter and Paul. This, we may suppose, was at the top; in the middle of the picture he had to find room for a jewelled cross occupied by doves, and at the bottom he depicted the cities of Jerusalem and Bethlehem with the sheep which issued from them. He mentions also palms which indicate that the new or heavenly Jerusalem is depicted.

Another early instance is the apsidal recess in the mausoleum of Galla Placidia where deer drink of the waters which spring from the base of the acanthus.

The richly decorated vestibule of the Lateran Baptistery must have been used, as Wilpert says, for the instruction (and exorcism) of candidates for baptism—not, as some think, for the *consignatio* or anointing with oil, which, being the conclusion of every bath, was the last act in the rite of baptism, after which the neophytes went directly into the church to receive their first communion. The English Reformers, obsessed by the notion that confirmation was entirely separate from baptism and consisted essentially in the laying on of hands, stigmatized the early practice of the Church as "a corrupt following of the apostles."

## APSIDAL CROSS

It will be remembered that St. Nilus rejected as "childish" the proposal of Olympiodorus to decorate a church with hunting scenes and innumerable crosses, counselling him instead to put *one* cross in the apse and to decorate the nave with scenes from the Old and New Testaments. Yet it is not likely that Olympiodorus was following a whim of his own which had no traditional support. We know that hunting scenes were depicted in the Cathedral at Aquileia, and we may suppose that they were not uncommon. In the mausoleum of S. Costanza the mosaics of the ring vault depicted the occupations of the four seasons (pl. 62), and the river at the bottom of the great mosaic in the cupola was enlivened with fishing scenes (pl. 61c). Although the Constantinian mosaic in the vestibule of the Lateran Basilica could not on so small a field display "innumerable" crosses, there are as many as could well be introduced. There are twelve "Latin" crosses in the lower border, and six jewelled crosses hang from the summit of the apse. Nevertheless, what Nilus suggested might in his time have been seen in the decoration of many of the Roman churches. We have already observed that immediately after the Peace a single cross was prominent in the apse. As a result of the vision which led to his conversion Constantine had naturally a great interest in the cross, and the incidental discovery at Jerusalem of the True Cross, which led to the erection of the richly jewelled cross on the rock identified as Calvary, fixed the attention of the people upon this central symbol of Christianity, which henceforth was regarded not simply as a sign of suffering and humiliation but of resurrection and triumph. There can be no doubt that this symbol figured conspicuously in the great hall of the Sessorian Palace which Helena transformed into the Church of the Holy Cross. Paulinus tells us that the cross was the central feature in the apse of his church at Nola. And we shall see soon that in the principal churches of Rome the nave was decorated, as Nilus desired, with stories from the Old and New Testaments.

## APSE OF THE LATERAN BASILICA

Rome, though it furnishes no example of a church completely decorated with mosaics, such as we have in churches of the fifth and sixth centuries at Ravenna, the Church of St. Mark in Venice, the Cathedral at Monreale and the Cappella Palatina in Palermo, affords, nevertheless, the best opportunity for the study of the history of mosaic art, furnishing as it does examples dating from almost every century during the long period in which it has flourished. It is a curious fact that the only church in Rome in which the mosaic decoration is nearly complete is the American Church dedicated to St. Paul in which I ministered for many years. The noble mosaics by Burne-Jones which decorate the apsidal end, and those made by George Breck for the west wall and the façade, leave nothing more to be wished for but the scenes from the Gospels which must some day cover the clerestory of the nave. Since the early mosaics in Rome are fragmentary, we have to put the scattered elements together and make the most of every suggestion they afford, if we would reconstruct imaginatively the glory of any one of the ancient churches.

Such being the case, I welcome without cavilling the argument by which Wilpert substantiates his opinion that the Constantinian mosaic in S. Giovanni

a. Section of the apsidal mosaic. S. Clemente, Rome. *ca.* 1125, but early Christian except for John and Mary, and Christ on the Cross.—b. Mosaic in the Baptistery of Albegna. After 350.

Pl. 58

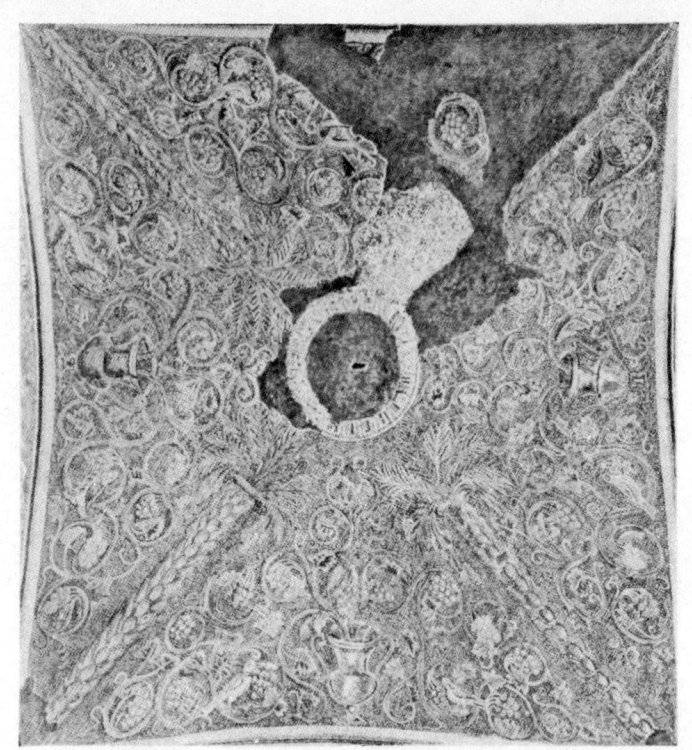

**a.** Mosaic in the vault of S. Matrona in S. Prisco, near Naples. First half of fifth century.
—**b.** Mosaic paving in the apse of a church at Ancona. Early fifth century.

Pl. 59

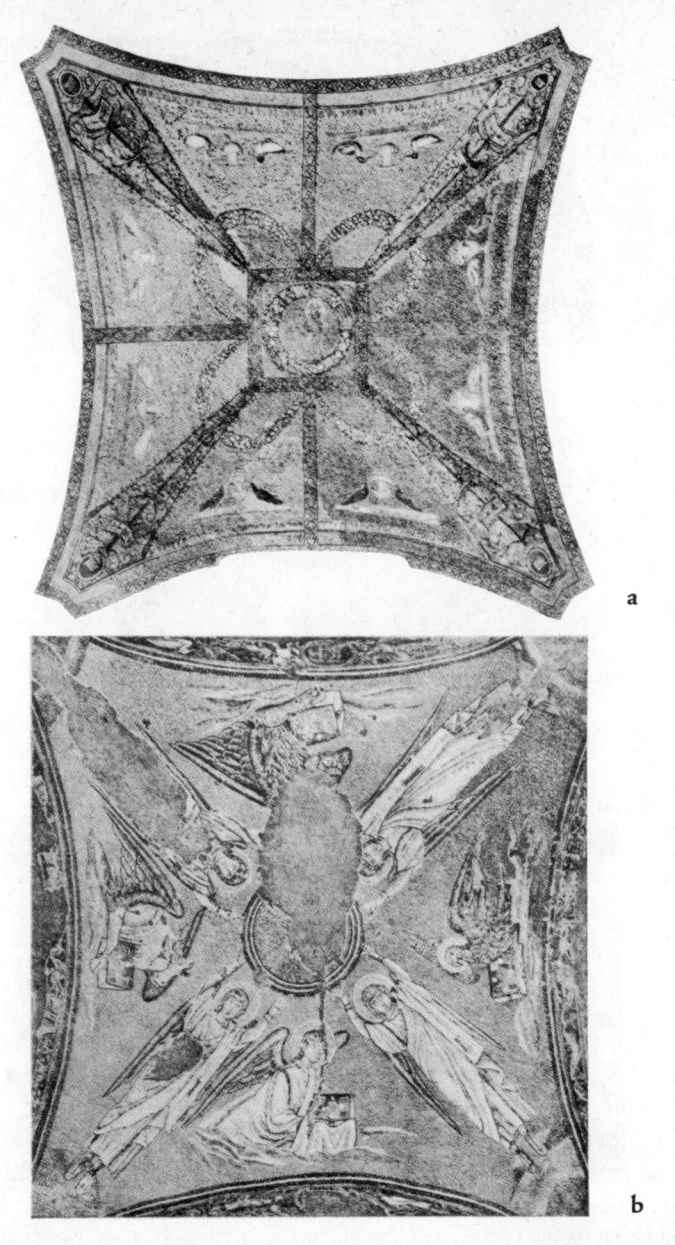

**a.** Mosaic in the vault of the Chapel of St. John the Evangelist, in the Lateran, founded by Pope Hilarius (461–468).—**b.** Archiepiscopal Palace, Ravenna, *ca.* 500. The monogram in the center is supported by four angels.

Pl. 60

**a.** The Good Shepherd. Mausoleum of Galla Placidia, Ravenna. Fifth century.—**b.** Wilpert's reconstruction of the fourth-century mosaic in the Lateran.—**c.** Sketch by Ugonio, in the Escorial, of mosaic in the dome of S. Costanza, Rome. (See p. 141.)

Pl. 61

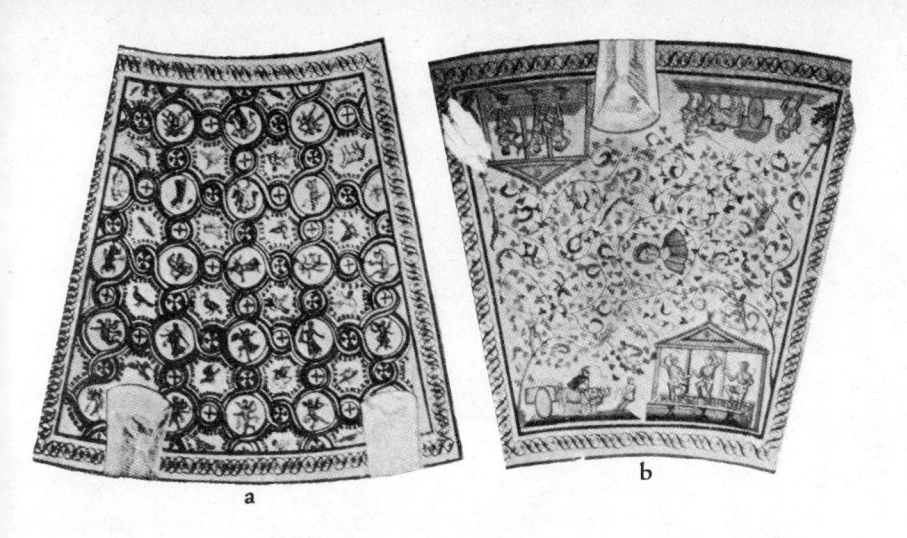

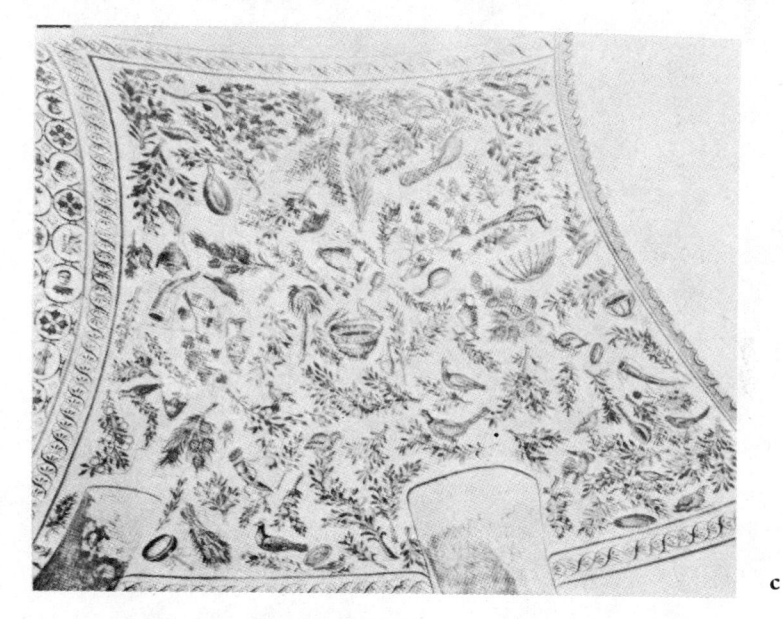

Three mosaics in the ring vault of the Mausoleum of S. Costanza, Rome.

Pl. 62

**a.** Apsidal mosaic of SS. Cosma and Damiano, Rome. Peter and Paul introduce these two Oriental saints with St. Theodore and Pope Felix, the donor.—**b.** Mosaic in the sanctuary of S. Apollinare in Classe. The sacrifices of Abel, Abraham, and Melchizedek are presented at the Christian altar. Seventh century.

a. Christ seated as Pantocrater upon the globe of the world flanked by SS. Peter and Paul, St. Hippolytus, St. Stephen, and Pope Pelagius, who presents a model of the church. S. Lorenzo, Rome. b. Abraham receives the "men" and sacrifices Isaac.—c. A representation of the Christian altar at which Abel and Melchizedek offer their sacrifices. S. Vitale, Ravenna.

Pl. 64

**a.** Mosaic on the arch of S. Maria Maggiore, Rome, built by Sixtus III, 432-440. In the middle of the (round) arch is the inscription XYSTUS EPISCOPUS PLEBI DEI below the throne supporting the Cross and flanked by the Apostles Peter and Paul and the four angelic beasts. **b.** Bronze medallion of Peter and Paul. Vatican Library, Rome. Third century.

Pl. 65

Five of the fourth-century mosaics in S. Maria Maggiore (see pp. 148-150.)—**a.** Joshua commands the sun and moon to stand still.—**b.** The walls of Jericho fall.—**c.** Melchizedek presents bread and wine to Abraham.

Pl. 66

a. Abraham receives the "three men," bids Sarah bake bread, and serves them with a "dressed calf."—b. The revolt of Korah and his company; Moses, Joshua, and Caleb protected by the glory of the Lord in front of the Tabernacle.

Pl. 67

S. Sabina, Rome. **a.** Female figures representing "the Church from the Circumcision" and "the Church from among the Gentiles." (See pp. 49, 128.)—**b.** Dedicatory inscription with female figures at ends. Fifth century.—**c.** *Opus sectile* in *pietra dura* decorating the wall. (See p. 143.)

Pl. 68

**a.** Mosaic on the triumphal arch (poorly restored). St. Paul's Church, Rome. Fourth century.—**b.** Center of the apsidal mosaic. S. Aquilino, Milan. *ca.* 350.

Pl. 69

**a.** Mosaic in the late and perfected Byzantine style, recently revealed over the royal door leading from the narthex into the Church of St. Sophia, Constantinople.—**b.** Mosaics in the Cappella Palatina, Palermo. Abraham entertains the angels; sacrifice of Isaac. *ca.* 1140. (See p. 2.)

Pl. 70

S. Maria Antiqua, Rome. Frescoes: **a.** Madonna and Child. Sixth century.—**b.** Crucifixion. Later than the seventh century.

Pl. 71

in Laterano was not essentially altered by the restoration made in the thirteenth century by Nicholas IV. The picture on plate 61b represents Wilpert's notion of the original mosaic. It excludes only the figures drawn on a smaller scale, which were certainly added by Nicholas. For one is his own portrait, the others, SS. Francis and Anthony, who appear behind Mary and the Baptist, are there to exalt the Franciscan order, which first attained the papal throne in the person of Nicholas. The Franciscan artist Turriti depicted himself and his helper, Jacopo Camerino, at the feet of the apostles who occupy the space between the windows. There is reason to think that Nicholas was conservative in his restoration, for the bust of Christ was left unchanged. In order to insure finer workmanship the mosaics of this image were laid not directly upon the wall but upon a slab of travertine, and this, perhaps because it was thought to be a miraculous picture, was carefully restored to its place. This instance gives some support to Wilpert's opinion that the square nimbus used for persons still living originated in the custom of painting a portrait head on a square of canvas and applying it to the fresco on the wall. As for the river with playing putti at the bottom of this mosaic, there can be no doubt that the restorers left it as it was or copied it carefully. It is thoroughly Constantinian in character. The hand of God at the top of the picture was suppressed by the restorer, but nothing could be more in keeping with the earliest Christian art than the cross upon Mount Calvary, and the deer which drink the water of life from Gihon, Phison, Tigris and Euphrates, which flow into a river identified by its river god as Jordanes. Here, as in S. Costanza (pl. 56c), the boats, the fish, the water fowl and the delightful putti reproduce a favorite theme of Hellenistic art, and only by name is the river transformed from the Nile to the Jordan. It is a theme which could not have occurred to an artist of the thirteenth century. The names which now identify the figures near the cross as "Mater Dei" and John (meaning the Baptist), those to the left of the beholder as Paul and Peter, and those on the right as John the Evangelist and Andrew, were perhaps added by the restorer; but the inscription upon the scroll which Paul carries must have been original, for it reads: SALVATOREM EXPECTAMUS DVM IC (We wait for a Saviour, the Lord Jesus Christ. 1 Thess. 4:15-18), and it was to the Saviour this church was originally dedicated. That the river here is named Jordan is more important than one might think, for the whole picture is an invitation to baptism, eloquently addressed to the unbaptized who, as we have seen, occupied the middle aisle. For this reason John the Baptist is put in a prominent place—so prominent that he ultimately was regarded as the patron of this church. In the sixth century Sergius III spoke of the Baptist as *genius loci*, which implies, I suppose, that the original dedication of this church to the Saviour had not yet been forgotten.

## ARCH OF S. MARIA MAGGIORE

Although usually the wall above the apse was, like the apse itself, devoted to heavenly or apocalyptic themes, the decoration of the apsidal arch in S. Maria Maggiore is of a very different character: it tells the story of Jesus's infancy. This is due to the fact that Sixtus III (432–440) desired to celebrate in this way the Council of Ephesus (431), which affirmed that the humanity and the divinity of Christ were united in His person, and hence by implication sanctioned the custom, already dear to many, of addressing Mary as Mother of God.

This church, as we have seen, was originally known simply as Basilica Liberiana, after the pope who presumably built it, but was soon associated with the manger at Bethlehem. It was therefore an appropriate place to celebrate the miraculous birth of Jesus, and this celebration naturally glorified the Virgin Mother. Probably at this time (the middle of the fifth century) the church was definitely associated with the name of Mary. It is not only the greatest (maggiore) but the earliest of the many churches in Rome which are called by her name. At the end of the thirteenth century the same Nicholas IV who transformed the mosaic in the apse of the Lateran Basilica, and by the aid of the same artist, Jacobo Turriti, altered the acanthus pattern in the apse of S. Maria Maggiore so far as was necessary in order to introduce in the center of it a picture representing the coronation of the Madonna. Christ and His Mother are seated side by side upon a throne, where He places the crown upon her head.

Of course, the fifth-century mosaic on the arch in front of the apse did not go so far in glorifying the Mother. The artist had so many stories to tell of the infancy of Jesus that they had to be presented on a scale too small to be clearly envisaged from the floor of the church, or in the illustration which is given here (pl. 65), and therefore a description is needed to identify the subject of each particular scene in the five zones. It begins at the top and goes from left to right, though this order is not always chronological.

(1) The Annunciation: Mary, guarded by four angels, is seated upon a throne near her dwelling when the Archangel Gabriel descends from heaven to announce his message. Joseph, issuing from his house has his doubts re-

moved by another angel (Lk. 1:26-37). (2) The Presentation in the Temple: Mary holding the Child, followed by two angels and by Joseph with a third angel, is met by Anna the prophetess and by Simeon who advances impetuously to receive the Child (Lk. 2:22-39). Before the door of the Temple the priests are waiting, and the "pair of turtledoves" are ready for the sacrifice which must be offered. It may be that the angel on the extreme right is warning Joseph to flee from Herod (Mt. 2:13-15), for just below is the reception of the Holy Family in Egypt. (3) The Visit of the Magi: Christ, already a boy (of more than two years, one would think), is seated on a throne, the star above Him, four angels behind, Mary and Anna seated on either side of Him, when *two* Magi come from Jerusalem to offer their gifts. (4) The Arrival in Egypt is represented in terms of an apocryphal gospel which tells of the reception of the Holy Family by Aphrodisius, the ruler of the city. Two angels accompany the Child, who is now beginning to walk. (5) Slaughter of the Innocents, the first martyrs, who are commemorated after Christmas along with St. Stephen: soldiers bring to Herod the unhappy mothers of Israel who carry their children of "two years old and under" (Mt. 2:16-18). The early Christian artists were reluctant to depict heart-rending scenes of suffering, and therefore in this picture the infants are not visibly put to death (cf. pl. 113a). (6) The Magi appear before Herod in Jerusalem (Mt. 2:1-12). Evidently the artist had not been able to find a place for this subject where it belonged in chronological order.

It will be noticed that the angels are very much in evidence in these pictures. This is one of the earliest instances in which they have wings. The Bible assumes no such thing in the case of ordinary angels. Indeed it is implied that they need a ladder to ascend to heaven and descend. In a mosaic in S. Apollinare Nuovo (pl. 73), which is almost one century later than this we are now considering, the angels have wings but still carry the staff which they needed as God's messengers when they had no wings.

The two lowest zones are occupied by Jerusalem and Bethlehem and the blessed sheep which issue from them. In the foregoing description one subject has been omitted because it is not included in our illustration. Indeed it is partly obscured by the Borgia arms. And yet its importance is indicated by the fact that it is the keystone of the arch. It represents the empty throne to which we have already devoted some attention.[1] In this instance the throne is flanked by Peter and Paul, and by the four living creatures, as though Christ were visibly seated upon it. On it, instead of the cross, we see the crown and the royal mantle, and "a book closed with seven seals" (Rev. 5:1). This last item

---
[1] See p. 86.

is so clearly apocalyptic that it gave offense to a sober-minded pope: Gelasius (492–496) condemned the use of it, and it did not appear again in the monumental art of Rome.

It is profitable to compare these scenes from the infancy of Jesus with the treatment of the same subjects on the cathedra of Maximinus (pl. 83–85), on the columns of S. Marco (pl. 97), on the altar frontal, seven hundred years later, in Salerno (pl. 112, 114), and in the manuscript illustrations which are presented here (pl. 133a).

## CHURCHES IN RAVENNA

I have no intention of going deeply into so big a subject. In any case, the baptisteries must be considered separately, in the next section, and the mosaics in the nave of S. Apollinare Nuovo are treated as a series by themselves. Here I remark only upon a few decorations made for the sanctuary which are illustrated in this book.

Ravenna was not a Roman city, either in its architecture or in its pictorial art, in its sarcophagi or in its mosaics, during any of the stages of its history—when Honorius (c. 402) moved his court thither from Rome, when it was the capital of the Gothic kingdom of Theodoric (493–526), and finally when the victory of Belisarius (540) made this city the Western Exarchate of the Eastern Empire and it was greatly enriched by Justinian and his Empress Theodora. The last stage was strongly marked by the influence of Eastern art, especially in the Church of S. Vitale, which was built by Justinian in the style he had perfected in Constantinople. Soon after that, when the tie with the East was broken, Ravenna languished, and because it had from that time forth no history, its historical monuments were preserved as they could not have been in a living town.

The mausoleum of Galla Placidia, the sister of Honorius, is the most perfect gem of mosaic art which has been preserved from the fifth century, for it is completely intact (pl. 44a, b, 61a). One can see from the few illustrations furnished here that in this first stage the decoration followed essentially the traditions of Roman art. The Gothic king, too, had obviously no other source of inspiration, and even the art introduced by Justinian was not un-Roman. We can say at the most that it was non-Roman; for the difference between Rome and Ravenna was hardly greater than between Rome and Milan, which also had relations with the East and was always proudly attached

# S. APOLLINARE NUOVO, RAVENNA

Built and adorned by Theodoric, 493–526 (see pp. 170-174)

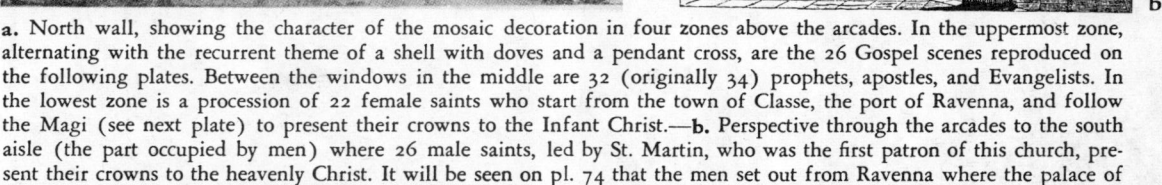

a. North wall, showing the character of the mosaic decoration in four zones above the arcades. In the uppermost zone, alternating with the recurrent theme of a shell with doves and a pendant cross, are the 26 Gospel scenes reproduced on the following plates. Between the windows in the middle are 32 (originally 34) prophets, apostles, and Evangelists. In the lowest zone is a procession of 22 female saints who start from the town of Classe, the port of Ravenna, and follow the Magi (see next plate) to present their crowns to the Infant Christ.—b. Perspective through the arcades to the south aisle (the part occupied by men) where 26 male saints, led by St. Martin, who was the first patron of this church, present their crowns to the heavenly Christ. It will be seen on pl. 74 that the men set out from Ravenna where the palace of Theodoric is chiefly in evidence. After Ravenna was restored to the Orthodox, the curtains were added to hide the Arian courtiers who watched the procession from the arcade, but here and there a hand in front of a column betrays their presence. Both processions move toward the altar.

Pl. 72

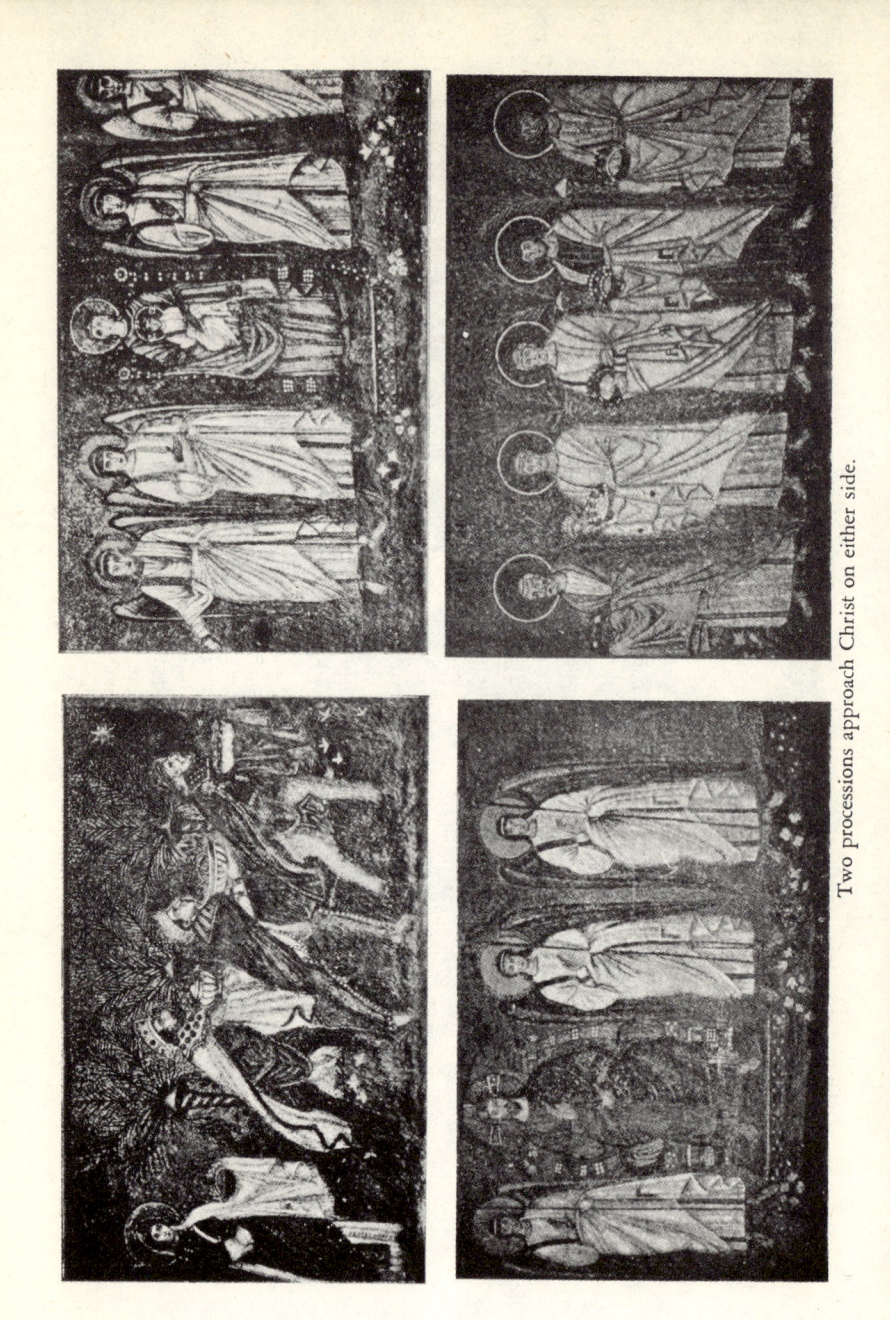

Two processions approach Christ on either side.

Pl. 73

**a.** The south wall with the palace of Theodoric.—**b.** The paralytic of Bethesda.—**c.** The demoniac of Gerasa.

Pl. 74

**a.** The paralytic of Capernaum.—**b.** Christ separating the sheep from the goats.—**c.** The widow's mite.—**d.** The Pharisee and the publican.—**e.** Raising of Lazarus.—**f.** The Samaritan woman.

Pl. 75

**a.** The Gentile woman beseeching Jesus to heal her lunatic daughter.—**b.** Jesus heals two blind men.—**c.** Jesus calls Peter and Andrew.—**d.** Jesus blesses the loaves and fishes.—**e.** Miracle of Cana (an inept restorer has represented the jars as baskets).—**f.** The Last Supper.

Pl. 76

**a.** Christ's discourse on the Mount of Olives.—**b.** The kiss of Judas.—**c.** Jesus led away to judgment.—**d.** Jesus before the High Priest.—**e.** Peter's denial foretold.—**f.** Peter's denial.

**a.** Judas brings back the thirty pieces of silver.—**b.** Pilate washes his hands.—**c.** Christ led to Calvary.—**d.** The women at the tomb.—**e.** Christ on the way to Emmaus.—**f.** Christ appears to all the apostles.

Pl. 78

to the differences which distinguished it. The art of Ravenna cannot without absurdity be called Byzantine.

In S. Vitale mosaic pictures of the Old Testament sacrifices which prefigure the Eucharist were appropriately placed in the presbytery (pl. 64b, c). Nothing of the sort is to be found in Rome; but presumably this is due to the fact that the basilicas provided no space for such pictures in the presbytery. The style is not un-Roman. A century later these pictures were repeated in S. Apollinare in Classe (pl. 63b), and there the figure of Bishop Ursicinus resembles perfectly the episcopal figures in Roman mosaics of the seventh century (pl. 145a). We shall see later that the Gospel scenes in S. Apollinare Nuovo (pl. 72-78) are exactly such as we might expect to find in Rome, if any such pictures had been preserved. In S. Vitale the figures of the Evangelists have what are called "Byzantine" traits. But what does this mean? Far more "Byzantine" is the gorgeous procession (pl. 146, 147) headed by Justinian and Theodora who carry into the church their votive offerings of gold, a chalice and a paten. But this is Byzantine only in the sense that the imperial couple and their courtiers are dressed according to the etiquette Diocletian had prescribed.

## BAPTISTERIES

Hitherto we have been engaged exclusively with the decoration of the apsidal end of the church, where the Eucharistic sacrifice was celebrated. We have found a great variety of themes, some of which (Majestas, the Great Commission, and the Throne) were described in connection with the sarcophagi. It is astonishing how many might be combined in one picture, and it is obvious that these many themes were fundamentally coherent.

Before considering the decoration of the nave, which because it was the people's part of the church required a very different treatment, we will deal here with the building designed for the performance of the other great sacrament, Baptism.

Because we are accustomed to see a little baptismal font in every parish church, we may wonder why a separate building was ever required for baptism, and why it was attached only to the bishop's church, the cathedral. In the first place, it is because baptism was literally a bath. This operation required space which the basilica did not afford, and all the more space because it was customary to baptize many persons at one time, preferably on the Eve of Easter. In the next place, in answer to the second query, we must remember that ordinarily it was the bishop who presided at this ceremony. The Church was obliged to recognize in theory the validity of lay baptism, and even of baptism by aspersion; but in order that this sacrament might be administered with the greatest solemnity the bishop retained the privilege of presiding over it, long after he had been obliged to relinquish to the presbyters the right to celebrate the Eucharist independently. The bishop presided. This does not mean that with his own hands he immersed the neophyte and signed his forehead with oil. He delegated the performance of these acts to presbyters or deacons. It was in this sense the bishop was said to baptize, and in the same sense to confirm. In the Eastern Churches it is still the presbyters who actually administer the sacraments of Baptism and Confirmation.

So long as baptism was a bath, the house in which it was administered naturally was assimilated to the round or octagonal bath houses which were in public and private use throughout the Empire. This had the advantage that it permitted the use of the dome, which symbolized the vault of heaven, and we shall see that the artists made the most of it. If the dome was felt to be appropriate to the tomb because it encouraged the hope of life after death, it was no less appropriate to the sacrament of regeneration.

It may be remarked that the earliest baptisteries were lighted very inadequately by the windows under the dome. This is explained by the fact that baptism was usually administered at night, on the Eve of Easter, so that for illumination the baptisteries depended upon lamps. The neophytes (newly enlightened) on leaving the well-lighted baptistery were introduced into the more splendidly lighted church where the Eucharist was celebrated and where they were to make their first communion.

## S. COSTANZA

We have to speak here of S. Costanza in Rome because, though it was not a baptistery, it had the shape of one, and the hints we have of the decoration of the dome help us to reconstruct the mosaic which has vanished from the Lateran Baptistery which Constantine built and adorned. It is in a very roundabout way we are able to form any idea of the decoration of the first monumental baptistery in Christendom.

S. Costanza was built by Constantine as the mausoleum for his family. Although neither he nor his mother Helena was buried there, his daughter Constantina was, and perhaps his sister Constantia, from whom it gets its name. Although the mosaics of the ring vault are well preserved (pl. 62), and the subjects in two little apses can be made out in spite of a barbarous restoration, not a trace of the mosaic of the dome remains—and that is what we need to throw light upon the character of the decoration which once adorned the dome in the Lateran Baptistery, of which also no vestige remains. In the case of S. Costanza, there were fortunately sketches made in the sixteenth century of the remnants of the mosaic which then were still visible, especially a sketch by Ugonio (pl. 61c) which is preserved in the Escorial. Because the design was symmetrical, even a few fragments of the picture enable us to form a pretty clear idea of this superb creation. Another sketch shows that there was a second row of Biblical scenes framed by the acanthus stems which spring from the caryatids flanked by tigers, rising from the river Jordan. The plan of this picture, as we shall see subsequently, corresponds closely to the description we have of the mosaic which once adorned the dome of the baptistery at Naples, built not long after the Lateran Baptistery and presumably copied from it.

Restoring the scheme as a whole, we find that there was room for twelve Biblical scenes in the lower zone, and for as many more in the smaller fields above. Ugonio identified rightly several of the lower pictures: Tobias with his fish, the vindication of Susanna, and the sacrifices of Cain and Abel. The picture next to Tobias, as I understand it, represents Susanna persecuted by the elders. Inasmuch as all of these subjects are from the Old Testament, it may be assumed that the twelve subjects in the upper zone were taken from the New Testament. Although no trace of them is left, Wilpert ventures to enumerate them, being guided only by analogy. I repeat his list: the Annunciation, the Adoration of the Magi, the Samaritan woman at Jacob's well, the Multiplication of the loaves, the Miracle of Cana, the Healing of a blind man, of a paralytic, of the woman with an issue of blood, the Raising of Lazarus, the Separation of the sheep and the goats—and two more which he was not bold enough to identify. It is evident that all of these subjects, actual or conjectural, would be as appropriate in a baptistery as in a tomb. In addition, the earliest baptisteries would likely contain, as do all the baptisteries we know, a picture of the baptism of Jesus.

## THE LATERAN BAPTISTERY

We may be sure that Constantine must have lavishly adorned the baptistery which he built at the beginning of his reign to accompany the great basilica of five aisles which he dedicated to the Saviour and presented to Pope Sylvester as his cathedral. This presumption is substantiated by the account in the *Liber Pontificalis* of the costly gifts of gold and silver which the emperor bestowed upon this baptistery. The immense octagonal font was of porphyry ornamented with silver. Seven silver deer poured water into the font. On the side opposite the original entrance, which was from the vestibule, one beheld a golden lamb, on either side of which were silver statues of Christ and of John the Baptist, who evidently pointed to Christ or to the lamb, for in his left hand he held a scroll on which was inscribed: *Ecce Agnus Dei, ecce qui tulit peccatum mundi.* Eight porphyry columns, collected by Constantine but subsequently discarded because they were of unequal lengths, were ultimately placed around the font by Sergius III. They gave no support to the edifice but carried an architrave with an inscription, and perhaps they served to support curtains. Pope Hilarius hung above the font a golden dove. In another place I give an account of the gold and silver ornaments bestowed upon the Lateran Basilica. The high walls of the baptistery were not meant for mosaics but for a rich incrustation of colored marbles, which was accounted more noble because it was more costly. Mosaics were used only for the ring vault and the dome—and they, alas, have disappeared without leaving a trace. We have not even a design or a description of them. Of course, the gold and silver have disappeared; for it is notorious that though moths and rust do not corrupt them, thieves will break in and steal. No works of art are so perishable. All the treasures of silver and gold which were lavished upon the churches of Rome by Constantine were carried off by Alaric.

It is not so commonly understood that marbles were likely to be stolen. They too had an intrinsic worth, though they are not what we call precious stones. They were brought from far, chiefly Greece and its islands, or from Proconnesus, that being easier than to transport them overland to Rome from the mountains of Carrara which now supply the whole of Italy. Porphyry and serpentine were brought from Egypt, although there are mountains of them in the southern Alps—as the alpinist will not forget who with his nailed boot steps incautiously upon a boulder . . . and falls as suddenly as if he had stepped on ice. These hard stones were the more precious because they could be shaped and polished only with diamond dust.

It is significant that contemporary descriptions of the Constantinian churches, while they exult over the silver and gold, and lay stress upon the beauty of the marbles, have nothing to say about the mosaics. Constantine himself, writing to the Bishop of Jerusalem, gave him a free hand to order the most costly marbles for columns, wall covering and floors, but said not a word about mosaics. No argument can be drawn from this silence. The fact is that mosaic pictures were not a costly decoration. The tesseræ could be made cheaply from a glass paste, and able artisans, even if they were not slaves, could be had for a low wage. Therefore, though many mosaics have perished with the dilapidation of the walls to which they were attached, none have been destroyed in order that they might be carried off. On the other hand, the early churches have been robbed of their marble incrustations so completely that only two examples are left: one in the Cathedral at Parenzo (barely discernible in pl. 50b), and another on the clerestory walls of S. Sabina (pl. 68c). Yet we know well, chiefly from the remains of patrician houses buried under the imperial palaces on the Palatine, how beautiful this work was, and what incredible labor it cost to piece together perfectly in intricate patterns (*opus sectile*) a stone veneer which includes, as does the example in S. Sabina, *pietra dura*, whether it be porphyry or serpentine. In Italy this precious material has been used over and over again. What we know as Florentine mosaic derives its materials from the marbles which once decorated the palaces and villas of Rome. When I was a student at Rome in 1899 and tramped often in the Campagna with Professor Lanciani, or with Thomas Ashby, who was a fellow student, I realized vividly what a great store of exotic marbles had been accumulated before the barbarian invasions. For a beginning was made that winter to restore to cultivation fields which since the sixth century had been given over to pasturage, and as we followed the plough we found almost anywhere fragments of the colored marble which once had incrusted the walls of the suburban villas such as once were scattered everywhere within ten miles or more of Rome. The few pieces I carried away in my pocket served to make a chess board which I have now on my desk. The Roman *opus sectile* was infinitely more precious than the slabs of marble veneer which we use today and which were used to such good effect on the palaces of Venice and upon S. Marco. To accomplish that effect one has only to saw two sheets of marble and place them side by side. If there is any diversification of color, a symmetrical pattern will be produced as surely as when a drop of ink is folded in a sheet of paper. Such marble incrustations as were once the glory of the Lateran Baptistery could not in our day be reproduced even on a small scale. Along with the silver and the gold they have disappeared completely. The mosaics also have disappeared, and we can only conjecture what they were.

## S. GIOVANNI IN FONTE AT NAPLES

Wilpert has acquired a plausible basis for such a conjecture by vindicating the great antiquity of the baptistery at Naples. For if the baptistery in this provincial city was built not long after the middle of the fourth century, it is safe to assume that it must have been influenced profoundly by the eminent precedent established by Constantine a few years earlier in Rome, the Baptistery of the Lateran. At all events, the ancient mosaics which are preserved in the baptistery at Naples are of themselves of great interest for the history of early Christian art.

The mosaics on the walls are fairly well preserved. Two of them are illustrated here. Four niches contain pictures of the living creatures, symbols of the Evangelists. But of far greater interest are the pictures on the flat wall above the niches which depict the Good Shepherd in paradise tending His flock, which includes not only sheep but deer. In two cases He carries a sheep on His shoulders—it is not only lambs that need His tender care—and the sheep which flank Him on either side are feeding in green pastures. In the other two cases the Shepherd leans upon His staff while He addresses the deer which come to drink of the river of the water of life. Between these scenes, on the four other walls of the octagon, there was room for eight apostles. The most admirable of these figures is shown on plate 34a.

Unfortunately, the mosaics in the dome have been preserved only in fragments. We can make out that a vine pattern, concentrating at the apex about the monogram flanked by Alpha and Omega, frames eight large trapezoids (disposed in two zones), in each of which there was room for one or more Biblical scenes. In five of these fields it is possible to identify seven New Testament subjects: (1) the Samaritan woman at the well, and the Transformation of water into wine; (2) the Multiplication of the loaves and fishes; (3) Christ giving the Law to Peter; (4) Christ sustaining Peter on the water, and the miraculous draft of fishes; (5) the Two Women at the sepulchre. Wilpert conjectures that the other fields contained: (6) the Healing of a blind man, and of the paralytic at the pool of Siloam; (7) the Baptism of Christ; (8) the Annunciation. He bases his conjecture upon the subjects which can be dimly discerned in the decoration of S. Matrona near Naples, which was built only fifty years later, and where also there are eight fields which presumably were filled with New Testament subjects, although only two can be securely identified: the head of Christ in a medallion, and the throne with its customary insignia.

This suggests that the throne of Christ was thought appropriate especially to baptisteries. In fact, the throne has a prominent place in the Baptistery of the Orthodox at Ravenna (S. Giovanni in Fonte), where it is repeated four times, alternating with the books of the Gospel supported upon the Holy Table and flanked by two chairs (pl. 32b, c). There too, as in the Baptistery of the Arians, the baptism of Christ occupies the center of the dome. In the Lateran Baptistery, where the baptism of Christ was represented by statues of silver, this subject was perhaps not repeated in mosaic, but there may well have been a representation of the throne. We have reason to suppose that the pictures in this first monumental baptistery, the gift of an emperor, were more complete and more carefully planned. What we can conjecture about them may be thought to justify Wilpert's view that they were designed as a commentary upon the so-called Apostles' Creed, the "Symbol" which each candidate for baptism was expected to recite from a pulpit (*renditio symboli*). The baptismal creed used in Rome from the beginning of the second century was as follows: "I believe in God the Father Almighty, and in Jesus Christ, who was born of the Holy Ghost by the Virgin Mary, who was crucified under Pontius Pilate and was buried, rose the third day, ascended into heaven, sitteth on the right hand of the Father, from whence He will come to judge the living and the dead, and in the Holy Ghost, a Holy Church, the forgiveness of sins, and the resurrection of the flesh." Although in this early creed there are already twelve articles of faith, the fiction which attributed each of them to one of the apostles had not yet been suggested.

## ST. JOHN LATERAN

The Lateran Basilica, the most venerable church in Christendom, has suffered from such radical changes that one might well despair of finding any hint of the character of the pictorial decoration bestowed upon it by the munificence of Constantine. The building has lost even the characteristic aspect of a basilica. When it threatened to collapse, the ancient columns were incorporated two by two in heavy pillars of masonry, before each of which there now stands the statue of an apostle—statues no better than those by Thorwaldsen in the Cathedral of Copenhagen. Yet we have seen that the apsidal mosaic has not totally lost its original form (pl. 61b). We happen to know that the mosaics between the clerestory windows of the nave represented twelve prophets alternating with the twelve apostles, and a curious chance enables us to infer what subjects once adorned the lower walls of the nave where now there are baroque reliefs in stucco. Constantine's artists depicted here twelve scenes from the Old and the New Testaments, which were destroyed by an earthquake in 896. At the Seventh Œcumenical Council (787) the legate of Pope Hadrian I, speaking in defense of the use of pictures in the churches, happened to mention that the first two pictures in the Lateran (presumably on opposite sides of the nave) represented Adam and Eve expelled from paradise, and the dying thief admitted to it. We have here an example of the conservatism which the Church of Rome has commonly blended with its innovations. For the first two of the baroque reliefs made in the seventeenth century correspond to this description. They replaced an earlier set of stucco reliefs which were made soon after the destruction of the mosaics, and evidently they repeated the same subjects. We may infer therefore that the Constantinian mosaics were one of the earliest examples of the *concordantia Veteris et Novi Testamenti* (Parallelism between the Old and New Testaments) which was a favorite subject in early Christian art. In this instance we have: (1) Adam and Eve / the Penitent Thief; (2) the Flood / the Baptism of Christ; (3) the Sacrifice of Abraham / Christ bearing the cross; (4) Joseph sold by his brethren / Christ betrayed by Judas; (5) the Passage of the Red Sea / Christ's ascent from Hades; (6) Jonah spewed out by the sea monster / Christ ascending to heaven.

The gifts of silver and gold with which, according to the *Liber Pontificalis*, Constantine enriched the Lateran Basilica may be taken as a measure of his munificence in decorating it with marbles and mosaics. The ciborium was an object of special admiration. Nothing of the sort had been seen before. The cupola was of pure gold, and it was covered with a gabled roof of silver. From it were suspended twenty silver dolphins (probably lamps), and it was further adorned, in some way, with seven silver altars, not to speak of other curious embellishments. All of this was, of course, carried off by Alaric. At the request of Sixtus III, Valentinian replaced it with a new ciborium of silver, of which we have no description. "Gold plates weighing 500 pounds" given by Constantine were probably used instead of marble to cover the lower walls of the apse. In front of the Constantinian ciborium (*in fronte* meaning perhaps in front of the gabled roof) was a silver statue of the Saviour seated in a chair, with a height of 5 feet (therefore life size) and a weight of 120 pounds. On either side (doubtless extending around the ciborium) were the twelve apostles in silver, of the same height, and weighing 90 pounds each. Behind (*a tergo respiciens in apside*) another figure of the Saviour, of the same height, weighing 140 pounds. Here He was flanked by four angels of the same height, each weighing 105 pounds, and each carrying the staff which was appropriate to messengers of God before angels were provided with wings. The fact that here Christ was twice represented by silver statues explains why the same theme was not repeated in the apsidal mosaic.

## MOSAICS IN ST. PETER'S

We know only in a general way the character of the mosaics with which Constantine, and probably his son Constantius, adorned the apsidal end of the church erected over the body of St. Peter, which was demolished in 1606 to make way for the colossal substitute which boasts the unique distinction that it contains not one original example of pictorial art. We know only from descriptions the mosaics of the old church, yet we can picture the apsidal mosaic pretty clearly because it is perfectly in line with others we have already considered. In the center of it Christ was depicted between Peter and Paul. Two palms and a meadow denote that the scene is in paradise. Two stags drink from the four rivers of life which proceed from the throne. In a lower zone a gemmed cross was supported upon a throne, and at the bottom twelve sheep coming from Jerusalem and Bethlehem approached the *Agnus Dei*. The apsidal arch, as was appropriate in this church, depicted many scenes from the life of Peter. The triumphal arch probably contained a medallion of Christ, with Peter on the left acclaiming Him, and with Constantine advancing on the right to present a model of the church. The symbols of the four Evangelists seem also to have been depicted here.

The façade of the basilica, facing east upon the atrium, was not till a century later decorated by Leo I (440-461) with the symbols of the Evangelists on either side of a medallion of Christ. According to Grisar this medallion (presumably when it was in a ruinous condition) was replaced by Sergius I (687-701) with the *Agnus Dei* which is to be seen in a sketch made in the eleventh century by a monk of Farfa. The *Liber Pontificalis* ascribes to Sergius the introduction of the *Agnus* in the Liturgy, and Grisar conjectures that both cases may be regarded as a reply to a decree of the Council of Trullo (692) by which the Eastern Churches in the spirit of iconoclasm forbade the use in art of the lamb as a symbol of Christ, a tradition especially dear, as we have seen, to the Church of Rome.

The clerestory of the nave was decorated with figures of the prophets, and the wall below it had Biblical scenes in two zones. According to the account of Grimaldi, which was accompanied by a rude sketch made not long before the demolition of the basilica, there were at least forty-four Old Testament scenes on the north wall (at the right as one entered the church), and presumably there were as many scenes from the New Testament on the opposite wall, but there is no evidence that they represented a *concordantia*. Probably they were the gift of Liberius, to whom were due the mosaics in the nave of S. Maria Maggiore which tell the story of Moses and Joshua, whereas in St. Peter's the series began with Noah. The south wall was evidently in a position so precarious that it could not have been preserved much longer; for it leaned so far to the south that the dust which had accumulated upon it hindered Grimaldi from identifying more than five subjects: (1) the Baptism of Christ; (2) the Raising of Lazarus; (3) the Crucifixion, on a large field occupying two zones; (4) the Descent into hell; (5) Christ's appearance to the Eleven—but the sketch shows another appearance of the risen Lord. By the time of Liberius (352-366) the illustrated octateuchs must have furnished the mosaic artists abundant suggestions for Old Testament scenes, and many New Testament subjects had already been dealt with in the catacombs, on the sarcophagi, and doubtless in the churches.

## NAVE OF S. MARIA MAGGIORE

The mosaics in the nave of S. Maria Maggiore (pl. 66, 67), which depict scenes from the books of Exodus and Joshua and are commonly ascribed to Liberius, are not notable for their decorative effect, but they are important because they are the earliest mosaic pictures we know which seek simply to illustrate episodes in Biblical history, and because they may be thought to reflect the character of the earliest manuscript illustrations. That these mosaics were copied from books may be inferred from consideration that they are not strictly decorative, and that the details are too small to make a telling effect upon one who sees them from the floor of the church. Mosaics when they are properly designed make the best effect from a distance.

In S. Maria Maggiore there were originally forty-two panels, most of them having pictures in two zones, but today there remain only thirty-seven, since Sixtus V destroyed five of them to magnify the approach to the two sepulchral chapels of his family which form a kind of transept. I comment here only upon the five which are illustrated in this book, and give merely a list of the others. The octateuchs, as will appear later, contain all these pictures and many more, and thirty-five subjects from the Old Testament are depicted on the altar frontal at Salerno.

Plate 66a. Joshua calls upon the sun and the moon to stand still till the battle is finished. The poetical character of this account was not recognized by the early Church, although in Hebrew the Mazoretic text is vocalized as poetry, and even in English there is rhythm in the lines:

*Sun, stand thou still on Gibeon,*
*And thou, Moon, in the Valley of Aijalon!*

In one picture, the walls of Jericho fall down; the Hebrew soldiers compass the city round about and Rahab appears on the ramparts, but the Ark and the trumpeters are shown in the lower zone (Josh. 6:1-200).

In another, Melchizedek offers to Abraham bread and wine (Gen. 14:18-20). The great amphora standing on the ground suggests the chalice commonly used on Christian altars (pl. 64c, 63b). In this instance Melchizedek is on foot and Abraham on horseback, where as in the Vienna Genesis both are on foot (pl. 120a).

In a third, Abraham receives the three "men" (Gen. 18:1-16). The central figure of the three is distinguished by a shining mandorla; the others have haloes. Abraham bows profoundly. Augustine, alluding to the Holy Trinity, says aptly, "He saw three, he worshipped one." At Abraham's bidding Sarah, coming out of the house (not a tent), prepares "cakes" for the divine guests, while he, running to the herd, "fetched a calf tender and good" which, when the servant had dressed it, he placed before the "men" upon a plate hardly large enough for a hare. This was a feast *al fresco* under the oaks of Mamre. It was there, as he sat in the door of his tent during the heat of the day, the Lord appeared unto him.

In a fourth, the revolt of Korah (Num. 16:1-5). In the upper zone Moses expostulates with Korah and his company. The lower zone represents a more serious revolt against Moses, Joshua and Caleb (Num. 14:1-10), who are protected from stoning by "the glory of the Lord" which appeared before the tent of meeting.

The other twenty-five panels represent the following subjects in the order here given, omitting those already described: (2) Separation of Lot and Abraham. (4) Isaac blesses Jacob.—Discovery of the trick. (5) Jacob comes to Laban.—His welcome. (6) Jacob serves for Rachel. (7) Jacob complains to Laban of his deceit.—He marries Rachel. (8) Jacob meets Esau.—Their reconciliation. (9) Jacob's agreement with Laban.—Separation of the flocks. (10) Jacob's device of the staves.—God bids him return to his home.—He tells his wives of this decision. (11) Sichem and Hemor beg Jacob for Dina.—Jacob sends them away. (12) Dina's brothers require the Sichemites to be circumcised.—Sichem and Hemor persuade the people by a harangue. (13) Moses as a boy brought back to Pharaoh's daughter.—He disputes with the wise men of Egypt. (14) Moses married to Sephora.—He meets God at the bush. (15) Crossing of the Red Sea. (16) Moses speaks with God—and with the people.—The catch of quail. (17) The bitter waters made sweet.—Meeting of Moses and Abimelech. (18) The battle of Raphedim.—Moses spreads out his arms, supported by Aaron and Hur. (20) Moses delivers the Law to the people.—His death.—Priests carrying the Ark of the covenant. (21) Crossing the Jordan.—Joshua sends the spies to Jericho. (22) The spies return, let down from the wall by Rahab.—Upper zone. They report to Joshua. (24) The people of Gibeon ask help of Joshua.—He goes to their aid. (25) Victory over the five kings.—The hail of stones. (27) Execution of the five kings of the Amorites.

## THE NAVE IN GENERAL

There is no reason to suppose that the decoration of the nave with Biblical subjects was not pretty generally in use throughout the Empire. In his *Dittochæon* Prudentius describes twenty-four pictures from the Old Testament and twenty-five from the New, forming a *concordantia*, which doubtless he had seen somewhere with his own eyes. The twenty-fifth scene which he ascribes to the New Testament must have been in the apse, the other pictures from the Old and New Testaments in the nave, and probably on opposite sides.

Choricius of Gaza, in two panegyrics addressed to Marcianus, the bishop of that city, describes rhetorically two of its churches as they appeared in the sixth century. In the case of the Church of St. Stephen he remarks chiefly upon the splendid columns and the marble incrustations on the walls, leaving us to suppose that there was no pictorial decoration except in the nave, where the river Nile was depicted on both sides, stretching presumably from the door to the apse. In the other church, that of St. Sergius, which evidently was the cathedral, there was a room for baptism at the north-west corner, and opposite that a room for "the bishop's salutation." Both churches had a square atrium surrounded by a colonnade which was approached through an imposing entrance (propylæum). No other beauty of the exterior seemed worthy of remark. Only upon entering the church of St. Sergius was one filled with wonder. First one beheld the apse, where the Mother and Child were depicted in mosaic, with the bishop on one side, and on the other the imperial donor holding a model of the church. Both of the lateral apses, which were required by the Antiochian liturgy, were adorned only with trees, flowers and birds. Choricius extols especially the marble incrustations of the walls, and enumerates the various parts of Greece or of the Greek islands from which the various sorts of marble were brought. We can infer that there were stories depicted on the lower wall of the nave, for he says, "I shall omit the stories on the wall and pass on to the roof," by which evidently he means the clerestory, and he mentions the Annunciation, the Visitation, the Birth of Jesus in a stable alongside an ox and an ass, the shepherds, the Marriage at Cana, "a woman healed of a lingering disease," the Man with a withered hand, the Centurion entreating for his sick servant, the son of the Widow of Nain, the Woman who anointed Christ's feet, Jesus rebuking the wind, the Healing of a demoniac, the Woman with an issue of blood, Lazarus, the Last Supper, Judas betraying his Lord, Jesus being led to the governor, the Mocking of Jesus, the Crucifixion, the Women at the sepulchre seeing the angel and the sleeping soldiers, and finally the Ascension.

We learn incidentally that portraits, even of living persons, were not uncommon in the churches, for Paulinus reports that his own portrait in mosaic adorned the church which his friend Sulpicius Severus built in honor of St. Martin at Primuliacum in Gaul, where of course the portrait of the patron must have occupied a more conspicuous place. Plate 60c reproduces a mosaic portrait of Ambrose made soon after his death in the church called by his name in Milan. So this fashion was in vogue a thousand years before the Italian Renaissance. We have seen in chapter II that in Syria even idealized portraits might give occasion to idolatry. In the West there was no such danger.

From time to time we have had occasion to speak of the so-called *martyria*, i.e., basilicas erected in honor of a particular martyr. They were common to the East and the West. They would naturally be adorned with pictures of the martyr's sufferings. Prudentius (born probably at Saragosa in 348) describes in his *Peristephanon* pictures of this sort which he himself had seen: in honor of Hippolytus at Rome, and in honor of the martyr Cassian at Imola (Forum Cornelii). We have seen that the early Christian artists were reluctant to depict the physical sufferings of Christ or even of the Holy Innocents; but it seems that not much delicacy was shown in depicting the pains of later martyrs.

We have reached a point now where something must be said about the nine cycles of Biblical subjects which are fully illustrated here. Four of them

MONUMENTAL ART

are presented on small objects, and one of them (on the doors of S. Sabina) is incompletely illustrated; but nowhere, not even in immense folios, have so many been reproduced as in this small book. It would be superfluous, of course, to describe these pictures when they are plainly presented to the eye; but many readers will want to have them interpreted, and that cannot be done adequately in the captions printed immediately below them. By way of interpretation nothing more than a list of the subjects is needed. I am not ambitious to do more, but I confess that I have been inclined to preen myself upon the fact that I publish so many pictures. To the student it certainly is useful to have a great number of pictures; and to have the *complete* cycles represented by the mosaics of S. Apollinare Nuovo, by the alabaster columns in S. Marco, by the ivory cathedra in Ravenna, by the ivory altar frontal in Salerno, and by the Rossano Gospel, so far as it has been preserved, is infinitely more satisfactory than to have a few specimens of each. I could wish that physically and financially it might have been possible to present in this small volume many more illustrations of early Christian art, but I find some satisfaction in the reckoning that hardly more than ten of the themes which emerged in the art of the first six centuries are not illustrated here in one way or another.

## S. APOLLINARE NUOVO

Plates 72 and 73 give a general notion of the scheme of mosaic decoration in S. Apollinare Nuovo, which was so complete that no place was left for marble incrustations except on the walls of the side aisles. It will be seen that on the north side, the women's side of the church, a procession of twenty-two virgin saints starts out from the town of Classe, the port of Ravenna, following the Magi to offer their crowns to the Mother and Child, whereas on the south side a procession of twenty-six male saints, led by St. Martin, approach the glorified Christ seated upon a throne guarded by four angels, having wings as well as the traveller's staff. The men set out from the city of Ravenna, where the palace of Theodoric is very much in evidence. Originally Theodoric and his courtiers were seen between the columns of the arcade. The curtains were added later to blot out the figures of these heretics when the victory of Belisarius restored Ravenna to Justinian and the Catholic Church. Nothing remains of them but here and there a hand barely visible in front of the columns. It is significant that in no other respect did this church and the Arian Baptistery have to be changed by Bishop Agnellus to make them suitable for

## S. APOLLINARE NUOVO

Catholic worship. Theodoric was the first Gothic king who had a genuine appreciation of Roman culture. But he was an Arian, and the Arian heresy was felt to be a breach so profound that it separated men socially and politically as well as religiously. Yet in view of the pictures in this church and in the baptistery it is evident that an Arian was not what we understand by the name Unitarian. This church was rededicated to the very Catholic saint, Martin of Tours. It was renamed S. Apollinare Nuovo when the fear of depredation by Saracen pirates required the removal of the body of this saint from the church named after him in Classe.

In the lower zone of the clerestory, between the windows, are thirty-two pictures (originally there were thirty-six), of prophets, apostles and evangelists. In the narrower zone above the windows there are twenty-six scenes from the Gospels which here are published in detail (pl. 74-78). They alternate with a recurrent decoration which consists of doves standing upon a fan-shell to which is attached a pendent cross. The series begins on the north wall near the door with the paralytic carrying his bed, and it ends at the opposite corner with the vacant tomb. Inasmuch as these scenes are not exactly in chronological order, it is thought that the choice of them may have been determined by the Gospels read during Lent. Here I have rearranged them so that the empty tomb does not come before the appearances of the risen Lord.

Here is the list, accompanied in some cases by a brief comment. The pictures are taken from an elephant folio edited by Corrado Ricci, reproducing photographs by Anderson.

In the first picture in the nave, the paralytic at the pool of Bethesda carrying his bed (Jn. 5:2-9). Commonly it is impossible to determine whether St. John's story is meant or the very different story told by St. Mark (2:1-12) and the other Synoptists. But in this series, as a unique exception, both stories are illustrated. The third picture (pl. 75a) evidently represents the paralytic at Capernaum, inasmuch as the sick man is let down through the roof. This story is by far the more poignant. It is significant, apart from its picturesque features, for the fact that Jesus said, "Son, thy sins are forgiven thee." The paralytic may have been cramped in body only because he had a cramp in his soul. We have tardily learned enough psychology to know that the absolution uttered by Jesus was the only effective therapy. It has seemed to me therefore that this picture, used so often in the catacombs, was the hieroglyph for the Sacrament of Absolution. But perhaps not. Perhaps the artists thought only of the physical miracle, which is the only point in St. John's story. This is a serious question, and if I had no such serious thoughts, I might be interested only, like other "Christian archæologists," in reckoning how many times the paralytic carries his bed upside down, and how many times right side up (cf. 25b and 36a).

The next picture is the demoniac of Gerasa, as the story is told in Mk. 5:1-9.

On the next page, 75a is the paralytic at Capernaum. The important detail that he was let down through the roof has not often been dealt with because it presented the painter with difficult problems—which have not been solved very successfully here.

Then in b, Christ separates the sheep from the goats (Mt. 25:32). Where the goats have no horns (as in this picture, in contrast to plate 24c), there is left only the beard to distinguish them from the sheep. In the case of humans it is not so easy as one might think to distinguish which are the goats. Only the most worthy Judge eternal can make that distinction infallibly; and doubtless many who here are excluded as goats are welcomed there as sheep.

Then in c is told the story of the widow's mite (Mk. 12:41-44). This is not merely a parable, it is an episode in the Gospel story, a sight which Jesus observed.

Then in d the story of the Pharisee and the publican in the Temple (Lk. 18:9-14). In the Gospel this is called a "parable," but this too is a sight which Jesus saw.

I call attention here to the fact that throughout this series Jewish men are consistently clad in the *pænula* (chasuble), except when they are priests. But the fact that Christ and His apostles were Jews the artist preferred to ignore.

Then in e the raising of Lazarus (Jn. 11:1-46). Following an old artistic tradition, Lazarus as a mummy stands in an ediculum; but here the artist was constrained to omit Mary and Martha, in consideration of the fact that at so great a distance above the floor subordinate figures would have the effect of confusing the picture.

Finally, in f, the Samaritan woman at the well (Jn. 4:4-26).

On the next page, 76a, is not, as Ricci thinks, the Woman with an issue of blood (Mk. 5:25-34) for she does not touch the hem of Christ's robe; neither is it, as Wilpert thinks, the Woman taken in adultery (Jn. 8:2-11), for Christ is not seated; rather it is the Gentile woman who in the region of Tyre and Sidon besought Jesus to heal her lunatic daughter (Mt. 15:21-28). One of the apostles seems to be saying, "Send her away, for she crieth after us"—meaning that Christ should grant her request in order to get rid of her.

In b, Jesus touches and heals the eyes of two blind men (Mt. 20:30-34). The men wear chasubles, and feeling their way with a stick they show that they are blind.

In picture c, Jesus calls Peter and Andrew to follow Him (Mt. 4:18-20).

But though these were the first men called, Christ has already standing beside Him another disciple decorously dressed in a white pallium, such as the early artists in the catacombs bestowed, with some plausibility, upon Christ and His apostles. In this series, however, Christ is distinguished from His apostles by wearing a purple pallium. He is a prince who faces every situation with imperturbable dignity. This was characteristic of the art of Ravenna (pl. 61a, 56a), and in Byzantium this tradition was maintained to the end.

In picture d, Jesus lays His hands upon the loaves and fishes to bless them (Mk. 6:34-44). It may be remarked that these were not "small fishes."

Of picture e Wilpert says, "Subject uncertain"; but Ricci, who was able to examine the mosaic close at hand, reports that here originally there were water jars, which an inept restorer has mistaken for baskets. So here we have the Miracle at Cana (Jn. 2:1-11), which as a symbol of the Eucharist was commonly associated with the Multiplication of the loaves.

Picture f is the Last Supper (Mk. 14:12-25). It follows appropriately the symbols of the Eucharist, and the connection with the feast in the wilderness is made clear by the two fish placed upon the table around which Jesus and the Twelve are seated, where the Lord as usual occupies the place of honor at the right horn of the sigma. The table is covered with a cloth such as was used on Christian altars (pl. 64b, c, 63b). This was the first Eucharist, and though Christ was present in the flesh, it was of Him, the Ichthys, the disciples partook.

On plate 77, in picture a, Jesus addresses the apostles on the Mount of Olives (Mk. 13:1-37)—it is not Gethsemane, as Wilpert thinks.

In b, Judas betrays the Lord with a kiss (Mk. 14:44-49). The band sent by the high priest comes with "swords and staves." On the other side Peter is about to draw his sword.

In c, Jesus is led away to the high priest—not by the soldiers who came to take Him, but by Jews who wear the *pænula*, one of which garments has an outlandish form.

In d, Jesus is brought before the high priest (Mk. 14:55-65). Here three priests sit as judges. The artist may have assumed that at a trial the judge would have assessors. But John (18:13) by mentioning Annas suggested that there were at least two high priests, and Mark had already said "all the chief priests." In this series the high priest is distinguished from others by wearing a mantle like a cope fastened by a morse in front of the breast, like Melchizedek (pl. 66c, 63b). He follows Jesus to the court of Pilate, and even to Calvary.

In e, Jesus foretells Peter's denial (Mk. 14:30).

In f, Peter indignantly denies the accusation of the comely maid-servant (Mk. 14:54, 66-72).

On plate 78, in picture a, Judas brings back to the high priest the pieces of silver (Mt. 27:3-5).

In b, Jesus is accused by the high priest, and Pilate washes his hands (Mt. 27:24).

In c, Jesus is led to Calvary, followed by the high priest and the Jews, while Simon carries the cross—which in this case appears to be no great burden (Mk. 15:20-22).

In d, the Two Women come to the empty tomb (an elegant *tempietta*) and are told by the angel that Christ is risen (Mk. 16:1-8). The sleeping soldiers are not represented here.

In e, Jesus discourses to the "two disciples" on the way to Emmaus (Lk. 24:13-35). The artist did not regard these disciples as apostles, for he clothes them with the *pænula*.

In f, Jesus appears a second time "within" the house, when the doors were shut: He shows the wound in His side, and Thomas, covering his hands in sign of adoration, exclaims, "My Lord and my God!" (Jn. 20:24-29).

## CATHEDRA OF MAXIMIANUS
### (Plates 79-89)

The chair of Maximianus, Bishop of Ravenna (d. 556), is one of the earliest extant monuments which tells the story of Jesus continuously. Here it is told in ivory carvings, on the columns of S. Marco in sculpture, and on the walls of S. Apollinare in mosaic. Besides the beautiful design of the border, in which birds and beasts enliven the pattern of the vine, there were originally thirty-nine pictorial panels. The five figures on the front represent John the Baptist flanked by the four Evangelists—whom I do not venture to identify. Ten panels on the sides tell the story of the patriarch Joseph; and originally there were twenty-four, of which only twelve remain, devoted to the story of Jesus. Eight of them were in front of the back rest and sixteen behind it. Even if the monogram can be tortured to read: MAXIMIANUS EPISCOPUS, the chair was certainly not made for this bishop, but before the end of the fifth century, and probably in Alexandria. Among the panels which have disappeared only eight are unaccounted for, since early writers mention the Visitation, the flight of Elizabeth (according to the Protevangelion of James), and the Marriage at Cana, as a sequel to the miracle. It is evident enough that all the

## CATHEDRA OF MAXIMIANUS

Ivory chair of Maximianus, Bishop of Ravenna (d. 556), made before his time, probably in Alexandria. The 22 panels on the following plates depict the story of Joseph and the story of Jesus.

Pl. 79

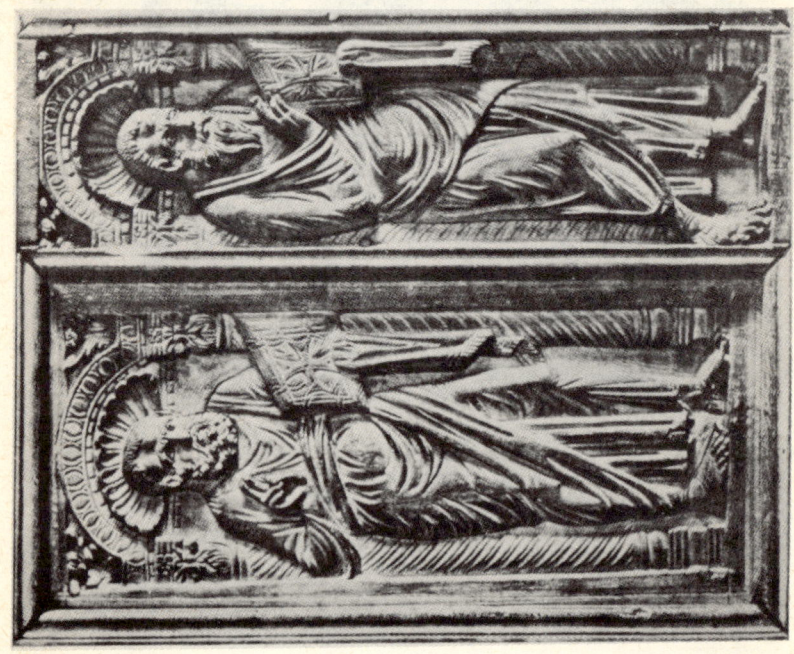

The four Evangelists who flank the figure of John the Baptist.

Pl. 80

a. Jacob rends his garments on seeing Joseph's coat stained with blood.—b. Joseph led down into the dry well.—c. Joseph sold to the Ismaelites.—d. Joseph sold by the Ismaelite merchants to Potiphar in Egypt.

Pl. 81

Pl. 82

**a.** Joseph rejects the advances of Potiphar's wife and, on her accusation, is dragged to prison.—**b.** Pharaoh's dream of the fat and lean cattle.—**c.** Joseph interprets Pharaoh's dream.—**d.** Joseph fills the sacks of his brothers with grain.

a. Joseph beholds his brother Benjamin.—b. Joseph embraces his father.—c. Annunciation.

Pl. 83

Pl. 84

a. Mary submits to the test of bitter water (apocryphal).—b. Joseph, being reassured in

a. The birth of Jesus; like the ox and ass, the withered hand of Salome, the midwife, is an apocryphal embellishment.—b. The Virgin and Child receive the Magi (the latter depicted on a piece now lost).

Pl. 85

Pl. 86

a. Christ blesses the loaves and fishes.—b. Feeding of the multitude.

Pl. 87

a. Christ healing the blind and lame.—b. The Samaritan woman at the well.

Pl. 88

a. Entry into Jerusalem.—b. Ivory Gospel cover from Murano. National Museum, Ravenna. (See pp. 176-177.)

Pl. 89

carvings were not executed by the same hand—but any student can make this discrimination as well as I.

The story of Joseph is told dramatically and with great skill, in spite of some crudeness in the design of the figures.

On plate 81, in picture a, Jacob rends his garments when he beholds the blood upon the coat of many colors he had made for his son Joseph (Gen. 37: 31-35). Little Benjamin stands beside him; but the woman clasping her knee is not Joseph's mother, since Rachel died in giving birth to Benjamin.

In b, Joseph is let down into the dry well by his jealous brothers, who, to persuade his father that the boy was devoured by wild beasts, kill a kid and dip in its blood his coat of many colors (Gen. 37:23, 24).

In c, Joseph is sold to Ismaelite (or Midianite) merchantmen who happen to pass that way with their camels (Gen. 37:25-28).

In d, the Ismaelites, arriving in Egypt, sell Joseph to Potiphar (Gen. 37:36).

On plate 82, in picture a, Joseph rejects the advances of Potiphar's wife, and on her false accusation he is dragged to prison (Gen. 39:13-20).

In b, Pharaoh dreams of the seven fat and the seven lean kine (Gen. 41:1-8).

In c, Joseph interprets Pharaoh's dream (Gen. 41:14-36).

In d, Joseph fills with wheat the sacks of his brethren (Gen. 42:25).

On plate 83, in picture a, Joseph beholds with emotion his brother Benjamin (Gen. 43:29).

In b, Joseph embraces his father Jacob (Gen. 46:28, 29). His body-guard and his brethren are equally astonished.

In c, the story of Jesus begins with the Annunciation (Lk. 1:26-38). The angel Gabriel, though he has wings, carries a staff, which may have been regarded as a symbol of his authority as the messenger of God.

On plate 84, in picture a, Joseph, to allay his suspicion of Mary, subjects her to the test of swallowing bitter water (an apocryphal invention).

In b, Joseph, being reassured in a dream, tenderly conducts his pregnant wife to Bethlehem (Lk. 2:1-5). In these scenes an angel is present as a symbol of divine protection.

On plate 85, in picture a, Joseph, along with the ox and the ass of the apocryphal gospels, looks with wonder at the child in the manger (Lk. 2:6, 7). Already the star shines upon the Infant. Mary, lying below on a mattress, heals the midwife Salome of a withered hand, which, according to an apocryphal embellishment, was her punishment for doubting the virginity of the mother.

In b, Mary and the Child (no longer in swaddling clothes) receive the visit of the Magi—who originally were depicted on a panel which is lost (Mt. 2:1-12).

On plate 86, in picture a, the Baptism of Jesus (Mk. 1:9-11). The dove descends abruptly, angels hold His garments, and a river-god stirs up the water to cover Him almost to the waist—a device for making visible a figure which is supposed to be totally immersed.

In b, Christ transforms the water into wine (Jn. 2:1-11). A servant carries a goblet to the master of the feast. Here, as in three other pictures of this series, Christ carries a rod surmounted by a cross. The addition of the cross was characteristic of Egypt, but the magic rod was a device in the frescoes of the catacombs to indicate where His power was shown.

On plate 87, in picture a, Christ blesses the loaves and the fishes (Mk. 6:1-14).

In b, the apostles distribute the loaves to the multitude (Mk. 6:39-44). Men and women are seated around a sigma, as at the Last Supper, and in the front of it the fish is conspicuous. This is the sequence we observed in the mosaics of S. Apollinare Nuovo.

On plate 88, in picture a, Christ heals a blind man by touching his eyes, while a man dreadfully lamed approaches with a crutch (Jn. 9:1-16; Mt. 21:14).

In b, Christ talks with the Samaritan woman at the well (Jn. 4:4-26).

On plate 89, in picture a, Christ, seated upon an ass, but not astride, enters Jerusalem in triumph (Mk. 11:1-11). A woman, who perhaps is the symbol of the city, sperads a carpet (not a garment) in His path. Two men wave palm branches (which were *not* strewn on the ground). The man standing in a tree is likely Zacchæus, who, though out of place, sometimes appears in this connection.

## GOSPEL COVER FROM MURANO
(Plate 89b)

The ivory Gospel cover from Murano, which is now in the National Museum at Ravenna, may be spoken of here, although it exemplifies the deterioration of art during the sixth century. It resembles the carvings on the cathedra of Maximianus and may be referred to Egypt. But the stiff figures are unduly elongated, partly because they must be made to fit the narrow spaces allotted to them. The staring frontal aspect of Christ and the apostles is characteristic of decadent art. The cross at the top is surrounded by a wreath and supported by floating angels. At the ends of the panel stand two imperial figures wearing the *paludamentum*, holding in the one hand the globe of the

STATUES & RELIEFS

Silver pyx of St. St. Ambrose. Used for the reserved Sacrament; preserved in the Chapel of S. Nazaro in S. Ambrogio, Milan. (See p. 160.)—a. Judgment of Solomon.—b. The Three Children in the fiery furnace.

Pl. 90

a. The lid represents Jesus' "hard saying" (Jn. 6:60).—b. Daniel's judgment of the elders.

Pl. 91

a. Gifts of the Magi.—b. Ivory diptych in Florence. Fifth century.

Pl. 92

world marked with the cross, and in the other (significantly) a rod tipped with the cross such as Christ carries. In the center Christ is seated upon a throne, having Peter and Paul on either side of Him and two other apostles (not angels) behind Him. Beneath this are the Three Children in the fiery furnace. An angel carrying a cross-tipped wand represents the divine intervention which quenched the fire. At the bottom is the story of Jonah, where the angel again intervenes. On the sides are four miracles of Christ: the Healing of a blind man, the Raising of Lazarus, the Cure of a demoniac, and the Paralytic carrying his bed.

Because these pictures are on so small a scale they have all the more need of interpretation.

## IVORY DIPTYCH AT FLORENCE

The ivory diptych in Florence which is reproduced on plate 92b also requires interpretation, and it well deserves it, for no better piece of work was produced in the fifth century.

The beauty of the right leaf is incontestable. Adam in an Eveless Eden innocently plucks the many delicious fruits he is permitted to eat, and he seems so well content with the company of the beasts that one wonders if another helpmeet really was needed. Evidently he understood the language of the beasts, and knowing thus their proper natures he was able to give them all appropriate names. Everyone must feel instinctively that it would have been inappropriate had he called the lion a lamb or the goat an eagle, and that it would have been ridiculous had he called the elephant a mouse. The artist, though he found delight in depicting Adam, ignored an implication of the Biblical record which Sir Thomas Browne emphasized when he called him "the man without a navel."

The picture of Eden being carved so beautifully, we cannot but wonder at the emaciated figures on the other leaf. The first impression suggests a defect of artistic skill. But in fact this picture is a perfect commentary upon the story of St. Paul's shipwreck on the island of Malta as it is told in Acts 28: 1-10. The four figures in the lowest row are evidently wasted with malarial fever and dysentery. The artist anticipated Dr. Ramsay's fairly recent discovery that the "barbarians" on that island, as well as the father of Publius the governor, were suffering from such diseases. These poor barbarians were as much astonished as was Publius and the native chieftain on seeing that Paul took no harm when the viper which had fastened on his hand was shaken into the fire. They were ready to think him a god. Publius is correctly dressed as a Roman official, the barbarians are dressed as such—they wear trousers. In the upper zone St. Paul, seated in a chair, instructs his disciples. The man with a book may be St. Luke.

As a striking contrast to this diptych we have on the same plate and on the two plates which precede it the silver pyx made for St. Ambrose in the fourth century. Here we have a superior artist who had not broken with classical traditions, but did not know the Scriptures nor the traditions of Christian art (pl. 90-92a).

## DOORS OF S. SABINA

The fifth-century reliefs on the wooden doors of S. Sabina in Rome are in some respects the most precious examples of early Christian art. This church was built and adorned under the pontificate of Cælestin by a man named Peter, a presbyter of Rome but a native of Dalmatia—as we learn from the mosaic inscription on the west wall.

In order to make the details visible, plate 93 reproduces only a part of the doors. Originally these doors had twenty-eight sculptured panels, twelve of them large and sixteen small. Now there are left only eight large and ten small panels. All of them are shown here except five of the small ones. Since all but one of the ten small panels which remain depict scenes from the New Testament, it seems likely that those which perished had to do with the Old Testament and formed a *concordantia*. We shall see that two (perhaps three) of the large panels were devoted to what we might call Church history, and that they too form a sort of *concordantia*. There is no reason to suppose that the subjects are now arranged as they were originally, but the notion that the beautiful frame, the vine pattern, was due to a restoration is now discarded. All the sculptured panels belong to the same age, though they are not all by the same hand. The finest of them are among the best productions of early Christian art. They are notable not only for artistic skill but for the thought which is revealed in them. It is remarkable that so many of these carvings on cyprus wood have been perfectly preserved, and we have no cause to wonder that ten panels have perished. Those at the bottom would suffer most from wear, as they did on the wooden doors of S. Ambrogio in Milan.

The eight large panels presented here give clear enough evidence of a

**a.** Part of the cyprus doors of S. Sabina, Rome. Earlier than 432.
**b.** Single small panel in doors of S. Sabina; one of the earliest representations of the Crucifixion.

Two panels from the doors of S. Sabina.—a. The Church.—b. The Empire.
—c. Ends of the ivory box at Brescia.

Pl. 94

**a.** Ivory tablet in Trier Seventh century. (See pp. 170-171.)—Ivory box in the British Museum. (See pp. 165-166.)—**b.** Pilate washes his hands; *Via crucis;* Peter's denial.—**c.** Judas hangs himself (one of the earliest crucifixions).—**d.** The women at the tomb.—**e.** Doubting Thomas.

Pl. 95

Top and sides of the ivory box at Brescia. Probably end of fourth century: 36 subjects.

purpose to draw a parallel between events related in the Old and the New Testaments. The Ascension of Christ and the ascent of Elijah (at the upper left and the lower right of the first door) are evidently meant to correspond and were probably placed side by side. The two panels which now are side by side at the top of the other door present two series of events which were commonly compared in early Christian art. Even formally they are designed to match one another, being divided into zones. In the first, Christ raises Lazarus, multiplies the loaves to feed the multitude in the wilderness, and turns water into wine. All of these subjects, including the resurrection of the dead, were associated with the Eucharist. On the other panel we have Moses, the leader of Israel, providing manna in the wilderness and striking water from the rock. We have seen that in the very earliest art the water struck from the rock suggested baptism. "That rock was Christ," said St. Paul (1 Cor. 10:4) in a passage which assimilates the Old Testament to the New: "baptized unto Moses in the cloud and in the sea, and did all eat the same spiritual meat, and did all drink the same spiritual drink." In Jn. 6:31f. the manna is contrasted with "the true bread from heaven." The parallelism adduced in these panels was not an invention of the artist, who had only to exploit an old tradition.

These two instances create a strong presumption that all the large panels were designed in pairs. The drowning of Pharaoh and his hosts in the Red Sea (depicted in the panel at the lower left, where also Moses confounds the Egyptians by turning his rod into a serpent) was probably matched by the drowning of Maxentius and his army in the Tiber at the battle of the Milvian Bridge, which was depicted on the sarcophagi as a parallel to the destruction of Pharaoh (pl. 21b, c), and was so understood by Constantine. The panel (lower left on the second door) which represents Moses tending the flock of Jethro, hearing God speak from the burning bush, and receiving the Law in the presence of Aaron, may have been matched by a picture of the Transfiguration, in which Moses as well as Elijah were involved. Four large panels remain unexplained. Of the two which are lost I can give no account, but two which remain and are perfectly preserved can, I think, be easily explained, although, because they are unique in Christian art, they leave archæologists in perplexity. The beautiful picture reproduced on plate 94a depicts Christ in glory, declaiming, "I am the Alpha and the Omega, the Beginning and the End," and holding in his left hand a scroll on which is depicted the Greek word *Ichthys* (fish). Above the firmament of heaven, the sun and the moon, He is surrounded by a wreath accompanied by the four symbols of the Evangelists. Below we see a female figure standing in the attitude of prayer, above whom Peter and Paul hold a wreath in which is inscribed a cross, the upper shaft of which, strangely enough, stretches beyond the wreath like a tongue of flame and points to Christ in glory to whom the woman looks aspiringly with upturned face. If the Ascension had not been represented on another panel, one might perhaps suppose that this was a unique version of it, and that the woman below the cross was Mary. But the presence of Paul in this scene would be an anachronism such as no Christian artist has ever been guilty of. I have prepared the reader to understand that essentially the orant expresses faith—faith exhibited in prayer, and we have seen that it is perfectly consonant with contemporary art, as exhibited in this very church (pl. 68) and in S. Pudenziana (pl. 57), to interpret the female figure here as the Church in prayer, aspiring in faith above earthly things, and above the heavenly dome, to Christ in Glory: the *Ichthys*, Jesus Christ Son of God Saviour.

But how does this match the other picture, which now is far separated from it on the door but here is placed beside it on plate 94b, and which represents what we regard as a secular subject? The figure clad in the *paludamentum* I take to be an emperor, though so far as we can see he wears no crown. He too stands in the attitude of prayer, and beside him stands a guardian angel. In the zones below the people acclaim him with the gesture we know as the Fascist salute, which is depicted also on the Arch of Constantine, where the people wear, as they do here on the upper zone, an exiguous toga, the dress which only Roman citizens might wear. In the lower zone the people wear the *pænula*, which was the common dress throughout the Empire. The building in the background is thought to be a church because it has a cross on the gable between the two towers. But churches had no such towers, except in northern Syria a century later, where they were copied from the palace. This is one of the reasons for ascribing the doors of S. Sabina to Syrian artists, who would be inclined to depict an imperial palace in this way. Nor is there any incongruity in placing a cross upon what was called "the sacred palace" of the emperor—though churches at that time had no cross upon their roofs. On plate 95a we see a picture of Christ in the lunette above the door of the imperial palace in Constantinople. Constantine and his successors were not disposed to relinquish the sacred character enjoyed by their pagan predecessors. They still claimed the title of Pontifex Maximus, though they interpreted it in a new way. The mediaeval notion of the Holy Roman Empire was a novelty only in name. Eusebius makes it clear that Constantine cherished such an idea and transmitted it to his successors. A faint reflection of this in more modern times was the divinity that doth hedge a king. The cross and the eagle were respectively the symbols of Church and State. The Church dared not usurp the secular power which the eagle implied, but on the other hand the emperor commonly carried the triumphal cross (pl. 106b, and coins on pl. 55). We can estimate from a trivial example how broadly current was the conception of the State as a sacred power alongside of the Church. It is furnished by a bit of silk damask found in Egypt (pl. 144c). In the upper zone it represents the imperial eagle attacking a noxious beast, and perfectly parallel to this we see in the lower zone the figure of Christ, holding the cross and piercing the dragon. It was thus that Constantine depicted himself at the very beginning of his reign in a statue which he erected in the Roman Forum, "holding in his hand," as Eusebius says, "the sign of salutary suffering." At the end of his reign the labarum, with its staff piercing a serpent, appeared upon his coins, with the motto *Spes publica*. The Church was inclined to exalt the Empire even when it was a pagan and a hostile power. Eusebius says, "By the express appointment of the same God two roots of blessing, the Roman Empire and the doctrine of Christianity, sprang up together for the benefit of men."

Berthier, in his monograph on the doors of S. Sabina, interprets this panel as a representation of Zacharias coming out of the Temple where an angel had foretold the birth of his son John (Lk. 1:5-23). No interpretation could be more inept; and yet the other misinterpretations, many and various as they are, do not deserve the least consideration. If these two panels were placed on the door, as they are here, side by side, the interpretation I put upon them would "spring into the eye," as the Germans say. For nothing could be plainer, it seems to me, than that one picture is the glorification of the Empire, and the other a just appreciation of the character of the Church exhibited in faith and prayer. I say a just appreciation, for here we have not an apotheosis of the Empire, and still less of the Church. Yet they are parallel to one another, and both are sacred.

I shall not say much about the ten small panels which have been preserved. It will be enough if I enumerate nine of them: (1) Habakkuk carried by an angel to Babylon by a lock of his hair, in order that he may give to Daniel in the lions' den the pottage he had prepared for himself; (2) the Magi; (3) Gethsemane; (4) Christ before Caiaphas; (5) Peter's denial; (6) Christ before Pilate; (7) the Women at the Tomb; (8) Christ's appearance to the Women in the Garden, and (9) to Three Disciples (including, as I think, doubting Thomas).

But about the tenth panel, the picture of the Crucifixion (pl. 93b), more

MONUMENTAL ART

must be said. It is significant, not only because it is one of the earliest pictures of the Crucifixion in early art, being second perhaps only to that on the ivory box in the British Museum (pl. 95c), but because here Christ is represented as standing in the attitude of prayer, His hands not nailed to the cross but (as in the case also of the thieves) to blocks of wood. The background indicates that this took place outside the walls of Jerusalem.

It is deplorable that the reliefs which tell the story of David on the wooden doors of S. Ambrogio in Milan have not been so well preserved, for they were doubtless made under the supervision of Ambrose, who was especially devoted to the author of the Psalms. They are in so ruinous a state that hardly any attention was paid to them till Adolph Goldschmidt deciphered these remnants with rare acumen and exemplary piety.

## THE IVORY BOX AT BRESCIA

Hardly any work of art in ancient or modern times has so many pictures in so small a space as the ivory box at Brescia. On this small box the artist found room for fifty-one subjects, including the fifteen medallions which appear to be portraits. It will be seen that the figures are beautifully executed. They cannot be later than the fifth century. It must suffice here to enumerate the thirty-six Biblical scenes, beginning with the small ends. Moses at the burning bush; the Three Children in the fiery furnace (with four persons standing behind them!); Moses receiving the Law, the strange story told in 1 Kings 13 about the man of God and the lion; Christ healing a blind man, raising Lazarus, and also the daughter of Jairus; Rebecca and Eliezer at the well; Jacob's dream; the golden calf and the festivity accompanying its worship ("the people sat down to eat and drink, and rose up to play," Ex. 32:6); Christ in Gethsemane; Christ foretells Peter's denial, is brought before the high priest, then before Pilate (who washes his hands), then is led away; an orant; Jonah asleep under the gourd; Moses and the brazen serpent (Num. 2:7-11); a tower (suggested perhaps by the Third Vision of Hermas); Sapphira lies to Peter; she falls dead; the young men carry her out (Acts 5:1-11); Judas hangs from a tree; Moses found in the ark of bulrushes (Ex. 2:1-6); Moses kills an Egyptian (Ex. 2:11-14); the manna in the wilderness (?); Jonah is thrown to the sea monster; Jonah is spewed out; a fish; Christ appears to Mary in the garden ("Touch me not"); Christ appears to all the apostles in the house and unfolds the Scriptures; Christ as the Good Shepherd ("the door of the sheep") defends His flock against the wolf while the hireling fleeth; a cock on a column recalls Peter's denial; Susanna as orant; Susanna watched by the elders; Daniel's judgment against the elders; Daniel between the lions.

Here is as good a place as any to remark upon a feature common to classical and Christian art which Wickhoff, speaking of manuscript illustrations, called "the continuous style." An example of it is to be seen here in the story of Sapphira. She appears twice in the same picture, the second situation being a sequence of the first. The reader will recognize that we have already seen several instances of this "style," in the story of Jonah, for instance, and we shall encounter many more in the manuscript illustrations. Wickhoff associates this style of pictorial narrative with the stories depicted continuously on the spirals of the columns of Trajan and Marcus Aurelius. On his assumption that the earliest Bible illustrations were painted continuously on rolls this comparison seemed very apt. Even now when this assumption is contested it remains true that the continuous style is characteristic of Christian art in general. I remark here only that this style of continuous narrative which seemed strange to us not many years ago has now become perfectly familiar through the strip pictures which are a reflection of the movies. There is now an effort made to popularize the Bible stories by telling them in the same way—unfortunately with the result of vulgarizing them, by the crudeness of the colors and by the outlandish styles in which the characters are dressed. Yet something of the sort ought to be done, and early Christian art shows how it could be done to good effect.

## THE IVORY BOX IN THE BRITISH MUSEUM

Another example of fifth-century art at its best is the ivory box in the British Museum which is illustrated on plate 95. It presents an instance of the continuous style in an exaggerated form. For on the first panel Pilate has not finished washing his hands before Jesus sets out upon the *via crucis*, accompanied by a soldier wearing the Pannonian cap, and encounters Peter who is in the act of denying that he knows Him. On the second panel Judas hangs from a tree near the cross, and while the soldier is offering Jesus the sponge, Joseph of Arimathea comes to bury Him. This is likely the earliest representation of the Crucifixion that has been preserved. Christ is naked but for a loincloth, as on the doors of S. Sabina, but here His arms are stretched out horizontally. This position is realistic enough in case the feet are supported or securely nailed to the cross. The third panel shows the Two Women seated by the open tomb where the soldiers sleep, but there is no angel. The tomb was often depicted in this form, but the frequency with which it was repeated shows that such objects of art were made by the dozen and by uninstructed artisans. In one case they so far misunderstood the situation that they placed the soldiers upon the roof of the edicule. The fourth panel presents the oft-repeated theme of Christ displaying the wound in His side to doubting Thomas (Jn. 20:24-29).

## COLUMNS OF THE CIBORIUM IN S. MARCO
*(Plates 97-101)*

The two carved columns of alabaster which support the ciborium in St. Mark's Church at Venice (but only the two front columns) are among the most interesting examples of Christian art in the fifth century. Archæologists, because they were deceived by the late Latin inscriptions which accompany the pictures, persisted in regarding these columns as mediæval—as the posterior pair certainly are, having been made in the thirteenth century to accompany the ancient pair. There can be no doubt about the antiquity of the two columns which are illustrated here, but their history is obscure. It is known that up to the year 1260 the ciborium in S. Marco had spiral columns resembling the columns which Constantine placed in front of the presbytery of S. Pietro. Such columns are to be seen in a mosaic of that year representing the interior of the church. We may infer therefore that the columns we now have were a part of the loot brought to Venice after the sack of Constantinople at the end of the fourth Crusade (1204), and adapted later to their present use. This implies that they were made in Constantinople. But there is nothing to distinguish them as "Eastern," and this is a great embarrassment to the proponents of the Eastern theory. To rebut the obvious inference that Eastern and Western art were pretty much the same, they have nothing to say but, "What else could one expect of such a 'melting-pot' as Constantinople?"

These columns are distinguished, however, by their artistic superiority. It is obvious that the work was shared by two artists, one of whom, generally accounted the abler, was responsible for the four lower zones on both columns, the other for the five zones above. The difference in their technique is more

## COLUMNS OF THE CIBORIUM IN S. MARCO

a. Joseph's doubt of Mary.—b. The birth of Jesus.—c. The Magi scrutinizing the stars, a sphere, and the Scriptures.—d. Mary invited to the marriage in Cana.—e. The marriage table is spread.—f. Mary tells the servants to do as Jesus bids.

Pl. 97

**a.** Water turned into wine.—**b.** The wine brought to the master of the feast.—**c.** Raising of Lazarus.—**d.** "He stinketh."—**e.** "Shut your mouth," said Jesus to the wind (Mk. 4:39).—**f.** Healing of the man born blind.

Pl. 98

a. The blind man washes his eyes at the pool of Siloam.—b. The woman with an issue of blood touches Christ's garment.—c. The Roman nobleman pleads for his son.—d. The nobleman's reverent gesture.—e. Christ heeds the petition of the Canaanitish woman for her demented daughter.—f. The Last Supper (a disciple brings the fish).

Pl. 99

a. Peter's denial; "The cock crows; Peter weeps," says the inscription.—b. Pilate behind the judge's desk and the standard bearers.—c. The scribes record the trial.—d. Pilate washes his hands.—e. The women at the sepulchre where the guards sleep.—f. "The lamb is crucified with evildoers."

Pl. 100

**a.** Christ descends into limbo.—**b.** "Christ seated in celestial glory."

## STATUES AND RELIEFS

**c.** Statue of St. Hippolytus (restored). Lateran Museum. Early third century. (See p. 31.)
—**d.** Statue of the Good Shepherd. Lateran Museum. Third century.

Pl. 101

**a.** Statuette of Christ (?). Museo delle Terme, Rome. Early third century. (See p. 13.)—
**b.** Christ in the attitude of a Greek poet. Part of a sarcophagus found in Constantinople. Fourth century.

Pl. 102

a. Lead ampulæ in which pilgrims brought oil from the Holy Sepulchre, which is depicted on them. Cathedral, Monza. Sixth century. (See p. 101.)—b. Bronze monogram from Aquileia. Latter half of the fourth century.

Pl. 103

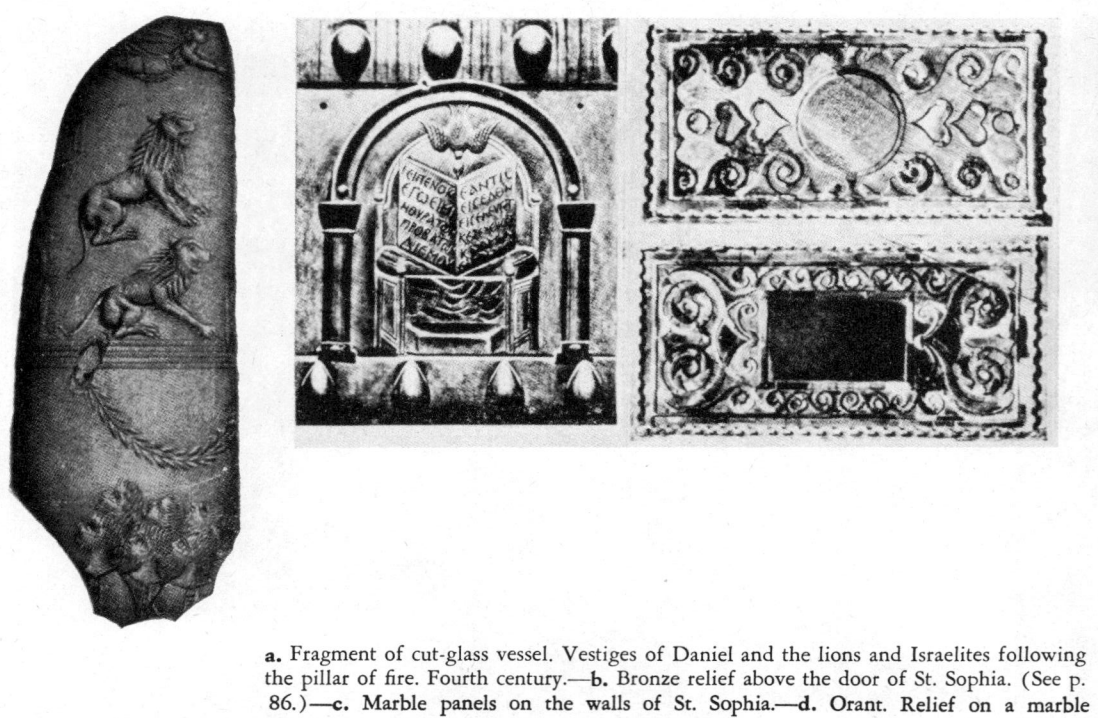

Pl. 104

**a.** Fragment of cut-glass vessel. Vestiges of Daniel and the lions and Israelites following the pillar of fire. Fourth century.—**b.** Bronze relief above the door of St. Sophia. (See p. 86.)—**c.** Marble panels on the walls of St. Sophia.—**d.** Orant. Relief on a marble parapet.

Ivory diptychs. **a.** An angel. British Museum. Fourth century.—**b.** Consul Anastasius (507). Paris.—**c.** Consul Areobiundus (566), Leningrad.—**d.** Archangel Michael (verso of diptych of Severus) (470). Leipzig.

Pl. 105

a. Consul Probus (405). Aosta.—b. Empress Ariadne (wife of Zeno, d. 491, and Anastasius, d. 518). Florence.—c. Consul Boëthius (487). Brescia.

Pl. 106

striking in photographs than in the original because the contrasts of light and shadow are intensified. It is easy to distinguish the two artists, but I wonder how many readers of this book will share the opinion that the artist responsible for the lower zones was in all respects the superior, or, as some say, "the most gifted artist of late antiquity." All of the pictures on plate 97 are by this artist, and all but figure e on plate 98 by the other. One must say that the upper zones are smoother, clearer and more pleasing. This would have been the judgment of late antiquity, which in fact allotted to this artist the more important zones. It may be said that the sculptor of the lower zones shows more originality and inventiveness. But what disposed modern critics to prefer him is a certain resemblance to tendencies of the late Renaissance which pleases our modern taste. Both artists exercised their inventiveness to an unusual degree in order to tell a story which overlapped the narrow niches formed by eight colonnettes in every drum.

I comment here only upon the illustrations provided in this book, which are all Wilpert has published from Venturi's photographs, though all the scenes are not included. For example, the Last Supper is accompanied by the Foot-washing, which is not shown here. I copy the late Latin inscriptions because, with one exception, they characterize the scenes correctly.

Plate 97a. *Suspitio de Maria*. Mary replies to Joseph's doubt by protesting her virginity.

Plate 97b. *Nativitas Jesu Christi*. The Birth of Jesus (Lk. 2:7)—the ox and the ass looking on.

Plate 97c. *Scrutatio prophetie*. Here, in fact, only one of the three Magi is engaged in searching the Scriptures (Mt. 2:1-12); another is intently scrutinizing a crystal globe, while the third plucks wisdom from the stars. Not in vain were they called "wise men."

Plate 97d. *Invitatur ad nuptias*. Mary is invited to the Marriage at Cana (Jn. 2:1, 2). This is the first of four pictures which deal with the same story in two zones.

Plate 97e. *Nuptiæ in Chana*. The tables are spread for the feast.

Plate 97f. Learning that the wine has given out, Mary instructs the servants to do as Jesus bids (Jn. 2:5).

Plate 98a. *De aqua vinum*. The water is turned into wine (Jn. 2:6, 7).

Plate 98b. The wine is brought to the master of the feast (Jn. 2:8-10).

Plate 98c. *Quatridivanū Dn̄s Lazarum suscitat*. The Raising of Lazarus—in two scenes (Jn. 11:1-46). The men on either side who lay hold of him by his grave clothes cover their noses—taking too literally the saying, "he stinketh."

Plate 98e. *Imperat ventis.* This sculptor, if he is not the superior artist, is at all events an excellent commentator. He agrees with Wellhausen that Codex Beza rightly omits the word "sea," with the understanding that it was only the wind Christ addressed, because only the wind (*pneuma*) could be regarded as a demon. And evidently the artist rightly interprets Mk. 4:39 to mean—not "Peace, be still," as we elegantly translate it—but, "Be quiet, shut your mouth!" Such words make sense when, as in this case, the wind is a demon blowing with distended cheeks.

Plate 98f. *Lutum fecit Dn̄s et unxit oculum ceci nati.* The Lord heals the man born blind by anointing his eyes with clay (Jn. 9:1-6). The story is told in two scenes, in the second of which,

Plate 99a. the man complies with the injunction to wash his eyes—in a basin which here represents the pool of Siloam.

Plate 99b. *Orat chananea.* Here, like many modern archæologists, the inscription confuses the Canaanitish woman of Mk. 7:24-30 with the woman who had an issue of blood and "touched" Christ's garment (Mk. 5:25-34). Perhaps the artist too was at fault in depicting the head of a demented (?) woman above the house.

Plate 99c. *Regulus orat pro filio.* A "nobleman" (traditionally known as Regulus and depicted here as a princely personage, wearing a diadem and accompanied by servants and soldiers) pleads for his son (Jn. 4:46-52). Christ by His gesture (like that of Thorwaldsen's statue labelled "Come unto me") grants all that is asked of Him.

Plate 99d. *Item de Regolo.* Regulus, on learning of his son's recovery, returns to express his gratitude, stretching forth his hands *under* his garment as a sign of the utmost respect, as one would receive a royal gift.

Plate 99e. *Sanat filia [m] chananea.* Here we have the Canaanitish woman (Mk. 7:24-30). Addressing Christ as "Lord," she makes the same gesture as Regulus. Her demented daughter is seen on the left. These last scenes celebrate Christ's gracious behavior towards three Gentiles. The woman with an issue of blood is supposed to have come from Cæsarea Philippi (Paneas), where she gratefully erected a statue of Jesus, which Eusebius is disposed to excuse on the ground that to a pagan this would seem a pious act, though to Christians it might seem idolatrous.

Plate 99f. *Cena Domini.* Because the Foot-washing follows this we know that it is the Lord's Supper—although, as in the case of the Marriage at Cana, the narrow niche affords not enough space to depict adequately the table and the guests. An apostle approaches, bearing upon a platter the fish.

## DIPTYCHS

Plate 100a. *Gallus canit. Flet Petrus.* When the cock crew, Peter went out and wept bitterly (Mk. 14:66-72).

Plate 100b. On the side not shown the inscription indicates that Jesus is scourged (*flagellatus*). Here Pilate, acting as judge, is properly seated behind a desk (cf. pl. 128, 129), and is accompanied by youths bearing the imperial standards. His wife, looking from a window, warns him, "Have nothing to do with that righteous man."

Plate 100c. Behind Pilate the clerks of the court inscribe the "acts" upon their tablets.

Plate 100d. *Lavat Pilatus manum.* Washing his hands, Pilate stands before a bowl into which water is poured by an attendant (Mt. 27:24).

Plate 100e. On the left, the women visit the tomb and find the guards asleep (Mk. 16:1-8). On the right, this story comes to the ears of the governor (Mt. 28:13, 14).

Plate 100f. *Agnus crucifigitur cum iniquis.* To avoid picturing the sufferings of Christ, the *Agnus Dei* is depicted in his stead on the cross, between the two thieves. Above the sun and the moon are personified, and below soldiers divide the garments.

Plate 101a. *Surgunt corpora sanctorum.* "Many bodies of the saints were raised" (Mt. 27:52). This is depicted on the left. On the right Christ descends to the limbus (1 Pet. 3:19), rescuing the patriarchs, while Hades bites his fingers in impotent rage.

Plate 101b. *Iesus sedit in gloria celesti.* Jesus is seated in glory, attended by the highest ranks of angelic beings, the "living creatures" of Ezekiel.


## DIPTYCHS

To show the ups and downs of art from the beginning of the fifth century to the middle of the sixth I have included here (pl. 105, 106) seven of the many diptychs which have been preserved. The movement in general was down rather than up; for, except for the diptych of the Empress Ariadne, the later examples are obviously coarser. Most of them are consular diptychs. The consulate, though it no longer conferred power, was a coveted honor, and for the distinction of having the year named after them, men were willing to give the customary largess to the people and to pay for the "games" in the circus. If they did not continue, like Cicero, to refer proudly to "my consulate," at least they could celebrate their entrance upon the office by presenting diptychs like these to powerful friends.

## MONUMENTAL ART

I can dismiss this subject briefly because, except for two angels, and a cross surmounting the globe in the hand of an empress, there is nothing Christian about these pictures—least of all the cruel spectacles in the circus, which were not discontinued until a young Christian named Telemachus made a heroic protest by throwing himself into the arena, where he was devoured by wild beasts.

Plate 105a. An angel, fifth century, in the British Museum.

Plate 105b. Anastasius, Consul in 507 (Paris). The consul holds in his hand the ceremonial handkerchief (*mappa*), which was to be thrown down as a signal for the games to begin—as a mayor or governor now throws out the baseball.

Plate 105c. Areobiundus, Consul in 506 (Leningrad). At the bottom is shown the fight with wild beasts, and the fans avidly watching it.

Plate 105d. The archangel Michael, verso of a diptych of the Consul Severus, 470 (Leipzig).

Plate 106a. Probus, Consul in 405 (Aosta).

Plate 106b. The Empress Ariadne, c. 500 (Florence). She was successively the wife of Zeno (471–491) and Anastasius (491–518). Absorbed as we are here in Christian art, we might forget that the eagle was the emblem of the Empire; but we are more prone to forget that the emperor also laid claim to the cross.

Plate 106c. Boëthius, Consul in 487 (Brescia). The money bags at his feet represent the largess he was about to distribute to the people.


## THE IVORY TABLET AT TRIER
### (Plate 95a)

This tablet was purchased by the city of Trier, where it is now conserved in the treasury of the Cathedral, because it was supposed to commemorate an event which happened in that place, the translation of the body of St. Roch. But though it is not possible to determine its age precisely, it really belonged to a very different time and place—probably to the seventh century, and certainly to Constantinople. Perhaps it was made about 690, when Justinian II was emperor. It represents two archbishops with the pallium seated in a chariot and holding a casket containing the relics of a saint which were translated to Constantinople for the dedication of a church. The church was new, for workmen are still engaged in laying the last tiles on the roof. It was a cathedral church, for it has a baptistery attached to it, and presumably the smaller basilica is a martyrium destined to receive the bones of the saint. The chariot (not unlike that of the Ethiopian eunuch, pl. 27a) is probably adorned with figures of the twelve apostles, for, if it has room for three on each side, it could have six on the back. Presumably it belonged to the Bishop of Constantinople, for if it had been lent by the emperor, it would have been adorned with eagles. The visiting bishop probably brought the relics to the city. Both men have striking features which suggest portraits. The emperor, followed by two courtiers, all holding candles, precedes the chariot on foot, and the procession is welcomed by the empress, who holds a great cross over her shoulder. One may notice that the bust of Christ is depicted (doubtless in mosaic) upon the façade of an immense palace which flanks the cathedral. This imperial palace is crowded to the roof with spectators, and from the windows of the first floor many people swing censers—the traditional accompaniment of a funeral (cf. pl. 151b). The artists in early times knew well how to tell a story. The Italian primitives preserved this art, but it was lost in the high Renaissance —and today it has been regained only in strip pictures.

## ALTAR FRONTAL IN SALERNO
*(Plates 107-118)*

In Southern Italy, where Salerno and Amalfi, as rivals of Venice, prospered exceedingly by maritime trade, art enjoyed an amazing continuity. The best evidence of this is the ivory altar frontal in the Cathedral of Salerno, which competent critics have dated anywhere from the fifth to the twelfth century, and which I am inclined to ascribe to the eleventh. It is composed now of thirty-eight small panels, or fragments of them, which depict thirty-five subjects from the Old Testament and thirty-eight from the New—not to speak of several panels (three at least) which have been lost. Originally these ivory panels may have been made for a chair such as that of Ravenna (pl. 79). Their provenance is uncertain. But wherever they were made, the fact that they have been ascribed to such different dates is an ostensible proof of the continuity of early Christian art. Though I reproduce here only one example of the mosaics in the Cappella Palatina in Palermo, it is enough to show how striking is the similarity between the ivories of Salerno and the mosaics made in the twelfth century for the Norman kings in the royal chapel at Palermo and in the Cathedral of Monreale. Four Carolingian ivories, which have an interest especially for students of ecclesiastical ritual, are introduced here to show how classical art had been transformed as early as the ninth century by the Germanic peoples of Northern Europe, whereas in Southern Italy, and of course in Byzantium, art pursued a more continuous course.

Although all the subjects depicted on the Salerno ivories are described briefly by the captions beneath them, it may be convenient to have a list of them here.

### OLD TESTAMENT SERIES

Plate 107d. The First Day: creation of light (Gen. 1:2-5).—The Second Day: creation of the heavens, represented by the angels (Gen. 1:8).

Plate 107e. The Third Day: creation of plants (Gen. 1:11, 12).—The Fourth Day: creation of sun, moon and stars (Gen. 1:16-19).

Plate 108a. The Fifth Day: creation of fishes and birds (Gen. 1:20-23).—The Sixth Day: creation of beasts (Gen. 1:24, 25).

Plate 108b. The Sixth Day: creation of Adam, and of Eve out of Adam (Gen. 1:26-28; 2:20-23).—The fall of man: the serpent tempts Eve, who eats the forbidden fruit and gives it to Adam (Gen. 3:1-6).

Plate 108c. Adam and Eve (wearing breeches) are driven from Eden (Gen. 3:24).—They both till the ground (Gen. 3:23).

Plate 108d. The sacrifices of Cain and Abel (Gen. 4:3-5).—Cain strangles his brother Abel (Gen. 4:8). The gesture he makes when rebuked by God implies denial: "Am I my brother's keeper?" (Gen. 4:9).

Plate 109a. Noah hears with consternation God's warning of the Flood and the injunction to build the Ark (Gen. 6:12-16).—Noah superintends the building of an ark much more elaborate than the cubical box of earlier art (Gen. 7:5). Upon it, alas, men labor who will not be saved by it; for there are six laborers, and Noah had only three sons.

Plate 109b. God shuts Noah in the Ark (Gen. 7:16).—The dove brings the olive branch, but the raven has not ceased to cling to the Ark (Gen. 8:6-12).

Plate 109c. Noah steps out of the Ark upon dry ground (Gen. 8:18).—Noah and his sons offer unto God a sacrifice of thanksgiving for their deliverance (Gen. 8:20). Here only the *hand* of God appears out of the rainbow; but elsewhere we see that this late artist had not the slightest scruple about representing God in human form.

Plate 109d. Noah and his sons bow down to receive God's blessing (Gen. 9:1); but as the Bible says nothing about a blessing upon the wives, they stand

Three small ivory panels. British Museum. Fifth century.—**a.** Water from the rock.—**b.** Raising of the daughter of Jairus.—**c.** Paul and Thecla; stoning of Paul (*Acta Pauli*).

## ALTAR FRONTAL AT SALERNO

Subjects from the Old and New Testaments. Probably eleventh century. (See pp. 279-296.)—**d.** First day: Light and darkness. Second day: Creation of Heaven.—**e.** Third day: Creation of plants. Fourth day: Creation of sun, moon, and stars.

Pl. 107

Pl. 108

a. Fifth day: Creation of fishes and birds; creation of beasts.—b. Sixth day: Creation of man; the fall of man.—c. Expulsion from Eden; tilling of the soil.—d. Offerings of Cain and Abel; Cain strangles Abel. "Am I my brother's keeper?"

a. Noah ordered to build; he builds the ark.—b. God shuts the ark; the dove with the olive branch.—c. Noah leaves the ark; he offers a sacrifice.—d. Blessing of Noah and his sons; Noah makes wine.

Pl. 109

**a.** Noah's drunkenness; the confusion of tongues.—**b.** Abraham builds an altar; Pharaoh with Sarah and Abraham.—**c.** Abraham pleads for Sodom; Sarah and Abimelech.—**d.** Sacrifice of Isaac; God blesses Abraham.

Pl. 110

**a.** Jacob's dream; Moses at the bush.—**b.** Moses' rod; Moses' leprous hand.—**c.** A fragment, God blesses Abraham.—**d.** A fragment, Moses receives the Law.

Pl. 112

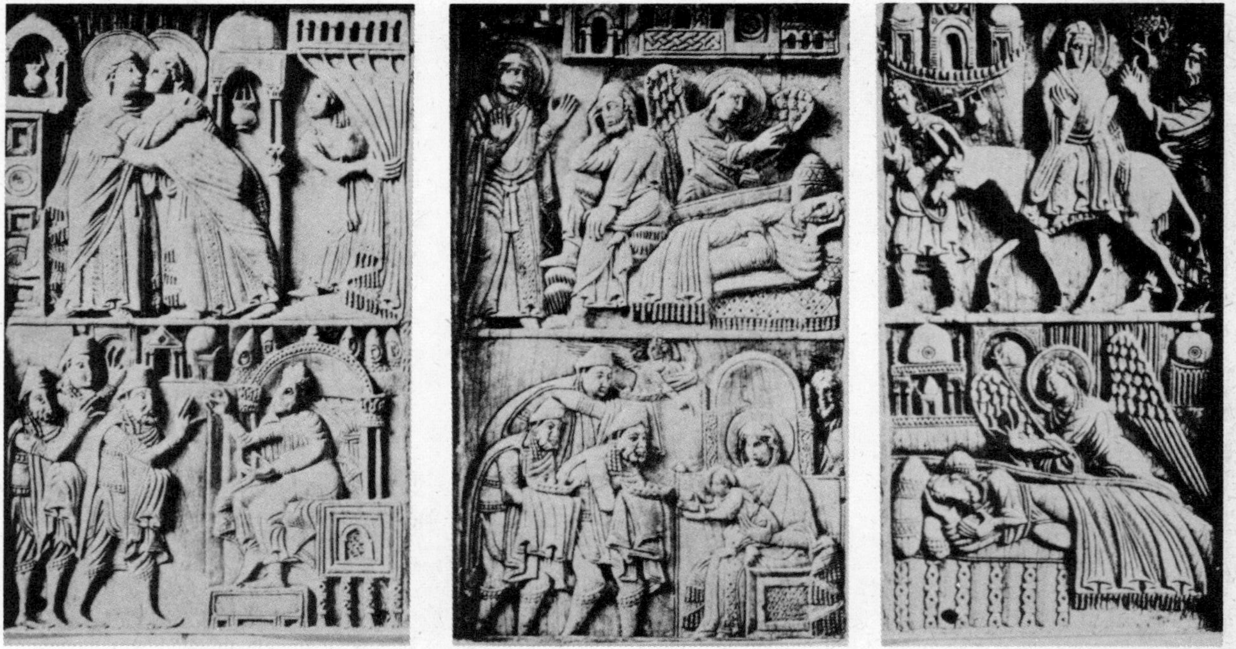

a. The Visitation; the Magi and Herod.—b. Joseph's doubt dispelled; the Magi at Bethlehem.—c. The journey to Bethlehem; "Flee into Egypt."

a. The angels and shepherds; slaughter of the innocents; Elizabeth and John hid in a mountain.—b. Birth of Jesus, with Salome at the right (apocryphal); arrival in Egypt.—c. Presentation in the Temple; the marriage at Cana.

Pl. 113

Pl. 114

**a.** Baptism of Jesus; the Transfiguration.—**b.** Call of Peter and Andrew; the healing of dropsy, blindness, and lameness.—**c.** Christ in glory; raising of the widow's son.

**a.** The Samaritan woman; raising of Lazarus; entry into Jerusalem.—**b.** Feeding of the multitude; Christ washing the disciples' feet.—**c.** The Crucifixion; the Last Supper; soldiers dividing Christ's garments; Joseph buries Christ.

Pl. 115

Pl. 116

a. Breaking bread at Emmaus; blessing the disciples at Bethany.—b. Christ and the two Marys; "When the doors were shut (Jn. 20:19-29).—c. Christ's appearance to all the apostles; Pentecost.

**a.** The blind man washes; the women at the tomb.—**b.** Healing of the paralytic (the angel descends); Christ in limbo.—**c.** The women report the Resurrection; Peter walks on the water.

Pl. 117

The Ascension, or Christ in glory (the only subject filling a whole panel).

Pl. 118

apart as spectators.—Noah discovers or invents the vine; he and his sons make wine, and, alas, he drinks too much. Even the best of boons can be abused.

I am fascinated by Edgar Dacqué's declaration that Noah was the inventor of the grape. Why should I not give it credence, seeing that he speaks like a scientist, and evidently is profoundly versed in geology and palæontology? He assumes that the first men, still closely related to nature, could see profoundly into the mechanism of life, and therefore were able to develop in the most unpromising plants qualities advantageous to mankind—to a degree that even Burbank did not dream of attaining. We do not know how long ago men succeeded in developing from an inconspicuous plant, which still is found by the seaside, all the sorts of cabbage we now eat—including cauliflower, broccoli and sprouts. But the primitive plant from which the grape was developed has not yet been discovered. Christian art, as well as the Scripture, consistently attributes this great invention to Noah, the ninth man after Adam, who by his father was prophetically named Comforter, because "he shall comfort us for our work and for the toil of our hands, by reason of the ground which the Lord hath cursed" (Gen. 5:29).

Plate 110a. While Noah lies uncovered in a drunken sleep, Shem and Japhet, walking backwards so as not to see his shame, cover him with a garment, and rebuke the youngest son Ham for looking upon his father's nakedness (Gen. 9:21-27). We do not often reflect that Noah, as well as Adam, was the father of us all. The Romans still felt the force of the tabu which Ham transgressed, for a son was not permitted to enter the same bath house with his father.—The Lord comes down to see the Tower of Babel and stops the proud work by creating a confusion of tongues (Gen. 11:1-9).

Plate 110b. Abraham builds an altar near Bethel, and in the attitude of a priest celebrating the Eucharist he offers a sacrifice to God (Gen. 12:8). Sarah weeps and Abraham expostulates when Pharaoh rebukes them for deceiving him by saying that they are brother and sister (Gen. 12:14-20).

Plate 110c. Abraham pleads in vain in behalf of Sodom (Gen. 18:20-32). The strange gesture God makes with His right hand (like that of Cain) means denial of the plea.—King Abimelech expostulates with Sarah for deceiving him as she had deceived Pharaoh (Gen. 20:1-18). These are spicy subjects which the illustrators of the Bible were not inclined to overlook (cf. pl. 134c, d).

Plate 110d. When Abraham is on the point of sacrificing his son Isaac, God checks him and points to the ram (Gen. 22:1-14). In this scene and the next the artist really had no need to depict God visibly, for the Bible says, "The angel of the Lord called to him out of heaven."—God blesses Abraham,

## MONUMENTAL ART

saying, "In thy seed shall all the nations of the earth be blessed" (Gen. 22: 14-18).

Plate 111a. Jacob's dream (Gen. 28:10-22). It is obvious that, if angels have wings, they do not need a ladder. But for this solecism we cannot blame the artist severely, seeing that all subsequent pictures reveal the same misconception of God's messengers, who not only descended from heaven but *first* ascended.—God speaks to Moses at the burning bush and commands him to take off his shoes (Ex. 3:1-6).

Plate 111b. Moses confounds the Egyptians by turning his rod into a serpent (Ex. 4:1-5).—Moses' hand becomes leprous (Ex. 4:6, 7).

Plate 111c, d. These are fragments which seem to belong to this series. Beside an altar, which like the Christian altar is covered with a ciborium, God blesses Abraham.—Moses receives the Law on Mount Sinai.

### NEW TESTAMENT SERIES

Plate 112a. The Visitation: Mary visits Elizabeth (Lk. 1:39-56). An inquisitive maidservant peeps from behind the curtain. One will note that picturesque details, architectural features, and adornment of every sort, which were sparingly used in early Christian art, are now very much in evidence, especially in the New Testament series.—The Magi come to Herod (Mt. 2: 1-8). The date of this picture is pretty closely indicated by the fact that the soldiers of Herod's bodyguard who look over the wall wear chain armor and pointed helmets.

Plate 112b. Joseph's suspicion of Mary, who protests her innocence, is dispelled by an angel while he sleeps (Mt. 1:18-25).—The three Magi bring their gifts to the Infant Jesus, who holds out His hands eagerly to receive them (Mt. 2:9-11).

Plate 112c. Mary journeys to Bethlehem upon an ass, and Joseph walking beside her holds her hand tenderly (Lk. 2:1-6).—Joseph is warned in a dream to flee with Mary and the Child into Egypt (Mt. 2:13-15).

Plate 113a. The angels announce the good news to the shepherds (Lk. 2: 8-20).—Slaughter of the Holy Innocents (Mt. 2:16-18). A soldier clad in mail treads upon four infants and is about to kill another before the eyes of Herod. Such poignant scenes of cruelty and suffering were no longer eschewed by Christian artists. The woman standing in what seems to be a tub but is meant to represent a city is "Rachel weeping for her children." Hidden from danger inside a mountain which opened to receive her (according to an apocryphal invention) are Elizabeth and her son John.

Plate 113b. Jesus is born in a stable (Lk. 2:7). But this stable is richly furnished; the ox gazes at the Babe wrapped in swaddling clothes like a mummy and lying in the manger where it was accustomed to eat; Joseph sits at the head of the bed, Salome, the midwife, at the foot.—Arrival in Egypt, where a figure which personifies hospitality, with a wine skin over his shoulder, pours into a bowl a drink for the Infant.

Plate 113c. The Presentation in the Temple (Lk. 2:22-38). It is at a Christian altar, ornamented on the front with a cross, that Simeon stands ready to receive the Child, and Anna the prophetess acclaims Him.—The marriage feast at Cana, where Jesus sits in the place of honor and, at Mary's prompting, commands the servants to fill the water pots (Jn. 2:1-11).

Plate 114a. The baptism of Jesus (Mt. 1:1-11). The dove descends, the hand of God appears, and angels hold the garments of Jesus.—The Transfiguration (Mk. 9:2-13).

Plate 114b. Christ calls Peter and Andrew to be His disciples (Mk. 1:16-18).—Christ heals a man suffering from dropsy, a blind man, and a lame one (Lk. 14:1-6; Mt. 21:14).

Plate 114c. Christ in glory, adored by two angels.—Christ raises the widow's son at Nain (Lk. 7:11-18).

Plate 115a. Christ discourses with the Samaritan woman at the well, and His disciples return bringing Him food (Jn. 4:4-42).—The raising of Lazarus (Jn. 11:1-46). The two sisters kneel at Christ's feet, and Hades blows a horn. Christ enters Jerusalem, children spreading their garments before Him and waving palm branches (Mk. 11:1-11).

Plate 115b. The miraculous feeding of the multitude (Mk. 6:31-44). Christ gives the loaves to His disciples, who distribute them to the people seated "in rows."—The Last Supper (Mk. 14:22-25), in the same sequence we have often seen. Christ, seated in the place of honor (but no longer on a couch), blesses one fish and the loaves. But no longer does He break the bread, for each disciple has his individual loaf—a very little loaf, such as each communicant commonly received at the Eucharist.—Christ washes His disciples' feet (Jn. 13:1-17).

Plate 115c. The Crucifixion (Mk. 15:22-41). Here for the first time, among the pictures shown in this book, we see Mary and St. John the Evangelist standing beneath the cross. It is noteworthy that the *colobion*, a long shirt (cf. pl. 71b) which was used early in the sixth century to cover the nakedness of Jesus, has by this time been discarded, never to appear again.— The soldiers divide among them the garments of Jesus (Mk. 15:24).—Joseph of Arimathea buries Christ's body in his own tomb (Mk. 15:42-47).

Plate 116a. A fragment. By the breaking of bread at Emmaus Christ is made known to the two disciples (Lk. 24:13-32).—A fragment. Christ blesses the twelve (!) apostles at Bethany (Lk. 24:50).

Plate 116b. Christ appears to the two women in the garden (Mt. 28:8-10; Jn. 20:14-18).—Christ appears to the eleven apostles "when the doors were shut," and shows His wounds to doubting Thomas (Jn. 20:19-29).

Plate 116c. Christ appears to all the apostles (Lk. 24:36-39; 1 Cor. 15:17). —The apostles (only eleven including Paul) on the day of Pentecost with tongues of fire on their heads (Acts 2:1-36). Peter holds a cross, Paul a book. Who holds the keys? It is Christ Himself, who is seated in the midst of them!

Plate 117a. Christ heals the blind man, who obeys the injunction to wash his eyes (Jn. 9:1-7).—The two women, bearing spices and swinging censers, come to the tomb and are told by the angel that Christ is risen (Mt. 28:1-8). The two soldiers sleep below the tomb. It may be noticed that the tomb, except for the elaborate superstructure, is well enough devised, but is so diminutive that it looks like a cinerary urn.

Plate 117b. Christ heals the paralytic, who stands up and carries his bed (Jn. 5:1-9). The angel plunges into the pool to "trouble the waters." Note that here the chronological sequence is not observed.—Christ descends to the limbus and frees the patriarchs (1 Pet. 3:19).

Plate 117c. The two women bring to the eleven apostles the report that the tomb is empty (Lk. 24:22, 23).—Peter essays to walk on the water (Mt. 14:27-31). But here Jesus is standing on the shore. Again an episode which belongs to "the days of His flesh" follows events which came after the Resurrection.

Plate 118. This is the only panel which is devoted to one subject only. It represents the *Majestas* of earlier art. Christ is enthroned in glory, framed in a mandorla supported by four angels. Below a group of men and women look up to Him. In the midst of the group a woman with upstretched arms is distinguished by a halo. This is Mary, making supplication for men. It is the *deesis* which Wilpert is fain to detect in earlier pictures, but which I have found only in the Rabula Gospel (pl. 124b), made near the end of the sixth century. It is not strange that we find it in the eleventh.

## THE SIGNIFICANCE OF
## ATTITUDE AND GESTURE

A few remarks about the significance of gestures in early Christian art might be appropriate anywhere. I put them here because in the ivory carvings we have been studying there are some striking instances.

It is often said that Italians speak with their hands. This is more nearly true than most people recognize. To the Sicilians a play without words is perfectly intelligible. It is a popular theatrical diversion. But this was once true of the whole Mediterranean basin where Christian art was developed. Even now in Italy one who would get rid of a beggar has only to shake indolently two fingers of the right hand which hangs limply by his side. The beggar is sure to see this almost invisible gesture, and likely he will depart. Frenchmen and Spaniards also talk with their hands; but they talk thus in vain to people who are not accustomed to listen with their eyes.

The early Christian artists had to rely upon attitude and gesture to make their figures vocal. These artists, even had they possessed the skill to express in the faces they depicted the feelings of the soul, could not have done so in the medium in which they worked. The scale of the ivory carvings was too small, and that of the mosaics, made of coarse tesseræ to be seen at a distance, was too great. So they expressed by attitude and gesture the feelings which moved their subjects. We, alas, not being accustomed to listen with our eyes, do not hear what they say, though they say it very clearly. Even archæologists often fail to discriminate between the woman who mutely touched Christ's garment, the Canaanitish woman who knelt at Christ's feet loudly imploring that He heal her daughter, and Mary who prostrated herself at His feet as an expression of gratitude for the raising of her brother Lazarus. The prevalent confusion about such subjects is due to a lack of attention, and Wilpert did well to devote a whole chapter in his work on mosaics to attitude and gesture. I will not say much about this subject here. Perhaps it is enough that I have emphasized its importance. But here and there in the course of this book I have called attention to significant gestures.

It is important to observe that a particular position of the fingers of the right hand, which in later times was associated exclusively with the act of benediction (and now is dissimilar in the Roman and in the Orthodox communions, though in both it is interpreted as a Trinitarian sign), indicated originally not benediction at all, but was a gesture ordinarily used by secular orators. Both forms were used indifferently in the East and the West as the gesture of Christ when addressing His disciples. He blessed them, indeed, but with the same gesture He also warned them and commanded them.

Goldschmidt, usually a good interpreter, gives a wrong interpretation of the scene reproduced on plate 110c. Understanding it to represent God as He makes a covenant with Abraham at the "smoking furnace" (Gen. 15:17-21), he does not know what to make of the strange gesture of God's right hand—which certainly does not look like benediction. Goldschmidt candidly admits that so marked a gesture must have a meaning. The meaning is plain enough when we recognize that this scene represents Abraham pleading in vain for Sodom (Gen. 18:20-32). In spite of the hypothetical concessions God made, His answer was substantially a denial of Abraham's request. Indeed, we see that the smoke has already commenced to envelop the doomed city. God's gesture of denial is the same that Cain makes on plate 108d. I have often seen such a gesture used in Italy. Not made so stiffly, it is true; but here the awkwardness is explained by the consideration that motion, a shaking of the hand, is essential to this gesture—and that, of course, cannot be indicated in sculpture. It may be that this gesture harks back to the Roman "thumbs down" whereby an emperor denied clemency to a defeated gladiator.

When I planned at one time to decorate with the story of Jesus the high clerestory walls in the American Church of St. Paul-within-the-walls where I ministered in Rome, I had to recognize that scenes so high up, so remote from the beholder, could be made intelligible only by treating the figures as silhouettes and relying upon dumb attitudes and gestures. But I despair of finding a modern artist who would make anything so good as the mosaics in the nave of S. Apollinare Nuovo. And even if the figures were to speak by their gestures, who among us would be able to hear them?

# VII

## BIBLE ILLUSTRATIONS

ALL PICTURES which represent subjects taken from the Bible may be called Biblical illustrations. With such pictures this book has been concerned hitherto. But when I speak of Bible illustrations I mean, of course, pictures which were incorporated in Biblical manuscripts, to explain or to adorn them.

The title I have chosen for this chapter indicates that I have not undertaken an ambitious task. If I had called it *Manuscript Miniatures* or *Illuminations*, the reader might justly expect a thorough disquisition upon a subject with which, alas, I am not competent to deal. Moreover, if such a theme were adequately treated, it could not be comprised within the limits of this handbook. Because it is a field thorny with controversy, I cannot even present the reader with a summary account of the opinions upon which modern scholars agree. Alas, there is not much agreement. The dates of illustrated manuscripts are as hotly disputed as their provenance and their artistic affinities. Even professors are afraid to stick their necks out. One of my "colleagues," who published admirable editions of illustrated manuscripts, does not venture to hint at the date to which he is inclined to ascribe them. I begged two of my most competent "colleagues" to contribute a compendious statement which I could insert here under the name of one or the other of them. I longed to adorn this book with such a jewel. But no, neither would so far commit himself. With difficulty I extracted from them a few plausible dates.

This is said in order to explain why there is no chapter here on manuscript miniatures or illuminations. But in any case I would avoid these words because they suggest a false idea of early Christian Biblical illustrations. The word miniature inevitably suggests, though etymologically it does not imply, a small and exquisite picture; and the word illumination properly means a decorative border or the decoration of an initial letter. Among the early Biblical illustrations there was nothing of this sort. The illustrations in Christian as well as pagan books attempted simply to depict an incident narrated in the text. Besides this, following a pagan convention, the manuscripts of the Gospels had to be adorned with such "portraits" of the Evangelists as the artist might derive from classical models, chiefly the conventional portraits of philosophers and tragedians.

Instead of a dissertation on manuscript illustrations I offer the reader a gift for which he ought to be more grateful: sixty-nine reproductions from ten different manuscripts.

Before proceeding, however, to examine these illustrations in detail, something must be said about early Bible illustrations in general and about the form of the manuscripts.

Book illustrations were not a Christian invention. The illustrated Virgil in the Vatican Library is ascribed to the fourth century, and no illustrated Biblical manuscript is as old. But because this art came into vogue at about the time when the Church was in the ascendant, it was by the Church it was developed, or at least conserved. In the same way it is true of the mosaic art that, though it did not originate in the Church, it was there only that it was developed to a high degree.

Whether the Jews began before the Christians to illustrate the Bible is still a subject of dispute, in spite of the third-century frescoes in the Synagogue at Dura. I am inclined to think that they did. For the frescoes at Dura prove at least that by the middle of the third century liberal Jews were no longer inhibited by the Second Commandment from producing pictorial art. Nowhere were the Jews at once so literary and so liberal as in Alexandria, and it is plausible to suppose that they began there as early as the third century to illustrate the Biblical story. If they did so, whether in manuscripts or in wall paintings, the Christian illustrators must have been influenced by them.

And a word must be said about the form of early books. Everyone knows that the earliest had the form of scrolls or rolls. That was convenient enough for continuous reading; but because the sheets could not be thumbed for the purpose of referring to particular passages, the form of the codex (separate leaves bound together) was used first of all for compilations of law, and was as obviously needed for the books of the Bible, even before its contents were distinguished by chapter and verse. The adoption of the codex was not likely earlier than the fourth century. Hence, in the earliest Christian art we find only the roll. Even after the codex had come into use, the roll figured in art almost as frequently because it was the traditional form. It was an anachronism to put in the hands of Christ a codex, though this was frequently done. One may consult the index *s. vv.* roll and codex. The liturgical books of the Church were, of course, in the form of the codex. The only exception is the *Exultat* roll which the deacon read at the ceremony of lighting the Easter candle. With exception of some parchment fragments and the Joshua Roll in the Vatican Library, all of the illustrated Bibles or Biblical books we now have are codices.

The difficulty about dating the illustrations found in Biblical books is not due so much to doubt about the date of the manuscript as to the fact that the copyists reproduced, and often with great fidelity, not only the text, but the illustrations which accompanied it. Hence manuscripts which are as late as the twelfth century may sometimes be taken as witnesses to the character of illustrations which were painted in the fifth century. This explains why the ivory carvings in Salerno conserve an antique style; for doubtless they in turn were copies from contemporary Bible illustrations which themselves had been copied from earlier manuscripts. Also there was a close correlation between book illustrations and the mosaics which adorned the churches, and in this case the dependence might have been on either side. Such illustrations as we have in the Vienna Genesis and in the Cotton Bible were made primarily for books, but they had an influence upon the mosaics. A book like the Vienna Genesis may have served as a model for the mosaics in the nave of S. Maria Maggiore, which as *mosaics* are not very telling; and it is thought that the Cotton Bible inspired the mosaics in the vestibule of S. Marco. On the other hand, pictures like those in the Rossano Gospel seem to have been copied from mosaics. This consideration immensely heightens their importance. For all the earlier mosaics in the East have been destroyed, either by the fury of iconoclastic emperors or by the zeal of Islam; the Bible illustrations and the ivories are the only evidence of them we have left. The Rossano Gospel gives us some idea of the decoration in hundreds of churches in the time of Justinian. It is thought today by persons upon whose judgment I am compelled to rely (like my "colleague" Professor Weitzmann) that the earliest illustrated Bibles had only small pictures scattered through the text, such as we see in the eleventh-century manuscript reproduced on plate 133a, and in the small figures which accompany the canon tables in the Rabula Gospel (pl. 123). But my meek disposition to bow to authority is somewhat disturbed by the reflection that other manuscripts as old as this have large pictures only, which are separate from the text.

The fact that the Joshua Roll, instead of being regarded as our oldest illustrated manuscript, is now, because of the character of the text, ascribed to the tenth century, demolishes the most ostensible support for Wickhoff's theory of the development of Bible illustrations—and yet his observations are still important. Even if no illustrated roll had been preserved, it would be plausible to assume that the earliest sort of book would be the first to be illustrated, and that in this case the artists would of course adopt the continuous style which had a broad vogue throughout the Empire before Trajan made use of it to tell the story of his conquests on the famous column he erected in Rome, where the emperor appears twenty-three times in the course of one campaign and in the whole course of the spiral picture recurs ninety times. It may still be true, as Wickhoff believed, that what he called the "continuous style" influenced the illustrations of the earliest Biblical manuscripts, even in codices. Perhaps he went too far when he affirmed that pictures which originated in a continuous roll were divided (not always adroitly) into separate pictures to fit such a codex as the Vienna Genesis. Yet the Vienna Genesis (pl. 120-122) exhibits the continuous style in most of its pictures, and like the mosaics in S. Maria Maggiore continues its stories in a lower zone. This is an effective way of telling a story by pictures, as is shown today by the popularity of strip pictures. Unfortunately, I have had some controversy with clergymen and religious publishers who in their zeal to get the Bible stories across adopt the crudest faults of the "funnies," without availing themselves of the advantages of the continuous style which is illustrated in early Christian art. Whether our artists are capable of using such a method I do not know.

## THE VIENNA GENESIS
### (Plates 120-122)

The Vienna Genesis, now that it is commonly ascribed to the fifth century (Wickhoff attributed it to the fourth, Riegl to the fifth, Gerstinger and Buberl to the sixth), can no longer be regarded as the oldest monument of Christian book illustration, a rank which belongs to the Itala Fragment (c. 360) and the pitiable remains of the Cotton Bible. Yet in view of the great number of its illustrations and their excellent state of preservation it still ranks high. "It deserves the first place," says Buberl, "among the three purple codices of the time of Justinian." The forty-eight illustrations (of which twelve are presented here) form the richest cycle of Old Testament illustrations preserved in any manuscript which antedates the iconoclasts. Since it must have had originally ninety-six sheets (instead of the twenty-four we have now), we can reckon that it had one hundred and ninety-two pictures, whereas the Byzantine octateuchs of the twelfth century allot to the First Book of Moses only one hundred and fifty pictures. Its home is sought in all the centers of Greek art, from Naples to Ravenna, from Constantinople to Alexandria and Antioch. Buberl decides in favor of Antioch, remarking that this was essentially a Greek city. John Chrysostom, though he was Bishop of Antioch, knew no Syriac.

As for the style of the pictures, I agree reluctantly with Buberl that the proportions of the figures are "stubby," that, though the background is finely

MANUSCRIPT ILLUSTRATIONS

The Cotton Bible. Early fifth century. (See p. 185.) **a.** The third day: Creation of Plants. —**b.** God speaks to Moses. (Two copies made in watercolor in the sixteenth century.)

Illustrations from the Vienna Genesis. Late sixth century. (See pp. 321-323.)—a. Melchizedek offers Abraham bread and wine.—b. God's promise to Abraham.—c. Lot departs from Sodom, and his wife becomes a pillar of salt.—d. The sin of Lot's daughters.

Pl. 120

Vienna Genesis.
a. Sarah and King Abimelech.—b. Esau returns from the chase and sells his birthright for a mess of pottage.—c. Jacob crosses the ford Jabbok.—d. Jacob strives with the "man" until break of day.

Pl. 121

Pl. 122

a. and b. The story of Joseph and Potiphar's wife.—c. Rebecca at the well.—d. Pharaoh's butler and baker. Vienna Genesis.

Illustrations from the Rabula Gospel. A Syriac manuscript made at Zagba, Mesopotamia, 506. —a. The Eusebian Canon Tables with the four Evangelists: Luke, Mark, John, Matthew. —b. Canon Tables with prophets: Jeremiah, Zechariah, Samuel, and Joshua; New Testament scenes; Annunciation.

Pl. 123

a. Crucifixion and Resurrection.—b. Incarnation and Ascension. Rabula Gospel.

Pl. 124

Illustrations of the Rossano Gospel. Latter part of the sixth century.—**a.** The raising of Lazarus.—**b.** Christ's entry into Jerusalem.—**c.** Cleansing the Temple.

Pl. 125

**a.** Parable of the wise and foolish virgins.—**b.** Christ as the good Samaritan.—**c.** Healing of the blind man at the pool of Siloam. Rossano Gospel.

Pl. 126

**a.** The Last Supper; Christ washes Peter's feet.—**b.** Christ administers the bread to the apostles.—**c.** Christ administers the chalice to the apostles. (In the sixth century it was thus that they came forward to receive the sacrament.) Rossano Gospel.

Pl. 127

**a.** Christ praying in Gethsemane and awakening the apostles. (Until the late Renaissance, this was the only attempt in art to represent night.)—**b.** Christ before Pilate; Judas brings back the money to the high priests and hangs himself. Rossano Gospel.

Pl. 128

a. Christ accused before Pilate.—b. "Jesus or Barabbas?"
Rossano Gospel.

Pl. 129

Two illustrations from a manuscript contemporary with the Rossano Gospel. Paris, Bibliothèque Nationale, Supp. grec. 1286.—**a.** The multiplication of the loaves and fishes, the seven baskets, the multitude being seated on the grass.—**b.** The head of John the Baptist is brought to Herod's feast and received by the daughter of Herodias. Two disciples take charge of his body. On the left Moses displays a scroll: "Whoso sheddeth man's blood, by man shall his blood be shed"; on the right is David whose scroll reads: "Precious in the sight of the Lord is the death of his saints."

Illustrations from the Joshua Roll.—a. The Ambassadors of Gibeon.—b. The messengers report to Joshua on Ai.

Pl. 131

The four Evangelists. Ms. 43, Stauronikta, Mt. Athos. (From A. M. Friend, Jr., *The Portraits of the Evangelists in Greek and Roman Manuscripts.*)—**a.** Matthew.—**b.** Mark.—**c.** Luke.—**d.** John. Though the ms. is late, the pictures are repeated from an early source.

Pl. 132

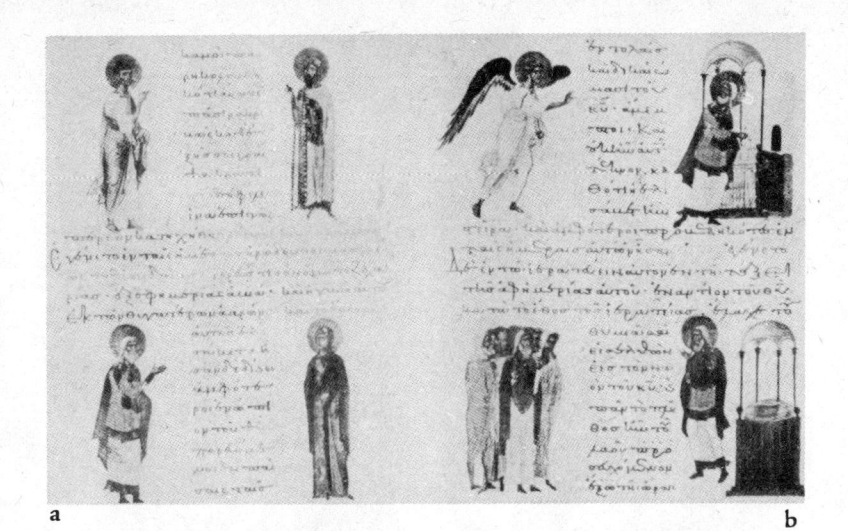

Two pages from a manuscript in the Bibliothèque Nationale, Paris. Ms. grec. 64. Eleventh century.—a. Theophilus and Herod; Zacharias and Elizabeth.—b. Zacharias at the altar; Zacharias and the people.—c. Page from the Paris Psalter. David playing the harp. Tenth century.

Pl. 133

Illustrations from the Octateuch of Smyrna. Eleventh or twelfth century.—**a**. Abraham leaves Haran.—**b**. Abraham builds an altar at Sichem and at Bethel.—**c**. Sarah taken by Pharaoh.—**d**. Sarah given back to Abraham.

Pl. 134

Octateuch of Smyrna.
a. Jacob's dream.—b. Jacob anoints the stone; "How dreadful is this place!"—c. The Hebrews leave Egypt laden with gifts.

Octateuch of Smyrna.
a. Pharaoh and his army; the Hebrews pass through the Red Sea.—b. The song of Miriam.—c. Pharaoh and his army drowned.—d. Aaron's rod buds.—e. Revolt of Korah.

Pl. 136

Octateuch of Smyrna.
a. Death of Miriam.—b. Water from the rock.—c. Death of Moses.—d. Joshua succeeds Moses.—e. Joshua sends spies who meet Rahab at Jericho.

**Octateuch of Smyrna.**
   a. The covenant with Rahab.—b. Rahab hides the spies on the roof, lets them down by a rope, and they hide in the mountains.

Pl. 138

## BIBLE ILLUSTRATIONS

painted in fifteen out of the forty-eight pictures, the dissolution of the feeling of space and the negation of perspective contrast sharply with the mosaics in the nave of S. Maria Maggiore (pl. 66, 67), and that the picturesque features in the mosaics of the arch of that same church (pl. 65) have only a weak echo in these Bible illustrations. Nevertheless, Buberl agrees with Wickhoff that the Vienna Genesis presents an instance of the mixture of the illusionistic style with more definite drawing, a conflict between naturalism and illusionism, "which furnishes a remarkable example of a transition in which all the efforts of art in the preceding centuries find an echo, and in which, on the other hand, the roots of a new art, the art of the Middle Ages, are already observable." Like Riegl, he regards it as an advance, not as a sign of decadence, as Wickhoff thought it. Buberl distinguishes eight artists. Gerstinger is content with six. That is a point upon which I can throw no light.

I call attention only to the fact that the continuous style is used in all the pictures. And in this connection I would remark upon the just distinction Wickhoff makes between what he calls the *continuierende* style, which is suitable for narrative, and the *distinguierende* (a separate scene without adjuncts), suitable for drama, and the *complementierende* (separate, but with allegorical or other adjuncts), which is suitable for epic pictures.

I publish here only a quarter of the pictures preserved in the Vienna Genesis, yet to them I must add some words of explanation, for fear they might remain an enigma to readers who are not well acquainted with early Christian iconography.

Plate 120a. The offering of Melchizedek (Gen. 14:18-20). Melchizedek, King of Salem, "priest of God Most High," here brings forth bread and wine from an altar, like that of the church with its ciborium, and blesses Abraham (cf. Heb. 7:1), whose wives and servants and flocks and herds descend the hill behind him.

Plate 120b. God's promise to Abraham (Gen. 15:1-6). Abraham in a vision during his sleep hears God say, "Fear not, Abraham, I am thy shield and thy exceeding great reward." But Abraham complains, "O Lord God, what wilt thou give me, seeing that I go childless, and he that is possessor of my house is the Damascene Eliezer" [the servant shown below]. A screen divides this scene from the next, where God "brought him forth abroad and said, Look now towards heaven and count the stars, if thou be able to count them: and he said unto him, So shall thy seed·be. And he believed the Lord, and He accounted it unto him for righteousness." In receiving this promise Abraham covers his hands as he did in receiving the offering of Melchizedek.

## BIBLE ILLUSTRATIONS

Plate 120c. An angel compels the family of Lot to leave the doomed city of Sodom (Gen. 19:12-16). While Lot and his family flee from the burning city, Lot's wife stops to look longingly back at her home and is turned into a pillar of salt (Gen. 19:23-26).

Plate 120d. The sin of Lot's daughters (Gen. 19:30-38). It had better be read in the sacred text, which is not prudish. The candor of the Bible is sometimes startling, but this can be embarrassing only to persons who cherish the fond belief that man is a virtuous animal.

Plate 121a. Sarah and King Abimelech (Gen. 20:1-18). Abimelech, King of Gerar, sees Sarah in a fascinating pose and falls in love with her. Abraham, fearing he might be slain by the amorous king, declares that she is his sister, and Abimelech takes her as one of his wives. But from a window of his castle he sees Abraham fondling Sarah, and a voice from God tells him she is Abraham's wife (as well as his sister). Among primitive people a most terrible tabu is erected against adultery, and the king in restoring Sarah to her husband showers upon him many gifts as "a covering of the eyes."

Plate 121b. Esau sells to Jacob his birthright for a mess of pottage (Gen. 25:27-34). Esau returns hungry from the chase, bringing no game, while Jacob comes home with his ass laden with grain. While Jacob is cooking his pottage on the fire, Esau offers his birthright as the first born of the twins in exchange for this food, and Jacob gives it to him.

Plate 121c. Jacob crosses the brook Jabbok (Gen. 32:3-23; 33:1-16). It was a perilous moment for Jacob because he was about to meet his offended brother Esau, who was accompanied by four hundred men. As the sheep and cattle had been sent on ahead, the artist rightly represents that only Lea and Rachel with their children follow Jacob across the bridge. But the bridge was his invention, since the Bible speaks of "the ford Jabbok." The brothers hasten impetuously to meet one another, and when they part, Jacob (appearing for the third time in this continuous picture) kisses Esau's hand—a correct expression of the obsequious manner of address the Bible ascribes to him.

Plate 121d. Jacob strives with the "man" till break of day (Gen. 32:24-32). Before the perilous encounter which ended happily in the previous picture, Jacob had a strange experience: when "he was left alone there wrestled a man with him until the breaking of the day." The man said, "Let me go, for the day breaketh" [when not only spooks but angels must vanish]. But Jacob said, "I will not let thee go, except thou bless me." As a blessing he was given the new name of Israel. The sun rose upon him as he passed over Penuel—the place where he had seen God face to face. I have no misgivings

BIBLE ILLUSTRATIONS

about this story, for I remember well that when I was a small boy I saw God in the swaying spray of a blackberry bush in full blossom.

Plate 122a. Joseph resists the solicitation of Potiphar's wife (Gen. 39:7-12). The lady lies upon a sumptuous bed in her elegant palace, but Joseph escapes from her, leaving his cloak in her hands. Without his cloak he joins the virtuous domestics who outside the door are spinning or playing with a pet dog. Below is depicted an idyll of domestic virtue and felicity: the good mother while she is spinning instructs her little son; one maid-servant is engaged in needlework; another holds the baby in her arms.

Plate 122b. Joseph is charged with attempt at adultery (Gen. 39:13-20). Potiphar returns home. Before he enters his wife's chamber she has instructed her household to corroborate her charge against Joseph. Below, they attest the truth of her story when she displays to her husband Joseph's cloak.

Plate 122c. Going far back in the story, we see Rebecca coming down from the city of Nahor in Mesopotamia to draw water from the well, which here is personified by a female figure pouring water from a jar. Again we see her giving water to quench the thirst of the servant Abraham had sent to find a wife for his son Isaac (Gen. 24:12-67).

Plate 122d. Pharaoh's feast (Gen. 40:1-23). Musicians enliven the occasion; the butler is reinstated; but, alas, the baker is to be seen hanging from a tree, while naughty boys throw stones at him.

### THE COTTON BIBLE
*(Plate 119)*

This precious Bible was injured so seriously by fire that, though critics may learn something from it, none of the pictures are well enough preserved to be reproduced here. The two illustrations shown here are water-color copies made in Paris by Daniel Rebel for the owner, M. Peirasc, in 1621, just before the Bible was sent to England. The loss of this book was irreparable, though, like the Vienna Genesis, it was a copy of an earlier original. It has been said already that the Cotton Bible may have served in its turn as a model for the Genesis mosaics in S. Marco. The two illustrations shown here remind one of Blake. Especially the first, in which three graceful angels signify the Third Day, in which God created plants. In the other God speaks to Moses.

## BIBLE ILLUSTRATIONS

### RABULA GOSPEL
*(Plates 123, 124)*

About the date and origin of this fragment of a Gospel we are left in no perplexity, for the monk who wrote it in Zagba in Mesopotamia gives his name as Rabula, and the date as 586. It is a Syriac Gospel which revises an old Syriac version made by Rabula. Of this important manuscript only six pages are shown here as specimens. The first four (pl. 123) are characteristic because of the elaborate decorations which frame the canon tables—tables which Eusebius made with the intent of harmonizing the Gospels. On the first two we have pictures of the four Evangelists; on the second pair, several prophets and the Annunciation. These elaborate frames may have furnished the suggestion for the decorative borders which became common after Carolingian times. For not only were manuscripts copied many times, but they might be copied in the remotest regions of the world and at a date long posterior to their origin—a consideration which adds greatly to the perplexity of students who seek to trace the origin of styles.

The only full-page pictures this book contains are reproduced on plate 124. They represent the Crucifixion and the Ascension. Both scenes are so far developed in the direction of mediæval art that, if we were not sure of the date, we might think them much later than the sixth century. Christ wears the colobion, while the thieves have only loincloths. Longinus pierces Christ's side with a spear, while another soldier offers Him a sponge soaked in vinegar. Mary and John appear here beneath the cross, opposite the three other women. Here at last the Fourth Gospel (Jn. 19:25-27) has triumphed over the Synoptists. The women who, according to Mt. 27:55, 56, were "beholding from afar," are brought immediately under the cross, and Mary the mother of Jesus (distinguished by a halo) stands alongside of John, not separated from him by the cross as in later art. In the lower zone the two women who come to anoint the body find the tomb empty, the watchmen asleep, and are told by the angel that He is risen. On the right Christ appears to the two women in the garden. The Ascension is like the *Majestas* on plate 118. Mary in the attitude of *deesis* stands in the center of the group. But here there are twelve persons, all of them men, therefore evidently the apostles. They are led by Peter and Paul, and from Mary they are separated by two angels—the "two men in white apparel, which said, Ye men of Galilee, why stand ye looking up into heaven? This Jesus who was received up from you into heaven shall so come in like manner as ye behold Him going into heaven" (Acts 1:9-11).

In spite of the extraordinary honor paid to Mary as Theotokos (Mother of God), it is astonishing to see her figuring here for the first time as a witness, the chief witness, of the Ascension. For we have seen how scrupulously the early Christian artists followed the indications of the Bible, which nowhere brings Mary into connection with the Ascension. But evidently this was not meant to be an historical picture, for St. Paul appears in it. This picture resembles in many respects the panel on the doors of S. Sabina (pl. 94a), where an orant (without a halo) symbolizes the Church. We have seen reason to believe that the artist who carved these doors was, like Rabula, a Syrian. I conjecture that more than a century later, when the symbol of the orant was no longer understood, it was misinterpreted as a figure of the Virgin Mary.

Why, without any Scriptural warrant, is the Virgin Mary (who here is distinguished by a halo) depicted beside the empty tomb engaged in lively discourse with the angel, and again kneeling before the risen Christ in the garden? Why does she appear at the Ascension, and why is St. Paul there? And, if Christ is God, why do the angels presume to crown Him? To such obscure questions Professor Albert Friend is able to give illuminating answers, which prove that these pictures, instead of being simply historical, were meant as an affirmation of the Chalcedonian doctrine. To me he has imparted the results of his astounding acumen as a detective; but the public must wait with patience until these results are published, when to the astonishment of the world it will be shown that the five large pictures in the Rabula Gospel were copied from the mosaics which once existed in the Church of Zion, which can plausibly be attributed to the Empress Eudoxia. Alas that such a one as I must write such a handbook as this—only because such a man as he will not stoop to so lowly a task.

### ROSSANO GOSPEL
*(Plates 125-129)*

A Gospel book, a part of which was preserved at Rossano, a small town in Calabria, is presumably of the same date as the Rabula Gospel, but of a very different character. It is a Greek Gospel, with relatively few pictures, but all of them large, arranged in a broad band which accompanies the text, having beneath them a row of prophets, which, except in the last picture, I have eliminated in order to save space. Only the two pictures of Pilate's judgment occupy a full page. It will be noticed that six of the pictures are in the continuous style. This Gospel is the more precious because it is the only manuscript in Greek which tells the story of Jesus in pictures. For this reason I reproduce here all the pictures which have been preserved. It may be observed that these pictures resemble in some respects the reliefs on the columns in S. Marco, and in other respects the mosaics in S. Apollinare Nuovo.

But here again we are left to our own devices if we would determine where this manuscript originated. Muñoz locates it in Asia Minor, Wulff, Dalton and Diehl in Byzantium, Lüdtke in Syria, Baumstark more precisely in Antioch, and Morey, of course, in Alexandria. It would be exceedingly embarrassing to me if I had to formulate a theory of my own. All that can be said with assurance is that it reflects the character of the pre-iconoclastic mosaics which might be found in any of the churches of the East after the reign of Justinian.

Since I publish here all the illustrations of this Gospel, I must say more in explanation of them than can be said in the captions printed beneath them.

Plate 125a. The raising of Lazarus (Jn. 11:1-46). Mary and Martha kneel at Christ's feet to express their gratitude and adoration. The "many Jews" who came with them are here depicted, some of them expressing astonishment and some consternation at the uncanny sight. Here, as on the columns of S. Marco (pl. 98c, d), it is assumed that someone must assist Lazarus to issue from the tomb, and here too this person, deducing falsely from verse 39 that "he already stinketh," covers his nose.

Plate 125b. Jesus, sitting sideways on an ass, is about to enter Jerusalem (Mk. 11:1-11). Behind him a boy breaks branches from an olive tree and hands them down to the disciples. Christ is met by "a great multitude" carrying palms (Jn. 12:12-13), by youths strewing garments in His path, and by a crowd of jubilant children.

Plate 125c. Christ cleanses the Temple (Mk. 11:15-17). "Those that sold the doves" are getting out hastily with their bird cages, the lambs are being disposed of, the money-changers are clearing their tables, and the artist remembers that Jesus "would not suffer that any man should carry a vessel through the Temple." He is a good commentator, for he understood, as not many do, that for this violent interference with the Temple ritual Jesus was challenged the next day by the "chief priests," saying, "By what authority doest Thou these things, and who gave Thee authority to do these things?" (Mk. 11:27, 28). Here, in the continuous style, this subsequent event is represented in the same picture—and on the left, because the Syrians wrote and read from right to left. Though this is a Greek manuscript, the picture may hark back to a Syrian original.

Plate 126a. The parable of the wise and the foolish virgins (Mt. 25:1-13).

Here Christ Himself is the bridegroom. The virgins carry not lamps but torches.

Plate 126b. The parable of the good Samaritan (Lk. 10:25-37). Although this story is called by St. Luke a "parable," and is certainly not an allegory, Jesus is not ineptly represented as the Good Samaritan. He appears a second time in this picture, giving money to the innkeeper when He reaches Jericho.

Plate 126c. The blind man on being healed washes in the pool of Siloam (Jn. 9:1-7), which hardly looks like a pool (cf. pl. 99a, 117b).

Plate 127a. The Last Supper (Mk. 11:12-25) and Christ washing Peter's feet (Jn. 13:1-17). The couch and the table have the traditional form of the sigma, but in place of the fish we see the bowl into which Judas "dips his hand" (Mt. 26:23).

Plate 127b, c. Christ gives the Holy Communion to the apostles—all twelve of them. This picture does not reflect the situation at the Last Supper, but rather the way in which Christians in the sixth century, and long after that, received the consecrated bread and wine at the Eucharist from the hand of the celebrant. The twelve apostles approach with joyful reverence, bending low but not kneeling, to receive the communion in both kinds. The bread they receive into their hands; the cup is put to their lips. This was a theme often used in Byzantine mosaics. It was an apt theme for the lower zone of the apse just behind the altar, and this picture proves that it was used in the church decoration prompted by Justinian. We are to understand that the apsidal mosaic from which this was copied formed one picture, in which the disciples converge from both sides, though Christ must be represented twice.

Plate 128a. Gethsemane (Mk. 13:32-42). Only in this picture, as a specimen, do I include the row of prophets which accompanied all of them. One of the prophets is evidently David, for he wears a crown. At the right of the picture we see Christ prostrated in prayer; at the left He awakens His disciples. Here again the sequence is from right to left, as on plate 125b, whereas on 127b and 128b (Judas) it is from left to right. The artist has attempted to paint a scene by night. Not till the seventeenth century was such a thing attempted again.

Plate 128b. In the upper zone Christ is brought before Pilate and accused by the high priest (Mk. 15:1-14). Pilate seated high upon his chair with the woolsack under him wears a diadem as the representative of the emperor. As a judge he has in front of him a table spread with a white cloth, upon which ink and writing utensils are placed. The cloth has embroidered upon it the portraits of the reigning emperors (*sacri vultus*), and behind the chair stand two iconophors carrying standards which also bear the images of the emperors. At the time of Jesus' trial there was, in fact, only one emperor, Tiberius; but in the sixth century men had become accustomed to having two or more at the same time. The high priest, accompanied by an orator, brings Jesus before the judge. Roman court officials stand on the other side, looking scornfully towards the Jews. The table and the iconophors recall one of the reliefs on the column of S. Marco (pl.100b). Pilate shows his embarrassment by resting his chin upon the scroll held in his right hand.

In the lower zone Judas brings back the thirty pieces of silver to the chief priests, and the elder of the two, with every sign of abhorrence, refuses to receive the money. In this continuous picture the sequence is to the right, where Judas is to be seen hanging pitiably from a tree.

Plate 129. The trial of Jesus (Mk. 15:15-20). Pilate is seated as before, but as the trial is now in progress the clerk of the court is diligently taking stenographic notes on a tablet he holds in his hand (cf. pl.100c). The Jews who now crowd in on both sides cry loudly for the condemnation of Jesus. But Pilate is now angry and determined. He seems to say, "Why, what evil hath He done?" The six figures in the lower zone are put there because the artist could not deal otherwise with the problem of perspective. They are supposed to be standing in front of Pilate. Barabbas, naked to the waist, and with hands tied behind his back as a dangerous criminal, is contorted by the effort to release himself from his guard.

On plate 130, I supplement the Rossano Gospel by a contemporary manuscript which is similar to it and is now in the National Library in Paris (Supp. grec. 1286). In this manuscript too the prophets figure, but at either end of the pictures instead of below. The first picture (pl. 130a) represents Herod's feast (Mk. 6:17-29). The head of John the Baptist is brought in on a platter ("charger") and received by the daughter of Herodias. Near at hand is the prison, where two of John's disciples watch over his body with every sign of consternation. Herod sits in the place of honor at the right horn of the sigma. The prophets and their prophecies are chosen appropriately. On the right is King David, whose scroll reads: "Precious in the sight of the Lord is the death of His saints" (Ps. 116:15). On the left is Moses, whose scroll reads: "Whoso sheddeth man's blood, by man shall his blood be shed; for in the image of God made He man" (Gen. 9:6).

The second picture (pl. 130b) represents the multiplication of the loaves and fishes (Mk. 6:34-44). The situation is like that in a mosaic in S. Apollinare Nuovo (pl. 76d), only here, as in the Rossano Gospel, Christ has a beard. The seven baskets of bread are in the middle. On the right sits the multitude, as on plate 115b.

## JOSHUA ROLL
### (Plates 138b, 131b)

The Joshua Roll in the Vatican Library is better preserved than any other Christian manuscript of this form, and it is the only roll which is illustrated. In this case the illustrations form a continuous band accompanying the text. What is left of this manuscript (perhaps about a half of the original) contains twenty-three sheets of parchment which now for safekeeping are separated and pressed between boards. It is sad to see this manuscript fallen from its high estate. For not long ago it was accounted one of the oldest and in many respects the most precious of illustrated Bibles; but now experts affirm that the writing is not earlier than the tenth century, and archæologists think they are generous if they admit that the pictures might have been copied from a sixth-century original. But I cannot get it through my head why it might not be referred just as well to an earlier original. Though it has now fallen into disrepute, there is something about it which strikes me as very ancient. If the roll was the earliest form of book, it is plausible to suppose that it was the first form illustrated. This is the only example we have of an illustrated roll; and even if the pictures are not so old as has been thought, they may teach us at least how such books were illustrated.

However that may be, the illustrations of the Joshua Roll certainly tell the story very well. I should like to reproduce more of them. But because they have not been adequately published I educe here only the two pictures which were contained in my first book. It will be seen that, whatever date be assigned to them, they have an interest of their own, the interest of definite and lively drawing. The movements are rapid and decided. The quick tempo reminds one of the Utrecht Psalter, which modern critics extol as a precursor of the style of Rembrandt.

Plate 132a. The ambassadors of Gibeon come to Joshua (Josh. 9:3-27). Two wily men of Gibeon (upper left-hand corner), pretending to come from a distant city, wearing old garments and clouted shoes, carrying rent wineskins and mouldy bread, hope by this ruse to make a covenant with Joshua which would save their town (upper right-hand corner), which actually was close to the place where the Israelites were encamped. They bow low before Joshua, who is completely taken in, and makes peace with them without asking "counsel of the mouth of the Lord." A male figure holding the horn of plenty symbolizes the fertility of the land. In the next section of this continuous picture Joshua, having learned of their deceit, rebukes the ambassadors, who, bowing more lowly than before, exculpate their people and obtain the promise that they shall not be slain but shall be made "bearers of wood and drawers of water" in the service of the Israelites.

Plate 131b. Joshua's messengers return to him with a report on the condition of the town of Ai (Josh. 7:2, 3).

### THE FOUR EVANGELISTS
(Plate 132)

We have many pictures of the Evangelists, because it was customary for bookmakers to publish at the beginning of a work the portrait of the author. But do not jump to the conclusion that the pictures of the Evangelists must be authentic portraits. These four "portraits" I take from Albert Friend's enchanting book on *The Portraits of the Evangelists in Greek and Roman Manuscripts*. I call it enchanting because it has something of the excitement of a detective story—which is the same as to say that it is like Henri Fabre's study of insects. In such a work the quest has greater interest than the achievement. But the result is interesting too, although it is negative. The conclusion is that the backgrounds are taken from theatrical scenery, and the "portraits" copied from what passed as the portraits of celebrated dramatists and philosophers. Professor Friend tells me that he has since succeeded in identifying them all.

### THE PARIS PSALTER
(Plate 133c)

The illustrations of the Paris Psalter, though they are found in a manuscript of the tenth or eleventh century, were regarded fifty years ago as copies of a fourth-century original. Although no one today derives them from so early a source, the one picture presented here is still precious as an example of the Greek way of illustrating an epic or an idyllic theme, in what Wickhoff calls the *complementierende* style: a unified picture with accessory figures which explain or enhance the significance of the central subject. Here David, in company with sheep and goats and his faithful dog, plays on the harp. A recumbent allegorical figure indicates the place: "the mountain of Bethlehem." "Harmony" is seated beside King David. Some of the accessories are too Greek for a Christian picture, for a nymph peeks from behind a column, which in the pagan manner is marked as sacred by a sash.

### THE OCTATEUCH OF SMYRNA
(Plates *134-138*)

Strangely enough, the most copious source of information about early Bible illustrations are the late Byzantine manuscripts which, because they contain the first eight books of the Old Testament, are called octateuchs. There are several of them, and because they agree generally in style and in their way of dealing with their subjects, we can infer confidently that they are copied from earlier originals, and with much plausibility that their models were very early. Because here the illustrations are small and are scattered in the text to which they refer, it is argued—but without anything like a compelling logic—that such was the way the earliest Christian manuscripts were illustrated.

I select from the Octateuch of Smyrna the twenty-five subjects (nineteen photographs) which are presented here. They are enough to give a fair notion of the character of the work as a whole; but because they are only selections from a far greater number, it would serve no purpose to give a list of them here.

In this case there is no dispute about the *provenance* of the manuscripts, since everyone agrees to call them Byzantine, implying that they were copied in Byzantium, which indeed was the only place in the East where they could have been made in the eleventh century when Islam prevailed everywhere else. And yet these pictures are not characteristically Byzantine. This is a reason for tracing them to earlier models.

But as to the date of these manuscripts, there is wide diversity of opinion. I note with dismay that one of my eminent "colleagues" affirms that the Octateuch of Smyrna cannot be dated later than the eighth century—and yet another, who is no less eminent, is presumptuous enough to date it in the eleventh. What then am I to think? I solace myself with the reflection that it really makes very little difference, so long as all are agreed upon the main point, that the illustrations represent an early stage of Christian art.

We hardly can pass a more favorable judgment upon illustrations than to say that they stand in no need of explanation. One cannot often say so much of modern pictures. Yet what are illustrations for except to illustrate. The illustrations in the Octateuch of Smyrna, when seen in connection with the text, or even with the short captions I have placed under them, tell the story very well. What I have to say about them is by way of comment—not explanation.

The story of Sarah and Pharaoh (pl. 134c, d) is so much like the story of Sarah and Abimelech as told in the Vienna Genesis (pl. 121a) that no further comment is needed here. I would remark, however, that in the picture of Jacob's dream (pl. 135a) the artist has duly noted the fact that the angels were "ascending and descending," but seems to have thought that only ascending angels had need of wings. I draw attention to plate 136d, where the tabernacle or "tent of meeting" is represented as a solidly built house. The artists had perhaps never seen a tent. Here the Hebrew altar has the form of the altar and ciborium of the Christian church. I take this to be the earliest form of ciborium, because it has the shape of the inverted cup which gave it its name. The dome of such a ciborium could not have been completed in masonry. It might have been made of wicker work (pl. 128b, 120a), like the primitive wattled hut with which it was perhaps associated. But it could also be made of metal, and we have seen that the earliest ciborium of which we have any record was made of gold and silver by Constantine for the Lateran Basilica. The story of Rahab and the spies is told with elaborate detail on plates 137e and 138a, b. Joshua sends them forth; they meet Rahab outside her house, which by a bush is marked as a wine shop, while her profession is indicated by a label; they make a covenant with her; she hides them on the flat roof when the messengers of the King of Jericho come to seek them; she lets them down by a cord from the wall of the city; they hide in the mountain (perhaps in the conspicuous tomb) until the pursuers have passed by without discovering them.

# VIII

# INDUSTRIAL ARTS

IN MY earlier book a chapter was devoted to what I called *Minor Arts*. But such minor arts as ivory carvings and manuscript illustrations have already been dealt with as invaluable indications on a small scale of the character of the monumental art which in the East has almost totally disappeared, and in the West is only partially preserved.

Therefore little is left for us to deal with here except what may properly be called industrial arts. That, of course, is a subject too big for a single volume. Fortunately, we have no reason to include so large a theme in the study of Christian art. It properly belongs to pagan archæology, for Christianity did nothing to further the progress of industry in the Roman Empire and was not able to check its decline. The Church was properly concerned only with the *Civitas Dei* and made no technological contributions to Græco-Roman civilization. Christians shared with their fellow citizens the secular customs which were characteristic of the culture in which they lived. They dressed like other men, and their houses, furniture, decoration and utensils were in no respect peculiar. It would appear therefore that there was no such thing as a Christian industrial art, nothing whatever that might properly be included under the title I have chosen for this chapter.

In fact, there is very little. But curiously enough, one very minor art fell almost exclusively into the hands of Christians. At least it can be said that only Christian examples have been found in large numbers. This is the art of decorating glass vessels, chiefly the *fond* of cups, with figures designed on gold leaf, which after it was applied to the glass was engraved, sometimes colored, and covered with a thin glaze. Of this art something must be said, if only for the reason that fifteen examples are illustrated here (pl. 141-142). The three hundred examples of this art published by Garrucci have a considerable importance for Christian iconography. For though they merely repeat subjects which are found in the frescoes of the catacombs or on the sarcophagi, they demonstrate the broad popularity of these subjects.

This art seems to have originated about the middle of the third century, and it had no considerable vogue after the end of the fourth. The subjects were drawn not only from the earliest cycle of sepulchral art in the catacombs (the Good Shepherd, Jonah, the miracles which attested God's power), but also from themes which emerged after the Peace (Adam and Eve, Daniel killing the dragon, etc.). It is characteristic of this art that Biblical subjects are supplemented by pictures which are purely personal, depicting a married couple, or a family group, or (as in the first illustration) a master artisan presiding over the workmen in his busy shop. We learn from this that such articles were commonly made to order. Often they display the names of the persons represented. Hence when they were pressed into the fresh plaster on the walls of the catacombs, the bottom of the cup might at least be preserved to identify the place where a dear one was buried. A revealing characteristic is the inscription PIE ZESES, which occurs very often. Though written in Roman letters, it is a Greek toast meaning Drink! Live!—just as we might say in a foreign tongue *Lebe wohl!* We infer from this that such cups were made for convivial occasions, such as marriage feasts and funeral banquets, which the Christians took over from the pagans. The fact that this art did not outlast the fourth century shows that the Church was soon obliged to suppress customs which did not comport with the sobriety Christianity enjoined. We know that the primitive custom of holding *agape* (love feasts) was eventually discarded because it encouraged disorderly conduct.

## TEXTILE ART
### (Plates 143, 144)

Of course weaving, tapestry and embroidery were not specifically Christian arts; yet something may be said about them here, not only as a contribution to a correct understanding of civil and ecclesiastical dress (a subject which will be treated briefly in the next chapter), but to illustrate the curtains and altar covers which were a conspicuous part of church decoration.

Textile art is the art which stands in the closest and most necessary relation to human life. It is a matter of course that in classical and in early Christian literature there are innumerable references to it. We know the names which were used to denote the texture and the color of different stuffs, and we have descriptions more or less detailed of textile decorations, with indications of their use. But such fabrics are the most perishable of all the materials used in the arts, and if the stuffs themselves are not preserved, the names which were familiar and clear to the ancients signify little to us. What significance can we attach, for instance, to the many words which denote various shades of "purple" or to the terms descriptive of different qualities of silk, or to the accounts of figured stuffs, if we do not know by what means they were

INDUSTRIAL ARTS

a. Bronze lamp. Jonah and the gourd.—b. Terra-cotta lamp. Martyr exposed to a lion.

Pl. 139

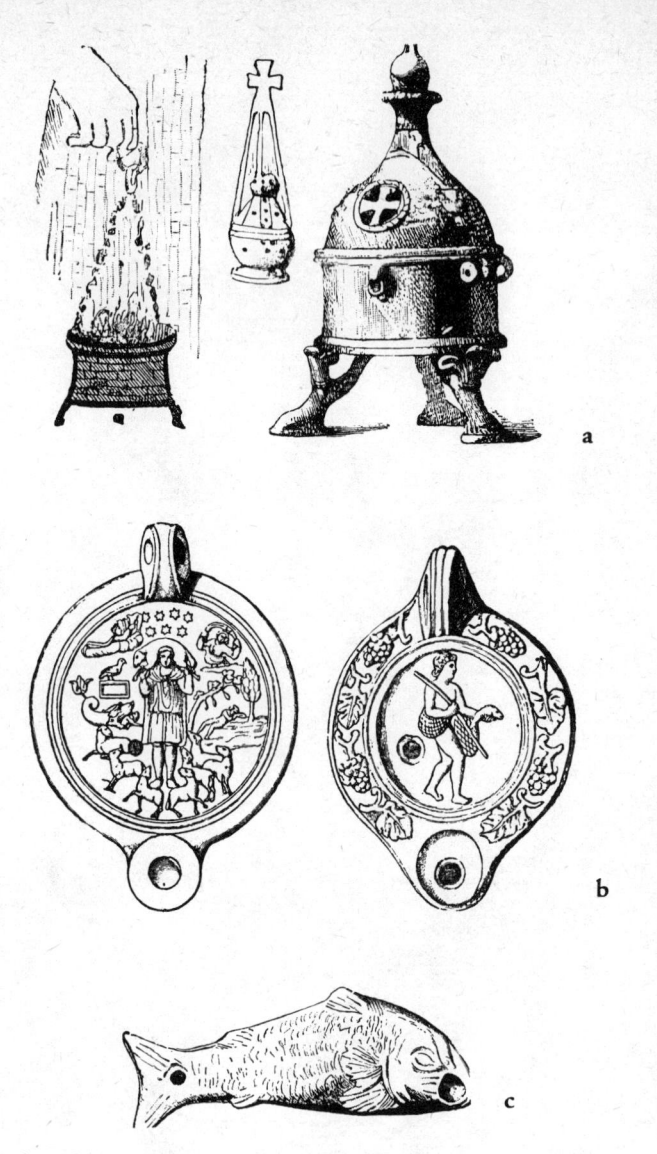

**a.** Censers of the fifth and sixth centuries.—**b.** Terra-cotta lamps with Christian symbols.—**c.** Terra-cotta fish used as a lamp.

Pl. 140

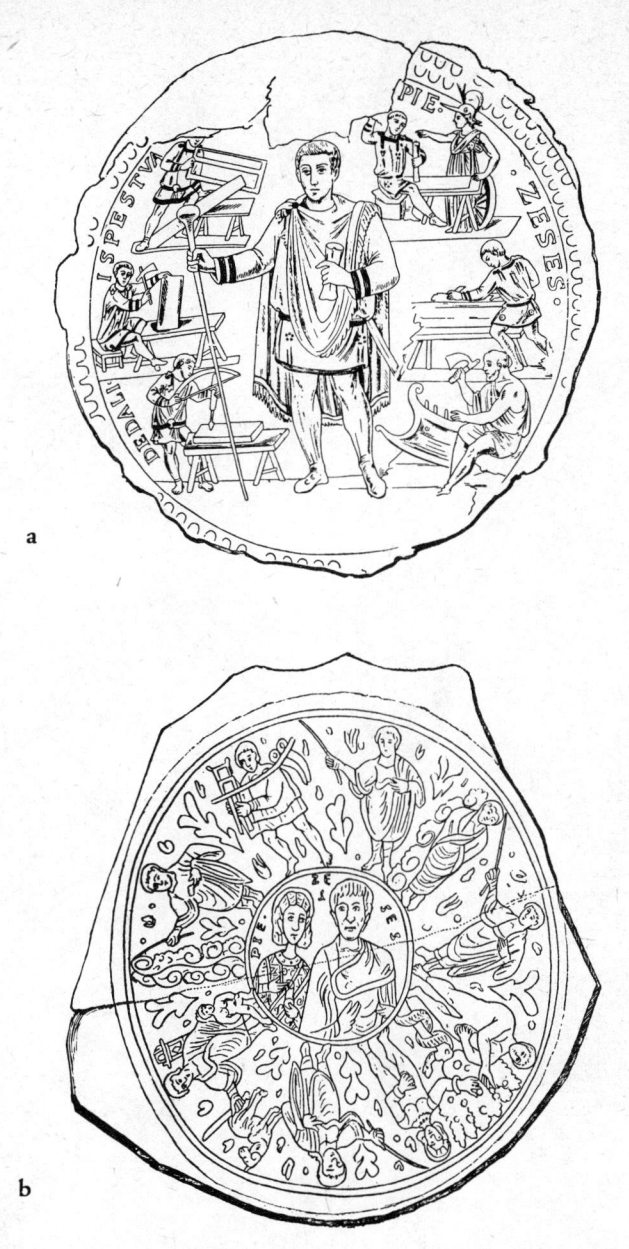

a. Gold glass with a toast to Dædalus, "inspector" of a carpenter shop.—b. Bottom of a gold glass with toast to a married couple and themes from early Christian art.

Pl. 141

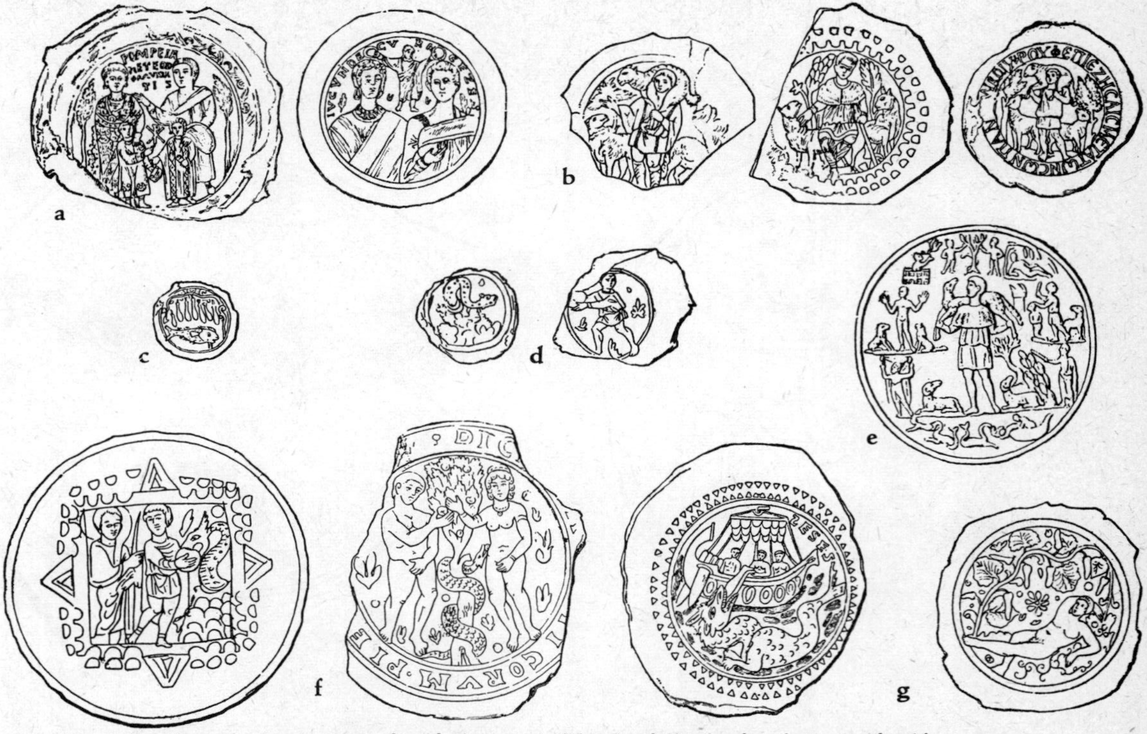

Pl. 142

a. Family groups on bottoms of gold glasses.—b. The Good Shepherd on bottoms of gold glasses.—c. Fish under gourds.—d. Daniel and the dragon.—e. Bronze medal.—f. Daniel and the dragon; Adam and Eve.—g. The story of Jonah.

EGYPTIAN TEXTILES
(pl. 143-144)
Fourth to seventh centuries. (See pp. 196-197.)

a. Stole with silk embroidery. Details: The Raising of Lazarus; Crucifixion; Mary Magdalen at the tomb. Seventh century.—b. *Clavus*. Silk embroidery. Seventh century.—c. *Segmentum* in tapestry. Seventh century.—d. *Segmenta* in tapestry. Third or fourth century.—e. "Egyptian cross," part of a *clavus* in tapestry.

Pl. 143

Pl. 144

a. A curtain. Tapestry or linen (reconstructed).—b. Curtain with design current from the third to sixth centuries. Victoria and Albert Museum, London.—c. Silk brocade. The Empire and the Church. Sixth century.

## INDUSTRIAL ARTS

executed? Painted representations of clothing, curtains, etc., have till lately constituted the only evidence which throws light upon classic textiles; and considering the character of most of the paintings which have been preserved for us, and the ruinous condition in which they have been transmitted, this evidence is far from being complete or reliable. Lately, however, there have been discovered in Egypt inexhaustible treasures of textile stuffs; and the examples which are now distributed among the great museums of the world are sufficient to illustrate every term used in this connection by classical or Christian authors. Unfortunately, the value of this great store of information is still only potential: the study of its relation to ancient literature and life has hardly been begun. This chapter is the poorer for lack of such study, which offers a rewarding field for investigation. In museums an immense amount of this material is stored in boxes and never seen.

But upon the face of them, and quite apart from the consideration of classical texts, these Egyptian finds bear clear witness to almost all phases of this important art from the third century to the seventh. One who is acquainted with the art of weaving can detect by an inspection of these fabrics the technical processes which were employed in making them. But the most important evidence they give is quite on the surface. They show at a glance the material, the texture, the quality, the colors and the forms which characterized ancient textiles and dress. They illuminate, for example, the character of the altar coverings and curtains which were an important part of church decoration. This, and the character of ancient dress, are the aspects of this subject which interest us most closely here.

But it is necessary in the first place to describe generally the character of these finds and to give some account of their discovery. The first find of this sort was made at the beginning of the nineteenth century at Sakkarah. There in 1801 a tunic was brought to light which came into the possession of the Louvre, and later other textiles of the same sort were collected in Turin and in the British Museum. But there was no methodical exploitation of the site, and it is at the end of the nineteenth century only that an overwhelming abundance of material has been furnished by the burial ground of Achmim in Upper Egypt, on the right bank of the Nile, the ancient Egyptian Chemmis (in Ptolemaic times Panopolis), renowned for its sculptors and masons as well as for linen weaving. This site has been exhausted—unfortunately not by intelligent exploration, but by indiscriminate pillage on the part of the Arabs who took no thought to preserve intact the contents of separate graves, and did not even preserve individual garments in their integrity, but simply stripped off the decorative patterns for which they were sure of finding a market. This was perhaps the richest site, but not the only one. Several other burying grounds have been explored with some success. Particularly noteworthy are the explorations at Antinoë, begun in 1897 by the Musée Guimet and finished the following year with the cooperation of the Chamber of Commerce of Lyons. These excavations were very fruitful, and of course were conducted under scientific direction. The finds were exhibited for a month in Paris and then divided between the two subscribing parties. They are not rich in distinctively Christian patterns, but they illustrate classical textiles very well, and afford a good basis for comparison with modern products.

These Egyptian finds have been studied in a short monograph by Gerspach, Director of the Gobelins. His professional judgment is of course very valuable. They have been studied from a broader and more distinctively archæological point of view by Dr. R. Forrer. His numerous works (the most important of which are named in the bibliography) are profusely illustrated, generally in color. Forrer's works refer exclusively to his own collection, which is thoroughly representative but has a special interest for us because it is rich in distinctively Christian patterns.

The excavations reveal a very simple mode of burial, which remained unchanged from the third to the seventh century. The body, with hardly any attempt at embalming, was clothed in ordinary garments, perhaps the best, bound to a cypress bed, and without a coffin or even a shroud was buried at the depth of about five feet in the dry sand which insured for so long a time the survival of the textiles which are found with the corpse. Hence for the most part we find only garments in these graves. If they were properly studied, they would furnish a complete picture of the dress of all classes from the third to the seventh century—not in Egypt alone, but generally throughout the empire, Egypt being the chief purveyor of linen garments in particular. Many of these garments, whether they are of linen, cotton, silk, or wool, are still fit to wear, and in most cases the color is well preserved.

Upon the evidence of these finds, Gerspach affirms that almost every product known to modern textile art was produced in great perfection by the ancients. An overwhelming proportion of the material is of linen or cotton. A colder country would show a greater proportion of woolen garments. But even here the weight and warmth of the woolen garments was sometimes extraordinary (to protect the body from heat, as is necessary today in that country), and linen was often woven like Turkish towelling (rough only on one side, however), to make warm tunics and palliums. The curtain illustrated on plate 144b has this texture. Cotton was sometimes woven like Canton flannel; or, by the same sort of weaving, a warmer garment with a more beautiful

## INDUSTRIAL ARTS

surface was produced by a woof of fine glossy wool. For greater warmth and perhaps protection against rain (though this would not often be needed in Egypt) a pure felt was used, or a felt beaten into a heavy woolen fabric. Light textures were the rule, but these were not often well preserved. The linen was sometimes finely woven, and always evenly. Light cotton tunics were common, and transparent fabrics were made of wool to be used as veils.

From first to last silk was very rare. Even in decorative pieces it is used only in the proportion of one per cent. How rare it was even in Rome we can judge from the mention of two tunics of half-silk (*subsericus*), an imperial gift made by Valerian and Gallienus to the Claudius who was to be their successor. Elagabalus was the first emperor who wore garments of pure silk (*holosericus*). At a later time silk was, of course, far more common in Rome than it would be in a small Egyptian city. As we find it in the Egyptian burying grounds it was employed mainly in the applied patches (*segmenta*) which were used for the adornment of commoner fabrics. Until after the fourth century it was generally used in one color, the sheen of the material giving sufficient delight to the ancients. It was always too thin for any but decorative uses. The Egyptian weavers resorted to various devices for economizing this rare substance. In the case of a light woolen veil in Forrer's collection the border is decorated by threads of silk shot through the woolen mesh. Another device consisted in winding linen threads with fine strands of silk, so that when woven they had the effect of a pure silk fabric. Perhaps in these two methods we may see the distinction the Romans made between the words *subsericus* and *tramosericus*. But they made a further distinction between *sericus* and *holosericus*.

Patterns woven in silk were made perhaps as early as the fourth century. Such ornaments were woven in the shape of a *clavus* with a round or lanceolate finial, ready to be attached to any garment. A piece of such a *clavus*, probably of the fifth century, is shown on plate 144c. The figures are in cream white, the natural color of the silk, against a silver-gray ground. Silk embroidery did not come into common use till the fifth century, and under "Byzantine" influence.

Linen was rarely dyed, and frequently it was unbleached. The dying of cotton, being easier, was more common. A brick-red dye made of tannin and iron was preferred. Wool, of course, was more often and more richly dyed, but always in solid colors, except when it was adorned with embroideries. It is well known that the pallium, like the toga, was commonly white, and was decorated only at the four corners. Palliums both of cotton and wool woven with broad stripes in different colors are found in the graves, but this was not the prevailing fashion, and this garment fell into disuse too early to be affected by the growing taste for striking color effects in dress. Women continued to use the palla much later, when it was the fashion to decorate the whole piece with a diapered pattern. The dalmatic was frequently adorned in the same way, and upon cotton the patterns were sometimes printed. On the other hand, the *pænula* (precursor of the chasuble) was always of one solid color, often some shade of "purple," though (as the mosaics also show) the natural chestnut brown of some of the Caucasian wools was often retained. For its sole decoration it has a fringe.

The richest dyes were not often lavished upon a whole piece of cloth. The choicest products of the dyer's craft appear only in the small patches of tapestry or embroideries (*clavus, segmentum, gammadia, paragauda*) which showed up like gems against the meaner fabric they decorated. It may be remarked as a peculiarity of the ancient use of textiles that the commonest fabrics (plain linen or wool) were used where we would expect the richest, as for altar cloths and curtains, whether in the church or the palace. This material was exalted by the borders (*paragaudæ*) and the *segmenta* which adorned it.

To our surprise we learn from the Egyptian finds that the decorative patches above mentioned (which we see often in ancient pictures) were not wrought by any of the stitches which are classed generally as embroidery, but were woven as tapestry. This tapestry was always made of colored wool upon a linen backing, and it was wrought precisely as were the Flemish tapestries and the Gobelins, upon an upright frame and from behind. When used upon a linen garment the decoration might be woven into the fabric, as they do now in Dalmatia. Upon cotton and wool it was always *appliqué*, as it often was upon linen. Lasting longer than the cloth it ornamented, it could readily be transferred to a new garment.

A simpler classical taste in color yielded in the fourth century to a preference for gaudy colors. Distinctively Christian designs belong, of course, to the later period. The refinement of classical taste is shown by moderation in the use of colors. It prized not a variety of color but the sheer beauty of a single precious dye, especially in the many colors classed as "purple," which applied to dark carmine red, reddish brown, violet, dark blue, and black. There is mention even of a "white purple." The pattern was pricked out by a strand of white linen thread. It was intricate in detail, though the total effect was simple. The designs were for the most part geometrical, combined with conventionalized vegetable forms, and animal figures were introduced within the frame of the main design. Plate 143d is the only illustration given here of classical *segmenta*. More ambitious pieces often represented mythological scenes, and later Christian subjects replaced them. It was the *segmentum* rather than the narrow *clavus* which gave room for artistic treatment and pictorial scenes. The *segmentum* was commonly round or square; but other shapes were used, and for the center of a curtain or a cover a star-shaped figure composed of superimposed squares was common. The way in which these pieces were employed for decorating a garment is described in the following chapter. Their use upon curtains, table covers, etc., was similar. Except for the *clavus* and the *tablion,* they were placed only in the center and at the corners. Plate 144b represents a curtain of about the fourth century—plain tapestry of brown "purple" wool woven into the linen. The angular figures which decorate the four corners were a very common ornament. They were called *gammadiæ* from their resemblance to the Greek letter gamma. *Segmenta* in the shape of the cross or of the monogram were often used upon garments, curtains and altar cloths. The letters which in early art are frequently to be seen as decorations of the pallium were tapestry *appliqués*. It is useless to seek in them for any other meaning beyond mere adornment. Plate 144a shows a more elaborate curtain with a distinctively Christian design, and of a later period. Even if it had not been found in Egypt, the Nile keys would betray its origin. The curtains represented in some of the mosaics at Ravenna (pl. 63b, 75d) are decorated with *segmenta;* others (pl. 147, 74a) have a diapered pattern covering the whole surface. The use of *appliqué* ornaments of a simple form such as we have mentioned lasted throughout many centuries. The only change was in the character of the tapestry itself. There was some deterioration in color during the fourth century, and still more in accuracy of design. The same patterns were repeated, but with less care in the execution of the geometrical designs and more conventionality in the treatment of animal forms. The decadent taste of the fifth and the following centuries found compensation for crudeness of design in a lavish use of colors. Not only were new colors employed, but they were used in vivid combinations. Side by side with the traditional classic patterns there came into use designs of an Oriental character which evidently were copied from imported fabrics but modified in various ways to suit the requirements of classic art, or adapted to the expression of Christian symbolism. The sacred tree of Assyria with its animal guardians is an example of such Oriental motifs. To the same influence we must ascribe the fashion of decorating the whole surface with small designs, especially the lozenge, the heart, the trefoil and the leaf (i.e., the diamonds, hearts, clubs and spades which we have on our cards), which were popular on Byzantine textiles in the tenth century and became common in the West after the Crusades. Though these figures had no relation to Christian symbolism, they were commonly used by the sixth century in ecclesiastical embroidery.

Hardly before the fifth century were Biblical subjects depicted upon the tapestries or embroideries which we find in Egypt, though we have seen that as early as the fourth century Asterius rebuked wealthy women for adorning their garments with pictures of Christ and His apostles, and with stories of His miracles. We are to understand that such pictures were wrought in tapestry upon the *segmenta* and were therefore not very ostentatious. The *Liber Pontificalis* does not mention such pictures before the eighth century, when such decoration had become very common; but by that time art had deteriorated to such a degree that the designs were hardly intelligible. Silk embroidery in Chinese flat stitch (feather stitch, as the Romans called it) came into use in the fifth century (pl. 143a, b, c). Plate 143a reproduces a unique object in Forrer's collection, which he takes to be an archepiscopal pallium of the sixth century. It is a narrow scarf of fine linen nearly two and a half yards long, adorned with nine silk embroideries and twelve patches (crosses, squares and lozenges) of plain silk, all of them *appliqué*. The three details shown here represent the raising of Lazarus, the Crucifixion, and Mary Magdalene with the angel at the tomb. On the other six pieces there are pictures of two angels, of Christ enthroned, Christ in prayer, Christ instructing a disciple, and healing a blind man. The embroideries are worked on a reddish-black ground in carmine red, golden yellow, light blue, white, and green. The other subjects in his collection which Forrer enumerates are: (from the Old Testament) Joseph the patriarch (of special interest to the Egyptians), Elijah in his chariot, the messengers with the grapes of Eshcol, Daniel among the lions, the sacrifice of Isaac; and (from the New Testament) the Annunciation, Mary visiting Elizabeth (pl. 143b), Mary holding the child Jesus (pl. 143c), the Magi (very frequent), Christ healing the paralytic, the Entrance into Jerusalem, the Resurrection, and the Good Shepherd. Orants and saints are often depicted. The commonest animal symbols are the dove, the lamb, the hart, the hare, the fowl, and the peacock.

Gold embroidery is rarely found in the Egyptian graves. But it was an ancient art, which was much used in Rome under the Empire. In the Christian basilicas it was used at a comparatively late time for the decoration of altar covers, etc. Early gold embroidery (as we learn from the few fragments which have been preserved) was wrought with fine threads of pure gold; the method later used is one which is now common: a fine linen thread was wrapped around with narrow strips of parchment or paper which had been coated with gold leaf. Of the stiff and heavy character of Roman gold embroidery we may get an idea from representations of the *toga picta* on consular diptychs (pl. 105, 106).

The Egyptian textiles would not be of much interest to us if they were examples only of a local tradition; but in fact they represent a cosmopolitan art and illustrate customs which prevailed throughout the Empire. Hardly anything reveals so clearly the uniformity of custom under the Empire than the fact that everywhere the same garments were worn and the same decorative patterns prevailed. The looms of Egypt received orders from Rome, and with them the classical patterns which were to be executed. This meant the subversion of local traditions. Among all the textiles from Achmim and other burial grounds there is hardly anything that has a distinctively Egyptian character. When Oriental designs were introduced, they became no less cosmopolitan than the classical patterns, for they promptly gained acceptance everywhere.

Notwithstanding a decline in taste and execution, textile embroidery in all its branches had a rapid material expansion in the fifth and sixth centuries, and with the decay of pictorial art in other fields these were the only objects always available to artisans as models for the conventional low reliefs in stone which from the fifth to the ninth century were one of the commonest monumental expressions of decorative art (pl. 51d). Almost all these low relief designs can be found in the textiles, and that this was their source can hardly now be questioned.

Plates 64 and 63b show that the simpler classical patterns were commonly used for church curtains and altar cloths even as late as the sixth century. We read of Biblical scenes depicted upon the curtains, and we have learned here in what way this was done. It only remains to describe how curtains and altar cloths were used in the churches.

Textile fabrics had in ancient times at least as large a use in the furnishing of private houses as they have with us, and their use in the churches reflects the customs of private life. In houses they were used for cushions and stools, as covering for seats, for tables and for the wall, as curtains at the doors, and as a canopy for shielding the atrium from the sun. They were also used as curtains for the colonnade which surrounded the atrium. All of these uses were repeated in the church. The cathedra of the bishop had its stool and its cushion; there were coverings for the seats of the presbyters, for the wall behind them, and for the altar; there were curtains at the doors of the church, before the presbytery, around the ciborium, and between the columns which separated the nave from the aisles. This lavish use of curtains was encouraged not only by the use of them in private houses but by the fact that they were used in the temples. The *Liber Pontificalis* gives a good notion of their use in the basilicas during the eighth and ninth centuries. The *Charta Cornutiana* (see below) shows that they were used in the same way during the fifth century, even in an unimportant church. The use of hangings must have been established as early as the fourth century, for it was in a measure required by the contemporary liturgy. They became so common an accessory of worship, particularly at the Eucharist, that we are left to wonder how the Western Church was able ultimately to dispense with them and with the separation of different orders in the congregation which they served to mark.

The *Charta Cornutiana* is a document of great interest to the archæologist. It is a deed of gift drawn up in the year 471 in favor of a village church in the neighborhood of Tivoli. The donor, Flavius Valila, known as Theodorius, bestows a piece of ground, silver utensils to the weight of about 54 pounds, bronze chandeliers, and three sets of curtains made of silk, half silk, and linen for high festivals, ordinary feasts, and weekdays. A distinction is made between hangings and covers. The covers (*pallea, mafortes*) were used upon the graves of saints, upon the altar, and upon other tables; the hangings (*vela*) were used for the purposes mentioned above. The various colors called "purple" are carefully distinguished.

No ancient monuments show so clearly the character of ancient altar cloths as do the mosaics in Ravenna (pl. 64c, 63b). The altar, a table with four legs, was covered on all sides with a white linen cloth, which presumably was decorated only in front. Plate 64c reveals a heavier and darker cover under the linen. The decoration is precisely what we have found among the Egyptian textiles and corresponds closely to the curtain illustrated on plate 144b. When the altar assumed a box form by the insertion of plates of stone between the legs, the patterns which had been used on linen altar covers were transferred to the stone, and this simple decoration was extended to the parapets of the choir and presbytery (pl. 51d).

Curtains were more important than the covers. The use of them in doors was a matter of course, but it seems strange to us that they were used between the columns of the ciborium to hide from the people the most solemn acts in the Liturgy. This practice must have been universal, and probably it began as early as the fourth century. At all events, the oldest ciboriums we have show devices for attaching curtain rods.

But this was only one feature of an elaborate system. In many churches of the fifth century we see holes in the columns of the nave about nine feet from the floor for the attachment of curtain rods. It is significant that they are on the outside, the side of the nave, for in the aisles they would have taken up the room which was needed for the worshippers who stood there, the men on the right and the women on the left. The fact that the isles rather than the nave was allotted to the faithful is one of the indications which suggests that the church in the house prescribed the character of the Christian basilica. At all events, the use of curtains in this place seems to reflect the custom which was familiar in the private house. There were still other curtains which at a certain moment in the Liturgy could be stretched across the nave in front of the presbytery. This elaborate mystery is still maintained in the Eastern Churches. In Greek and Russian churches the curtain has been replaced by the iconostasis, which has curtains only for the central door. The Armenians still use a curtain, which is drawn in front of the presbytery at the beginning of the Canon.

How curtains were hung, and how they were drawn, is illustrated on plates 80a and 81d. In colonnades, where freedom of passage was not important, they were simply knotted in the middle. In doors they might be knotted and then fastened to the door post on one side, or they might be double so that they could be drawn to both sides.

About carpets there is nothing to be said. The mosaic floor was the carpet. Nothing more was needed in the church, for the people commonly stood in prayer. We know that they always stood to listen to the sermon.

# IX

## CIVIL AND ECCLESIASTICAL DRESS

It is not the art of dress I propose to discuss here, but the fashions of dress which are disclosed in early Christian art, the dress which the Christians of course wore because everybody else did, but which ultimately, as an instance of religious conservatism, became the distinctive dress of the clergy.

It is deplorable that modern artists (I mean for the last millennium) have so meager a notion of Greek and Roman dress; but it is not astonishing, seeing that archæologists tell them so little about it, and are themselves so imperfectly informed. The public, though it has a faint notion of the Greek pallium and the Roman toga (ridiculously conceived, however, as a cotton sheet), has no notion at all of the fashions of dress which prevailed after the second century, the period covered by the numerous illustrations presented here. To enable the student to suck all the advantage he can from these pictures, I have taken pains to indicate in the index where every sort of garment is depicted. By this I spare myself the task of writing a lengthy disquisition upon ancient dress. I might perhaps wish to say here more than I do about ecclesiastical dress, if I had not included a chapter on this subject in a book I recently wrote on the Liturgy. Wilpert has devoted several chapters to the articles of civil and ecclesiastical dress which are depicted in pagan and early Christian art, and because of his knowledge of the Roman monuments he speaks with more authority than anyone else. His precedent justifies me in including such a subject here, but I will say only what is necessary to orient the student in his own research.

Beginning at the top, I speak first of hats. It may be observed that very few hats are illustrated here. This in a negative way confirms the fact that by the Greeks and Romans they were not much used. Yet men like fishermen who were much exposed to the sun wore broad-brimmed hats, and Hermes, as a messenger, is distinguished by a hat with a narrow brim. No such hats are illustrated here, but in one picture (pl. 22b) we can barely discern that a fisherman wears a skull cap. Soldiers, of course, wore helmets, and royal persons crowns or diadems. As a protection against rain or cold a hood (*cucullus*) was commonly attached to the outer garment, such as the *pænula* (chasuble), but here only one late instance of this is discernible (pl. 150a). A hood was always attached to the *birrus*, which was a rough coat worn by laborers, and

# MONUMENTAL ART

a. Mosaic in the Oratory of St. Venantius attached to the Lateran Baptistery. *ca.* 642. Like the pictures before it and one following, it illustrates civil and ecclesiastical dress. — b. Fresco in the cemetery of Callistus above the tomb of Pope Cornelius. Pope Sixtus and Bishop Optatus. Sixth century.

Mosaic in S. Vitale, Ravenna. The Emperor Justinian with his officers carries a golden paten and is met by the bishop and two priests. Sixth century.

Pl. 146

Mosaic in S. Vitale, Ravenna. The Empress Theodora with her court enters the church to present a golden chalice. Sixth century.

Pl. 147

Covers of the Sacramentary of Metz. Bibliothèque Nationale, Paris. Made for Bishop Drogo (826–855). This is the earliest extant representation of the order of the Mass and of the other sacramental acts of the bishop. The original sequence presumably has not been preserved. 1) The clergy reverence the altar on entering the church [?] (2nd row, right); 2) all are seated during the Epistle (1st, left); 3) the bishop kisses the Gospel (2nd, left); 4) all stand during the Creed (2nd, middle); 5) oblations: the bishop receives the bread at the parapet of the presbytery and presents it at the altar where a deacon hands him a cruet of wine (3rd, left); 6) the clergy bow before the altar while it is censed (1st, middle); 7) Consecration (3rd, middle); 8) the kiss of peace (1st, right); 9) Communion (3rd, right).

Pl. 148

1) Baptism of Jesus (1st, middle); 2) Christ blessing the disciples (2nd, middle); 3) Ascension (1st, right); 4) consecration of a church (2nd, right); 5) blessing of the oil (2nd, left); 6) blessing of water for baptism (3rd, middle); 7) baptism of a child (3rd, right); 8) confirmation of a youth (3rd, left); 9) laying of hands on two deacons (1st, left).

Pl. 149

Ivory covers of a Missal. Frankfurt a.M. Ninth century. (See p. 53.)—a. A bishop (Gregory the Great?) instructs a choir of monks.—b. The bishop about to begin the Canon as the assistants finish the *Ter sanctus*.

Pl. 150

## MONUMENTAL ART

Frescoes in the Lower Church of S. Clemente, Rome. **a.** St. Clement saying mass. A man and a woman present the oblations (bread in the form of a hoop—cf. the pretzel form in pl. 128). The group at the right refers to the legend of a man named Sisinius who scornfully accompanied his wife to church and was converted by St. Clement.—**b.** Translation of the body of St. Clement. Pope Nicholas I, attended by SS. Cyril and Methodius, accompanies the bier and later says Mass. The words on the book are at the end of the Canon: *Per omnia secula seculorum* and *Pax Domini sit semper* [*vobiscum*]. About the end of the eleventh century.

because of its humble associations was adopted by monks. The traditional ornament of the mediaeval cope is a vestigial evidence that it once had a hood. It is well known (though there are no illustrations of it here) that Germans and Dacians on the northern border of the Empire wore conical hats of felt or fur. Here we have examples only of the Phrygian cap, which the Romans associated with Persia and therefore bestowed upon the Magi, so long as they were not known as the Three Kings but as priests of the ancient Persian religion.

On the other hand, women commonly covered the head with a veil, which did not ordinarily cover the face. Many instances of it are illustrated here. For it was not seemly for women to appear in public without covering the head. Even Rahab the harlot wore a veil (pl. 137e, 138a, b). No wonder then that St. Paul insisted upon the observance of this custom (1 Cor. 11:2-16).

It goes without saying that no sort of headdress was worn by the clergy: the pope had no tiara, the bishop no mitre, the presbyter no biretta. Only in the latest picture shown here (pl. 151b) has the pope a conical hat. Yet before the mitre came into use it was sometimes felt to be inconvenient that there was no way to distinguish a bishop from a presbyter. In the ninth century the artist of the ivory covers of the Sacramentary of Metz (pl. 149) distinguished the bishop by bestowing upon him a halo (upper left-hand corner)—but this was a questionable expedient. It would have been better to put a mitre on his head.

About footgear nothing much need be said, since no clear illustrations are provided—except on plates 105 and 106, where we see that shoes were worn with the toga, and sandals of a sort by soldiers. Sandals were commonly worn with the pallium, but we see on plate 34c that Ambrose as a bishop wore shoes. When I add that in ancient times respectable women wore shoes, I have said all that I have to say about footgear.

A loincloth (*cinctus, ventrale, perizoma* in Greek) was a fundamental and invariable article of dress; but to be clad only in that was to be "naked" (Jn. 21:7).

Over the loincloth was worn a shirt (*tunica, chiton*). In its original form nothing could be simpler: an oblong piece of cloth (either linen or wool) which was drawn around the body and fastened above the shoulders by a *fibula* (safety pin) on either side. In this form it had no sleeves. If they were wanted, the tunic was sewed like our shirts. In any case, the tunic was usually girdled (*tunica cincta*), and though the girdle might be laid aside for comfort at home, it was not seemly to go abroad without it—except in Africa, and in Rome so far as such a foreign custom might be tolerated. Commonly the tunic was just long enough to reach below the knee when it was girdled, though soldiers wore it shorter. There was need here of some nicety in the arrangement of the folds—all the more because the *clavus* must fall perpendicularly. Women wore a long tunic (*tunica talaris*) reaching to the ankles, and with long sleeves. At first such a tunic was accounted effeminate when used by men; but by the end of the second century it was thought more dignified for elderly persons (pl. 101c). From this we derive the alb, which is the fundamental ecclesiastical vestment. Except in very warm climates a second tunic of wool was worn over linen. Perhaps because he lived in Africa it was remarked as peculiar to St. Augustine that he wore a woolen tunic. The Emperor Augustus, being sensitive to cold, wore in winter a heavy toga (which of course was of wool), four tunics, an undershirt, a woolen chestcloth, short hose and leggings. This example shows that more need was felt of clothing in Rome than the multitude of naked statues might lead one to suppose.

Over the tunic was thrown an outer garment of wool. That too was a rectangular piece of cloth which needed no sewing but only a pin over the left shoulder. The *palla* worn by women had the same form, but in early times the border was thrown over the head to serve as a veil. Greek statues show how graceful a garment the pallium might be, though doubtless not all who wore it knew how to make the most of it.

Something must be said about the Roman *toga*, although it is rarely illustrated in Christian art. It appears but once in the frescoes of the catacombs, and on the sarcophagi only in the portrait busts of the deceased. In its origin it doubtless differed not at all from the pallium. But the Romans were led by pride to make their dress so distinctive that it was too cumbersome to wear. By law Romans were obliged to wear it, but they complained that one was "packed in a toga rather than clad in it," and so many evaded the law that a satirist said that Romans possessed togas only to be buried in them. The toga, when developed to a cumbersome size, had the form of an ellipse of from eight to ten feet in its smaller diameter and twice as much in the greater. It had to be folded along the greater diameter. Then like the pallium it was thrown over the left shoulder, drawn around the body and then fastened by the *nodus* where it passed over the left shoulder again. Then began the trouble of adjusting the folds and the *sinus* according to the fashion, and for this a talented slave was needed. The common people, of course, evaded such difficulties by wearing a very scanty toga, which was little more than a badge of citizenship. But the consular toga, the only form which survived the fourth century, was still more complicated; for so heavily was it embroidered in gold that it had to be folded (*contabulata*) in broad bands which displayed only the ornament, and after it had been drawn around the body in the usual manner it was passed around again with the pattern fully displayed, and the end rested on the left arm (pl. 105, 106). It survived in the Byzantine court as an insignium of imperial dignity, but by that time it had become a mere scarf, the *lorum*.

The pallium, on the other hand, is illustrated here very abundantly. It was worn generally by Christians because it comported with their cosmopolitan religion. In his tractate *De pallio* Tertullian attributes to the pallium the proud boast, "Every liberal study is covered by my four corners." It was in fact the dress of philosophers, who sometimes expressed their preference for the simple life by wearing it without a tunic. It was so worn by Justin Martyr and other Christian teachers. Only at the end of his book does Tertullian reveal that he is a Christian, when he exclaims, "Rejoice, O Pallium, and be glad: a better philosophy has taken thee into her service since thou hast begun to clothe the Christians."

Early Christian art, following a convention which was invariably observed, clothed Jesus and the apostles in a white pallium, and this tradition prevailed even when the pallium had ceased to be used as a common article of dress. Perhaps it was not an artificial convention; for Christ and His apostles might well have worn this garment, which was in use throughout the empire. At all events it was better than the modern pseudo-archæological fashion of depicting Jesus and the apostles in a garb which certainly was not known in Palestine in their days; for it was not then inhabited by nomadic Arabs. The architecture, the dress, and the culture of Galilee were predominantly Greek, and the Greek language was generally known. But doubtless this convention was carried too far when it prescribed that Abraham and Moses and other sacred characters of the Old Testament must likewise be dressed in the pallium. That is an anachronism. But it is not so deplorable as Sargent's pictures of the prophets in the Boston Library. They are nothing but bundles of clothes—yet once, in homage to a great artist, they were admired.

Owing to the sacred associations the pallium had for Christians, it was retained as a badge when it had ceased to be worn as a garment. By the same process of *contabulatio* which transformed the toga it became the *pallio sacro*, the scarf of white wool which the pope bestows upon archbishops. It is hung over the chasuble, since it would not be visible beneath it (pl. 145). In its later form it was turned into a yoke, with ends hanging down before and behind (pl. 150, 151). Wilpert's important study of ancient dress began with this demonstration of the origin of the sacred pallium.

Already it has been hinted that as early as the second century the toga and the pallium had begun to yield ground to competitors which eventually supplanted them. Obviously, soldiers could not fight when dressed in a toga or pallium, therefore they wore a short cape, the chlamys, which was fastened over the right shoulder and left that arm free. It was such a cape the soldiers threw mockingly over the shoulders of Jesus. In Christian art it appears only as the dress of the Magi, who, being Persians, were properly clothed in what was reputed to be the Persian dress. From this cape was developed a much longer cloak, the *paludamentum,* which became the uniform of the imperial court and of the higher officers of the army. Of this there are many illustrations here. On plate 146 it may be compared with the dress of ecclesiastics; for there we see two deacons wearing the dalmatic above a long tunic, and a bishop who wears the sacred pallium above his chasuble. A square patch (*tablion*) sewed upon the front of the *paludamentum* was a distinction worn by the emperor and his higher officials.

The bureaucratic tendency of the empire resulted by the sixth century in the imposition of a distinctive uniform upon almost all classes of citizens. By that time the clergy too were distinguished by their dress. Yet the garments they wore in the church still did not differ from those of the ordinary citizen substantially, but in an extra touch of quality and elegance.

Another foreign mantle, the *lacerna,* was introduced into the Roman army by Lucullus. But it was then an article of luxury, used only by the higher officers, and its exotic origin was not soon forgotten. Unlike the chlamys, it was fastened in front of the breast by a large breastpin. It was often described by the generic name *amictus.* It was used by early Christian artists, aptly enough, in depicting Melchisedek and the Jewish high priests. The Vulgate in Ecclesiasticus 50:12 represents that the high priest Simon, son of Onias, wore the *amictus.* The artists followed this clue. From this garment was derived, at a very late period in the Middle Ages, the ecclesiastical cope.

But it was not by these garments the toga and pallium were superseded in civil use. First of all it was by the dalmatic, which essentially was a tunic, but longer than usual, and with wide sleeves. It was also heavier, therefore suitable as an outer garment, and it had a clear advantage in the fact that it could not fall off. It was worn over the tunic, and the *clavus,* since it was no longer visible on the tunic, was transferred to the dalmatic. Far less comely, but even more practical as a protection against rain, was the *pænula* (*phainoles,* later called *casula,* meaning cosy little house—whence our word chasuble). It was made of heavy woolen stuff, even of leather, for essentially it was a raincoat, like the Mexican poncho, or the loden cloak carried by tourists in the Alps. It was such a garment, so appropriate to travellers, St. Paul inadvertently left behind him at Troas (2 Tim. 4:13). As a raincoat it was in common use before the Christian era, but it was slow in gaining favor as a garment for daily use. About the end of the second century, when a Christian soldier was chided for wearing his chasuble in church, Tertullian defended him on the ground that it was a regimental uniform which he was not permitted to lay aside in a public place. We see from this that the chasuble was yet far from being regarded as a Eucharistic vestment or as a distinction of the bishop. The earliest portrait we have of a bishop (pl. 101c) shows Hippolytus wearing the alb and the pallium. Nearly two hundred years later, the mosaic portrait of Ambrose, Bishop of Milan, shows him in the chasuble (*pænula*). Sumptuary laws had proved impotent to check the growing popularity of this garment. In 382 even senators were permitted to wear it, except in conducting public business. By that time women as well as men were wearing the *pænula*, of various shapes and sizes. In the catacombs there is a picture which Wilpert stigmatizes as an example of the "baroque *pænula*," exceedingly full behind, but with only a small triangle in front. Strangely enough, this shape reappears in an eleventh-century fresco in the Lower Church of S. Clemente (pl. 151). The graves of Achmim furnish various forms, including the fiddleback chasuble of modern Roman use, and the Benedictine scapular. The type which was worn by bishops in the fifth century was full and large, covering the arms to the wrist. This is attested by many of the monuments reproduced here. There is also a literary proof of some interest. The familiar pictures which represent St. Martin of Tours cutting off ostentatiously a piece of his cloak and giving it to a beggar does not do justice to this saint. As his friend Sulpicius Severus tells the story, no one but the beggar knew what he did, when from beneath his outer garment he extracted the woolen tunic he was wearing. This could have been done secretly only if he was wearing a full chasuble. It implies also that the "tunic" was fastened in the antique fashion merely by *fibulæ*.

On plate 150 one can plainly see, and in other instances can descry obscurely, that under his chasuble the bishop wears the dalmatic of the deacon, over that the stole of the presbyter, and under it the alb. Of course, under all that he wore what the Spaniards call *ropa íntima*, the customary undergarments. Today we wear still more than that: the black cassock, which is quite superfluous, and the breeches or trousers, which are perfectly incongruous with the classical dress. Yet, absurd as this may seem, it is significant, as the concretion of the history of two millenniums.

In the ninth century or earlier, when everybody wore the chasuble, how was the bishop to be distinguished—unless he was an archbishop and wore the sacred pallium? We can hardly get it through our heads that the chasuble in itself was not a distinctive dress. We rub our eyes when we read that the deacons on entering the church laid aside the chasubles they had been wearing in the street, in order to don the dalmatic. And what change did the bishop make, or the presbyter? He laid aside the common chasuble in which he had come, and put on a finer one, richer in its material and more dignified in form. The difference was only that between an everyday coat and the Sunday-go-to-meeting dress. The difference is observable on plate 150, where everybody except the deacons wears a chasuble, but the chasuble of the bishop is distinguished by its elegance. On plates 148, 149, the elegance of the bishop's dress was not so well depicted by the artist.

I have said nothing about trousers, pants, or breeches, which to us seem an indispensable part of male attire. Everybody knows that such garments distinguished the northern barbarians. Yet there are many illustrations of them here. For such things were often worn by Roman soldiers, and pantaloons (tight trousers) were used by Asiatic peoples and were commonly attributed to the Magi.

I have said all this very briefly because I can expect such readers as are interested in the subject to consult the index and by its aid to follow through the numerous illustrations of each garment which is here mentioned.

# A SELECT BIBLIOGRAPHY

Grouped by subjects and in the order of their relative importance.

## I

### WORKS OF HISTORIC IMPORTANCE

GIOVANNI B. DE ROSSI.   *La Roma sotterranea cristiana.* 3 vols., plates and atlas. Rome, 1864–77. A fourth volume was prepared after the master's death by his pupil, Orazio Marucchi. The plates have been superseded by Josef Wilpert's more accurate reproductions. The name "Roma sotterranea" had been used by Antonio Bosio for his work on the catacombs which was published in 1632, and it was again used by Wilpert for his book on the frescoes.

———   *Musaici cristiani e saggi dei pavimenti delle chiese di Roma anteriori al secolo XV.* Portfolio, pub. in 27 parts containing 53 colored plates. Rome, 1872–99. This work has been superseded by Wilpert's publication of the mosaics by the aid of photography.

———   *Inscriptiones christianæ urbis Romæ.* 3 vols., folio. *Rome,* 1861–88.

———   *Bullettino di archeologia cristiana* (continued as *Nuovo Bullettino di archeologia cristiana,* 1895–1922) contains much of De Rossi's work from 1863 to the time of his death in 1894.

EDMOND F. LE BLANT.   *Inscriptions chrétiennes de la Gaule antérieures au VIIIe siècle.* 2 vols., folio. Paris, 1856-65.

———   *Nouveau recueil des inscriptions chrétiennes de la Gaule antérieures au VIIIe siècle.* Paris, 1892.

———   *Etude sur les sarcophages chrétiens antiques de la ville d'Arles.* Folio. Paris, 1878.

———   *Les Sarcophages chrétiens de la Gaule.* Folio. Paris, 1886.

RAFFAELE GARRUCCI.   *Storia della arte cristiana nei primi otto secoli della chiesa.* 6 vols., folia, 500 plates (with about 2000 line drawings). Prato, 1872–81. This work is still indispensable even though we are accustomed to rely upon photographs.

## II

### ENCYCLOPÆDIAS

FERNAND CABROL. (F. Cabrol and H. Leclercq, ed.).   *Dictionnaire d'archéologie chrétienne et de liturgie.* 27 vols. Paris, 1907–37. Notable especially for the articles by Dom Henri Leclercq.

The excellent encyclopædias mentioned in my earlier book are now out of date.

A SELECT BIBLIOGRAPHY

## III
## COMPENDIOUS MANUALS

Orazio Marucchi.   Eléments d'archéologie chrétienne. 3 vols. Paris, Rome, 1899–1903.

——— Manuale di archeologia cristiana. 4th Italian ed., revised by Giulio Belvederi. Rome, 1933.

Henri Leclercq.   Manuel d'archéologie chrétienne depuis les origines jusqu'au VIII$^e$ siècle. 2 vols. Paris, 1907.

Carl M. Kaufmann.   Handbuch der christlichen Archäologie; Einführung in die Denkmälerwelt und Kunst des Urchristentums. 3d ed., Paderborn, 1922.

Victor Schultze.   Grundriss der christlichen Archäologie. Munich, 1919.

## IV
## THE CATACOMBS
(additional to works mentioned under I and III)

Orazio Marucchi.   Le catacombe romane; opera postuma. Rome, 1932.

Paul Styger.   Die römischen Katakomben; archäologische Forschungen über den Ursprung und die Bedeutung der altchristlichen Grabstätten. Berlin, 1933.

——— Römische Märtyrergrüfte. 2 vols. Berlin, 1935.

Josef Wilpert.   Papstgräber und die Cäciliengruft. Freiburg i.B., 1900. (See other works by this author mentioned under V.)

Bellarmino Bagatti.   Il Cimitero di Commodilla o dei Martiri Felice ed Adautto presso la Via Ostiense. Rome, 1936.

Hans Lietzmann.   Petrus und Paulus in Rom; liturgische und archäologische Studien. Bonn, 1915.

Walter Lowrie.   SS. Peter and Paul in Rome. New York, Oxford, 1940.

Paul Styger.   Il monumento apostolico di Via Appia. Rome, 1917.

Adriano Prandi.   La memoria apostolorum in catacumbas. Rome, 1936.

Hans Achelis.   Römische Katakombenbilder in Catania. Berlin, Leipzig, 1932.

——— Die Katakomben von Neapel. Portfolio in 6 parts. Leipzig, 1935–36.

Carlo Cecchelli.   Ipogei eretici e sincretici. Rome, 1927.

——— Monumenti cristiano-eretici di Roma. Rome, 1944.

Johann P. Kirsch.   Le catacombe romane. Rome, 1933.

## V
## PAINTINGS IN THE CATACOMBS
(additional to works mentioned under I)

Josef Wilpert.   Roma Sotterranea, die Malereien der Katakomben Roms (also in Italian). 2 vols., folio. Freiburg i.B., 1903.

——— Ein Cyclus christologischer Gemälde aus der Katakombe der Heiligen Petrus u. Marcellinus. Freiburg i.B., 1891.

# A SELECT BIBLIOGRAPHY

———  *Die gottgeweihten Jungfrauen in den ersten Jahrhunderten der Kirche.* Freiburg i.B., St. Louis, Mo., 1892.

———  *Fractio Panis; die älteste Darstellung des eucharistischen Opfers in der "Cappella greca."* Freiburg i.B., St. Louis, Mo., 1895.

———  *Die Malereien der Sacramentskapellen in der Katakombe des heiligen Callistus.* Freiburg i.B., 1897.

PAUL STYGER.  *Die altchristliche Gräberkunst; Versuch der einheitlichen Auslegung.* Munich, 1927.

## VI

### SARCOPHAGI

JOSEF WILPERT.  *I Sarcofagi cristiani antichi.* 3 vols., folio. Rome, 1929–36.

KARL GOLDMANN.  *Die ravennatischen Sarkophage.* Strassburg, 1906.

GERHART RODENWALDT.  "Antike Säulensarkophage," in *Römische Mitteilungen,* XXXVIII-XXXIX, 1923–24, pp. 2ff.

A. DE WAAL.  *Der Sarkophag des Junius Bassus in den Grotten von St. Peter; eine archäologische Studie.* Folio. Rome, 1900.

FRIEDRICH GERKE.  *Der Sarkophag des Junius Bassus.* Berlin, 1936.

WALTER ALTMANN.  *Architektur und Ornamentik der antiken Sarkophage.* Berlin, 1902.

## VII

### ARCHITECTURE

HEINRICH HOLTZINGER.  *Die altchristliche Architektur in systematischer Darstellung; Form, Einrichtung und Ausschmückung der altchristlichen Kirchen, Baptisterien und Sepulcralbauten.* Stuttgart, 1899 (Part II, 1899). This is an admirable work.

GEORG G. DEHIO and G. VON BETZOLD.  *Die kirchliche Baukunst des Abendlandes.* 2 vols. and folio atlas in 5 vols. Stuttgart, 1887–1901. Only a small part has to do with the early period.

AUGUSTE CHOISY.  *Histoire de l'architecture.* 2 vols. Paris, 1899. The second volume is invaluable for the technique of church building in the East and West.

GIOVANNI T. RIVOIRA.  *Le origini della architettura lombarda e delle sue principali derivazioni nei paesi d'oltr'Alpe.* 2 vols. Rome, 1901–1907.

———  *Roman Architecture and Its Principles of Construction under the Empire* (with an appendix on the evolution of the dome up to the XVIII century). Translated from the Italian by G. McN. Rushforth. Oxford, 1925.
This is a demonstration that the techniques employed in Byzantine and in Gothic architecture were already used in Rome before the fifth century.

F. WITTING.  *Die Anfänge christlicher Architektur; Gedanken über Wesen und Entstehung der christlichen Basilika.* Strassburg, 1902.

C. J. MELCHIOR DE VOGÜÉ.  *Syrie centrale; architecture civile et religieuse du I<sup>er</sup> au VII<sup>e</sup> siècle.* 2 vols. Paris, 1865–1877.

## A SELECT BIBLIOGRAPHY

HOWARD C. BUTLER. *Architecture and Other Arts.* (Publications of an American archæological expedition to Syria in 1899-1900, Part 2.) Folio. New York, 1903.

——— *Early Churches in Syria, Fourth to Seventh Centuries,* edited and compiled by E. Baldwin Smith. Folio. Princeton, 1929.

HERMANN W. BEYER. *Der syrische Kirchenbau.* Berlin, 1925.

RICHARD KRAUTHEIMER. *Corpus basilicarum christianarum Romæ. The Early Christian Basilicas of Rome.* Text in English. Vol. I, folio. Città del Vaticano, 1937. (Alas, no other volumes have been published.)

——— "The Beginnings of Early Christian Architecture," in *The Review of Religion,* Jan. 1939, pp. 127-148.

ALOIS RIEGEL. "Zur Entstehung der altchristlichen Basilica," in *Jahrbuch der Mitteilungen der k.k. Zentralkommission z. Erforschung u. Erhaltung der Kunstund historisch. Denkmale,* N. F. I, pp. 195-216. Vienna, 1903.

W. GERBER. *Altchristliche Kultbauten Istriens und Dalmatiens.* Dresden, 1912.

ALFONS MARIA SCHNEIDER. *Die Hagia Sophia zu Konstantinopel.* Berlin, 1939.

EMERSON H. SWIFT. *Hagia Sophia.* New York, 1940.

JEAN EBERSOLT and A. THIERS. *Les églises de Constantinople.* 2 vols. Paris, 1913.

AUGUST HEISENBERG. *Grabeskirche und Apostelkirche, zwei Basiliken Konstantins.* 2 vols. Leipzig, 1908.

HUGUES VINCENT and F. M. ABEL. *L'église de l'Eléona.* Paris, 1911.

——— *Jerusalem; recherches de topographie, d'archéologie et d'histoire.* 5 vols. Paris, 1912-1926.

——— *Bethléem; le sanctuaire de la Nativité.* Paris, 1914.

——— *Emmaüs; sa basilique et son histoire.* Paris, 1932.

JOHN W. CROWFOOT. *Churches at Jerash. A Preliminary Report of the Joint Yale-British School Expeditions of Jerash, 1928-1931.* Oxford, 1931.

——— *Early Churches in Palestine.* Oxford, 1941.

CARL HERMANN KRAELING, ed. *Gerasa, City of the Decapolis; an account embodying the record of a joint excavation conducted by Yale University and the British School of Archæology in Jerusalem (1928-1930), and Yale University and the American Schools of Oriental Research (1930-1931, 1933-1934).* New Haven, 1938.

PAUL MICKLEY. *Die Konstantin-Kirchen im Heiligen Lande. Eusebius-Texte übersetzt und erläutert (Das Land der Bibel,* Bd. 4, H. 3-4). Leipzig, 1923.

CARL WATZINGER. *Denkmäler Palästinas; Einführung in die Archäologie des Heiligen Landes.* 2 vols. Leipzig, 1933-1935.

JEAN CLÉDAT. *Le monastère et la nécropole de Baouît.* 3 vols. (Vol. I issued in 2 parts, 1904-06.) Cairo, 1904-1916.

JAMES E. QUIBELL. *Excavations at Saqqara.* Cairo, 1908-12.

MIKHAIL I. ROSTOVTZEFF. *Dura-Europos and its Art.* Oxford, 1938.

C. HOPKINS. "The Christian Church" in *Preliminary Report of Fifth Season of Work October 1931-March 1932 of the Excavations at Dura-Europos conducted*

A SELECT BIBLIOGRAPHY

by Yale University and the French Academy of Inscriptions and Letters, pp. 237-252; also published separately, New Haven, 1934.

P. V. C. BAUR. "The Paintings in the Christian Chapel," *ibid.*, pp. 254-283.

H. PEARSON and C. KRAELING. "The Synagogue at Dura-Europos" in *Preliminary Report of Sixth Season of Work* (1932–33), etc.; also published separately, New Haven, 1936.

THEODOR EHRENSTEIN. *Über die Fresken der Synagoge von Dura-Europos.* Vienna, 1937.

JAMES H. BREASTED. *Oriental Forerunners of Byzantine Painting; First-Century Wall Paintings from the Fortress of Dura on the Middle Euphrates.* Chicago, 1924.

## VIII
## MOSAICS
(additional to De Rossi's work)

JOSEF WILPERT. *Die römischen Mosaiken und Malereien der kirchlichen Bauten vom IV. bis zum XIII. Jahrhundert.* 4 vols., folio. Freiburg i.B., 1916. It needs to be remarked that the first two volumes contain disquisitions on early Christian art in general which, in my opinion, are by far the best exposition of this subject.

MARGUERITE VAN BERCHEM and ETIENNE CLUZOT. *Mosaïques chrétiennes du IV$^e$ au X$^e$ siècle.* Geneva, 1924.

EUGÈNE MÜNTZ. *La mosaïque chrétienne pendant les premiers siècles.* I. *La technique.* II. *La mosaïque dans les catacombes.* Nogent-le-Rotrou, 1893.

JULIUS KURTH. *Die Mosaiken der christlichen Ära.* I. *Die Wandmosaiken von Ravenna.* Berlin, 1905. 2d ed., Munich, 1912.

CORRADO RICCI. *Ravenna.* Bergamo, 1913.

―――― *Tavole storiche dei musaici di Ravenna.* Folio, with plates in elephant folio. Rome, 1930–37.

HANS DÜTSCHKE. *Ravennatische Studien; Beiträge zur Geschichte der späten Antike.* Leipzig, 1909.

THOMAS WHITTEMORE. *The Mosaics of St. Sophia at Istanbul.* 3 vols. Oxford, 1935–38. (Additional volumes to follow.)

OTTO DEMUS. *Die Mosaiken von San Marco in Venedig, 1100–1300.* Baden bei Wien [*c.* 1935].

JEAN PAUL RICHTER and A. CAMERON TAYLOR. *The Golden Age of Classic Christian Art.* London, 1904.

## IX
## CHARACTER AND ORIGIN OF CHRISTIAN ART
(additional to the exposition of Wilpert mentioned in VIII)

JOSEF STRZYGOWSKI. *Orient oder Rom; Beiträge zur Geschichte der spätantiken und frühchristlichen Kunst.* Leipzig, 1901.

ALOIS RIEGL. *Die spätrömische Kunst-Industrie, nach den Funden in Österreich-*

## A SELECT BIBLIOGRAPHY

*Ungarn.* 2 vols. Vienna, 1901–23; 2d ed., Vienna, 1927, a posthumous edition with a supplement by Otto Pächt.

These are the two books which, at the beginning of the century, diverted the study of Christian archæology into divergent paths. In the next group are gathered the works which follow more or less zealously the lead of Strzygowski; in the second group are those which resolutely take the opposite way; in the third group are those which take no part in this controversy; and in the fourth category a few works of late classical art which have a bearing on our study.

### I.

JOSEF STRZYGOWSKI. *Origin of Christian Church Art; New Facts and Principles of Research.* Translated by O. M. Dalton and H. J. Braunholtz. Oxford, 1923.

It is not necessary to cite here the many works of this lively author, for from these lectures which were delivered in England one may get a notion of the restless movements of his mind and of the problems to which he rightly drew attention. His subsequent movements were sometimes so eccentric that even devoted disciples have hesitated to follow him.

ORMONDE M. DALTON. *East Christian Art; A Survey of the Monuments.* Oxford, 1925. (A follower of Strzygowski whose zeal is tempered by discretion.)

——— *Byzantine Art and Archæology.* Oxford, 1911.

CHARLES DIEHL. *Manuel d'art byzantin.* Paris, 1910. 2d ed., rev. and augm., Paris, 1925.

This is an eloquent book but is not so recent as the date of the second edition might suggest.

OSKAR K. WULFF. "Ein Gang durch die Geschichte der altchristlichen Kunst mit ihren neuen Pfadfindern," in *Repertorium für Kunstwissenschaft,* Bd. 34, 1911, pp. 281-314.

——— *Altchristliche und byzantinische Kunst.* Vol. I, *Die altchristliche Kunst von ihren Anfängen bis zur Mitte des I. Jahrhunderts.* Berlin-Neubabelsberg [c. 1914] (not much changed in the second edition, Potsdam, 1936).

LUDWIG VON SYBEL. *Christliche Antike; Einführung in die altchristliche Kunst.* 2 vols. Marburg, 1906–09.

——— "Das Werden der christlichen Kunst," in *Repertorium für Kunstwissenschaft,* 1916–17.

——— *Frühchristliche Kunst, Leitfaden ihrer Entwicklung.* Munich, 1920.

GUILLAUME DE JERPHANION. *La voix des monuments; notes et études d'archéologie chrétienne.* Paris, 1930.

PAUL STYGER. *Die altchristliche Gräberkunst; Versuch der einheitlichen Auslegung.* Munich, 1927.

E. BALDWIN SMITH. *Early Christian Iconography.* Princeton, 1918.

CHARLES R. MOREY. *Early Christian Art; an Outline of the Evolution of Style and Iconography in Sculpture and Painting from Antiquity to the Eighth Century.* Princeton, 1942.

——— *Mediæval Art.* New York, 1942.

## A SELECT BIBLIOGRAPHY

2.

FRANZ WICKHOFF. *Römische Kunst* (with a preface by M. Dvořák). Berlin, 1912. This is Wickhoff's introduction to his edition of *Die Wiener Genesis*. It was translated into English by Mrs. S. A. Strong with the title *Roman Art*, London, 1900.

―――― *Schriften Franz Wickhoffs*, ed. by M. Dvořák. 3 vols. Berlin, 1912.

ALOIS RIEGL. *Stilfragen; Grundlegungen zu einer Geschichte der Ornamentik*. Berlin, 1893.

―――― "Spätrömisch oder orientalisch?" in *Allgemeine Zeitung*, 1905, Beilage, Nos. 93, 94.

―――― *Gesammelte Aufsätze*, ed. by Karl M. Swoboda (posthumous publication). Augsburg-Vienna, 1929.

MAX DVOŘÁK. "Alois Riegl," in *Mitteilungen der k.k. Zentralkommission z. Erforschung u. Erhaltung*, etc., III. Folge, Bd. 4, pp. 255-276. Vienna, 1904.

―――― "Die Entstehung der christlichen Kunst" in *Wiener Jahrbuch für Kunstgeschichte*, Bd. 2 (XVI), 1923, pp. 1-13.

―――― *Katakombenmalerei*. Munich, 1924.

―――― *Gesammelte Aufsätze zur Kunstgeschichte*, ed. by Johannes Wilde and Karl M. Swoboda (with a supplement by Otto Pächt). Munich, 1929.

―――― *Kunstgeschichte als Geistesgeschichte; Studien zur abendländischen Kunstentwicklung*. Munich, 1924. (Note Chapter I, "Katakombenmalerei, die Anfänge der christlichen Kunst," pp. 3-40.)

AUGUST SCHMARSOW. *Grundbegriffe der Kunstwissenschaft am Übergang vom Altertum zum Mittelalter kritisch erörtert und in systematischem Zusammenhange dargestellt*. Leipzig, Berlin, 1905, 1922.

JOSEF WILPERT. *Principienfragen der christlichen Archäologie*. Freiburg i.B., St. Louis, Mo., 1889.

―――― *Erlebnisse und Ergebnisse im Dienste der christlichen Archäologie*. Freiburg i.B., 1930.

―――― "Early Christian Sculpture; Its Restoration and Its Modern Manufacture," in *Art Bulletin*, December 1926, pp. 89-141. New York, 1926.

CARLO CECCHELLI. "Il problema 'Orient oder Rom,'" in *Atti della Congregazione Nazionale di Studii Romani*. Rome, 1927.

A. PLEHN. "Neue Stilerklärung," in *Gegenwart*, LXII, pp. 280-282.

ERNST HEIDRICH. *Beiträge zur Geschichte und Methode der Kunstgeschichte*. Basel, 1917.

JOSEF SAUER. *Wesen und Wollen der christlichen Kunst*. Freiburg i.B., 1926.

F. PANOFSKY. "Der Begriff des Kunstwollens," in *Zeitschrift für ästhetische und allgemeine Kunstwissenschaft*, XVI, Heft 4, 1921, pp. 216-222, and XVIII, 1924, pp. 129-169.

HANS TIETZE. *Die Methode der Kunstgeschichte; ein Versuch*. Leipzig, 1913.

K. MANNHEIM. "Beiträge zur Theorie der Weltanschauungs-Interpretation," in *Jahrbuch für Kunstgeschichte*, I, 1921-22.

## A SELECT BIBLIOGRAPHY

WILHELM NEUSS. *Stilfragen.* Berlin, 1893.

——— *Die Kunst der alten Christen.* Augsburg, 1926.

F. WITTING. *Von Kunst und Christentum, Plastik und Selbstgefühl; von antikem und christlichem Raumgefühl; Raumbildung und Perspektive; Historisch-ästhetische Abhandlung.* Strassburg, 1903.

HANS BERSTL. *Das Raumproblem in der altchristlichen Malerei.* Bonn, 1920.

F. SAXL. "Frühes Christentum und spätes Heidentum in ihren künstlerischen Ausdrucksformen," in *Jahrbuch für Kunstgeschichte*, Bd. II (XVI), 1923, pp. 63-121.

MARCEL LAURENT. *L'art chrétien primitif.* 2 vols. Brussels, 1911.

KARL KÜNSTLE. *Ikonographie der christlichen Kunst.* 2 vols. Freiburg i.B., 1926-28.

MAX HUGGLER. *Mythologie der altchristlichen Kunst.* Strassburg, 1929.

HELMUT LOTHER. *Realismus und Symbolismus in der altchristlichen Kunst.* Tübingen, 1931.

HERMANN W. BEYER. *Die Eigenart der christlichen Kunst im Rahmen der Spätantike.* Stettin, 1931.

WALTER ELLIGER. *Die Stellung der alten Christen zu den Bildern in den ersten vier Jahrhunderten.* Leipzig, 1930.

——— *Forschungen zur Kunstgeschichte und zur christlichen Kunst.* Leipzig, 1931.

——— *Zur Entstehung und frühen Entwicklung der altchristlichen Bildkunst.* Leipzig, 1934.

### 3.

HANS ACHELIS. *Der Entwicklungsgang der altchristlichen Kunst.* Leipzig, 1919.

ALBERT J. GAYET. *L'art copte; Ecole d'Alexandrie—architecture monastique, sculpture, peinture, art somptuaire; illustrations de l'auteur.* Paris, 1902.

WLADIMIR DE GRÜNEISEN. *Les caractéristiques de l'art copte.* Florence, 1922.

JOHANNES REIL. *Die altchristlichen Bildzyklen des Lebens Jesu.* Leipzig, 1910.

FRANZ J. DÖLGER. IXΘYS. *Das Fischsymbol in frühchristlicher Zeit.* 4 vols. Rome, Freiburg i.B., 1910. (Vols. II and III: *Der heilige Fisch in den antiken Religionen und im Christentum.* Münster i.W., 1922. Vol. IV, illustrations only. Münster, i.W., 1927.)
This is a study in comparative religion and was followed by five volumes of "religionsgeschichtliche Studien," entitled *Antike und Christentum*, Münster i.W., 1929-36.

LOUIS BRÉHIER. *L'art chrétien, son developpement iconographique des origines à nos jours.* Paris, 1918.
Only a small part of this book deals with the early Christian period.

WLADIMIR DE GRÜNEISEN. *Sainte Marie Antique.* Rome, 1911.
The frescoes were reproduced by J. Wilpert in his work, *Mosaiken und Malereien.*

## A SELECT BIBLIOGRAPHY

### 4.

EUGENIE STRONG (Mrs. S. A. Strong).   *Roman Sculpture from Augustus to Constantine.* London, New York, 1907. Italian translation: *La scultura romana da Augusto a Constantino.* 2 vols. Florence, 1923-1926.

FRITZ WIRTH.   *Römische Wandmalerei vom Untergang Pompejis bis ans Ende des dritten Jahrhunderts.* Berlin, 1934.

A. SCHOBER.   "Der landschaftliche Raum im Hellenischen Relieffeld," in *Jahrbuch für Kunstgeschichte,* II, 1923, pp. 36-51.

MARY H. SWINDLER.   *Ancient Painting, from the Earliest Times to the Period of Christian Art.* New Haven, London, 1929.

GIULIO E. RIZZO.   *La pittura ellenistico-romana.* Milan, 1929.

### X
## MANUSCRIPT ILLUSTRATIONS

N. K. KONDAKOV.   *Histoire de l'art byzantin consideré principalement dans les miniatures.* 2 vols. in one. Paris, 1886-1891.

GUIDO BIAGI, ed.   *Reproductions from Illuminated Manuscripts; Fifty Plates from MSS. in the R. Medicean Laurentian Library.* Florence, 1914.

WILHELM RITTER VON HÄRTEL and FRANZ WICKHOFF, ed.   *Die Wiener Genesis.* Folio. Vienna, 1895.

FRANZ WICKHOFF.   *Beschreibendes Verzeichnis der Illuminierten Handschriften in Österreich.* 8 vols. Leipzig, 1905-38.

HANS GERSTINGER, ed.   *Die Wiener Genesis.* Vienna, 1931.

—— *Die griechische Buchmalerei.* Vienna, 1926.

PAUL BUBERL.   *Das Problem der Wiener Genesis.* Vienna, 1936.

—— *Die byzantinischen Handschriften.* Leipzig, 1937.

ARTHUR HASELOFF.   *Codex purpureus Rossanensis.* Folio. Berlin, 1898.

GÜNTHER HASELOFF.   *Die Psalterillustrationen im 13. Jahrhundert.* Kiel, 1938.

ANTONIO MUÑOZ.   *Il codice purpureo di Rossano e il frammento sinopense.* Folio, in color. Rome, 1907.

D. C. HESSELING.   *Miniatures de l'octateuque grec de Smyrne: Manuscrit de l'école Evangélique de Smyrne.* Leyden, 1909.

FIODOR I. USPENSKI.   *L'octateuque du Sérail* (text in Russian separate from the plates). Sophia, 1907.

JOHN A. HERBERT.   *Schools of Illumination; Reproductions from Manuscripts in the British Museum.* 6 vols., folio. London, 1914-30.

J. HENRY MIDDLETON.   *Illuminated Manuscripts in Classical and Mediæval Times, their Art and their Technique.* Cambridge, 1892.

ERNEST T. DEWALD.   *The Illustrations of the Utrecht Psalter.* Folio. Princeton, 1932.

ERNEST T. DEWALD, A. M. FRIEND, JR., and KURT WEITZMANN, ed.   *The Illustrations in the Manuscripts of the Septuagint.* 2 vols., folio. Princeton, 1941-42.

## A SELECT BIBLIOGRAPHY

A. M. FRIEND, JR.　　*The Portraits of the Evangelists in Greek and Latin Manuscripts.* Folio. Princeton, 1929.

KURT WEITZMANN.　　*Byzantinische Buchmalerei des IX. und X. Jahrhunderts.* Folio. Berlin, 1935.

CARL NORDENFALK.　　*Die spätantiken Kanontafeln; kunstgeschichtliche Studien über die Eusebianische Evangelienkonkordanz in den vier ersten Jahrhunderten ihrer Geschichte.* Göteborg, 1938.

——— *Vier Kanontafeln eines spätantiken Evangelienbuches.* Göteborg, 1937.

HUGO BUCHTHAL.　　*The Miniatures of the Paris Psalter; a Study in Middle Byzantine Painting.* London, 1938.

KARL LEHMANN-HARTLEBEN.　　*Die Trajanssäule; ein römisches Kunstwerk zu Beginn der Spätantike.* 2 vols., folio. Berlin, 1926.

## XI

### IVORY, WOOD AND GLASS

JOHN O. WESTWOOD.　　*A Descriptive Catalogue of the Fictile Ivories in the South Kensington Museum, with an Account of the Continental Collections of Classical and Mediæval Ivories.* London, 1876.

ORMONDE M. DALTON.　　*Catalogue of Early Christian Antiquities and Objects from the Christian East in the Department of British and Mediæval Antiquities and Ethnography of the British Museum.* London, 1901.

CORRADO RICCI.　　*Raccolte artistiche di Ravenna.* Bergamo, 1905.

MARCEL LAURENT.　　*Les ivoires prégothiques conservés en Belgique.* Paris, 1912.

GEORG STUHLFAUTH.　　*Die altchristliche Elfenbeinplastik.* Freiburg i.B., 1896.

JOSEF SAUER.　　*Die altchristliche Elfenbeinplastik.* Leipzig, 1922.

LOUIS WEBER.　　*Einbanddecken, Elfenbeintafeln, Miniaturen, Schriftproben aus Metzer liturgischen Handschriften.* Folio. Metz, 1913.

ADOLPH GOLDSCHMIDT.　　*Die Elfenbeinskulpturen aus der Zeit der karolingischen und sächsischen Kaiser, VIII.-IX. Jahrhundert.* 4 vols., folio. Berlin, 1914-26.

——— *Die byzantinischen Elfenbeinskulpturen des X.-XIII. Jahrhunderts,* bearb. von A. Goldschmidt and Kurt Weitzmann. 2 vols., folio. Berlin, 1930-34.

——— *Die Kirchentür des heiligen Ambrosius in Mailand.* Strassburg, 1902.

JOACHIM J. BERTHIER.　　*L'église de Sainte-Sabine à Rome.* Rome, 1910.

RICHARD DELBRÜCK.　　*Die Consulardiptychen und verwandte Denkmäler.* Berlin, Leipzig, 1929.

CARLO CECCHELLI.　　*La Cattedra di Massimiano ed altri avorii romano-orientali.* Portfolio. Rome, 1936-37.

RAFFAELE GARRUCCI.　　*Vetri ornati di figure in oro, trovati nei cimiteri dei cristiani primitivi di Roma.* Rome, 1858.

HERMANN VOPEL.　　*Die christlichen Goldgläser.* Freiburg i.B., 1899.

A SELECT BIBLIOGRAPHY

## XII

## TEXTILES AND DRESS

Robert Forrer. *Die Gräber- und Textilfunde von Achmim-Panopolis.* Strassburg, 1891.

—— *Die frühchristlichen Alterthümer aus dem Gräberfelde von Achmim-Panopolis.* Strassburg, 1893.

Alois Riegl. *Die ägyptischen Textilfunde im k. k. österreichischen Museum für Kunst und Industrie. Allgemeine Characteristik und Katalog.* Vienna, 1889.

Josef Wilpert. *Die Gewandung der Christen in den ersten Jahrhunderten; vornehmlich nach den Katakomben-Malereien dargestellt.* Cologne, 1898.

—— *Un capitolo di storia di vestiario.* In two parts, folio. Rome, 1909.

Joseph Braun. *Die liturgische Gewandung im Occident und Orient nach Ursprung und Entwicklung, Verwendung und Symbolik.* Freiburg i.B., 1907.

—— *Die liturgischen Paramente in Gegenwart und Vergangenheit.* Freiburg i.B., 1924.

Henri Leclercq. Articles on ecclesiastical dress in F. Cabrol's *Dictionnaire d'archéologie chrétienne et de liturgie.*

## XIII

## LITERARY SOURCES

A quantity of material is to be found in the first volume of Garrucci's *Storia della arte cristiana.*

Many of the texts are presented in a convenient form in the following publications:

Friedrich W. Unger. *Quellen der byzantinischen Kunstgeschichte* (No. 12 in Quellenschriften für Kunstgeschichte und Kunsttechnik des Mittelalters und der Renaissance). Vienna, 1878.

Julius von Schlosser. *Quellenbuch zur Kunstgeschichte des abendländischen Mittelalters* (Quellenschriften für Kunstgeschichte und Kunsttechnik des Mittelalters und der Neuzeit. N. F., 7). Vienna, 1896.

Eugène Müntz. *Les sources de l'archéologie chrétienne dans les bibliothèques de Rome, de Florence et de Milan* (Extrait des mélanges d'archéologie et d'histoire publiés par l'Ecole française de Rome). Rome, 1888.

This work gives a convenient conspectus of this class of literature.

## XIV

## ARCHÆOLOGICAL REVIEWS

It is a matter of course that much of the advanced work in this field was first registered in such reviews as the *American Journal of Archæology*, the *Art Bulletin*, the *Bullettino di archeologia cristiana. Byzantinische Zeitschrift, Jahrbuch des deutschen archäologischen Instituts* and in the *Mitteilungen* of the same Institute, in *Repertorium für Kunstwissenschaft*, and in the *Römische Quartalschrift für christliche Altertumskunde und für Kirchengeschichte*—but it is equally a matter of course that in a book of this nature I do not make many references to such articles.

# INDEX

Abericus, 35, 56f.
Abrahams sacrifice, 40
Acanthus, 132
Achmim-Panopolis, 197ff.
Acilii, 30, 40
Adam and Eve, 40, 72f.
" in Eden, 159
Adoration of the shepherds, 60
*Agape*, 26, 46, 92, 196
*Agnus Dei*, 43, 84, 127, 147
Alexander Severus, 11
Alexandria, 43, 180
Alpha and Omega, 84, 112
Altar, 54, 100f., 104, 203
Altar cloth, 101, 203f.
Altar frontal, Salerno, 2, 171ff.
*Ambo—see* Pulpit
Ambrose, 151, 211
" silver pyx, 160
*Amictus*, 210
*Ampula*, 101
Anastasis, 116ff., 129
Anchor, 55
Angels, 137
Annunciation, 43, 60, 136
Antioch, 89, 182
Apocalyptic, 8, 84, 138
Apollonic, 5, 71
Apostles, 112, 129, 209
Apse, 91, 134f.
" of S. Pudenziana, 126ff.
Apsidal cross, 133
" mosaics, 8
Aquila and Priscilla, 31
Archaeology, 1, 19f.
Architecture, 19, 87
*Arcosolium*, 24ff.
*Arenaria*, 24
Ariadne, Empress, 169, 170
Arles, Synod of, 9
Ascension, 161
Asterius, 13, 202
Athanasius, 59
Attitude and gesture, 177ff.
Atrium, 92, 104

Balaam, 43, 61
Baptism, 43, 53,. 57ff., 72, 73, 78, 133, 135, 139ff.
Baptistery, 106f., 139
" at Dura, 16, 44
" at Naples, 144
" at Ravenna, 144
" of Lateran, 12, 132ff., 141ff.
Basil, 13
Basilica, 88ff.
" the name, 88
*Bema—see* Pulpit
Bethlehem, 128f.
Bible, 7, 41, 43
" illustrations, 43, 179ff.
Birth of Jesus—*see* Nativity
Books, 180
Bordeaux Pilgrim, 88, 114
Breads, 52
Brescia, ivory box, 69, 164f.
British Museum, 165
Burial, mode of, 22f., 198
Burial societies, 22
Burial *sub divo*, 39
*Byrrus—see Lacerna*
"Byzantine," 6, 15, 17, 85f., 123f., 138f., 172, 193

Calvary, 116ff., 127
Canaanitish woman, 77
Cap, 76 206; *see* Phrygian
*Capella greca*, 26, 53
" *Palatina*, 15, 134, 171
Catacombs, 6f., 20ff., 39f., 61; *see* Cemeteries
Cathedral, 26, 101f., 107, 203
" of Maximianus, 2, 156ff.
Cathedral of Aquileia, 133
" of Cefalù, 15
" of Monreale, 15, 124, 171, 134
" of Salerno, altar frontal, 171ff.
" of Torcello, 15
Ceilings, 99
Celestial banquet, 43, 51ff.
Cemeteries, 6ff., 20ff., 23, 29

224

# INDEX

Cemetery of Callistus, 24, 26, 31
" of Domitilla, 24, 29
" of Priscilla, 30f., 40
Central plan, 121ff.
*Charta Cornutiano*, 204
Chasuble—*see* Paenula
Children, the Three, 40, 45, 62f., 71
Chlamys, 210
Christ, and apostles, 61
" as Judge, 43, 61
" before Pilate, 71
" enters Jerusalem, 71
" gives the Law, 66, 81f., 100
" and miracles, 78f.
" and Passion, 79
" portraits of, 11f., 71, 135
" Resurrection of, 38, 61, 65, 80, 109; *see* Anastasis
" statues of, 12ff.
Chrysostom, 13, 182
Church and Empire, 162
" etymology, 87
" property, 21f.
" symbols of, 49
" towers, 96
Churches listed:
  Anastasis, 116ff., 128
  Apostles, in Rome, 108
  at Dura, 15, 44, 89, 91
  of Eleona, 119
  at Gaza (S. Sergius), 115, 150
  at Madaba, 25, 117
  at Mamre, 119
  Holy Sepulchre—*see* Anastasis
  Nativity, at Bethlehem, 115ff., 128
  of N. Syria, 95, 102, 118, 121ff.
  S. Agnese, Rome, 117
  S. Apollinare Nuovo, 79, 152ff., 180, 188
  S. Clemente, 106, 132
  S. Costanza, 133, 140f.
  S. Croce, 107
  S. John Lateran, 106, 134, 145ff.
  S. Lorenzo, 109
  S. Marco, Venice, 15, 79, 113, 124, 134, 166ff., 185, 188
  S. Maria Maggiore, 108, 136f., 148ff., 181ff.
  S. Paul's, 106, 108

Churches listed—*continued*
  S. Peter's, 106, 109, 147
  S. Pudenziana, 114, 126ff.
  of the Resurrection, 129
  S. Sabina, 128, 143, 160ff., 187
  S. Sophia, 86, 112f., 124f., 128
Ciborium, 100, 166ff., 194
Classe, 153
Classic art, 3, 5
*Clavus*, 199f., 208
Clement of Alexandria, 10, 54, 56
Cloak—*see* Amictus
Codex, 180
"Colleagues," 179
Colonnades, 98, 104, 113, 129, 150
*Columbaria*, 22f.
Columns in S. Marco, Venice, 166ff.
Commission, the Great—*see* Missio
*Concordantia*, 14, 148, 150, 160
*Confessio*, 101
Constantine, 2, 10f., 14, 24, 48, 62, 68, 70, 84, 97, 108f., 111ff., 115, 128, 134, 140, 142, 194
Constantinople, 13, 15, 112, 166
Consular Diptychs—*see* Diptychs
*Contabulatio*, 208f.
Continuous style, 165f., 181ff.
Cope, 210
*Corno*, 89
Cotton Bible, 182, 185
Council of Ephesus, 10, 108, 136
Council of Nicaea, 14, 113
Creed, Apostles', 60
Cremation, 23
Cross, 14, 98, 100, 110ff., 133ff., 163
Crown, 61
" of thorns, 61
Crucifixion, 45, 61, 110, 163f.
Crypt of the popes, 36
Cubiculum, 4, 36
Curtains, 103, 198, 203ff.
Cyprian, 58
Cyril of Jerusalem, 57

Dalmatic, 200
Damascus, 27, 35ff.
Daniel and Susanna, 64
" and the lions, 7, 11, 40, 48, 64, 71, 74, 77
David, 40

225

## INDEX

Deer drinking, 133, 135
Deliverance, the divine, 41f., 45
Demoniac, 41
Didactic, 48, 79, 100
Diocletian, 90
Diptychs, 159f., 169f.
Dome, 99, 113, 117f.
Doors, 104, 203
" of S. Ambrogio, 160
" S. Sabina, 160ff.
Dress; see Tunic, *Pallium*, Toga, Dalmatic, Chlamys, *Paludamentum*, *Paenula*, etc.
" ecclesiastical, 206ff.
Dura, church and baptistery, 15, 44, 89, 91f.
" synagogue, 15, 43, 180
Dwelling house, 98, 105

*Ecclesia, ex circumcisione*, 128
" *ex gentibus*, 128
Edessa, 12, 89
Egypt, 6, 197f.
Eleona, church, 119
Elijah, 40, 72, 160
Elvira, Synod of, 9
Emperor, 63, 162, 170f.
Epigraphy—see Inscriptions
Epiphanius, 15, 119
Eschatology, 40, 54, 83f.
Etheria, 114f.
Ethiopian eunuch—see Philip
Eucharist, 22, 43, 52, 53ff., 78
Eudoxia, Empress, 116, 187
Eusebius, 11, 50, 84, 88ff., 115ff., 128, 162, 186
Evangelists, 192
Everlasting life—see Immortality
*Exedra*—see Galleries

Faith symbol of, 46f.
Fall—see Adam and Eve
Feeding the multitude, 54; see Miracle
Fish, 51f., 55ff.
Fisherman, 56, 59
Fishing scenes, 56, 59, 133
Flavii, 29
Florence, ivory diptych, 159ff.
*Fossor*, 25, 43
*Fractio Panis*, 53

Frescoes, 1, 39ff.
Frontal aspect, 6, 17, 158

Galla Placidia, mausoleum, 121, 133, 138
Galleries in catacombs, 21
*Gammadiae*, 201
Gesture, 88f.; *also see* Hand
Gold and silver, 142, 146
Gold embroidery, 202
Gold glass, 11, 195
Golgotha—see Calvary
Good Shepherd, 7, 11, 12, 42ff., 50, 74
Gospel cover, 158
Gourd, 65
Gradual, 102
*Grammaticus—see Paedagogus*
Great Commission—see *Missio*
Gregory Nazianzen, 13
Gregory of Nyssa, 13
Gregory the Great, 16

Habakkuk, 77; carried to Babylon, 64; see Daniel
Halo, 135
Hand of God, 133, 135
Hat, 76, 206
Helena, 107, 134, 140
Hellenistic art, 2, 12, 17, 48, 73, 135
Herod, 63
Hieroglyphs, 5, 45, 55
Hieropolis, 56
Hildebrand, 131
Hippolytus, 12, 13, 50, 151, 211
Holy Innocents—see Slaughter of
Holy Roman Empire, 162
Holy Sepulchre—see Anastasis
Hope, 38f., 60
House of the Church, 87f.
House, private, 98
Hunting scenes, 14, 133
Husband and wife, 69, 72
*Hypogeum*, 22, 30, 40

Iconoclasm, 5, 14
Icons—see Images
Idolatry, 10, 38, 50
Illuminations, manuscript, 179
Images, 12, 14f.
*Imago clypeata*, 68
Immortality, 38f., 57, 60

226

## INDEX

Impressionism, 5f.
Industrial arts, 195ff.
Infancy of Jesus; *see* Nativity; *also* Magi
Inhumation, 23
Inscriptions, 27ff., 56
*Introductio*, 61
Irenaeus, 11, 12, 55, 56
Isaac—*see* Abraham's sacrifice
Islam, 181
Ivories, 164f., 170ff., 181
IXθYS, 55f., 112, 161f.; *see* Fish

Jacob at the brook Jabbok, 184
Jairus' daughter, 40, 79
Jamblichus, 17
Jericho, the walls fall, 148
Jerome, 13, 74, 118
Jerusalem, 114, 128f.
" and Bethlehem, 115ff., 128, 133 137
" mosaic map, 117
Jews and art, 9, 15f., 43, 180
Job, 40, 66f.
John Baptist, 135
Jonah, 40, 64f., 74
Joshua Roll, 180, 181, 191
Judgment, general, 83, 85
" particular, 61, 83
Junius Bassus, 66, 70ff.
Justin Martyr, 75, 80, 92, 119
Justinian, 18, 117f., 121ff., 182, 188

Key, symbol of authority, 131
Korah, 149
*Kuntswollen*, 3ff., 93

Labarum, 111
*Lacerna*, 210—*see Amictus*
Lamps, 101
Last Supper, 52ff.
Law, Christ gives the, 66, 82f.
Lazarus, 40, 66, 78f.
*Liber Pontificalis*, 25, 89, 103, 113, 142, 146f., 202, 204
Liberius, 107
Licinius, 90
Life of Jesus, 60, 78f.
Lights over Altar, 57
Liturgy, 55, 92f., 205
*Loculus*, 24

Logos, 72
Lombard architecture, 94, 122f.
Lord's Supper—*see* Eucharist
*Lucinarium*, 25

Magi, 7, 38, 62f., 79, 137
Magic, 96, 98
*Majestas*, 80, 84ff.
Manger, 79
Marble, 142
*Martyrium*, 117f., 129, 151
Martyrs, 26ff., 33f., 101
Mary—*see* Virgin and Child
" and John at the Cross, 132
Mausoleum of S. Costanza, 140
" of Galla Placidia, 121, 133, 138
Maximianus, Cathedra of, 2, 157f.
Meetinghouse, 87
Melchizedek, 149
Mercy, 83f.
Milan, S. Aquilino, 126
Miniatures, 179
Minucius Felix, 89
Miracle of the loaves, 78
Miracles, 42, 78f.
*Missio*, 80, 114, 126f.
Modernistic churches, 94
Monogram, 110ff.
Mosaics, 2, 105, 115, 124, 134, 142f., 181
Moses at the bush, 40
" receives the Law, 66
" (Peter) strikes water from rock, 40, 74
Murano, Gospel Cover, 158f.
*Mysteria*, 57
Mystery cults, 39, 97
Myth, 5, 63

Narrative, 48
Nativity, 79, 136; *see also* Church of Anastasis
Nave, decoration, 150f.
Nebuchadnezzar, 40, 63
Nicholas IV, 135
Nicomedia, 90
Nilus, 14, 133
Nimbus—*see* Halo
Noah and the ark, 40, 65f., 74
Numinous, 96

227

# INDEX

Octateuch of Smyrna, 193ff.
Oecumenical authority, 131
Olympidorus, 14, 133
*Opus sectile*, 143
Orant, 45ff., 76
Orientalists, 2
Orientation, 109
Origen, 10, 75, 119
Orpheus, 42
Ox and ass, 79

Paedagogus, 75f.
*Paenula*, 200, 206ff.
Palace, 96, 162
Palermo, mosaics, 2
Palestine, 39, 114ff.
*Palla*, 208
*Palla sacra*, 209
*Pallium*, 199, 209
*Paludamentum*, 158, 210
Pantocrator, 85
Papal crypt, 26, 31
Paradise, 53
Paralytic with bed, 40, 58
Paris, Bibl. Nat., Ms., Suppl. grec. 1286, 190
Paris Psalter, 192
Paul and Peter—*see* Peter
" at Malta, 159
" with Sword, 130f.
" arrest of, 74f.
Paulinus of Nola, 16, 93, 110, 132ff., 151
Pectorius, 56
*Peribolos*, 104
Peter and Paul, 8, 71, 74, 129ff.
" as a good shepherd, 50
" in Rome, 26
" with keys, 131
" arrest of, 74, 76f.
Peter Damianus, 131
Philip and the eunuch, 73f.
Phrygian cap, 63
Pilate, 11, 72
Portraits of apostles, 131
" of evangelists, 179
" of Jesus, 11f.
" of saints, 13, 151
" on sarcophagi, 71f.

Prayer, attitude of, 45
" for the dead, 33, 35
" to the departed, 33
Presbytery, 102
Presentation, 137
*Propylaeum*, 104, 129, 150
*Prothesis*, 104
Prudentius, 13, 151
Pudens, 105, 126f., 128
Pulpits, 102
Purple, 200

Rabula Gospel, 181, 186f.
Ravenna, 117, 123f., 134, 138f., 201
"Reading man," 75
Red Sea, 42
Relics, 101
Resurrection—*see* Christ, Resurrection
Riegl, A., 3ff.
*Refrigerium*, 26, 51
Roman art, 6
Romanticism, 21
Rome, 134
Roof, 139
Rossano Gospel, 152, 181, 187ff.

Sacrament chapels, 58
Sacraments, 78
Sakkara, 197
Salerno, altar frontal, 171ff., 181
Samaritan woman, 40, 58
Sarcophagi, Christian, 63, 68ff., 129
" pagan, 68
*Schola*, 91
Seasons, 40, 133
Second Commandment, 9ff., 15, 180
*Segmentum*, 199ff.
Sepulchral art, 6f., 38ff.
Sessorian Palace, 107, 134
Severus Alexander—*see* Alexander
Shepherds at the manger, 43, 79
*Sigma*, 52, 54
Silk, 199
Silver and gold, 142, 146
Sirens—*see* Ulysses
Slaughter of the Innocents, 137
Space, sense of, 98f.
Spiral columns, 166
Stained glass, 125

## INDEX

Statues, 12, 50
*Stile bello*, 71, 72
Strzygowski, 3, 120
*Sub divo*, 39
Sun worship, 62, 111
Susanna, 40, 64
Symbolism, 5f., 56f., 58f.
Synagogue, 91
" at Dura, 15
Syria, 6, 17f.
Syria, North, 91, 95, 102

*Tablion*, 201, 210
Tapestry, 110, 196ff.
Thecla, 60
Temple, Jewish, 95
" Pagan, 95
Tertullian, 10, 31, 45, 56, 58, 110, 211
Textile art, 196ff.
Theodora, 139
Throne of Christ, 85f., 137, 144f.
*Tituli*, 25, 89, 105
Tobias, 40
Trajan, 181

*Triclia*, 26, 130
Trier, ivory tablet, 170f.
Trinity, 72, 117
Tufa, 23
Tunic, 108f., 208

Ulysses and the sirens, 75

Vienna Genesis, 181, 182ff., 193
Virgil, Vatican Library, 180
Virgin and Child, 43, 61, 136
Visitation, 60

Water clock, 76
Wilpert, 1, 2, 4, 65, 76f., 132ff., 155, 176, 206, 211
Wine, 52
Wise and foolish virgins, 43
Woman with an issue, 13, 40, 77
Women at the Sepulchre—*see* Christ, Resurrection

Zahn, 84, 128
Zion, 187

Revised June, 1965

# harper ☧ torchbooks

## HUMANITIES AND SOCIAL SCIENCES

### American Studies: General

THOMAS C. COCHRAN: The Inner Revolution: Essays on the Social Sciences in History TB/1140
EDWARD S. CORWIN: American Constitutional History. Essays edited by Alpheus T. Mason and Gerald Garvey TB/1136
A. HUNTER DUPREE: Science in the Federal Government: A History of Policies and Activities to 1940 TB/573
OSCAR HANDLIN, Ed.: This Was America: As Recorded by European Travelers in the Eighteenth, Nineteenth and Twentieth Centuries. Illus. TB/1119
MARCUS LEE HANSEN: The Atlantic Migration: 1607-1860. Edited by Arthur M. Schlesinger; Introduction by Oscar Handlin TB/1052
MARCUS LEE HANSEN: The Immigrant in American History. Edited with a Foreword by Arthur M. Schlesinger TB/1120
JOHN HIGHAM, Ed.: The Reconstruction of American History TB/1068
ROBERT H. JACKSON: The Supreme Court in the American System of Government TB/1106
JOHN F. KENNEDY: A Nation of Immigrants. Illus. Revised and Enlarged. Introduction by Robert F. Kennedy TB/1118
RALPH BARTON PERRY: Puritanism and Democracy TB/1138
ARNOLD ROSE: The Negro in America: The Condensed Version of Gunnar Myrdal's An American Dilemma TB/3048
MAURICE R. STEIN: The Eclipse of Community: An Interpretation of American Studies TB/1128
W. LLOYD WARNER and Associates: Democracy in Jonesville: A Study in Quality and Inequality ‖ TB/1129
W. LLOYD WARNER: Social Class in America: The Evaluation of Status TB/1013

### American Studies: Colonial

BERNARD BAILYN: The New England Merchants in the Seventeenth Century TB/1149
JOSEPH CHARLES: The Origins of the American Party System TB/1049
LAWRENCE HENRY GIPSON: The Coming of the Revolution: 1763-1775. † Illus. TB/3007
LEONARD W. LEVY: Freedom of Speech and Press in Early American History: Legacy of Suppression TB/1109

PERRY MILLER: Errand Into the Wilderness TB/1139
PERRY MILLER & T. H. JOHNSON, Eds.: The Puritans: A Sourcebook of Their Writings
Vol. I TB/1093; Vol. II TB/1094
KENNETH B. MURDOCK: Literature and Theology in Colonial New England TB/99
WALLACE NOTESTEIN: The English People on the Eve of Colonization: 1603-1630. † Illus. TB/3006
LOUIS B. WRIGHT: The Cultural Life of the American Colonies: 1607-1763. † Illus. TB/3005

### American Studies: From the Revolution to the Civil War

JOHN R. ALDEN: The American Revolution: 1775-1783. † Illus. TB/3011
RAY A. BILLINGTON: The Far Western Frontier: 1830-1860. † Illus. TB/3012
GEORGE DANGERFIELD: The Awakening of American Nationalism: 1815-1828. † Illus. TB/3061
CLEMENT EATON: The Freedom-of-Thought Struggle in the Old South. Revised and Enlarged. Illus. TB/1150
CLEMENT EATON: The Growth of Southern Civilization: 1790-1860. † Illus. TB/3040
LOUIS FILLER: The Crusade Against Slavery: 1830-1860. † Illus. TB/3029
DIXON RYAN FOX: The Decline of Aristocracy in the Politics of New York: 1801-1840. ‡ Edited by Robert V. Remini TB/3064
FRANCIS J. GRUND: Aristocracy in America: Social Class in the Formative Years of the New Nation TB/1001
ALEXANDER HAMILTON: The Reports of Alexander Hamilton. ‡ Edited by Jacob E. Cooke TB/3060
DANIEL R. HUNDLEY: Social Relations in Our Southern States. ‡ Edited by William R. Taylor TB/3058
THOMAS JEFFERSON: Notes on the State of Virginia. ‡ Edited by Thomas P. Abernethy TB/3052
BERNARD MAYO: Myths and Men: Patrick Henry, George Washington, Thomas Jefferson TB/1108
JOHN C. MILLER: Alexander Hamilton and the Growth of the New Nation TB/3057
RICHARD B. MORRIS, Ed.: The Era of the American Revolution TB/1180
R. B. NYE: The Cultural Life of the New Nation: 1776-1801. † Illus. TB/3026
GEORGE E. PROBST, Ed.: The Happy Republic: A Reader in Tocqueville's America TB/1060

† The New American Nation Series, edited by Henry Steele Commager and Richard B. Morris.
‡ American Perspectives series, edited by Bernard Wishy and William E. Leuchtenburg.
* The Rise of Modern Europe series, edited by William L. Langer.
‖ Researches in the Social, Cultural, and Behavioral Sciences, edited by Benjamin Nelson.
§ The Library of Religion and Culture, edited by Benjamin Nelson.
Σ Harper Modern Science Series, edited by James R. Newman.
° Not for sale in Canada.

1

FRANK THISTLETHWAITE: America and the Atlantic Community: *Anglo-American Aspects, 1790-1850* TB/1107
A. F. TYLER: Freedom's Ferment: *Phases of American Social History from the Revolution to the Outbreak of the Civil War. 31 illus.* TB/1074
GLYNDON G. VAN DEUSEN: The Jacksonian Era: 1828-1848. † *Illus.* TB/3028
LOUIS B. WRIGHT: Culture on the Moving Frontier TB/1053

## American Studies: Since the Civil War

RAY STANNARD BAKER: Following the Color Line: *American Negro Citizenship in Progressive Era.* ‡ *Illus. Edited by Dewey W. Grantham, Jr.* TB/3053
RANDOLPH S. BOURNE: War and the Intellectuals: *Collected Essays, 1915-1919.* ‡ *Edited by Carl Resek* TB/3043
A. RUSSELL BUCHANAN: The United States and World War II. † *Illus.* Vol. I TB/3044; Vol. II TB/3045
ABRAHAM CAHAN: The Rise of David Levinsky: *a documentary novel of social mobility in early twentieth century America. Intro. by John Higham* TB/1028
THOMAS C. COCHRAN: The American Business System: *A Historical Perspective, 1900-1955* TB/1080
THOMAS C. COCHRAN & WILLIAM MILLER: The Age of Enterprise: *A Social History of Industrial America* TB/1054
FOSTER RHEA DULLES: America's Rise to World Power: 1898-1954. † *Illus.* TB/3021
W. A. DUNNING: Essays on the Civil War and Reconstruction. *Introduction by David Donald* TB/1181
W. A. DUNNING: Reconstruction, Political and Economic: 1865-1877 TB/1073
HAROLD U. FAULKNER: Politics, Reform and Expansion: 1890-1900. † *Illus.* TB/3020
JOHN D. HICKS: Republican Ascendancy: 1921-1933. † *Illus.* TB/3041
ROBERT HUNTER: Poverty: *Social Conscience in the Progressive Era.* ‡ *Edited by Robert d'A. Jones* TB/3065
HELEN HUNT JACKSON: A Century of Dishonor: *The Early Crusade for Indian Reform.* ‡ *Edited by Andrew F. Rolle* TB/3063
ALBERT D. KIRWAN: Revolt of the Rednecks: *Mississippi Politics, 1876-1925* TB/1199
WILLIAM L. LANGER & S. EVERETT GLEASON: The Challenge to Isolation: *The World Crisis of 1937-1940 and American Foreign Policy*
Vol. I TB/3054; Vol. II TB/3055
WILLIAM E. LEUCHTENBURG: Franklin D. Roosevelt and the New Deal: 1932-1940. † *Illus.* TB/3025
ARTHUR S. LINK: Woodrow Wilson and the Progressive Era: 1910-1917. † *Illus.* TB/3023
ROBERT GREEN MCCLOSKEY: American Conservatism in the Age of Enterprise: 1865-1910 TB/1137
GEORGE E. MOWRY: The Era of Theodore Roosevelt and the Birth of Modern America: 1900-1912. † *Illus.* TB/3022
WALTER RAUSCHENBUSCH: Christianity and the Social Crisis. ‡ *Edited by Robert D. Cross* TB/3059
CHARLES H. SHINN: Mining Camps: *A Study in American Frontier Government.* ‡ *Edited by Rodman W. Paul* TB/3062
TWELVE SOUTHERNERS: I'll Take My Stand: *The South and the Agrarian Tradition. Intro. by Louis D. Rubin, Jr.; Biographical Essays by Virginia Rock* TB/1072
WALTER E. WEYL: The New Democracy: *An Essay on Certain Political Tendencies in the United States.* ‡ *Edited by Charles B. Forcey* TB/3042
VERNON LANE WHARTON: The Negro in Mississippi: 1865-1890 TB/1178

## Anthropology

JACQUES BARZUN: Race: *A Study in Superstition. Revised Edition* TB/1172
JOSEPH B. CASAGRANDE, Ed.: In the Company of Man: *Twenty Portraits of Anthropological Informants. Illus.* TB/3047
W. E. LE GROS CLARK: The Antecedents of Man: *An Introduction to the Evolution of the Primates.* ° *Illus.* TB/559
CORA DU BOIS: The People of Alor. *New Preface by the author. Illus.* Vol. I TB/1042; Vol. II TB/1043
RAYMOND FIRTH, Ed.: Man and Culture: *An Evaluation of the Work of Bronislaw Malinowski* ǁ ° TB/1133
L. S. B. LEAKEY: Adam's Ancestors: *The Evolution of Man and His Culture. Illus.* TB/1019
ROBERT H. LOWIE: Primitive Society. *Introduction by Fred Eggan* TB/1056
SIR EDWARD TYLOR: The Origins of Culture. *Part I of "Primitive Culture."* § *Introduction by Paul Radin* TB/33
SIR EDWARD TYLOR: Religion in Primitive Culture. *Part II of "Primitive Culture."* § *Introduction by Paul Radin* TB/34
W. LLOYD WARNER: A Black Civilization: *A Study of an Australian Tribe.* ǁ *Illus.* TB/3056

## Art and Art History

WALTER LOWRIE: Art in the Early Church. *152 illus. Revised Edition* TB/124
EMILE MÂLE: The Gothic Image: *Religious Art in France of the Thirteenth Century.* § *190 illus.* TB/44
MILLARD MEISS: Painting in Florence and Siena after the Black Death: *The Arts, Religion and Society in the Mid-Fourteenth Century. 169 illus.* TB/1148
ERICH NEUMANN: The Archetypal World of Henry Moore. *107 illus.* TB/2020
DORA & ERWIN PANOFSKY: Pandora's Box: *The Changing Aspects of a Mythical Symbol. Revised Edition. Illus.* TB/2021
ERWIN PANOFSKY: Studies in Iconology: *Humanistic Themes in the Art of the Renaissance. 180 illustrations* TB/1077
ALEXANDRE PIANKOFF: The Shrines of Tut-Ankh-Amon. *Edited by N. Rambova. 117 illus.* TB/2011
JEAN SEZNEC: The Survival of the Pagan Gods: *The Mythological Tradition and Its Place in Renaissance Humanism and Art. 108 illustrations* TB/2004
OTTO VON SIMSON: The Gothic Cathedral: *Origins of Gothic Architecture and the Medieval Concept of Order. 58 illus.* TB/2018
HEINRICH ZIMMER: Myth and Symbols in Indian Art and Civilization. *70 illustrations* TB/2005

## Business, Economics & Economic History

REINHARD BENDIX: Work and Authority in Industry: *Ideologies of Management in the Course of Industrialization* TB/3035
GILBERT BURCK & EDITORS OF FORTUNE: The Computer Age TB/1179
THOMAS C. COCHRAN: The American Business System: *A Historical Perspective, 1900-1955* TB/1080
THOMAS C. COCHRAN: The Inner Revolution: *Essays on the Social Sciences in History* TB/1140
THOMAS C. COCHRAN & WILLIAM MILLER: The Age of Enterprise: *A Social History of Industrial America* TB/1054

ROBERT DAHL & CHARLES E. LINDBLOM: Politics, Economics, and Welfare: *Planning and Politico-Economic Systems Resolved into Basic Social Processes*
TB/3037
PETER F. DRUCKER: The New Society: *The Anatomy of Industrial Order* TB/1082
EDITORS OF FORTUNE: America in the Sixties: *The Economy and the Society* TB/1015
ROBERT L. HEILBRONER: The Great Ascent: *The Struggle for Economic Development in Our Time* TB/3030
ABBA P. LERNER: Everybody's Business: *Current Assumptions in Economics and Public Policy* TB/3051
ROBERT GREEN MCCLOSKEY: American Conservatism in the Age of Enterprise, 1865-1910 TB/1137
PAUL MANTOUX: The Industrial Revolution in the Eighteenth Century: *The Beginnings of the Modern Factory System in England* ° TB/1079
WILLIAM MILLER, Ed.: Men in Business: *Essays on the Historical Role of the Entrepreneur* TB/1081
PERRIN STRYKER: The Character of the Executive: *Eleven Studies in Managerial Qualities* TB/1041
PIERRE URI: Partnership for Progress: *A Program for Transatlantic Action* TB/3036

## Contemporary Culture

JACQUES BARZUN: The House of Intellect TB/1051
JOHN U. NEF: Cultural Foundations of Industrial Civilization TB/1024
NATHAN M. PUSEY: The Age of the Scholar: *Observations on Education in a Troubled Decade* TB/1157
PAUL VALÉRY: The Outlook for Intelligence TB/2016

## History: General

L. CARRINGTON GOODRICH: A Short History of the Chinese People. *Illus.* TB/3015
DAN N. JACOBS & HANS H. BAERWALD: Chinese Communism: *Selected Documents* TB/3031
BERNARD LEWIS: The Arabs in History TB/1029
SIR PERCY SYKES: A History of Exploration. ° *Introduction by John K. Wright* TB/1046

## History: Ancient and Medieval

A. ANDREWES: The Greek Tyrants TB/1103
P. BOISSONNADE: Life and Work in Medieval Europe: *The Evolution of the Medieval Economy, the Fifth to the Fifteenth Centuries.* ° *Preface by Lynn White, Jr.*
TB/1141
HELEN CAM: England before Elizabeth TB/1026
NORMAN COHN: The Pursuit of the Millennium: *Revolutionary Messianism in Medieval and Reformation Europe and its Bearing on Modern Leftist and Rightist Totalitarian Movements* TB/1037
G. G. COULTON: Medieval Village, Manor, and Monastery
TB/1022
HEINRICH FICHTENAU: The Carolingian Empire: *The Age of Charlemagne* TB/1142
F. L. GANSHOF: Feudalism TB/1058
EDWARD GIBBON: The Triumph of Christendom in the Roman Empire *(Chaps. XV-XX of "Decline and Fall," J. B. Bury edition).* § *Illus.* TB/46
MICHAEL GRANT: Ancient History ° TB/1190
DENYS HAY: The Medieval Centuries ° TB/1192
J. M. HUSSEY: The Byzantine World TB/1057
SAMUEL NOAH KRAMER: Sumerian Mythology TB/1055

FERDINAND LOT: The End of the Ancient World and the Beginnings of the Middle Ages. *Introduction by Glanville Downey* TB/1044
G. MOLLATT: The Popes at Avignon: 1305-1378 TB/308
CHARLES PETIT-DUTAILLIS: The Feudal Monarchy in France and England: *From the Tenth to the Thirteenth Century* ° TB/1165
HENRI PIERENNE: Early Democracies in the Low Countries: *Urban Society and Political Conflict in the Middle Ages and the Renaissance. Introduction by John H. Mundy* TB/1110
STEVEN RUNCIMAN: A History of the Crusades. Volume I: *The First Crusade and the Foundation of the Kingdom of Jerusalem. Illus.* TB/1143
FERDINAND SCHEVILL: Siena: *The History of a Medieval Commune. Introduction by William M. Bowsky*
TB/1164
HENRY OSBORN TAYLOR: The Classical Heritage of the Middle Ages. *Foreword and Biblio. by Kenneth M. Setton* TB/1117
F. VAN DER MEER: Augustine The Bishop: *Church and Society at the Dawn of the Middle Ages* TB/304
J. M. WALLACE-HADRILL: The Barbarian West: *The Early Middle Ages, A.D. 400-1000* TB/1061

## History: Renaissance & Reformation

JACOB BURCKHARDT: The Civilization of the Renaissance in Italy. *Introduction by Benjamin Nelson and Charles Trinkaus. Illus.*
Vol. I TB/40; Vol. II TB/41
ERNST CASSIRER: The Individual and the Cosmos in Renaissance Philosophy. *Translated with an Introduction by Mario Domandi* TB/1097
FEDERICO CHABOD: Machiavelli and the Renaissance
TB/1193
EDWARD P. CHEYNEY: The Dawn of a New Era, 1250-1453. * *Illus.* TB/3002
R. TREVOR DAVIES: The Golden Century of Spain, 1501-1621 ° TB/1194
DESIDERIUS ERASMUS: Christian Humanism and the Reformation: *Selected Writings. Edited and translated by John C. Olin* TB/1166
WALLACE K. FERGUSON et al.: Facets of the Renaissance
TB/1098
WALLACE K. FERGUSON et al.: The Renaissance: *Six Essays. Illus.* TB/1084
JOHN NEVILLE FIGGIS: The Divine Right of Kings. *Introduction by G. R. Elton* TB/1191
JOHN NEVILLE FIGGIS: Political Thought from Gerson to Grotius: 1414-1625: *Seven Studies. Introduction by Garrett Mattingly* TB/1032
MYRON P. GILMORE: The World of Humanism, 1453-1517.* *Illus.* TB/3003
FRANCESCO GUICCIARDINI: Maxims and Reflections of a Renaissance Statesman (Ricordi). *Trans. by Mario Domandi. Intro. by Nicolai Rubinstein* TB/1160
J. H. HEXTER: More's Utopia: *The Biography of an Idea*
TB/1195
JOHAN HUIZINGA: Erasmus and the Age of Reformation. *Illus.* TB/19
ULRICH VON HUTTEN et al.: On the Eve of the Reformation: *"Letters of Obscure Men." Introduction by Hajo Holborn* TB/1124
PAUL O. KRISTELLER: Renaissance Thought: *The Classic, Scholastic, and Humanist Strains* TB/1048
PAUL O. KRISTELLER: Renaissance Thought II: *Papers on Humanism and the Arts* TB/1163

NICCOLÒ MACHIAVELLI: History of Florence and of the Affairs of Italy: *from the earliest times to the death of Lorenzo the Magnificent. Introduction by Felix Gilbert*  TB/1027
ALFRED VON MARTIN: Sociology of the Renaissance. *Introduction by Wallace K. Ferguson*  TB/1099
GARRETT MATTINGLY et al.: Renaissance Profiles. *Edited by J. H. Plumb*  TB/1162
MILLARD MEISS: Painting in Florence and Siena after the Black Death: *The Arts, Religion and Society in the Mid-Fourteenth Century. 169 illus.*  TB/1148
J. E. NEALE: The Age of Catherine de Medici °  TB/1085
ERWIN PANOFSKY: Studies in Iconology: *Humanistic Themes in the Art of the Renaissance. 180 illustrations*  TB/1077
J. H. PARRY: The Establishment of the European Hegemony: 1415-1715: *Trade and Exploration in the Age of the Renaissance*  TB/1045
J. H. PLUMB: The Italian Renaissance: *A Concise Survey of Its History and Culture*  TB/1161
GORDON RUPP: Luther's Progress to the Diet of Worms °  TB/120
FERDINAND SCHEVILL: The Medici. *Illus.*  TB/1010
FERDINAND SCHEVILL: Medieval and Renaissance Florence. *Illus.*  Volume I: *Medieval Florence*  TB/1090
Volume II: *The Coming of Humanism and the Age of the Medici*  TB/1091
G. M. TREVELYAN: England in the Age of Wycliffe, 1368-1520 °  TB/1112
VESPASIANO: Renaissance Princes, Popes, and Prelates: *The Vespasiano Memoirs: Lives of Illustrious Men of the XVth Century. Introduction by Myron P. Gilmore*  TB/1111

## History: Modern European

FREDERICK B. ARTZ: Reaction and Revolution, 1815-1832. * *Illus.*  TB/3034
MAX BELOFF: The Age of Absolutism, 1660-1815  TB/1062
ROBERT C. BINKLEY: Realism and Nationalism, 1852-1871. * *Illus.*  TB/3038
CRANE BRINTON: A Decade of Revolution, 1789-1799. * *Illus.*  TB/3018
J. BRONOWSKI & BRUCE MAZLISH: The Western Intellectual Tradition: *From Leonardo to Hegel*  TB/3001
GEOFFREY BRUUN: Europe and the French Imperium, 1799-1814. * *Illus.*  TB/3033
ALAN BULLOCK: Hitler, A Study in Tyranny. ° *Illus.*  TB/1123
E. H. CARR: The Twenty Years' Crisis, 1919-1939: *An Introduction to the Study of International Relations* °  TB/1122
GORDON A. CRAIG: From Bismarck to Adenauer: *Aspects of German Statecraft. Revised Edition*  TB/1171
WALTER L. DORN: Competition for Empire, 1740-1763. * *Illus.*  TB/3032
CARL J. FRIEDRICH: The Age of the Baroque, 1610-1660. * *Illus.*  TB/3004
RENÉ FUELOEP-MILLER: The Mind and Face of Bolshevism: *An Examination of Cultural Life in Soviet Russia. New Epilogue by the Author*  TB/1188
M. DOROTHY GEORGE: London Life in the Eighteenth Century  TB/1182
LEO GERSHOY: From Despotism to Revolution, 1763-1789. * *Illus.*  TB/3017
C. C. GILLISPIE: Genesis and Geology: *The Decades before Darwin* §  TB/51

ALBERT GOODWIN: The French Revolution  TB/1064
ALBERT GUERARD: France in the Classical Age: *The Life and Death of an Ideal*  TB/1183
CARLTON J. H. HAYES: A Generation of Materialism, 1871-1900. * *Illus.*  TB/3039
J. H. HEXTER: Reappraisals in History: *New Views on History and Society in Early Modern Europe*  TB/1100
A. R. HUMPHREYS: The Augustan World: *Society, Thought, and Letters in Eighteenth Century England*  TB/1105
ALDOUS HUXLEY: The Devils of Loudun: *A Study in the Psychology of Power Politics and Mystical Religion in the France of Cardinal Richelieu* § °  TB/60
DAN N. JACOBS, Ed.: The New Communist Manifesto *and Related Documents. Third edition, revised*  TB/1078
HANS KOHN, Ed.: The Mind of Modern Russia: *Historical and Political Thought of Russia's Great Age*  TB/1065
KINGSLEY MARTIN: French Liberal Thought in the Eighteenth Century: *A Study of Political Ideas from Bayle to Condorcet*  TB/1114
SIR LEWIS NAMIER: Personalities and Powers: *Selected Essays*  TB/1186
SIR LEWIS NAMIER: Vanished Supremacies: *Essays on European History, 1812-1918* °  TB/1088
JOHN U. NEF: Western Civilization Since the Renaissance: *Peace, War, Industry, and the Arts*  TB/1113
FREDERICK L. NUSSBAUM: The Triumph of Science and Reason, 1660-1685. * *Illus.*  TB/3009
JOHN PLAMENATZ: German Marxism and Russian Communism. ° *New Preface by the Author*  TB/1189
RAYMOND W. POSTGATE, Ed.: Revolution from 1789 to 1906: *Selected Documents*  TB/1063
PENFIELD ROBERTS: The Quest for Security, 1715-1740. * *Illus.*  TB/3016
PRISCILLA ROBERTSON: Revolutions of 1848: *A Social History*  TB/1025
ALBERT SOREL: Europe Under the Old Regime. *Translated by Francis H. Herrick*  TB/1121
N. N. SUKHANOV: The Russian Revolution, 1917: *Eyewitness Account. Edited by Joel Carmichael*
Vol. I  TB/1066;  Vol. II  TB/1067
A. J. P. TAYLOR: The Habsburg Monarch, 1809-1918: *A History of the Austrian Empire and Austria-Hungary* °  TB/1187
JOHN B. WOLF: The Emergence of the Great Powers, 1685-1715. * *Illus.*  TB/3010
JOHN B. WOLF: France: 1814-1919: *The Rise of a Liberal-Democratic Society*  TB/3019

## Intellectual History

HERSCHEL BAKER: The Image of Man: *A Study of the Idea of Human Dignity in Classical Antiquity, the Middle Ages, and the Renaissance*  TB/1047
R. R. BOLGAR: The Classical Heritage and Its Beneficiaries: *From the Carolingian Age to the End of the Renaissance*  TB/1125
J. BRONOWSKI & BRUCE MAZLISH: The Western Intellectual Tradition: *From Leonardo to Hegel*  TB/3001
ERNST CASSIRER: The Individual and the Cosmos in Renaissance Philosophy. *Translated with an Introduction by Mario Domandi*  TB/1097
NORMAN COHN: The Pursuit of the Millennium: *Revolutionary Messianism in medieval and Reformation Europe and its bearing on modern Leftist and Rightist totalitarian movements*  TB/1037

G. RACHEL LEVY: Religious Conceptions of the Stone Age and Their Influence upon European Thought. Illus. Introduction by Henri Frankfort TB/106
ARTHUR O. LOVEJOY: The Great Chain of Being: A Study of the History of an Idea TB/1009
MILTON C. NAHM: Genius and Creativity: An Essay in the History of Ideas TB/1196
ROBERT PAYNE: Hubris: A Study of Pride. Foreword by Sir Herbert Read TB/1031
RALPH BARTON PERRY: The Thought and Character of William James: Briefer Version TB/1156
BRUNO SNELL: The Discovery of the Mind: The Greek Origins of European Thought TB/1018
ERNEST LEE TUVESON: Millennium and Utopia: A Study in the Background of the Idea of Progress. ‖ New Preface by the Author TB/1134
PAUL VALÉRY: The Outlook for Intelligence TB/2016

### Literature, Poetry, The Novel & Criticism

JAMES BAIRD: Ishmael: The Art of Melville in the Contexts of International Primitivism TB/1023
JACQUES BARZUN: The House of Intellect TB/1051
W. J. BATE: From Classic to Romantic: Premises of Taste in Eighteenth Century England TB/1036
RACHEL BESPALOFF: On the Iliad TB/2006
R. P. BLACKMUR et al.: Lectures in Criticism. Introduction by Huntington Cairns TB/2003
RANDOLPH S. BOURNE: War and the Intellectuals: Collected Essays, 1915-1919. ‡ Edited by Carl Resek TB/3043
ABRAHAM CAHAN: The Rise of David Levinsky: a documentary novel of social mobility in early twentieth century America. Introduction by John Higham TB/1028
ERNST R. CURTIUS: European Literature and the Latin Middle Ages TB/2015
GEORGE ELIOT: Daniel Deronda: a novel. Introduction by F. R. Leavis TB/1039
ETIENNE GILSON: Dante and Philosophy TB/1089
ALFRED HARBAGE: As They Liked It: A Study of Shakespeare's Moral Artistry TB/1035
STANLEY R. HOPPER, Ed.: Spiritual Problems in Contemporary Literature § TB/21
A. R. HUMPHREYS: The Augustan World: Society, Thought and Letters in Eighteenth Century England ° TB/1105
ALDOUS HUXLEY: Antic Hay & The Giaconda Smile. ° Introduction by Martin Green TB/3503
ALDOUS HUXLEY: Brave New World & Brave New World Revisited. ° Introduction by Martin Green TB/3501
HENRY JAMES: Roderick Hudson: a novel. Introduction by Leon Edel TB/1016
HENRY JAMES: The Tragic Muse: a novel. Introduction by Leon Edel TB/1017
ARNOLD KETTLE: An Introduction to the English Novel. Volume I: Defoe to George Eliot TB/1011
Volume II: Henry James to the Present TB/1012
ROGER SHERMAN LOOMIS: The Development of Arthurian Romance TB/1167
JOHN STUART MILL: On Bentham and Coleridge. Introduction by F. R. Leavis TB/1070
PERRY MILLER & T. H. JOHNSON, Editors: The Puritans: A Sourcebook of Their Writings
Vol. I TB/1093; Vol. II TB/1094
KENNETH B. MURDOCK: Literature and Theology in Colonial New England TB/99

SAMUEL PEPYS: The Diary of Samuel Pepys. ° Edited by O. F. Morshead. Illus. by Ernest Shepard TB/1007
ST.-JOHN PERSE: Seamarks TB/2002
O. E. RÖLVAAG: Giants in the Earth TB/3504
GEORGE SANTAYANA: Interpretations of Poetry and Religion § TB/9
C. P. SNOW: Time of Hope: a novel TB/1040
HEINRICH STRAUMANN: American Literature in the Twentieth Century. Third Edition, Revised TB/1168
DOROTHY VAN GHENT: The English Novel: Form and Function TB/1050
E. B. WHITE: One Man's Meat. Introduction by Walter Blair TB/3505
MORTON DAUWEN ZABEL, Editor: Literary Opinion in America Vol. I TB/3013; Vol. II TB/3014

### Myth, Symbol & Folklore

JOSEPH CAMPBELL, Editor: Pagan and Christian Mysteries Illus. TB/2013
MIRCEA ELIADE: Cosmos and History: The Myth of the Eternal Return § TB/2050
C. G. JUNG & C. KERÉNYI: Essays on a Science of Mythology: The Myths of the Divine Child and the Divine Maiden TB/2014
DORA & ERWIN PANOFSKY: Pandora's Box: The Changing Aspects of a Mythical Symbol. Revised Edition. Illus. TB/2021
ERWIN PANOFSKY: Studies in Iconology: Humanistic Themes in the Art of the Renaissance. 180 illustrations TB/1077
JEAN SEZNEC: The Survival of the Pagan Gods: The Mythological Tradition and its Place in Renaissance Humanism and Art. 108 illustrations TB/2004
HELLMUT WILHELM: Change: Eight Lectures on the I Ching TB/2019
HEINRICH ZIMMER: Myths and Symbols in Indian Art and Civilization. 70 illustrations TB/2005

### Philosophy

HENRI BERGSON: Time and Free Will: An Essay on the Immediate Data of Consciousness ° TB/1021
H. J. BLACKHAM: Six Existentialist Thinkers: Kierkegaard, Nietzsche, Jaspers, Marcel, Heidegger, Sartre ° TB/1002
CRANE BRINTON: Nietzsche. New Preface and Epilogue by the Author TB/1197
ERNST CASSIRER: The Individual and the Cosmos in Renaissance Philosophy. Translated with an Introduction by Mario Domandi TB/1097
ERNST CASSIRER: Rousseau, Kant and Goethe. Introduction by Peter Gay TB/1092
FREDERICK COPLESTON: Medieval Philosophy ° TB/376
F. M. CORNFORD: From Religion to Philosophy: A Study in the Origins of Western Speculation § TB/20
WILFRID DESAN: The Tragic Finale: An Essay on the Philosophy of Jean-Paul Sartre TB/1030
PAUL FRIEDLÄNDER: Plato: An Introduction TB/2017
ÉTIENNE GILSON: Dante and Philosophy TB/1089
WILLIAM CHASE GREENE: Moira: Fate, Good, and Evil in Greek Thought TB/1104
W. K. C. GUTHRIE: The Greek Philosophers: From Thales to Aristotle ° TB/1008
F. H. HEINEMANN: Existentialism and the Modern Predicament TB/28

EDMUND HUSSERL: Phenomenology and the Crisis of Philosophy. *Translated with an Introduction by Quentin Lauer* TB/1170

IMMANUEL KANT: The Doctrine of Virtue, *being Part II of The Metaphysic of Morals. Translated with Notes and Introduction by Mary J. Gregor. Foreword by H. J. Paton* TB/110

IMMANUEL KANT: Groundwork of the Metaphysic of Morals. *Translated and analyzed by H. J. Paton* TB/1159

IMMANUEL KANT: Lectures on Ethics. § *Introduction by Lewis W. Beck* TB/105

QUENTIN LAUER: Phenomenology: *Its Genesis and Prospect* TB/1169

GEORGE A. MORGAN: What Nietzsche Means TB/1198

MICHAEL POLANYI: Personal Knowledge: *Towards a Post-Critical Philosophy* TB/1158

WILLARD VAN ORMAN QUINE: Elementary Logic. *Revised Edition* TB/577

WILLARD VAN ORMAN QUINE: From a Logical Point of View: *Logico-Philosophical Essays* TB/566

BERTRAND RUSSELL et al.: The Philosophy of Bertrand Russell. *Edited by Paul Arthur Schilpp*
  Vol. I TB/1095; Vol. II TB/1096

L. S. STEBBING: A Modern Introduction to Logic TB/538

ALFRED NORTH WHITEHEAD: Process and Reality: *An Essay in Cosmology* TB/1033

WILHELM WINDELBAND: A History of Philosophy
  Vol. I: *Greek, Roman, Medieval* TB/38
  Vol. II: *Renaissance, Enlightenment, Modern* TB/39

## Philosophy of History

NICOLAS BERDYAEV: The Beginning and the End § TB/14

NICOLAS BERDYAEV: The Destiny of Man TB/61

WILHELM DILTHEY: Pattern and Meaning in History: *Thoughts on History and Society.* º *Edited with an Introduction by H. P. Rickman* TB/1075

RAYMOND KLIBANSKY & H. J. PATON, Eds.: Philosophy and History: *The Ernst Cassirer Festschrift. Illus.* TB/1115

MILTON C. NAHM: Genius and Creativity: *An Essay in the History of Ideas* TB/1196

JOSE ORTEGA Y GASSET: The Modern Theme. *Introduction by Jose Ferrater Mora* TB/1038

KARL R. POPPER: The Poverty of Historicism º TB/1126

W. H. WALSH: Philosophy of History: *An Introduction* TB/1020

## Political Science & Government

JEREMY BENTHAM: The Handbook of Political Fallacies: *Introduction by Crane Brinton* TB/1069

KENNETH E. BOULDING: Conflict and Defense: *A General Theory* TB/3024

CRANE BRINTON: English Political Thought in the Nineteenth Century TB/1071

EDWARD S. CORWIN: American Constitutional History: *Essays edited by Alpheus T. Mason and Gerald Garvey* TB/1136

ROBERT DAHL & CHARLES E. LINDBLOM: Politics, Economics, and Welfare: *Planning and Politico-Economic Systems Resolved into Basic Social Processes* TB/3037

JOHN NEVILLE FIGGIS: The Divine Right of Kings. *Introduction by G. R. Elton* TB/1191

JOHN NEVILLE FIGGIS: Political Thought from Gerson to Grotius: 1414-1625: *Seven Studies. Introduction by Garrett Mattingly* TB/1032

F. L. GANSHOF: Feudalism TB/1058

G. P. GOOCH: English Democratic Ideas in Seventeenth Century TB/1006

J. H. HEXTER: More's Utopia: *The Biography of an Idea. New Epilogue by the Author* TB/1195

ROBERT H. JACKSON: The Supreme Court in the American System of Government TB/1106

DAN N. JACOBS, Ed.: The New Communist Manifesto *and Related Documents* TB/1078

DAN N. JACOBS & HANS BAERWALD, Eds.: Chinese Communism: *Selected Documents* TB/3031

ROBERT GREEN MCCLOSKEY: American Conservatism in the Age of Enterprise, 1865-1910 TB/1137

KINGSLEY MARTIN: French Liberal Thought in the Eighteenth Century: *Political Ideas from Bayle to Condorcet* TB/1114

JOHN STUART MILL: On Bentham and Coleridge. *Introduction by F. R. Leavis* TB/1070

JOHN B. MORRALL: Political Thought in Medieval Times TB/1076

JOHN PLAMENATZ: German Marxism and Russian Communism. º *New Preface by the Author* TB/1189

KARL R. POPPER: The Open Society and Its Enemies
  Vol. I: *The Spell of Plato* TB/1101
  Vol. II: *The High Tide of Prophecy: Hegel, Marx, and the Aftermath* TB/1102

HENRI DE SAINT-SIMON: Social Organization, The Science of Man, and Other Writings. *Edited and Translated by Felix Markham* TB/1152

JOSEPH A. SCHUMPETER: Capitalism, Socialism and Democracy TB/3008

CHARLES H. SHINN: Mining Camps: *A Study in American Frontier Government.* ‡ *Edited by Rodman W. Paul* TB/3062

## Psychology

ALFRED ADLER: The Individual Psychology of Alfred Adler. *Edited by Heinz L. and Rowena R. Ansbacher* TB/1154

ALFRED ADLER: Problems of Neurosis. *Introduction by Heinz L. Ansbacher* TB/1145

ANTON T. BOISEN: The Exploration of the Inner World: *A Study of Mental Disorder and Religious Experience* TB/87

HERBERT FINGARETTE: The Self in Transformation: *Psychoanalysis, Philosophy and the Life of the Spirit.* || TB/1177

SIGMUND FREUD: On Creativity and the Unconscious: *Papers on the Psychology of Art, Literature, Love, Religion.* § *Intro. by Benjamin Nelson* TB/45

C. JUDSON HERRICK: The Evolution of Human Nature TB/545

WILLIAM JAMES: Psychology: *The Briefer Course. Edited with an Intro. by Gordon Allport* TB/1034

C. G. JUNG: Psychological Reflections TB/2001

C. G. JUNG: Symbols of Transformation: *An Analysis of the Prelude to a Case of Schizophrenia. Illus.*
  Vol. I: TB/2009; Vol. II TB/2010

C. G. JUNG & C. KERÉNYI: Essays on a Science of Mythology: *The Myths of the Divine Child and the Divine Maiden* TB/2014

JOHN T. MCNEILL: A History of the Cure of Souls TB/126

KARL MENNINGER: Theory of Psychoanalytic Technique TB/1144

ERICH NEUMANN: Amor and Psyche: *The Psychic Development of the Feminine* TB/2012

ERICH NEUMANN: The Archetypal World of Henry Moore. 107 illus. TB/2020
ERICH NEUMANN: The Origins and History of Consciousness Vol. I Illus. TB/2007; Vol. II TB/2008
C. P. OBERNDORF: A History of Psychoanalysis in America TB/1147
RALPH BARTON PERRY: The Thought and Character of William James: Briefer Version TB/1156
JEAN PIAGET, BÄRBEL INHELDER, & ALINA SZEMINSKA: The Child's Conception of Geometry ° TB/1146
JOHN H. SCHAAR: Escape from Authority: The Perspectives of Erich Fromm TB/1155

## Sociology

JACQUES BARZUN: Race: A Study in Superstition. Revised Edition TB/1172
BERNARD BERELSON, Ed.: The Behavioral Sciences Today TB/1127
ABRAHAM CAHAN: The Rise of David Levinsky: A documentary novel of social mobility in early twentieth century America. Intro. by John Higham TB/1028
THOMAS C. COCHRAN: The Inner Revolution: Essays on the Social Sciences in History TB/1140
ALLISON DAVIS & JOHN DOLLARD: Children of Bondage: The Personality Development of Negro Youth in the Urban South || TB/3049
ST. CLAIR DRAKE & HORACE R. CAYTON: Black Metropolis: A Study of Negro Life in a Northern City. Revised and Enlarged. Intro. by Everett C. Hughes
Vol. I TB/1086; Vol. II TB/1087
EMILE DURKHEIM et al.: Essays on Sociology and Philosophy: With Analyses of Durkheim's Life and Work. || Edited by Kurt H. Wolff TB/1151
LEON FESTINGER, HENRY W. RIECKEN & STANLEY SCHACHTER: When Prophecy Fails: A Social and Psychological Account of a Modern Group that Predicted the Destruction of the World || TB/1132
ALVIN W. GOULDNER: Wildcat Strike: A Study in Worker-Management Relationships || TB/1176
FRANCIS J. GRUND: Aristocracy in America: Social Class in the Formative Years of the New Nation TB/1001
KURT LEWIN: Field Theory in Social Science: Selected Theoretical Papers. || Edited with a Foreword by Dorwin Cartwright TB/1135
R. M. MACIVER: Social Causation TB/1153
ROBERT K. MERTON, LEONARD BROOM, LEONARD S. COTTRELL, JR., Editors: Sociology Today: Problems and Prospects || Vol. I TB/1173; Vol. II TB/1174
TALCOTT PARSONS & EDWARD A. SHILS, Editors: Toward a General Theory of Action: Theoretical Foundations for the Social Sciences TB/1083
JOHN H. ROHRER & MUNRO S. EDMONSON, Eds.: The Eighth Generation Grows Up: Cultures and Personalities of New Orleans Negroes || TB/3050
ARNOLD ROSE: The Negro in America: The Condensed Version of Gunnar Myrdal's An American Dilemma TB/3048
KURT SAMUELSSON: Religion and Economic Action: A Critique of Max Weber's The Protestant Ethic and the Spirit of Capitalism. || ° Trans. by E. G. French; Ed. with Intro. by D. C. Coleman TB/1131
PITIRIM A. SOROKIN: Contemporary Sociological Theories. Through the First Quarter of the 20th Century TB/3046
MAURICE R. STEIN: The Eclipse of Community: An Interpretation of American Studies TB/1128
FERDINAND TÖNNIES: Community and Society: Gemeinschaft und Gesellschaft. Translated and edited by Charles P. Loomis TB/1116
W. LLOYD WARNER & Associates: Democracy in Jonesville: A Study in Quality and Inequality TB/1129
W. LLOYD WARNER: Social Class in America: The Evaluation of Status TB/1013

# RELIGION

## Ancient & Classical

J. H. BREASTED: Development of Religion and Thought in Ancient Egypt. Introduction by John A. Wilson TB/57
HENRI FRANKFORT: Ancient Egyptian Religion: An Interpretation TB/77
G. RACHEL LEVY: Religious Conceptions of the Stone Age and their Influence upon European Thought. Illus. Introduction by Henri Frankfort TB/106
MARTIN P. NILSSON: Greek Folk Religion. Foreword by Arthur Darby Nock TB/78
ALEXANDRE PIANKOFF: The Shrines of Tut-Ankh-Amon. Edited by N. Rambova. 117 illus. TB/2011
H. J. ROSE: Religion in Greece and Rome TB/55

## Biblical Thought & Literature

W. F. ALBRIGHT: The Biblical Period from Abraham to Ezra TB/102
C. K. BARRETT, Ed.: The New Testament Background: Selected Documents TB/86
C. H. DODD: The Authority of the Bible TB/43
M. S. ENSLIN: Christian Beginnings TB/5
M. S. ENSLIN: The Literature of the Christian Movement TB/6
JOHN GRAY: Archaeology and the Old Testament World. Illus. TB/127
H. H. ROWLEY: The Growth of the Old Testament TB/107
D. WINTON THOMAS, Ed.: Documents from Old Testament Times TB/85

## The Judaic Tradition

MARTIN BUBER: Eclipse of God: Studies in the Relation Between Religion and Philosophy TB/12
MARTIN BUBER: Moses: The Revelation and the Covenant TB/27
MARTIN BUBER: Pointing the Way. Introduction by Maurice S. Friedman TB/103
MARTIN BUBER: The Prophetic Faith TB/73
MARTIN BUBER: Two Types of Faith: the interpenetration of Judaism and Christianity ° TB/75
ERNST LUDWIG EHRLICH: A Concise History of Israel: From the Earliest Times to the Destruction of the Temple in A.D. 70 ° TB/128
MAURICE S. FRIEDMAN: Martin Buber: The Life of Dialogue TB/64
FLAVIUS JOSEPHUS: The Great Roman-Jewish War, with The Life of Josephus. Introduction by William R. Farmer TB/74
T. J. MEEK: Hebrew Origins TB/69

## Christianity: Origins & Early Development

AUGUSTINE: An Augustine Synthesis. Edited by Erich Przywara TB/335
ADOLF DEISSMANN: Paul: A Study in Social and Religious History TB/15

EDWARD GIBBON: The Triumph of Christendom in the Roman Empire (Chaps. XV-XX of "Decline and Fall," J. B. Bury edition). § Illus. TB/46
MAURICE GOGUEL: Jesus and the Origins of Christianity.° Introduction by C. Leslie Mitton
Volume I: *Prolegomena to the Life of Jesus* TB/65
Volume II: *The Life of Jesus* TB/66
EDGAR J. GOODSPEED: A Life of Jesus TB/1
ADOLF HARNACK: The Mission and Expansion of Christianity in the First Three Centuries. Introduction by Jaroslav Pelikan TB/92
R. K. HARRISON: The Dead Sea Scrolls: *An Introduction* ° TB/84
EDWIN HATCH: The Influence of Greek Ideas on Christianity. § Introduction and Bibliography by Frederick C. Grant TB/18
ARTHUR DARBY NOCK: Early Gentile Christianity and Its Hellenistic Background TB/111
ARTHUR DARBY NOCK: St. Paul ° TB/104
F. VAN DER MEER: Augustine the Bishop: *Church and Society at the Dawn of the Middle Ages* TB/304
JOHANNES WEISS: Earliest Christianity: *A History of the Period A.D. 30-150.* Introduction and Bibliography by Frederick C. Grant Volume I TB/53
Volume II TB/54

## Christianity: The Middle Ages and The Reformation

JOHANNES ECKHART: Meister Eckhart: *A Modern Translation by R. B. Blakney* TB/8
DESIDERIUS ERASMUS: Christian Humanism and the Reformation: *Selected Writings.* Edited and translated by John C. Olin TB/1166
ÉTIENNE GILSON: Dante and Philosophy TB/1089
WILLIAM HALLER: The Rise of Puritanism TB/22
JOHAN HUIZINGA: Erasmus and the Age of Reformation. *Illus.* TB/19
A. C. MCGIFFERT: Protestant Thought Before Kant. Preface by Jaroslav Pelikan TB/93
JOHN T. MCNEILL: Makers of the Christian Tradition: *From Alfred the Great to Schleiermacher* TB/121
G. MOLLAT: The Popes at Avignon, 1305-1378 TB/308
GORDON RUPP: Luther's Progress to the Diet of Worms ° TB/120

## Christianity: The Protestant Tradition

KARL BARTH: Church Dogmatics: *A Selection* TB/95
KARL BARTH: Dogmatics in Outline TB/56
KARL BARTH: The Word of God and the Word of Man TB/13
WINTHROP HUDSON: The Great Tradition of the American Churches TB/98
SOREN KIERKEGAARD: Edifying Discourses. *Edited with an Introduction by Paul Holmer* TB/32
SOREN KIERKEGAARD: The Journals of Kierkegaard. ° *Edited with an Introduction by Alexander Dru* TB/52
SOREN KIERKEGAARD: The Point of View for My Work as an Author: *A Report to History.* § Preface by Benjamin Nelson TB/88
SOREN KIERKEGAARD: The Present Age. § *Translated and edited by Alexander Dru. Introduction by Walter Kaufmann* TB/94
SOREN KIERKEGAARD: Purity of Heart TB/4
SOREN KIERKEGAARD: Repetition: *An Essay in Experimental Psychology.* Translated with Introduction & Notes by Walter Lowrie TB/117

SOREN KIERKEGAARD: Works of Love: *Some Christian Reflections in the Form of Discourses* TB/122
WALTER LOWRIE: Kierkegaard: *A Life* Vol. I TB/89
Vol. II TB/90
PERRY MILLER & T. H. JOHNSON, Editors: The Puritans: *A Sourcebook of Their Writings* Vol. I TB/1093
Vol. II TB/1094
F. SCHLEIERMACHER: The Christian Faith. *Introduction by Richard R. Niebuhr* Vol. I TB/108
Vol. II TB/109
F. SCHLEIERMACHER: On Religion: *Speeches to Its Cultured Despisers.* Intro. by Rudolf Otto TB/36
PAUL TILLICH: Dynamics of Faith TB/42
EVELYN UNDERHILL: Worship TB/10
G. VAN DER LEEUW: Religion in Essence and Manifestation: *A Study in Phenomenology.* Appendices by Hans H. Penner Vol. I TB/100; Vol. II TB/101

## Christianity: The Roman and Eastern Traditions

A. ROBERT CAPONIGRI, Ed.: Modern Catholic Thinkers I: *God and Man* TB/306
A. ROBERT CAPONIGRI, Ed.: Modern Catholic Thinkers II: *The Church and the Political Order* TB/307
THOMAS CORBISHLEY, S. J.: Roman Catholicism TB/112
CHRISTOPHER DAWSON: The Historic Reality of Christian Culture TB/305
G. P. FEDOTOV: The Russian Religious Mind: *Kievan Christianity, the tenth to the thirteenth centuries* TB/70
G. P. FEDOTOV, Ed.: A Treasury of Russian Spirituality TB/303
DAVID KNOWLES: The English Mystical Tradition TB/302
GABRIEL MARCEL: Homo Viator: *Introduction to a Metaphysic of Hope* TB/397
GUSTAVE WEIGEL, S. J.: Catholic Theology in Dialogue TB/301

## Oriental Religions: Far Eastern, Near Eastern

TOR ANDRAE: Mohammed: *The Man and His Faith* TB/62
EDWARD CONZE: Buddhism: *Its Essence and Development.* ° Foreword by Arthur Waley TB/58
EDWARD CONZE et al., Editors: Buddhist Texts Through the Ages TB/113
ANANDA COOMARASWAMY: Buddha and the Gospel of Buddhism. *Illus.* TB/119
H. G. CREEL: Confucius and the Chinese Way TB/63
FRANKLIN EDGERTON, Trans. & Ed.: The Bhagavad Gita TB/115
SWAMI NIKHILANANDA, Trans. & Ed.: The Upanishads: *A One-Volume Abridgment* TB/114
HELLMUT WILHELM: Change: *Eight Lectures on the I Ching* TB/2019

## Philosophy of Religion

RUDOLF BULTMANN: History and Eschatology: *The Presence of Eternity* ° TB/91
RUDOLF BULTMANN AND FIVE CRITICS: Kerygma and Myth: *A Theological Debate* TB/80
RUDOLF BULTMANN and KARL KUNDSIN: Form Criticism: *Two Essays on New Testament Research.* Translated by Frederick C. Grant TB/96

MIRCEA ELIADE: The Sacred and the Profane   TB/81
LUDWIG FEUERBACH: The Essence of Christianity. § Introduction by Karl Barth. Foreword by H. Richard Niebuhr   TB/11
ADOLF HARNACK: What is Christianity? § Introduction by Rudolf Bultmann   TB/17
FRIEDRICH HEGEL: On Christianity: Early Theological Writings. Edited by Richard Kroner and T. M. Knox   TB/79
KARL HEIM: Christian Faith and Natural Science   TB/16
IMMANUEL KANT: Religion Within the Limits of Reason Alone. § Introduction by Theodore M. Greene and John Silber   TB/67
JOHN MACQUARRIE: An Existentialist Theology: A Comparison of Heidegger and Bultmann. ° Preface by Rudolf Bultmann   TB/125
PAUL RAMSEY, Ed.: Faith and Ethics: The Theology of H. Richard Niebuhr   TB/129
PIERRE TEILHARD DE CHARDIN: The Phenomenon of Man °   TB/83

## Religion, Culture & Society

JOSEPH L. BLAU, Ed.: Cornerstones of Religious Freedom in America: Selected Basic Documents, Court Decisions and Public Statements. Revised and Enlarged Edition   TB/118
C. C. GILLISPIE: Genesis and Geology: The Decades before Darwin §   TB/51
KYLE HASELDEN: The Racial Problem in Christian Perspective   TB/116
WALTER KAUFMANN, Ed.: Religion from Tolstoy to Camus: Basic Writings on Religious Truth and Morals. Enlarged Edition   TB/123
JOHN T. MCNEILL: A History of the Cure of Souls   TB/126
KENNETH B. MURDOCK: Literature and Theology in Colonial New England   TB/99
H. RICHARD NIEBUHR: Christ and Culture   TB/3
H. RICHARD NIEBUHR: The Kingdom of God in America   TB/49
RALPH BARTON PERRY: Puritanism and Democracy   TB/1138
PAUL PFUETZE: Self, Society, Existence: Human Nature and Dialogue in the Thought of George Herbert Mead and Martin Buber   TB/1059
WALTER RAUSCHENBUSCH: Christianity and the Social Crisis. ‡ Edited by Robert D. Cross   TB/3059
KURT SAMUELSSON: Religion and Economic Action: A Critique of Max Weber's The Protestant Ethic and the Spirit of Capitalism. ‖ ° Trans. by E. G. French; Ed. with Intro. by D. C. Coleman   TB/1131
ERNST TROELTSCH: The Social Teaching of the Christian Churches °   Vol. I TB/71; Vol. II TB/72

# NATURAL SCIENCES AND MATHEMATICS

## Biological Sciences

CHARLOTTE AUERBACH: The Science of Genetics Σ   TB/568
A. BELLAIRS: Reptiles: Life History, Evolution, and Structure. Illus.   TB/520
LUDWIG VON BERTALANFFY: Modern Theories of Development: An Introduction to Theoretical Biology   TB/554
LUDWIG VON BERTALANFFY: Problems of Life: An Evaluation of Modern Biological and Scientific Thought   TB/521
HAROLD F. BLUM: Time's Arrow and Evolution   TB/555
JOHN TYLER BONNER: The Ideas of Biology. Σ Illus.   TB/570
A. J. CAIN: Animal Species and their Evolution. Illus.   TB/519
WALTER B. CANNON: Bodily Changes in Pain, Hunger, Fear and Rage. Illus.   TB/562
W. E. LE GROS CLARK: The Antecedents of Man: An Introduction to the Evolution of the Primates. ° Illus.   TB/559
W. H. DOWDESWELL: Animal Ecology. Illus.   TB/543
W. H. DOWDESWELL: The Mechanism of Evolution. Illus.   TB/527
R. W. GERARD: Unresting Cells. Illus.   TB/541
DAVID LACK: Darwin's Finches. Illus.   TB/544
J. E. MORTON: Molluscs: An Introduction to their Form and Functions. Illus.   TB/529
ADOLF PORTMANN: Animals as Social Beings. ° Illus.   TB/572
O. W. RICHARDS: The Social Insects. Illus.   TB/542
P. M. SHEPPARD: Natural Selection and Heredity. Illus.   TB/528
EDMUND W. SINNOTT: Cell and Psyche: The Biology of Purpose   TB/546
C. H. WADDINGTON: How Animals Develop. Illus.   TB/553

## Chemistry

J. R. PARTINGTON: A Short History of Chemistry. Illus.   TB/522
J. READ: A Direct Entry to Organic Chemistry. Illus.   TB/523
J. READ: Through Alchemy to Chemistry. Illus.   TB/561

## Communication Theory

J. R. PIERCE: Symbols, Signals and Noise: The Nature and Process of Communication   TB/574

## Geography

R. E. COKER: This Great and Wide Sea: An Introduction to Oceanography and Marine Biology. Illus.   TB/551
F. K. HARE: The Restless Atmosphere   TB/560

## History of Science

W. DAMPIER, Ed.: Readings in the Literature of Science. Illus.   TB/512
A. HUNTER DUPREE: Science in the Federal Government: A History of Policies and Activities to 1940   TB/573
ALEXANDRE KOYRÉ: From the Closed World to the Infinite Universe: Copernicus, Kepler, Galileo, Newton, etc.   TB/31
A. G VAN MELSEN: From Atomos to Atom: A History of the Concept Atom   TB/517
O. NEUGEBAUER: The Exact Sciences in Antiquity   TB/552
H. T. PLEDGE: Science Since 1500: A Short History of Mathematics, Physics, Chemistry and Biology. Illus.   TB/506
HANS THIRRING: Energy for Man: From Windmills to Nuclear Power   TB/556
WILLIAM LAW WHYTE: Essay on Atomism: From Democritus to 1960   TB/565

A. WOLF: A History of Science, Technology and Philosophy in the 16th and 17th Centuries. º *Illus.*
Vol. I TB/508; Vol. II TB/509
A. WOLF: A History of Science, Technology, and Philosophy in the Eighteenth Century. º *Illus.*
Vol. I TB/539; Vol. II TB/540

## Mathematics

H. DAVENPORT: The Higher Arithmetic: *An Introduction to the Theory of Numbers* TB/526
H. G. FORDER: Geometry: *An Introduction* TB/548
GOTTLOB FREGE: The Foundations of Arithmetic: *A Logico-Mathematical Enquiry* TB/534
S. KÖRNER: The Philosophy of Mathematics: *An Introduction* TB/547
D. E. LITTLEWOOD: Skeleton Key of Mathematics: *A Simple Account of Complex Algebraic Problems* TB/525
GEORGE E. OWEN: Fundamentals of Scientific Mathematics TB/569
WILLARD VAN ORMAN QUINE: Mathematical Logic TB/558
O. G. SUTTON: Mathematics in Action. º *Foreword by James R. Newman. Illus.* TB/518
FREDERICK WAISMANN: Introduction to Mathematical Thinking. *Foreword by Karl Menger* TB/511

## Philosophy of Science

R. B. BRAITHWAITE: Scientific Explanation TB/515
J. BRONOWSKI: Science and Human Values. *Revised and Enlarged Edition* TB/505
ALBERT EINSTEIN et al.: Albert Einstein: Philosopher-Scientist. *Edited by Paul A. Schilpp* Vol. I TB/502
Vol. II TB/503
WERNER HEISENBERG: Physics and Philosophy: *The Revolution in Modern Science* TB/549
JOHN MAYNARD KEYNES: A Treatise on Probability. º *Introduction by N. R. Hanson* TB/557
KARL R. POPPER: The Logic of Scientific Discovery TB/576
STEPHEN TOULMIN: Foresight and Understanding: *An Enquiry into the Aims of Science. Foreword by Jacques Barzun* TB/564
STEPHEN TOULMIN: The Philosophy of Science: *An Introduction* TB/513
G. J. WHITROW: The Natural Philosophy of Time º TB/563

## Physics and Cosmology

DAVID BOHM: Causality and Chance in Modern Physics. *Foreword by Louis de Broglie* TB/536
P. W. BRIDGMAN: The Nature of Thermodynamics TB/537
P. W. BRIDGMAN: A Sophisticate's Primer of Relativity TB/575
A. C. CROMBIE, Ed.: Turning Point in Physics TB/535
C. V. DURELL: Readable Relativity. *Foreword by Freeman J. Dyson* TB/530
ARTHUR EDDINGTON: Space, Time and Gravitation: *An outline of the General Relativity Theory* TB/510
GEORGE GAMOW: Biography of Physics Σ TB/567
MAX JAMMER: Concepts of Force: *A Study in the Foundation of Dynamics* TB/550
MAX JAMMER: Concepts of Mass *in Classical and Modern Physics* TB/571
MAX· JAMMER: Concepts of Space: *The History of Theories of Space in Physics. Foreword by Albert Einstein* TB/533
EDMUND WHITTAKER: History of the Theories of Aether and Electricity
Volume I: *The Classical Theories* TB/531
Volume II: *The Modern Theories* TB/532
G. J. WHITROW: The Structure and Evolution of the Universe: *An Introduction to Cosmology. Illus.* TB/504

---

Code to Torchbook Libraries:

| | |
|---|---|
| TB/1+ | : The Cloister Library |
| TB/301+ | : The Cathedral Library |
| TB/501+ | : The Science Library |
| TB/1001+ | : The Academy Library |
| TB/2001+ | : The Bollingen Library |
| TB/3001+ | : The University Library |

## A LETTER TO THE READER

Overseas, there is considerable belief that we are a country of extreme conservatism and that we cannot accommodate to social change.

Books about America in the hands of readers abroad can help change those ideas.

The U. S. Information Agency cannot, by itself, meet the vast need for books about the United States.

You can help.

Harper Torchbooks provides three packets of books on American history, economics, sociology, literature and politics to help meet the need.

To send a packet of Torchbooks [*] overseas, all you need do is send your check for $7 (which includes cost of shipping) to Harper & Row. The U. S. Information Agency will distribute the books to libraries, schools, and other centers all over the world.

I ask every American to support this program, part of a worldwide BOOKS USA campaign.

I ask you to share in the opportunity to help tell others about America.

EDWARD R. MURROW
Director,
U. S. Information Agency

[*retailing at $10.85 to $12.00]

PACKET I: *Twentieth Century America*
   Dulles/America's Rise to World Power, 1898-1954
   Cochran/The American Business System, 1900-1955
   Zabel, Editor/Literary Opinion in America (two volumes)
   Drucker/The New Society: *The Anatomy of Industrial Order*
   Fortune Editors/America in the Sixties: *The Economy and the Society*

PACKET II: *American History*
   Billington/The Far Western Frontier, 1830-1860
   Mowry/The Era of Theodore Roosevelt and the
      Birth of Modern America, 1900-1912
   Faulkner/Politics, Reform, and Expansion, 1890-1900
   Cochran & Miller/The Age of Enterprise: *A Social History of
      Industrial America*
   Tyler/Freedom's Ferment: *American Social History from the
      Revolution to the Civil War*

PACKET III: *American History*
   Hansen/The Atlantic Migration, 1607-1860
   Degler/Out of Our Past: *The Forces that Shaped Modern America*
   Probst, Editor/The Happy Republic: *A Reader in Tocqueville's America*
   Alden/The American Revolution, 1775-1783
   Wright/The Cultural Life of the American Colonies, 1607-1763

*Your gift will be acknowledged directly to you by the overseas recipient.
Simply fill out the coupon, detach and mail with your check or money order.*

---

**HARPER & ROW, PUBLISHERS • BOOKS USA DEPT.**
49 East 33rd Street, New York 16, N. Y.

Packet I ☐    Packet II ☐    Packet III ☐

Please send the BOOKS USA library packet(s) indicated above, in my name, to the area checked below. Enclosed is my remittance in the amount of _____ for _____ packet(s) at $7.00 each.

_____ Africa             _____ Latin America
_____ Far East           _____ Near East

Name_____

Address_____

_____

---

NOTE: *This offer expires December 31, 1966.*